CONDITIONAL CASH TRANSFERS

A World Bank Policy Research Report

CONDITIONAL CASH TRANSFERS

REDUCING PRESENT AND FUTURE POVERTY

Ariel Fiszbein and Norbert Schady

with

Francisco H.G. Ferreira,
Margaret Grosh, Nial Kelleher,
Pedro Olinto, and Emmanuel Skoufias

THE WORLD BANK
Washington, D.C.

©2009 The International Bank for Reconstruction and Development / The World Bank
1818 H Street NW
Washington DC 20433
Telephone: 202-473-1000
Internet: www.worldbank.org
E-mail: feedback@worldbank.org

Library of Congress Cataloging-in-Publication Data

Fiszbein, Ariel, 1960–
   Conditional cash transfers : reducing present and future poverty /
Ariel Fizbein, Norbert Schady.
     p. cm.
   Includes bibliographical references and index.
    ISBN 978-0-8213-7352-1 — ISBN 978-0-8213-7353-8 (electronic)
   1. Transfer payments—Latin America—Case studies.   2. Economic assistance, Domestic—Latin America—Case studies.   3. Poverty—Government policy—Latin America—Case studies.   I. Schady, Norbert Rüdiger, 1967-   II. Title.
   HC130.P63F564 2009
   338.91098—dc22

                                         2008047645

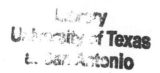
Cover design: Drew Fasick
Cover image: *Chorale and Landscape* by Paul Klee, 1921, 125 (gouache, pencil, and oil on paper, 35 x 31 cm); Zentrum Paul Klee, Bern, private loan. Used with permission. © 2009 Artists Right Society (ARS) New York/ VG Bild-Kunst, Bonn.

Contents

Boxes

Figures

Tables

Foreword

THE POTENTIAL IMPACT OF THE GLOBAL FINANCIAL CRISIS OF 2008 on living standards in the developing world has given renewed emphasis to the importance of social safety net programs. The right policies can be a smart investment in an uncertain world. This report reviews the evidence on conditional cash transfers (CCTs)—safety net programs that have become popular in developing countries over the last decade. It concludes that CCTs generally have been successful in reducing poverty and encouraging parents to invest in the health and education of their children.

The CCT programs studied in the report span a range of low- and middle-income countries; large and small programs; and those that work at local, regional, and national levels. Although there are important differences between countries and regions in how CCTs are used, they all share one defining characteristic: they transfer cash while asking beneficiaries to make prespecified investments in child education and health.

The largest CCTs, such as Brazil's Bolsa Família and Mexico's Oportunidades, cover millions of households. In Chile and Turkey, CCTs are focused more narrowly on extremely poor and socially excluded people, whereas CCTs in Bangladesh and Cambodia have been used to reduce gender disparities in education. Most recently, CCT pilot programs are being implemented in Sub-Saharan Africa to help alleviate the plight of millions of orphans in the wake of the continent's devastating HIV/AIDS epidemic. CCTs are proven versatile programs, which largely explains why they have become so popular worldwide.

This report considers the impact that CCTs have had on current poverty, education, health, and nutrition outcomes. It draws heavily on a large number of carefully constructed impact evaluations of CCT programs. As the authors note, it would not have been possible to write this report without the efforts made by the administrators of CCT programs themselves, a number of academics, and staff at international organizations, including the World Bank, to encourage and sustain these evaluations, and to make the results widely available. This clearly is a legacy worth sustaining.

By and large, CCTs have increased consumption levels among the poor. As a result, they have resulted in sometimes substantial reductions in poverty among beneficiaries—especially when the transfer has been generous, well targeted, and structured in a way that does not discourage recipients from taking other actions to escape poverty. Because CCTs provide a steady stream of income, they have helped buffer poor households from the worst effects of unemployment, catastrophic illness, and other sudden income shocks. And making cash transfers to women, as virtually all CCTs do, may have increased the bargaining power of women (itself an important goal in many contexts).

In country after country, school enrollment has increased among CCT beneficiaries—especially among the poorest children, whose enrollment rates at the outset were the lowest. CCT beneficiaries also are more likely to have visited health providers for preventive checkups, to have had their children weighed and measured, and to have completed a schedule of immunizations. These are important accomplishments. Nevertheless, the report shows that the evidence of CCT impacts on *final* outcomes in health and education—achievement and cognitive development rather than school enrollment, child height for age rather than growth monitoring—is more mixed. An important challenge for the future is better understanding what complementary actions are necessary to ensure that CCTs have greater impact on these final outcomes. This report argues that these complementary actions broadly fall into two categories: policies that improve the quality of the supply of health and education services, and policies that help promote healthier and more stimulating environments for children in their homes.

Even the best-designed CCT program cannot meet all the needs of a social protection system. It is, after all, only one branch of a larger tree that includes workfare, employment, and social pension programs. The report therefore considers where CCTs should fit within a country's social protection strategy.

As the world navigates a period of deepening crisis, it has become vital to design and implement social protection systems that help vulnerable households weather shocks, while maximizing the efforts of developing countries to invest in children. CCTs are not the only programs appropriate for this purpose, but as the report argues, they surely can be a compelling part of the solution.

Justin Lin
Senior Vice President and Chief Economist
The World Bank

Joy Phumaphi
Vice President, Human Development Network
The World Bank
January 2009

Acknowledgments

THIS POLICY RESEARCH REPORT WAS MANAGED BY ARIEL FISZBEIN and Norbert Schady. Contributing members of the report were Francisco H.G. Ferreira, Margaret Grosh, Nial Kelleher, Pedro Olinto, and Emmanuel Skoufias. Substantial contributions were provided by Maria Victoria Fazio, Deon Filmer, Emanuela Galasso, Margaret Koziol, Phillippe Leite, Mette Nielsen, and Christine Weigand.

The report benefited from comments from an advisory committee, which included Harold Alderman (World Bank), Orazio Attanasio (University College, London), Jere Behrman (University of Pennsylvania), Timothy Besley (London School of Economics), Santiago Levy (Inter-American Development Bank), Christina Paxson (Princeton University), and Laura Rawlings (World Bank).

François Bourguignon, in his role as chief economist of the World Bank, provided strong encouragement and intellectual support to the report. The report was written under the direction and general supervision of Elizabeth King (research manager) and Martin Ravallion (director, Development Research Group).

The authors have benefited from comments and useful input from Vivi Alatas, Colin Andrews, Caridad Araujo, Jehan Arulpragasam, Felipe Barrera, Maria Isabel Beltran, Nazmul Chaudhury, David Coady, Dante Contreras, Rafael Cortez, Aline Coudouel, Amit Dar, Gaurav Datt, Damien de Walque, Carlo del Ninno, Gershon Feder, Roberta Gatti, Paul Gertler, Rebekka Grun, Phillip Hay, Budi Hidayat, Jason Hobbs, Robert Holzmann, Emmanuel Jimenez, Theresa Jones, Peter Lanjouw, Benedicte Leroy De la Briere, Dan Levy, Maureen Lewis, Anja Linder, Kathy Lindert, Humberto Lopez, William Maloney, Andrew Mason, Alessandra Marini, Annamaria Milazzo, Amna Mir,

Fernando Montenegro, Juan Martin Moreno, Edmundo Murrugarra, Shinsaku Nomura, Berk Ozler, Lucy Payton, Mansoora Rashid, Helena Ribe, Dena Ringold, Manuel Salazar, Tahseen Sayed, Nistha Sinha, Hedy Sladovich, Emma Sorensson, David Steel, Cornelia Tesliuc, Alan Winters, and Elif Yukseker.

Financial support from the Development Impact Evaluation Initiative, the Knowledge for Change Program, and the Spanish Impact Evaluation Fund helped greatly in the preparation of this report.

Acronyms

AFDC	Aid to Families with Dependent Children
AIN-C	Atención Integral de la Niñez en la Comunidad
ATM	automated teller machine
BDH	Bono de Desarrollo Humano
BEDP	Basic Education Development Project
BANHCAFE	Banco Hondureño del Café
BANSEFI	Banco del Ahorro Nacional y Servicios Financieros
CCT	conditional cash transfer
CESSP	Cambodia Education Sector Support Project
CSP	Child Support Program
CT-OVC	Cash Transfer for Orphans and Vulnerable Children
EMA	Education Maintenance Allowance
FFE	Food for Education
FISDL	Fondo de Inversión Social para el Desarrollo Local
FSSAP	Female Secondary School Assistance Program
GDP	gross domestic product
GNP	gross national product
HIV/AIDS	human immunodeficiency virus/acquired immunodeficiency syndrome
JFPR	Japan Fund for Poverty Reduction
JPS	Jaring Pengamanan Sosial
LATE	local average treatment effect
MEGS	Maharashtra Employment Guarantee Scheme
NGO	nongovernmental organization
OAP	Old-Age Pension
OVC	Orphans and Vulnerable Children

PATH	Program of Advancement through Health and Education
PCE	per capita expenditure
PCI	per capita income
PESP	Primary Education Stipend Program
PESRP	Punjab Education Sector Reform Program
PETI	Programa de Erradicação do Trabalho Infantil
PKH	Program Keluarga Harapan
PRAF	Programa de Asignación Familiar
RDD	regression discontinuity
ROSC	Reaching Out-of-School Children
RPS	Red de Protección Social
SCAE	Subsidio Condicionado a la Asistencia Escolar–Bogotá
SEDGAP	Secondary Education Development and Girls Access Program
SES	socioeconomic status
SRMP	Social Risk Mitigation Project
SUF	Subsidio Unitario Familiar
TAE/ILAE	Tarjeta de Asistencia Escolar/Incentivo a la Asistencia Escolar
TANF	Temporary Assistance for Needy Families
TVIP	Test de Vocabulario en Imágenes Peabody
UCT	unconditional cash transfer
WDI	*World Development Indicators*

All dollar amounts are in U.S. dollars, unless otherwise indicated.

Overview

CONDITIONAL CASH TRANSFERS (CCTS) ARE PROGRAMS THAT transfer cash, generally to poor households, on the condition that those households make prespecified investments in the human capital of their children. Health and nutrition conditions generally require periodic checkups, growth monitoring, and vaccinations for children less than 5 years of age; perinatal care for mothers and attendance by mothers at periodic health information talks. Education conditions usually include school enrollment, attendance on 80–85 percent of school days, and occasionally some measure of performance. Most CCT programs transfer the money to the mother of the household or to the student in some circumstances.

Countries have been adopting or considering adoption of CCT programs at a prodigious rate. Virtually every country in Latin America has such a program. Elsewhere, there are large-scale programs in Bangladesh, Indonesia, and Turkey, and pilot programs in Cambodia, Malawi, Morocco, Pakistan, and South Africa, among others. Interest in programs that seek to use cash to incentivize household investments in child schooling has spread from developing to developed countries—most recently to programs in New York City and Washington, DC.

In some countries, CCTs have become the largest social assistance program, covering millions of households, as is the case in Brazil and Mexico. CCTs have been hailed as a way of reducing inequality, especially in the very unequal countries in Latin America; helping households break out of a vicious cycle whereby poverty is transmitted from one generation to another; promoting child health, nutrition, and schooling; and helping countries meet the Millennium Development Goals. Do those and other claims make sense? Are they supported by

1

the available empirical evidence? What does all of this imply for the way in which countries that have CCTs should structure or reform the programs? What about countries that do not have CCTs but are considering implementing them, often in circumstances very different from those in which the programs were first introduced?

This report seeks to answer those and other related questions. Specifically, it lays out a conceptual framework that considers the economic and political rationale for CCTs; it reviews the very rich evidence that has accumulated on CCTs, especially arising from impact evaluations; it discusses how the conceptual framework and the evidence on impacts should inform the design of CCT programs in practice; and it considers where CCTs fit in the context of broader social policies.

The report shows that there is good evidence that CCTs have improved the lives of poor people. Transfers generally have been well targeted to poor households, have raised consumption levels, and have reduced poverty—by a substantial amount in some countries. Offsetting adjustments that could have blunted the impact of transfers—such as reductions in the labor market participation of beneficiaries—have been relatively modest. Moreover, CCT programs often have provided an entry point to reforming badly targeted subsidies and upgrading the quality of safety nets. The report thus argues that CCTs have been an effective way to redistribute income to the poor, while recognizing that even the best-designed and best-managed program cannot fulfill all of the needs of a comprehensive social protection system. CCTs therefore need to be complemented with other interventions, such as workfare or employment programs and social pensions.

The report also considers the rationale for conditioning the transfers on the use of specific health and education services by program beneficiaries. Conditions can be justified if households are underinvesting in the human capital of their children—for example, if they hold incorrect beliefs about the returns to these investments; if there is "incomplete altruism" between parents and their children; or if there are large externalities to investments in health and education. Political economy considerations also may favor conditional over unconditional transfers: taxpayers may be more likely to support transfers to the poor if they are linked to efforts to overcome poverty in the long term, particularly when the efforts involve actions to improve the welfare of children.

CCTs have led poor households to make more use of health and education services, a key objective for which they were designed.

Nevertheless, the evidence on improvements in final outcomes in health and education is more mixed. Thus CCTs have increased the likelihood that households will take their children for preventive health checkups, but that has not always led to better child nutritional status; school enrollment rates have increased substantially among program beneficiaries, but there is little evidence of improvements in learning outcomes. These findings suggest that to maximize their potential effects on the accumulation of human capital, CCTs should be combined with other programs to improve the quality of the supply of health and education services, and should provide other supporting services. They also suggest the need to experiment with conditions that focus on outcomes rather than on the use of services alone.

The CCT Wave

Interest in and the scope of CCT programs have grown enormously in the last 10 years. The maps shown in figure 1 reveal the expansion between 1997 and 2008.

Paralleling the rise in the number of countries with CCT programs has been an increase in the size of some programs. Mexico's PROGRESA started with approximately 300,000 beneficiary households in 1997, but now covers 5 million households. (This program was renamed Oportunidades in 2001. In this report we will refer to the program as Oportunidades.) Brazil started with municipal Bolsa Escola programs in Brasilia and the municipality of Campinas. Those programs led to replication by local governments, followed by formulation of sector-specific federal programs, and then their unification and reform. Today the federal Bolsa Família program serves 11 million families (46 million people). In other countries, the increase in size has been less explosive but still notable. In Colombia, for instance, the program's initial goal was 400,000 households, but it had expanded to cover 1.5 million beneficiary households by 2007.

CCTs vary a great deal in scope. Some programs are nationwide, others are niche programs that serve a regional or narrow target population, and yet others are small-scale pilot efforts. Some programs require that households receiving transfers comply only with schooling conditions; others, especially programs in Latin America and the Caribbean, require that households comply with both schooling and

Figure 1 CCTs in the World, 1997 and 2008

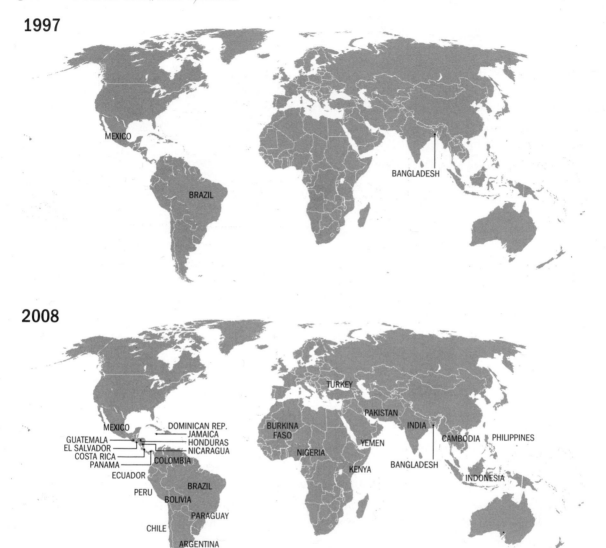

Source: World Bank.

health conditions. Table 1 presents a partial list of the CCT programs considered in this report. The list is not exhaustive in that it does not cover all existing programs. There are additional programs in operation for which little information was available, and some programs fit the CCT label less well than do others.

Table 1   Matrix of Program Size and Extent of Conditions

Program size/Target	Conditions	
	Education and health	Education only
Nationwide	Bolsa Família (Brazil)	Bolsa Escola (Brazil)
	Oportunidades (Mexico)	Jaring Pengamanan Sosial (Indonesia)
	Bono de Desarrollo Humano (Ecuador)	
	Familias en Acción (Colombia)	
	Program of Advancement through Health and Education (Jamaica)	
Niche (regional or narrow target population)	Chile Solidario	Female Secondary School Assistance Program (Bangladesh)
	Social Risk Mitigation Project (Turkey)	Japan Fund for Poverty Reduction (Cambodia)
		Education Sector Support Project (Cambodia)
		Basic Education Development Project (Yemen)
Small scale/pilot	Programa de Asignación Familiar (Honduras)	Subsidio Condicionado a la Asistencia Escolar–Bogotá (Colombia)
	Cash Transfer for Orphans and Vulnerable Children (Kenya)	Punjab Education Sector Reform Program (Pakistan)
	Atención a Crisis (Nicaragua)	
	Red de Protección Social (Nicaragua)	

Source: Authors' compilation.

The role of CCT programs in social policy varies from place to place as a consequence of differences in both program design and the context in which they operate. Most obviously, CCT programs vary with respect to pertinent measures of size. In terms of absolute coverage, they range from 11 million families (Brazil) to 215,000 households (Chile) to pilot programs with a few thousand families (Kenya, Nicaragua). In terms of relative coverage, they range from approximately 40 percent of the population (Ecuador) to about 20 percent (Brazil, Mexico) to 1 percent (Cambodia). In terms of budget, the costs range from about 0.50 percent of gross domestic product (GDP) in such countries as Brazil, Ecuador, and Mexico to 0.08 percent of GDP (Chile). The generosity of benefits ranges from 20 percent of mean household consumption in Mexico, to 4 percent in Honduras, and to even less for programs in Bangladesh, Cambodia, and Pakistan.

Many of the CCT programs in middle-income countries have pursued an integrated approach to poverty reduction, balancing goals of social assistance and human capital formation. They cover children from birth (or before) through the mid-teens, with conditions on health care use for children from birth to age 5 or 6 and with conditions on school enrollment thereafter. Programs usually are administered by ministries of social welfare or freestanding agencies under the presidency. Examples of that type of CCT include the programs in Brazil, Colombia, El Salvador, Jamaica, Mexico, Panama, and Turkey.

Mexico's Oportunidades is one of the iconic cases. The program started early, its evolution has been carried out thoughtfully, and it has been successful. What really makes Mexico's program iconic are the successive waves of data collected to evaluate its impact, the placement of those data in the public domain, and the resulting hundreds of papers and thousands of references that such dissemination has generated.

Brazil also is exemplary in its use of CCTs. It started early, its programs have evolved enormously, and the current program (Bolsa Família) is similar to Mexico's program in coverage and importance. In various respects, Brazil's Bolsa Família program provides something of an interesting contrast to the Mexican case—the issue of federalism is more in the forefront; it takes a softer, more gradual tack on conditions; and puts a shade more emphasis on redistribution than on human capital formation. Also, unlike Oportunidades, the Brazilian programs did not explicitly incorporate impact evaluations in their design; as a result, much less is known about the effect they have had on consumption, poverty, health, nutrition, and education.

Chile Solidario works in a very different way to fill a different niche. The program is targeted only to extremely poor people, about 5 percent of Chile's population. It differs notably from the classic CCT design by customizing conditions. Families initially work intensely with social workers to understand actions that could help them get out of extreme poverty. They then commit to action plans that become the household-specific conditions for receiving the benefit. The cash transfer itself really is intended only to motivate clients to make use of social workers' services. Thus far, Chile Solidario is a model unto itself, although other programs are moving to emulate it to a degree.

Another branch of the CCT program family focuses on education in low-income countries. The programs usually cover a more narrow segment of education—some only secondary (Bangladesh's Female Secondary School Assistance Program [FSSAP], Cambodia's Japan Fund for Poverty Reduction [JFPR], and Cambodia Education Sector Support

Project [CESSP]), some only primary (programs in Bolivia and Kenya and proposals in Nigeria and Tanzania), and occasionally both (Indonesia's Jaring Pengamanan Sosial [JPS] program). The genesis of these programs is rather varied. In Bangladesh, the FSSAP was part of a strategy to close a then-significant gender gap in education. In Indonesia, the JPS program was instituted following the East Asian financial crisis to prevent students from dropping out. In Kenya and Tanzania, the programs are geared especially to coping with the crisis of orphans and vulnerable children, a crisis that has burgeoned in the wake of HIV/AIDS.

CCT programs require the same systems as other transfer programs: at minimum, (1) a means to establish the eligibility of clients and enroll them in the program, and (2) a mechanism to pay their benefits. Strong monitoring and evaluation systems also are desirable. CCTs further require a means to monitor compliance with conditions and to coordinate among the several institutions involved in operating the program. In general, CCT programs have handled these systems rather well and, in some cases, they have been leaders in modernizing social assistance practice.

Almost all CCTs have tried to target their benefits rather narrowly to the poor through a combination of geographic and household targeting (mostly via proxy means testing). Moreover, many programs use community-based targeting or community vetting of eligibility lists to increase transparency. In many cases, CCTs have been the drivers for developing poverty maps or household targeting systems in their countries, or for upgrades to them. Indeed, it would not be an exaggeration to say that CCTs have moved forward the state of the art and standards for targeted programs generally.

A number of CCT programs have had unusually proactive management based on cutting-edge technical systems, especially with respect to monitoring and evaluation. Two features inherent to CCTs—the number of actors involved and the need for extensive information management to verify compliance with conditions—may have interacted in ways that have spurred creative development in monitoring and management. This excellence in systems, and the high degree of transparency in documentation and information that characterizes most programs, has contributed to the attraction of CCTs, although they are not inherent to them. The evaluation culture around CCTs is quite strong, well beyond traditional practice in social policy. Many programs have conducted impact evaluations with credible counter-factuals. Of those programs, a large share used experimental methods, at least initially. This culture of evaluation is spreading not only from one CCT program to another, but also from CCTs to other programs within the same countries.

The role and design of CCT programs is evolving. Early successes with the basic model are prompting countries to address second and third rounds of challenges, including the following: Should the emphasis on expanding the supply of services be complemented with efforts to improve the quality of those services? Should the range or definition of conditions be changed, for example, to reward performance instead of, or in addition to, mere service use? What can be done to ensure that youth who are aging out of the school support provided by the program can get jobs or further training? What should be the balance between targeting younger and older children? In some countries, CCT programs themselves are addressing these challenges through adjustments to their basic design; in other cases, they are catalyzing changes in other programs.

The Arguments for CCTs

Although market-driven economic growth is likely to be the main driver of poverty reduction in most countries, markets cannot do it alone. Public policy plays a central role in providing the institutional foundations within which markets operate, in providing public goods, and in correcting market failures. In addition to laying the foundations for economic growth, policy can supplement the effects of growth on poverty reduction, and one of the instruments that governments can use to that end is direct redistribution of resources to poor households. Direct cash transfers have opportunity costs (in terms of forgone alternative public investments) and may have some perverse incentive effects on recipients, but there is a growing body of evidence that in some cases transfers may be both equitable and efficient.

Conditional cash transfers make payments to poor households on the condition that those households invest in the human capital of their children in certain prespecified ways. Because attaching a constraint on the behavior of people one is trying to help is an unorthodox approach for economists, this report reviews the conceptual arguments for making cash transfers conditionally.

There are two broad sets of arguments for attaching conditions to cash transfers. The first set applies if private investment in children's human capital is thought to be too low. The second set applies if political economy conditions show little support for redistribution unless it is seen to be conditioned on "good behavior" by the "deserving poor."

Under the first group of arguments, private investment in human capital can be "too low" in two different senses. First, it can be below even the *private* optimal level for the individual children in question if household decision makers hold persistently misguided beliefs about either the nature of the process of investments in child education and health or the subsequent returns to these investments. For instance, parents may believe that earnings respond to education less elastically than they actually do. In practice, there is some evidence of this from developing countries. Among 15- to 25-year-olds in Mexico, the expected returns to schooling (calculated from questions asked of respondents) are substantially lower than the realized returns (the Mincerian returns calculated from a household survey), especially among children of fathers with low education levels (Attanasio and Kaufmann 2008). In the Dominican Republic, eighth-grade students estimate the rate of return to secondary school to be only one quarter to one third of the rate derived from an income survey (Jensen 2006).

Parents also may discount the future more heavily than they should, perhaps especially with regard to the returns on investments in their children—a case of "incomplete altruism." A slightly different but equally plausible version of this problem is a conflict of interest between the parents themselves as opposed to, or in addition to, one between parents and children. Mothers' objectives may be more closely aligned with those of all her children or, perhaps, especially with those of her daughters.[1] That alignment often is given as a justification for giving the cash transfer to the mother rather than to the father, as is common practice in most CCT programs. In many countries in South Asia, girls' schooling lags well behind that of boys, even though the returns to female education—both in wages, and in terms of child health—are at least as large as those for males. Low levels of investment in girls' schooling may be rational from the viewpoint of parents who are thinking of their own welfare (either because girls are more costly in terms of dowries or because boys are more likely to take care of their parents than are girls who move to their husbands' homes upon marriage), but they are *prima facie* evidence of a socially inefficient outcome. CCTs that compel parents to send their daughters to school are one way to address inefficient and inequitable gender disparities.

In general, these informational, principal-agent, or behavioral arguments can be seen as providing microfoundations for much older paternalistic arguments for redistribution in-kind or with strings attached.

The second sense in which private investments in children's health and education can be "too low" is that the private optimal level may be below the *social* optimal level. That situation could occur if there are positive externalities from education and health across households. Empirically, many health investments have important external benefits.[2] In the case of education, externalities might arise if there are increasing returns to skilled labor in production, at the aggregate level, or if education lowers crime.

How large these externalities are and whether (conditioned) cash transfers are the most effective instruments to correct for them, however, remains to be determined. In most countries, education and health services are already heavily subsidized. In many cases, they are publicly provided free of charge. To argue for an additional subsidy that compensates households for some of the indirect or opportunity costs of using these services, on the basis of the externality alone, would require showing that those externalities are quite large.

The political economy family of arguments centers around the notion that targeting tends to weaken the support for redistribution because it reduces the number of beneficiaries relative to the number of those who are taxed to finance the program. Whereas the response most commonly considered in the literature is to establish broad-based redistribution that includes the middle class, an alternative is to appeal to the altruistic motive of voters: the same people who object to targeted transfers as "pure handouts" might support them if they are part of a "social contract" that requires recipients to take a number of concrete steps to improve their lives or those of their children.

The notion that CCT programs constitute a new form of social contract between the state and beneficiaries is apparent in the use of the term *co-responsibilities* (instead of conditions) in a majority of programs, at least in Latin America. When conditions are seen as co-responsibilities, they appear to treat the recipient more as an adult capable of agency to resolve his or her own problems. The state is seen as a partner in the process, not a nanny. This latter interpretation is particularly plausible when the counterfactual to a CCT is not an automatic, transparent, unconditional cash grant seen as a citizen's entitlement (which is close to the textbook concept of an unconditional transfer), but is instead a myriad of ad hoc and mostly in-kind transfers intermediated through various service providers, nongovernmental organizations, and local governments. Under those circumstances, conditioning the transfers on "good behavior" *may* be perceived as less paternalistic than the alternative of conditioning transfers on say, voting for a certain party or belonging to a given social organization.

Moreover, the fact that the conditions are focused on building the human capital of children (rather than simply supporting parents) adds to CCTs' political acceptability as an instrument to promote opportunities; after all, it is hard to blame children for being poor. In that sense, using public resources to support the human capital development of poor children makes a CCT a poverty reduction program rather than a social assistance one. Making payments to mothers also resonates with well-accepted beliefs (mostly supported by evidence, as shown above) that women will tend to put funds to better use than will men.

The conclusion is that even in situations where a narrow technical assessment might suggest that an unconditional transfer is more appropriate than a CCT (say, because there is no evidence of imperfect information or incomplete altruism in poor families), conditions might be justified because they lead to a preferable political economy equilibrium. The political process may make significant cash transfers to the poor close to impossible unless those transfers are tied somehow to clear evidence of beneficiaries' "positive behaviors." The Latin American experience suggests that in the absence of dramatic political shifts, the increasing trend toward cash-based redistribution schemes has been associated with the use of some form of conditioned grants.

In sum, when there is a strong rationale to redistribute, a CCT can be justified under two broad sets of conditions: first, when private investment in human capital among the poor is suboptimal from a social point of view and, second, when conditions are necessary for political economy reasons (that is, redistribution is politically feasible only when conditioned on good behavior). This framework can be extended by identifying critical questions that can guide the decision whether to have a CCT program, as depicted in figure 2.

The Impacts of CCT Programs

Beginning with the Mexican program Oportunidades, an important feature of CCT programs has been strong emphasis on credible evaluations of their impact on various outcomes. This report draws heavily

Figure 2 Decision Tree Approach to Identifying CCT Programs as the Right Policy Instrument

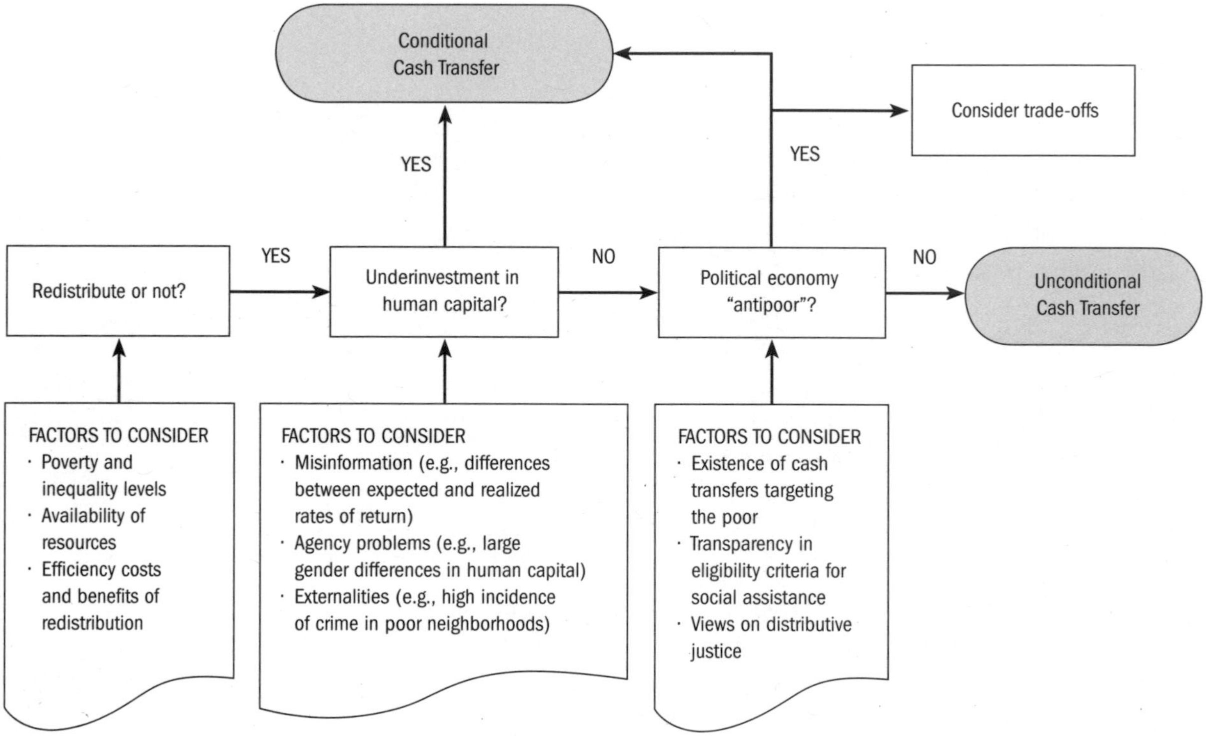

Source: Authors' illustration.

on those evaluations. Indeed, it would not have been possible to write the report without the efforts of the program administrators themselves, international donors, and academics around the world to ensure the high quality of many of the evaluations. The accumulating evidence of positive impacts has been instrumental both in sustaining existing programs and in encouraging the establishment of similar programs in other developing countries.

Most CCTs seek both to reduce consumption poverty and to encourage investments in the education and health of children. The report carefully considers the evidence of programs' impacts on those two dimensions of well-being.

The Impact on Consumption, Poverty, and Labor Market Participation

By and large, CCTs have had positive effects on household consumption and on poverty (as measured by the headcount index, the poverty gap, or the squared poverty gap). Tables 2 and 3 summarize the evidence.

Table 2 Impact of CCTs on per Capita Consumption, Various Years

Consumption	Brazil 2002	Cambodia 2007	Colombia 2002	Colombia 2006	Ecuador 2003	Ecuador 2005	Honduras 2000	Honduras 2002	Mexico 1998	Mexico Jun. 1999	Mexico Oct. 1999	Nicaragua 2000	Nicaragua 2001	Nicaragua 2002
Median daily per capita consumption of control households (current US$)	0.83	0.89	0.85	1.19	1.12	1.13	0.79	0.68	0.59	0.58	0.59	0.63	0.53	0.52
Daily per capita transfer (current US$)	0.06	0.02	0.12	0.13	0.08	0.08	0.06	0.06	0.12	0.14	0.13	0.16	0.15	0.15
Ratio of transfer to consumption (%)[a]	8	2–3	17	13	8	7	9	11	21	20	19	29	31	30
Impact on per capita consumption for the median household (%)	7.0**	B	A	10.0**	A	B	A	7.0*	B	7.8**	8.3**	A	29.3**	20.6**

Source: Authors' calculations for all countries in the table except Colombia. For Colombia, see Institute for Fiscal Studies, Econometría, and Sistemas Especializados de Información (2006).

Note: The estimated impacts presented here are not always equal to the unconditional double difference estimates because some regressions control for other correlates. The impact for Honduras was obtained from 2002 regression only. The impacts for Mexico are all for single equation cross-sectional regressions for each year. The lack of impact in 1998 is likely the result of the fact that this survey was carried out just a few months after the start of the program. Figures are in US$ obtained through the official exchange rates observed at the time of the surveys. In the case of Oportunidades in Mexico, the 1998 figures are for a few months after the start of the program. In the case of Bolsa Alimentação in Brazil, per capita consumption figures are for more than a year after the start of the program.

a. The transfer amounts as a proportion of per capita expenditures (or consumption) are not the same across all tables in the report because of differences in the surveys used, including their coverage and year.

A. Baseline, before households in CCT treatment group received transfers.

B. No significant impact on consumption.

* Significant at the 10 percent level.

** Significant at the 5 percent level.

Table 3 Impact of CCTs on Poverty Measures, Various Years

Poverty measure		Colombia		Honduras		Mexico			Nicaragua		
		2002	2006	2000	2002	1998	Jun. 1999	Oct. 1999	2000	2001	2002
Headcount index	Control	0.95	0.90	0.88	0.91	0.89	0.93	0.94	0.84	0.91	0.90
	Impact	A	−0.03*	A	B	0.02**	−0.01**	0.00	A	−0.07**	−0.05**
Poverty gap	Control	0.58	0.54	0.49	0.54	0.47	0.55	0.56	0.43	0.50	0.50
	Impact	A	−0.07**	A	−0.02*	0.01*	−0.03**	−0.02**	A	−0.13**	−0.09**
Squared poverty gap	Control	0.53	0.43	0.30	0.36	0.28	0.35	0.36	0.26	0.32	0.32
	Impact	A	−0.02**	A	−0.02*	B	−0.03**	−0.03**	A	−0.12**	−0.09**

Source: Authors' calculations.

Note: We exclude Cambodia and Ecuador from this table because the CCT did not have an effect on median consumption in those countries and so it is not surprising that it did not reduce poverty. We also exclude the Brazilian Bolsa Alimentação program because the evaluation sample is not representative of the program's target population, which makes the analysis of the impact on poverty less informative. For Honduras, Mexico, and Nicaragua, calculations were done via regression of household level Foster-Greer-Thorbecke indicator on treatment dummy and other explanatory variables. Using the evaluation sample of each program, we compute $P(i,t,a) = (z − y(i,t) / z)a * \text{Poor}(i,t)$, for alpha = 0, 1, and 2; and for each household, where $y(i,t)$ is household i's level of consumption per capita at year t, z is the country-specific poverty line, and $\text{Poor}(i,t)$ is an indicator function that equals 1 if the household is poor and equals 0 otherwise. For Honduras, the poverty line used was Lps 24.6 per capita per day in 2000 lempiras. Expenditure values for 2002 were deflated to 2000 lempiras. For Nicaragua, we used C$13.87 per capita per day in 2000 córdobas. Expenditure values for 2001 and 2002 were deflated to 2000 córdobas. For Mexico, we used the value of the Canasta Básica of 1997, which was M$320 per capita per month. We inflated this value of the Canasta Básica for 1998 and 1999 using the Canasta Básica Price Index found at: http://www.banxico .org.mx/polmoneinflacion/estadisticas/indicesPrecios/indicesPreciosConsumidor.html. Therefore, for October 1998, we used M$320 × 1.134. For June 1999, we used M$320 × 1.280. For October 1999, we used M$320 × 1.314. For Colombia (see Institute for Fiscal Studies, Econometria, and Sistemas Especializados de Información 2006), the estimated impacts presented here are not equal to the unconditional double difference estimates because regressions control for other correlates. The impact for Honduras was obtained from 2002 regression only. The impacts for Mexico are all for single equation cross-sectional regressions for each year.

A. Baseline, before households in CCT treatment group received transfers.

B. No significant impact on poverty measure.

* Significant at the 10 percent level.

** Significant at the 5 percent level.

Table 2 shows that the largest consumption impacts are found when the transfer amount is generous (as with the Red de Protección Social [RPS] program in Nicaragua). Moreover, because transfers generally are well targeted to the poor, the effects on consumption have translated into impacts on poverty, as is shown in table 3. Some of the reductions in poverty are quite large. In Nicaragua, for example, poverty fell by 5–9 points (using the 2002 data).

Another way of measuring the impact of CCTs on welfare is to compare the cumulative distribution of consumption per capita between those who receive the transfer and those who do not. The advantage of this method is that it does not rely on the selection of a poverty line, which can be somewhat arbitrary. If the cumulative distribution for recipient households lies completely to the right of the distribution for control households—so-called first-order stochastic dominance—current welfare is unambiguously improved by CCTs. That is clearly the case for RPS beneficiaries in Nicaragua, as shown in panel A of figure 3. Panel B shows an improvement that is much smaller for Honduras— a finding that is not surprising given the smaller magnitude of the transfer.

Moreover, CCTs have affected not only the overall level of consumption, but also the *composition* of consumption. There is a good deal of

Figure 3 Impact of CCTs on the Distribution of Consumption, Nicaragua and Honduras, 2002

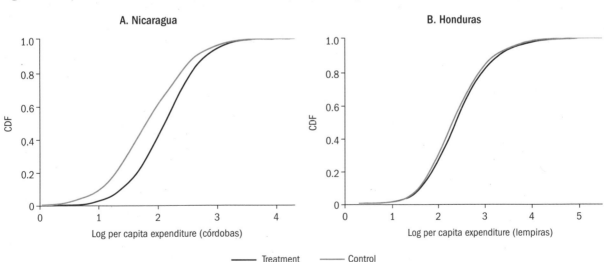

Source: Authors' calculations.
Note: CDF = cumulative distribution function.

evidence that households that receive CCTs spend more on food and, within the food basket, on higher-quality sources of nutrients than do households that do not receive the transfer but have comparable overall income or consumption levels.[3]

An important concern when CCTs first were launched was that they would result in large reductions in the labor market participation of adults—either because beneficiaries would choose to consume more leisure at higher income levels or because they would cut back on work in order to continue to appear to be "poor enough" to be eligible for transfers. In practice, CCTs appear to have had at most modest disincentive effects on adult work. Research on Cambodia, Ecuador, and Mexico shows that adults in households that received transfers did not reduce their work effort.

Although CCTs generally have not resulted in reductions in the labor market participation of adults, they have led to substantial decreases in child labor—as was intended by many of the programs. Reduced child work by CCT beneficiaries has been found in Brazil, Cambodia, Ecuador, Mexico, and Nicaragua. In some cases, the reductions are quite large. In Cambodia, for example, the average child receiving the transfer was 10 percentage points less likely to work for pay.[4]

In addition to possible reductions in labor market participation, a number of behavioral changes by households could have blunted the impact of CCTs on consumption and on poverty. In practice, all of these offsetting adjustments to transfers appear to have been small. Thus CCTs generally have not crowded out remittances and other transfers; they have had only small impacts on fertility, at least in the short run; and they have not had substantial local general equilibrium effects, such as increases in prices or wages. Finally, there is some evidence that CCT program beneficiaries invest part of the transfer, that the returns to these investments can result in higher consumption levels in the medium term (in Mexico, but not in Nicaragua), and that transfers made by CCT programs help households smooth consumption during adverse shocks. [5]

The Impact of CCTs on Education and Health Outcomes

In country after country, CCTs have led to significant and, in some cases, substantial increases in the use of services (tables 4 and 5). School enrollment rates have increased among program beneficiaries, especially among those who had low enrollment rates at the beginning. These impacts are found in the middle-income countries where CCT programs were first implemented (for example, Mexico); in lower-income countries in Latin America (for example, Honduras and Nicaragua); and in low-income countries in other regions (for example, Bangladesh, Cambodia, and Pakistan). CCT programs also have had a positive

Table 4 Impact of CCTs on School Enrollment and Attendance, Various Years

Country	Program	Age/Gender/ Grade	Baseline enrollment (%)	Impact[a]	Transfer (% of PCE)[b]	Evaluation method	Reference
Latin American and Caribbean countries							
Chile	Chile Solidario	Ages 6–15	60.7	7.5*** (3.0)	7	RDD	Galasso (2006)
Colombia	Familias en Acción	Ages 8–13	91.7	2.1** (1.0)	17	PSM, DD	Attanasio, Fitzsimmons, and Gómez (2005)
		Ages 14–17	63.2	5.6*** (1.8)			
Ecuador	Bono de Desarrollo Humano	Ages 6–17	75.2	10.3** (4.8)	10	IV, randomized	Schady and Araujo (2008)
Honduras	Programa de Asignación Familiar	Ages 6–13	66.4	3.3*** (0.3)	9	Randomized	Glewwe and Olinto (2004)
Jamaica	Program of Advancement through Health and Education	Ages 7–17	18 days[c]	0.5** (0.2)	10	RDD	Levy and Ohls (2007)
Mexico	Oportunidades	Grades 0–5	94.0	1.9 (25.0)	20	Randomized	Schultz (2004)
		Grade 6	45.0	8.7*** (0.4)			
		Grades 7–9	42.5	0.6 (56.4)			
Nicaragua	Atención a Crisis	Ages 7–15	90.5	6.6*** (0.9)	18	Randomized	Macours and Vakis (2008)
Nicaragua	Red de Protección Social	Ages 7–13	72.0	12.8*** (4.3)	27	Randomized	Maluccio and Flores (2005)

continued

Table 4 continued

Country	Program	Age/Gender/ Grade	Baseline enrollment (%)	Impact[a]	Transfer (% of PCE)[b]	Evaluation method	Reference
Non–Latin American and Caribbean countries							
Bangladesh	Female Secondary School Assistance Program	Ages 11–18 (girls)	44.1	12.0** (5.1)	0.6	FE	Khandker, Pitt, and Fuwa (2003)
Cambodia	Japan Fund for Poverty Reduction	Grades 7–9 (girls)	65.0	31.3*** (2.3)	2–3	DD	Filmer and Schady (2008)
Cambodia	Cambodia Education Sector Support Project	Grades 7–9 (girls)	65.0	21.4*** (4.0)	2–3	RDD	Filmer and Schady (2009c)
Pakistan	Punjab Education Sector Reform Program	Ages 10–14 (girls)	29.0	11.1*** (3.8)	3	DDD	Chaudhury and Parajuli (2008)
Turkey	Social Risk Mitigation Project	Primary school	87.9	–3.0* n.a.	6	RDD	Ahmed et al. (2007)
		Secondary school	39.2	5.2 n.a.			

Source: Authors' compilation.

Note: DD = difference-in-differences; DDD = difference-in-difference-in-differences; FE = fixed effects; IV = instrumental variables; n.a. = not available; PCE = per capita expenditure; PSM = propensity score matching; RDD = regression discontinuity design. This table contains unweighted means for the coefficients for Colombia ages 8–13 and 14–17, Chile ages 4–5 and 6–15, and Mexico grades 0–5 and 7–9. The standard errors in each case are the square roots of the averaged variances of these estimates.

a. The column for "impact" reports the coefficient and standard error (in parentheses); the unit is percentage points, with the exception of the Jamaican PATH program, where the unit is days.

b. The transfer amounts as a proportion of per capita expenditures (or consumption) are not the same across all tables in the report because of differences in the surveys used, including their coverage and year.

c. Impacts were measured in Jamaica only for student attendance over a 20-day reference period. The baseline enrollment rate prior to PATH was 96 percent.

* Significant at the 10 percent level.

** Significant at the 5 percent level.

*** Significant at the 1 percent level.

effect on the use of preventive health services, although the evidence is less clear-cut than with school enrollment.

Moreover, because CCT program effects on utilization are concentrated among households who were least likely to use services in the absence of the intervention, CCTs have contributed to substantial reductions in preexisting disparities in access to education and health. In Bangladesh, Pakistan, and Turkey, where school enrollment rates among girls were lower than among boys, CCTs have helped reduce this gender gap. In Cambodia, the JFPR program eliminated sharp socioeconomic gradients in enrollment among eligible households—although the coverage of the program was quite small. And in Nicaragua, the CCT impact on both school enrollment and growth monitoring was largest among extremely poor households, as shown

Table 5 Impact of CCTs on Health Center Visits by Children, Various Years

Country	Program	Outcome	Age range (years)	Baseline level (%)[a]	Impact[b]	Transfer (% of PCE)[c]	Evaluation method	Reference
Chile	Chile Solidario	Regular checkups	0–6	17.6	2.4 (2.7)	7	RDD	Galasso (2006)
Colombia	Familias en Acción	Child taken to growth and development monitoring	0–1	n.a.	22.8*** (6.7)	17	PSM, DD	Attanasio et al. (2005)
			2–4	n.a.	33.2*** (11.5)			
			4+	n.a.	1.5* (0.8)			
Ecuador	Bono de Desarrollo Humano	Child had growth control in last 6 months	3–7	n.a.	2.7 (3.8)	10	R	Paxson and Schady (2008)
Honduras	Programa de Asignación Familiar	Child taken to health center at least once in past month	0–3	44.0	20.2*** (4.7)	9	R	Morris, Flores, et al. (2004)
Jamaica	Program of Advancement through Health and Education	Number of visits to health center for preventive reasons in past 6 months	0–6	0.205	0.278*** (0.085)	10	RDD	Levy and Ohls (2007)
Mexico	Oportunidades	Number of visits to all health facilities in past month	0–2	0.219	−0.032 (0.037)	20	R	Gertler (2000)
			3–5	0.221	0.027 (0.019)			

continued

Table 5 continued

Country	Program	Outcome	Age range (years)	Baseline level (%)[a]	Impact[b]	Transfer (% of PCE)[c]	Evaluation method	Reference
Nicaragua	Atención a Crisis	Child weighed in last 6 months	0–6	70.5	6.3*** (2.0)	18	R	Macours, Schady, and Vakis (2008)
Nicaragua	Red de Protección Social	Child taken to health center at least once in past 6 months	0–3	69.8	8.4 (5.9)	27	R	Maluccio and Flores (2005)
		Child taken to health center and weighed in past 6 months	0–3	55.4	13.1* (7.5)			

Source: Authors' calculations.

Note: DD = difference-in-differences; n.a. = not available; PCE = per capita expenditure; PSM = propensity score matching; R = randomized; RDD = regression discontinuity design. This table contains weighted means for the coefficients for Chile, combining rural and urban estimates. The standard error in this case is the square root of the averaged variances of these estimates.

a. The unit for baseline level corresponds to the proportion of children who have been taken to the health center, with the exception of Jamaica and Mexico, where the unit corresponds to the number of visits.

b. The column for "impact" reports the coefficient and standard error (in parentheses); the units are percentage points, with the exception of Jamaica, where the unit is the number of visits to the health center in the past six months, and Mexico, where the unit is the number of visits to the health center in the past month.

c. The transfer amounts as a proportion of per capita expenditures (or consumption) are not the same across all tables in the report because of differences in the surveys used, including their coverage and year.

* Significant at the 10 percent level.

*** Significant at the 1 percent level.

in figure 4. As Amartya Sen (1985) and others have noted, poverty takes many forms—including an inability to develop basic "capabilities" in education and health. Providing all citizens in a country with an equality of opportunities is an important policy goal, and CCTs have helped level the playing field between rich and poor, more and less favored.

Although there is clear evidence that CCTs have increased the use of education and health services, evidence on the impact of CCTs on "final" outcomes in education and health is more mixed. Some (but by no means all) evaluations have found that CCTs contributed to improvements in child height among some population groups; there is also some evidence that program beneficiaries have better health status.[6]

Figure 4 Heterogeneity of Impacts by Socioeconomic Status, Nicaragua, 2000

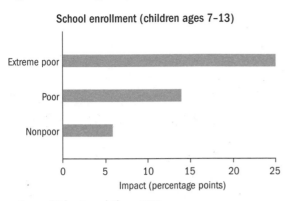

School enrollment (children ages 7–13)

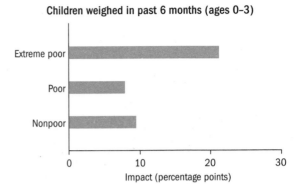

Children weighed in past 6 months (ages 0–3)

Source: Maluccio and Flores 2005.

Turning to education outcomes, adults with more exposure to the Oportunidades program in Mexico have completed more years of schooling than have those with less exposure; however, the likely increase in wages that can be expected to occur because of this added schooling is small. Also, a number of evaluations have concluded that the higher enrollment levels have not resulted in better performance on achievement tests, even after accounting for selection into school.[7] This pattern of program effects—increases in enrollment, without more learning—is not particular to CCTs. Nevertheless, the results are sobering because they suggest that the potential for CCTs to improve learning *on their own* may be limited. The evidence is somewhat more encouraging regarding the impact of CCT programs on cognitive development in early childhood (Macours, Schady, and Vakis 2008; Paxson and Schady 2008). This suggests that very early intervention might produce larger payoffs than one would expect, for example, by looking at the pattern of program effects on school enrollment by age or school grade.

There are various reasons why CCTs may have had only modest effects on "final" outcomes in education and health. One possibility is that some important constraints at the household level are not addressed by CCTs as currently designed; these constraints could include poor parenting practices, inadequate information, or other inputs into the production of education and health. Another possibility is that the quality of services is so low, perhaps especially for the poor, that increased use alone does not yield large benefits.

Policy and Design Options

Earlier in this overview, we discussed the circumstances under which a CCT is desirable. Given that a CCT is put in place, how should it be designed? We now turn to questions of CCT program design, including the selection of beneficiaries, the monitoring of conditions, the size of the transfer, and the complementary interventions that are needed.

Defining the Target Population

Selecting eligible beneficiaries is the first question any policy maker considering a CCT must address. A CCT should be designed to target *poor households* (for whom there is a stronger rationale to redistribute) *that underinvest in the human capital of their children.*

In practice, selecting the target population for a CCT first implies defining the criteria for eligibility based on poverty. The challenges of selecting the "right" targeting method and setting cut-off points for eligibility (that is, who qualifies as poor) are similar to those faced in the design of any social assistance program.

Defining the second criterion for targeting (that is, households that underinvest in the human capital of their children) is more complicated. In general, when households have qualified based on poverty criteria, CCT programs continue to make transfers as long as those households have children of the "right" ages and send them to school and/or take them to a health center. In some cases, it may be worthwhile to use a more narrow demographic target to direct transfers to population subgroups that appear to have the largest human capital gaps. This more narrow approach could imply targeting poor households with children transitioning from primary to secondary school in some countries, and poor households with young children in regions with high rates of malnutrition in others.

There may be trade-offs between redistributive and human capital goals resulting from alternative targeting approaches. In a setting in which a large share of the poor population experiences significant and similar human capital gaps, trade-offs are likely to be small. On the other hand, when human capital gaps are highly concentrated on a relatively small proportion of the poor, designing a CCT to maximize impact on human capital accumulation may limit its ability to act as a redistributive mechanism.

Selecting the Appropriate Conditions and the Size of the Transfer

Is the increase in the use of education and health services that results from CCTs purely a result of the income effects inherent in the transfer? Answering this question has important implications for the extent to which conditions are implemented and monitored, and the degree to which noncomplying households are penalized. As it turns out, evidence from a variety of sources (including comparisons across programs or countries, accidental glitches in program implementation, intentional features of program design, and structural models of household behavior) suggests that the impact of CCT programs on service use cannot be explained by the cash component of the program alone. [8] The conditions are thus important, at least in terms of increasing levels of school enrollment and the use of preventive health care.

However, service use is generally a means to an end. Thus the first step in selecting the "right" conditions is a review of the evidence on links between service use and the desired outcomes. Is getting children into health facilities the most effective way to improve their nutrition and health more broadly? Or is giving mothers nutrition and parenting information and training more effective?

Conditioning the cash transfer on the achievement of outcomes themselves is another possibility, particularly when links between such behaviors as service use and outcomes are unknown or complex, but outcomes are judged to be mostly within beneficiaries' control. In the future, experimentation with alternative incentive schemes (through small-scale pilot programs, for example) should become increasingly important. This could be done by adding performance bonuses to the basic benefits households receive for satisfying attendance conditions.

A second question is how to set the appropriate transfer amount. As discussed above, larger transfers generally have produced bigger improvements in consumption (or income) poverty—a result that seems reasonable. In terms of education and health outcomes, the critical questions are (1) how income-elastic are the outcomes? and (2) do larger transfers result in bigger behavioral changes by recipient households? In terms of enrollment in Cambodia, the marginal return to transfers appears to diminish very quickly—even though the "baseline" transfer is quite small (Filmer and Schady 2009a). More generally, however, the appropriate transfer amount for a CCT is likely to depend on the relative weight given to the program's redistribution and human capital goals, and is likely to vary across outcomes and settings. Structural modeling and small-scale experimentation can help policy makers identify and quantify the trade-offs (Bourguignon, Ferreira, and Leite 2003; Attanasio, Meghir, and Santiago 2005; Todd and Wolpin 2006a).

Entry and Exit Rules

The design of an effective program also requires careful consideration of rules for entry and exit. This is necessary to avoid confusion among prospective beneficiaries and to minimize the potential for manipulation and abuse. Entry and exit rules also are important because they can have unintended incentive effects, particularly related to labor force participation. To date, CCTs have used a proxy means rather than an income threshold to target benefits, and so the correspondence between program eligibility and labor supply is weaker than in many welfare programs in developed countries. However, the better a proxy means is at distinguishing "poor" from "nonpoor" households, the more highly it will be correlated with income and consumption—and the more likely it is to provide disincentives for adult labor market participation. Potential solutions include the use of time limits on benefits (as in Chile or in the United States under the Temporary Assistance for Needy Families [TANF] program), and the adoption of graduated benefits (whereby there is only a partial reduction of benefits after recertification shows households have ceased to be eligible under original criteria) in order to avoid "cliffs" and the associated negative incentive effects on labor supply.

Complementary Interventions

In many developing countries, the delivery of education and health services is dysfunctional. Poor infrastructure, absenteeism, and lack of adequate supplies are not unusual problems in schools and health centers. Achieving the human capital goals of CCT programs will require adaptation of the supply of services. In some countries, this adaptation may require governments or other actors to provide services where none existed before. Improving quality is perhaps an even greater challenge, and some governments have attempted to address this by offering monetary incentives to providers of health and education services for good performance. Reforms to increase access and the coverage of services frequently have been undertaken in parallel with or as an integral part of the CCT program.

In addition to the poor quality of services, other constraints at the household level may make it difficult for CCTs to improve final outcomes in health and education. Figure 5 makes this point for Ecuador. The figure shows the scores of children on a test of cognitive development in early childhood. At age 3, most children in the Ecuador sample are only modestly behind the reference population. By age 6, the age when they enter first grade, children in the two poorest deciles of the national distribution of wealth are almost three standard deviations behind where they should be. The implication is clear: a CCT by itself or even in combination with high-quality schools is unlikely to remedy such disadvantages. This is particularly important because recent theoretical and empirical research suggests that the returns to investments

Figure 5   Cognitive Development by Wealth Decile in Ecuador, 2003–04

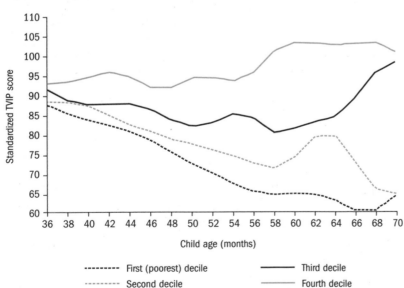

Source: Paxson and Schady 2007.

Note: TVIP = Test de Vocabulario en Imágenes Peabody. Each line corresponds to one decile from the national distribution of wealth, from the first (poorest) decile, to the fourth. The test is coded so that a score of 100 corresponds to the average performance in a reference population, and the standard deviation is 15.

later in the life cycle will be limited if children do not have adequate levels of cognitive, social, and emotional development in early childhood (Cunha et al. 2006; Knudsen et al. 2006).

Under these circumstances, interventions that seek to improve parenting practices and the quality of the home environment are likely to be particularly important. Oportunidades and some other CCTs attempt to expose parents to new information and practices by conditioning transfers on participation in talks (known as *pláticas*). The conditioned cash helps ensure that parents attend and participate in the *pláticas*. However, the cash-condition package offered by CCT programs may not be enough, and a comprehensive program that relies on more active participation by social workers and others may be needed.

CCTs in the Context of Social Protection Policies

CCT programs are just one option within the arsenal of social protection programs that can be used to redistribute income to poor households. They *cannot* be the right instrument for all poor households—for example, they cannot serve the elderly poor, childless households, or households whose children are outside the age range covered by the CCT. Redistribution to those groups is better handled through other means. In the case of the elderly poor, the potential labor supply disincentives from cash transfers are likely to be low, and the justification for further investments in human capital is questionable. As a result, social (or noncontributive) pensions often are the preferred instrument used by both developed and developing countries to provide assistance to elderly poor people.

Also, a CCT is unlikely to be the best instrument for social risk management. CCTs have been used to help cushion the negative impact of various types of crises on the poor. But their focus on long-term investments in human capital and their reliance on administrative targeting mean that CCT programs generally are not the best instrument to deal with transient poverty. Transfer programs that do not involve long-term commitments (such as those implicit in CCT conditions), that are self-targeted (and thus do not involve complex administrative decisions for entry or exit into the program), and that involve beneficiaries in activities that can help address the source of the shock (for example, job-related activities) appear to be better suited than are CCTs as instruments for managing risk.

Thus in most country contexts, CCT and other cash transfer programs are likely to coexist and should be seen as complements, rather than substitutes, addressing different household characteristics and the nature of the poverty those households experience. It is not surprising that policy makers and program managers for CCTs in Latin America, the region where such programs have the longest tradition and the most established status, increasingly are casting CCTs as part of a broader system of social protection. Doing so requires making the basic design features of programs compatible—for example, the transfer size in a CCT must be set in relation to that of other cash transfers to limit distortions, ensure horizontal equity, and make programs politically acceptable.

Finally, the potential administrative synergies across cash transfer programs are large. Perhaps the most obvious examples are common systems for administrative targeting and common systems to make payments to beneficiaries (such as with electronic cards). Numerous countries also are considering or experimenting with a common outreach and service platform—one-stop shops that beneficiaries of all social protection programs can use to access benefits and interact with program administrators.

Conclusion

CCT programs often are described in both extremely positive and negative terms. Our review of the CCT experience so far confirms that the programs have been effective in the sense that there is solid evidence of their positive impacts in reducing short-term poverty and increasing the use of education and health services. Those achievements should not be minimized because they are powerful proof that well-designed public programs can have significant effects on critical social indicators. CCTs also have had positive institutional externalities—most notably, through their emphasis on monitoring and evaluation, whereby they have helped strengthen a results culture within the public sector, at least within social policies. That strengthening is clearly a legacy worth sustaining. At the same time, our review provides ample reasons to be cautious and avoid transforming the obvious virtues of CCTs into a blind advocacy campaign in support of them.

Fifty years ago, Albert Hirschman (1958) argued that development is a "chain of disequilibria" whereby the expansion of one sector creates backward or forward pressures that can provide the necessary stimulus for the expansion of another sector, which is still underdeveloped. Those links operate not only through the standard motivation for profit, but also by building political pressure for government action. CCT programs have increased poor people's demand for services and have the potential to unleash a broader process to transform health, education, and social protection services. It is still too early to tell whether the current wave of CCT programs will produce those results, but the experience so far provides room for hope.

CHAPTER ONE

Introduction

COUNTRIES HAVE BEEN ADOPTING OR CONSIDERING ADOPTING conditional cash transfer (CCT) programs at a prodigious rate. In some countries, including Brazil, Ecuador, and Mexico, CCTs have become the largest social assistance program, covering millions of households. They have been hailed as a way of reducing inequality, especially in the very unequal countries in Latin America; of helping households break out of a vicious cycle whereby poverty is transmitted from one generation to another; of promoting child health, nutrition, and schooling; and of helping countries meet the Millennium Development Goals. Nancy Birdsall, of the Center for Global Development, calls CCTs "as close as you can come to a magic bullet in development" (Dugger 2004). Conversely, an article in the *Institute of Development Studies Bulletin* refers to CCTs as "superfluous, pernicious, atrocious and abominable" (Freeland 2007, p. 75), arguing that they represent an impractical way to improve the use of social services (particularly in low-income countries) and are immoral because they may deprive the neediest people of the assistance they deserve.

Do these and other claims make sense? Are they supported by the available empirical evidence? What does all of this imply for the way in which countries that have CCTs should structure or reform those programs? What about countries that do not have CCTs but are considering implementing them, often in circumstances very different from those in which they were first introduced?

This report seeks to answer these and other related questions. Specifically, it lays out a conceptual framework for thinking about the economic rationale for CCTs; it reviews the very rich evidence that has accumulated on CCTs, especially that arising from impact evaluations; it discusses how the conceptual framework and the evidence on impacts should inform the design of CCT programs in practice; and it discusses how CCTs fit in the context of broader social policies.

The report shows there is considerable evidence that CCTs have improved the lives of poor people. Transfers generally have been well targeted to poor households, have raised consumption levels, and have reduced poverty—in some countries by a substantial amount. Offsetting adjustments that could have blunted the impact of transfers, such as reductions in beneficiaries' participation in the labor market, appear to have been relatively modest. Moreover, CCT programs often have provided an entry point to reforming badly targeted subsidies and upgrading the quality of safety nets. The report thus argues that CCTs have been an effective way of redistributing income to the poor, although it recognizes that even the best-designed and best-managed CCTs cannot fulfill all of the needs of a comprehensive social protection system. They need to be complemented with other interventions, such as social pensions and workfare or employment programs.

The report also considers the rationale for conditioning transfers on the use of specific health and education services by program beneficiaries. Using such conditions (as opposed to making unconditional cash transfers) can be justified as a means to reinforce incentives for households to invest more in the human capital of their children—for example, when there is inadequate information about the returns to these investments, myopia, "incomplete altruism" between parents and their children, or externalities that are not taken into account by households. More generally, political economy considerations sometimes may favor conditional over unconditional transfers. For example, both taxpayers and beneficiaries may be more likely to support transfers to the poor if those transfers are linked to efforts to overcome poverty in the long term, particularly actions to improve the welfare of their children.

CCTs also have led poor households to make more use of health and education services, a key objective that CCTs were intended to accomplish. Nevertheless, the evidence on improvements in final outcomes in health and education is more mixed. Thus, CCTs have increased the likelihood that households take their children for preventive health check-ups, but doing so has not always led to better child nutritional status; and school enrollment rates have increased substantially among program beneficiaries, but there is little evidence of improvements in learning outcomes. These findings suggest that to maximize their potential effects on poor households' accumulation of human capital, CCTs should be combined with programs to improve the quality of the supply of health and education services and provide other supporting services. The evidence also suggests the need to experiment with conditions that focus on outcomes rather than on use of services alone.

The CCT Wave

The common definition of a conditional cash transfer program is one that transfers cash to poor households if they make prespecified investments in the human capital of their children.[1] In general, this has involved attaching "conditions" to transfers. Health and nutrition conditions often require periodic checkups or growth monitoring and vaccinations for children less than 5 years of age, perinatal care for mothers, and attendance by mothers at periodic health information talks. Education conditions usually include school enrollment and attendance at 80 or 85 percent of school days, and occasionally some measure of performance. Most CCT programs transfer the money to the mother of the household, or occasionally to the student.

CCT programs have two clear objectives. First, they seek to provide poor households with a minimum consumption floor. Second, in making transfers conditional, they seek to encourage the accumulation of human capital and to break a vicious cycle whereby poverty is transmitted across generations.

Interest in and the scope of CCT programs has grown enormously in the last 10 years. The maps shown in figure 1.1 give a feel for this expansion—although they understate the expansion because the whole of Brazil and Mexico are shown as active in 1997, when the Brazilian Bolsa Escola programs were run only by a handful of municipalities and Mexico's Oportunidades program was confined to very poor rural areas. Those programs did not become national for several years. Ten years later, 29 developing countries had some type of CCT program in place (in some cases, more than one) and many other countries were planning one. The range of polities interested covers all continents, although the longest established and most evaluated programs are found predominantly in middle-income countries in Latin America.

Paralleling the rise in the number of countries with programs has been an increase in the size of some programs. Mexico's program started with about 300,000 beneficiary households in 1997, but now

Figure 1.1   CCTs in the World, 1997 and 2008

1997

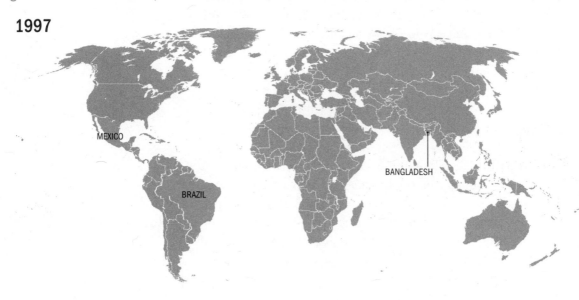

2008

Source: World Bank.

covers 5 million households. Brazil started with municipal Bolsa Escola programs in Brasilia and the municipality of Campinas. These led to replication by local governments, followed by the formulation of sector-specific federal programs, and then their unification and reform. Today, the federal Bolsa Família program serves 11 million families or 46 million people. In other countries, the increase in size has been less explosive, but still notable. In Colombia, for instance, the program's initial goal was 400,000 households, but it had expanded to cover 1.5 million households by 2007.

Many social policy analysts also see a parallel in the move to CCTs in developing countries and the welfare-to-work agenda in the United States and Europe, as embodied by reforms that led to the Revenu Minimum d'Insertion in France, the Temporary Assistance for Needy Families (TANF) reforms in the United States, and the New Deal in the United Kingdom. Like CCTs in the developing world, all of these programs require "desired behavior" in exchange for income support. In settings with highly informal labor markets, the conditions on children's health and schooling are easier to monitor than job search and work requirements and thus are sensible adaptations of the basic notion of linking social assistance to positive behavioral change.

Table 1.1 presents a partial list of CCT programs that are considered in this report. The list is not exhaustive: there are additional CCT

Table 1.1 Matrix of Program Size and Extent of Conditions

Program size/Target	Conditions	
	Education and health	Education only
Nationwide	Bolsa Família (Brazil)	Bolsa Escola (Brazil)
	Oportunidades (Mexico)	Jaring Pengamanan Sosial (Indonesia)
	Bono de Desarrollo Humano (Ecuador)	
	Familias en Acción (Colombia)	
	Program of Advancement through Health and Education (Jamaica)	
Niche (regional or narrow target population)	Chile Solidario	Female Secondary School Assistance Program (Bangladesh)
	Social Risk Mitigation Project (Turkey)	Japan Fund for Poverty Reduction (Cambodia)
		Education Sector Support Project (Cambodia)
		Basic Education Development Project (Yemen)
Small scale/pilot	Programa de Asignación Familiar (Honduras)	Subsidio Condicionado a la Asistencia Escolar–Bogotá (Colombia)
	Cash Transfer for Orphans and Vulnerable Children (Kenya)	Punjab Education Sector Reform Program (Pakistan)
	Atención a Crisis (Nicaragua)	
	Red de Protección Social (Nicaragua)	

Source: Authors' compilation.

programs in operation for which little information was available and there are some programs that fit the CCT label less well than others—for example, the Bono de Desarrollo Humano (BDH) program in Ecuador never actually has monitored compliance with the education and health conditions, even though a social marketing campaign stressed that beneficiaries were responsible for ensuring that their children were enrolled in school and were taken to health centers for preventive checkups. More information on the programs in table 1.1, as well as on other CCT programs in the developing world, is provided in program-by-program "at-a-glance" tables in appendix A.

Even without including every program, table 1.1 shows that CCTs vary a great deal in scope. Some programs are nationwide, others are niche programs, and yet others are small-scale pilot programs. Table 1.1 also shows that some programs have required that households receiving transfers comply only with schooling conditions; others, especially programs in Latin America and the Caribbean, have required that households comply both with schooling and with health conditions.

Theme and Variations

The role of CCT programs in social policy is different from place to place, as a consequence of differences in both their design and the context in which they operate. Most obviously, CCT programs vary with respect to the pertinent measures of size. In terms of absolute coverage, they range from 11 million families (Brazil), to 215,000 (Chile), to pilot programs with a few thousand families (Kenya, Nicaragua). In terms of relative coverage, programs cover a range from about 40 percent of the population (Ecuador), to approximately 20 percent (Brazil, Mexico), to 1 percent (Cambodia). In terms of budget, programs cost from about 0.50 percent of gross domestic product (GDP) in countries such as Brazil, Ecuador, and Mexico to 0.08 percent of GDP in Chile. The generosity of benefits ranges from 20 percent of mean household consumption in Mexico, to 4 percent of mean household consumption in Honduras, and to even less for the programs in Bangladesh, Cambodia, and Pakistan.

CCT programs are expected to fill different niches in social policy. In some countries (Brazil, Jamaica, Mexico), the CCT program offers large-scale social assistance and grew out of a reform and expansion of other social assistance programs.

In Mexico, Oportunidades was established to replace consumption subsidies that were badly targeted and had limited impact on poverty. By the mid-1990s, the Mexican government had 15 food subsidy programs. Of those programs, 11 were targeted at urban and rural populations and 4 had no explicit targeting mechanism (see Levy and Rodríguez [2004]; Levy [2006]). More than half of social funding was allocated to bread and tortilla subsidies in urban areas—a great deal of which was absorbed by nonpoor urban households. Food subsidies were an inefficient way to redistribute welfare to the rural poor, who often lived in small, hard-to-access communities. Approximately 60 percent of poor rural families received no support from the federal government (Rodríguez 2003). There was little coordination across programs, administrative tasks were duplicated, there was a noticeable imbalance in spending that favored urban areas, and there was no systematic evaluation to analyze the effectiveness of such programs.

Oportunidades was an innovation in Mexican social policy. In place of inefficient subsidies and poorly targeted cash transfers, the program made explicit a commitment to give beneficiaries the freedom to choose how they used the transfers as long as they committed to certain behaviors, namely education, health, and nutrition behaviors that were viewed as investments in human capital.

In Brazil, several states began to experiment with new forms of social assistance in the mid-1990s. In 1995, two programs (Bolsa Escola and the Guaranteed Minimum Family Income Program) were initiated in the Distrito Federal (Brasilia) and Campinas, respectively. The federal government started the Programa de Erradicação do Trabalho Infantil (PETI) in 1996. Two years later, the government began to provide transfers to municipalities that were running CCTs.

By 2001, CCTs with education conditions expanded to more than 100 municipalities and provided support to approximately 200,000 families (Lindert et al. 2007). In that same year, the federal government decided to create a national version of the Bolsa Escola program. It also initiated the Bolsa Alimentação (2001), a conditional cash transfer for pregnant women and lactating women with children; the Auxílio Gás (2002), an unconditional cash transfer intended to dampen the effects on poor families as cooking gas subsidies were phased out; and the Cartão Alimentação (2003), a general cash transfer to the extremely poor population to promote food consumption and prevent hunger. Bolsa Família was created in 2003 by merging Bolsa Escola, Bolsa

Alimentação, Cartão Alimentação, and Auxílio Gás. That consolidation of programs signaled an effort to improve the efficiency of the social safety net and to broaden federal support for poverty-targeted programs.

In other countries, such as Chile, programs are smaller and are meant to fill the cracks between and tie together a large number of existing social services. In some countries, CCT programs stand independently (Honduras, Jamaica), in others they provide links to a large and sometimes increasing array of other services (Chile, Colombia, Mexico). In several countries, CCT programs are still small pilot efforts (Kenya, Nicaragua). In still other countries, the programs' roots are in the education sector (Cambodia) or are a hybrid of social assistance and education (Bangladesh, Kenya). Some of the nascent programs will focus more on the nutrition of young children.

Many of the programs in middle-income countries have pursued an integrated approach to poverty reduction, balancing goals of social assistance and human capital formation. They cover children from birth (or prenatally) through their mid-teens, with conditions on health care use for children from birth to ages 5 or 6 and with conditions on school enrollment thereafter. Targeting usually is done with a proxy means test, sometimes combined with geographic targeting. In most cases, programs are administered by ministries of social welfare or freestanding agencies under the presidency. Examples of that type of CCT include Argentina, Brazil, Colombia, El Salvador, Jamaica, Mexico, Panama, and Turkey. Mexico has one of the iconic programs in this class. The program started early, its evolution has been carried out thoughtfully, and it has been successful. What really makes Mexico's program iconic is the successive waves of data collected to evaluate its impact, the placement of these data in the public domain, and the hundreds of papers and thousands of references to them that this easy access has generated.

Brazil's efforts also have been exemplary. The program started early, has evolved enormously, and is equally large in coverage and importance. Brazil's CCT provides something of an interesting contrast to the Mexican case in various respects—the issue of federalism is more to the fore in the program; it takes a softer, more gradual tack on conditions; and it puts a shade more emphasis on redistribution than on human capital formation. Also, unlike the Mexican program, the Brazilian programs did not explicitly incorporate impact evaluations in their design; as a result, much less is known about the impact they have had on consumption, poverty, health, nutrition, and education than is true of Mexico's program. Table 1.2 shows some of the more salient similarities and differences between the Oportunidades program in Mexico and the Bolsa Família program in Brazil.

There is another branch of the CCT program family that focuses on education in low-income countries. The programs usually cover a

Table 1.2 Implementation of "Similar" Programs: Contrast between Mexico and Brazil

Program feature	Mexico	Brazil
More-similar features		
Program size	5 million families 25% of the population	11 million families 25% of the population
Definition of conditions	Education: • School enrollment and minimum attendance rate of 85%, both monthly and annually • Completion of high school (for savings account)	Education: • At least 85% school attendance in a 3-month period for children aged 6–15
	Health: • Compliance by all household members with the required number of health center visits and mother's attendance at health and nutrition lectures	Health: • Children 0–7: vaccination and follow-up of nutritional development • Pregnant women: pre- and postnatal visits, health and nutrition seminars
Less-similar features		
Targeting system	Geographic targeting used to determine which rural areas participated initially	Geographic targeting used to assign ration of slots in registry of poor households
	Proxy means test used for household targeting within localities and in urban areas	Means test used as household targeting system
	Program itself does targeting and program registration	Municipalities do program targeting and program registration
Evaluation	Explicitly taken into account in program design	No systematic attempt to integrate evaluation of program impact into design
Benefit structure	Differentiated by age, grade, gender	Differentiated by poverty level
Payment mechanism	In cash at program-specific payment points	Via debit card usable at banks, ATM machines, and lottery points
Enforcement of conditions	Rigorous, reduction in benefits at first round of noncompliance	Warning system, noncomplying households seen as in need of additional "care" and problem solving

Source: Authors' compilation.

narrower segment of education—some only secondary (Bangladesh's Female Secondary School Assistance Program [FSSAP]; Cambodia's Japan Fund for Poverty Reduction [JFPR] and Education Sector Support Project [CESSP]), some only primary (Bolivia, Kenya, and proposals in Nigeria and Tanzania), and occasionally both (Indonesia's Jaring Pengamanan Sosial [JPS] program). The genesis of these programs is rather varied. In Bangladesh, the FSSAP was part of a strategy to close the then significant gender gap in education. Doing so was seen as an important policy objective: in 1981, the female literacy rate (approximately 13 percent) was about half the literacy rate among men (26 percent). As a result, a series of stipend and tuition waiver programs was made available to girls as long as they attended school regularly, made passing grades, and remained unmarried. In addition, the Food for Education (FFE) program was initiated in 1995 to provide in-kind food transfers to poor households as long as they sent their children to primary school (Ravallion and Wodon 2000). The FFE in-kind transfer was converted to a cash transfer in 2002, and was renamed as the Primary Education Stipend Program.

In Indonesia, the JPS program was instituted following the East Asian financial crisis in order to prevent children from dropping out. In Kenya and Tanzania, the programs are geared especially to coping with the crisis of orphans and vulnerable children that has burgeoned in the wake of HIV/AIDS. In many cases, the administrative structure behind these programs is less sophisticated than it is for the big Latin American programs. This is a result of several things. First, because these are primarily education programs and often are run through the education ministry, there are fewer actors to coordinate. Second, daily attendance is not always a condition of receipt of the transfer, and that simplifies administration. Third, the programs are newer and situated in lower-capacity countries so simpler systems are to be expected. To compensate for the lack of a complex administrative structure, the role of the community in implementing the programs is often greater than it is in the Latin American programs.

Chile Solidario works in a very different way to fill a different niche. The program is targeted to only the extremely poor, about 5 percent of Chile's population. It differs notably from classic CCT programs by customizing its conditions. Families initially work intensely with social workers to understand actions that could help them get out of extreme poverty, and then they commit to action plans that become the household-specific conditions of the benefit. The diagnosis covers a total of 53 different so-called minimum conditions grouped along seven dimensions (identification and legal documentation, family dynamics, education, health, housing, employment, and income). Households receive a comparatively small cash transfer, with the amount declining periodically during the two years of active participation, and then a still lower amount for an additional three years following the program. However, they receive preferential access to the full range of Chilean social assistance programs from the time they join Chile Solidario through the end of the three-year follow-up period. Additional, though small, transfers come from those other social programs; the transfer from Chile Solidario itself is really intended only to motivate clients to avail themselves of the services of the social worker. Chile Solidario is thus far a model unto itself, although other programs are moving to emulate it to a degree.[2]

The different goals and contexts of the programs suggest that somewhat different benchmarks may be pertinent to judge them, and different weights should be given to results in different dimensions—for example, reduction in consumption poverty versus improvements in human development outcomes. Primary school enrollment in Colombia and Mexico already exceeded 90 percent before the CCT programs. Enrollment increased slightly due to the CCTs, but dramatic gains were not possible because the base was already so high. Those programs, however, emphasized their role in social assistance and, with large transfers and well-targeted and extensive coverage, they are successful at it. The Bangladesh stipend for girls in secondary school was designed as a gender-targeted education program. It makes small cash payments, however; and given its focus on increasing girls' enrollments, it did not contemplate poverty targeting. Thus, without an understanding of the program and its original goals, one could consider it a failure by the standards of social assistance.

Variation can occur not only among countries, but even within a single program over time. For example, in the 10 years of its existence, Mexico's Oportunidades has undergone continuous evolution of implementation systems in order to respond to changing needs as the program expanded and as administrative systems were built. The role of geographic targeting was reduced as the program achieved national coverage, the role of community targeting was eliminated, and the role of the proxy means test increased accordingly. Carrying out the proxy means test and eligibility procedures moved from contracted agencies to in-house staff. Both eligibility and compliance monitoring were moved from a paper-based system to computerized systems, and most of the data now flows via the Internet. The timeline for bringing people into the program has been reduced from 6–8 months to 4–8 days, and a set of benefits held in a savings account was added to the cash payment.

The role and design of CCT programs is evolving in many countries. Early successes with the basic model are bringing countries to address a second and third round of challenges, including these:

- Should the emphasis on expanding the supply of services be complemented with efforts to improve the quality of those services, in tandem with the demand-increasing action of the CCT?
- Should the range or definition of conditions be changed, for example, to reward performance instead of, or in addition to, service use?
- What can be done to ensure that youth who are aging out of the school support provided by the program can attain jobs or receive further training?
- What should be the balance between targeting younger and older children?

In some countries, CCT programs themselves are addressing those challenges through adjustment to their basic design; in other cases, they are catalyzing changes in other programs.

Outline of the Report and Issues Covered

This report seeks to bring together existing knowledge about CCTs. Starting with the Mexican program Oportunidades, an important feature of CCT programs has been the strong emphasis they have placed on credible evaluations of their impact on various outcomes. The report draws heavily on those evaluations, and expands on earlier efforts to assess the performance of CCT programs using evidence from impact evaluations (see Das, Do, and Özler 2005; Rawlings and Rubio 2004). Indeed, it would not have been possible to write this report without the efforts of the programs themselves, international donors, and academics around the world to ensure the high quality of many of the evaluations. (See appendix B for further discussion of CCT impact evaluations.)

The accumulating evidence of positive impacts has been instrumental both in sustaining existing programs and in encouraging the establishment of similar programs in other developing countries.[3] Nevertheless, although the initial group of evaluations provided solid evidence of impact along several key dimensions, important policy and operational questions remain. First, much of what is known about CCTs is based on evaluations of programs in Latin America, especially Mexico. It is not clear, therefore, whether CCTs could be expected to have similar impacts in other settings, especially in countries that are significantly poorer and that tend to have weaker institutions. Although much of the evidence discussed in this report is based on studies of Latin American programs, we have made a special effort to discuss the evidence from countries in other regions, especially programs in Bangladesh and Cambodia.

Second, as CCT programs have become larger—in several countries they represent a substantial share of public budgets dedicated to poverty reduction—demand for evidence on their results has grown beyond the initial emphasis on a small number of outcomes. For example, policy makers and academics increasingly are focusing on possible long-term effects of the transfers, as well as on changes in "final" outcomes (say, learning rather than school enrollment, or nutritional status rather than frequency of growth monitoring checkups). This report pays particular attention to these outcomes, which have been discussed less extensively in the literature on CCTs.

Third, the fact that CCT programs are being implemented in very diverse country settings raises many questions regarding their design: the role of conditions, the appropriate means of targeting, the right size of the transfer, and the best way to coordinate CCT programs with the supply of services are just a few of the important questions being asked. Again, we make special efforts to analyze the possible importance of these features of program design in explaining changes in outcomes, and to consider carefully the appropriate role of a CCT within a country's social assistance system (although that is a complex agenda that goes beyond the goals of this report).

The rest of the report proceeds as follows. Chapter 2 provides a conceptual framework in which to think about CCTs. The chapter focuses particularly on when it makes sense to condition transfers on household investments in child human capital. It discusses three broad sets of circumstances under which CCTs are likely to be particularly attractive. The first set of circumstances is a case in which parents invest less in the human capital of their children than is warranted by the private returns to those investments. That situation might happen because parents value their own welfare more than that of their children; are poorly informed about the returns to investments in education, health, and nutrition; or are myopic and discount the future very heavily. In the second set of circumstances, there are externalities to human capital investments, as might be true if there are spillovers from having a better-educated or more healthy population that are not taken into account by rational individuals when they make decisions about investments. The third set of circumstances is one in which there are political economy considerations that justify imposing conditions on transfers, as might be the case, for example, when it is easier to sustain a budget for a program if transfers are perceived not as a handout but as a quid pro quo whereby a government gives households cash if—and only if—these households act "responsibly" and invest in their children.

Following that conceptual discussion, chapter 3 describes in detail how CCT programs work. Virtually all CCT programs have attempted to direct their benefits to the poor so the chapter begins with a discussion of the targeting instruments used in different programs. It then describes the benefit systems, including who receives the payment, how payment takes place, and what payment levels are in practice. The chapter continues by describing how programs have monitored conditions and the extent to which households are penalized for noncompliance. The final two sections of the chapter discuss the importance of monitoring and evaluation and how CCTs have coordinated with other actors in the social sectors.

Redistribution of resources to the poor is one of the two fundamental goals of most CCT programs, and chapter 4 presents the evidence of CCT impact on consumption poverty. The chapter discusses the impacts in the short term and, for two countries (Mexico and Nicaragua), in the medium term. Many policy makers originally had concerns that the effects of CCTs on household consumption would be relatively small as households made offsetting adjustments. As the chapter discusses, however, those adjustments—in terms of reductions in adult labor supply, in remittances, or in household access to other social programs—have been modest. As a result, the impact of CCTs on consumption poverty is largely determined (at least in the short run) by the size of the transfer and the extent to which programs effectively can ensure that the cash reaches poor households.

The second fundamental goal of CCTs is to encourage households to invest in the human capital of their children. Chapter 5 turns to the evidence on the impact that CCTs have had on outcomes in education, health, and nutrition. The chapter begins by showing that CCTs have had significant effects on the use of education and health services, and that those effects often have been substantial in magnitude. It then discusses the evidence of CCT effects on "final" outcomes in education and health. The chapter shows that the evidence on the impact of CCTs on these outcomes is somewhat mixed. Thus, CCTs appear to have had a modest impact on years of schooling completed by adults; they reduced the incidence of low child height for age in some countries and among some populations but not others; and they had little effect on learning outcomes among either school-age children or adults. Addressing those shortcomings is likely to require a combination of efforts: redefining conditions, perhaps including incentives for performance, not only service use; improving the quality of the supply of services; and complementing CCTs with interventions that help households overcome other barriers to adequate child nutrition, development, and learning. The chapter closes by discussing whether CCT program impacts that are observed are the result of the "income" effect associated with the transfer or the "price" effect that results from the conditions.

Chapter 6, the final chapter of the report, returns to the conceptual framework presented in chapter 2. In particular, with the evidence from chapters 4 and 5 in hand, it discusses when CCT programs are likely to be the right policy instrument. It then turns to a discussion of how CCT programs should be designed—for example, in terms of the population covered, the conditions that are monitored, and the magnitude of the transfer. The chapter closes by considering where CCTs fit in the context of social policies. An important message of the chapter is that CCTs have shown themselves to be effective and versatile programs. However, they are most likely to be effective in stimulating investments in child human capital and in providing a social safety net when they work closely with other programs. The chapter reviews some of the ongoing efforts by developing countries in this area. It also argues that there are other interventions—workfare or employment programs, pensions—that need to complement even the best-designed and best-managed CCT.

CHAPTER TWO

The Economic Rationale for Conditional Cash Transfers

CCTS ARE CASH TRANSFERS THAT ARE (1) TARGETED TO THE POOR and (2) made conditional on certain behaviors of recipient households. More specifically, these cash transfers are conditioned on minimum levels of use of health and education services, generally by (or for the benefit of) the children in the household. Typical requirements include enrollment and actual attendance at schools (for example, minimum attendance rates of 85 percent are required in Brazil's Bolsa Família and a similar restriction applies in Mexico's Oportunidades). Programs that have a health component also may require that children make regular visits to a health center and receive immunizations, and that pregnant women and lactating mothers keep a predetermined number of appointments at local clinics or attend informational sessions (*pláticas*) on hygiene and nutrition.

This chapter provides a conceptual understanding of how CCTs work. Governments have scarce resources and CCTs—whether they increase service use or not—compete for funds with other worthwhile projects, such as buying school equipment or upgrading rural roads. Why is giving people money to keep their children in (possibly very bad) schools a good use of public funds? Wouldn't it be better to buy more books and supplies or to improve teacher training so as to raise the quality of the education provided in those schools?

Even if there are good arguments for spending part of the government's budget on direct cash transfers to households, does it really make sense to attach conditions to the cash? After all, if attending those schools (or walking 5 miles to the local clinic to have the baby weighed) contributed more to expected future well-being than an alternative use of the child's time, wouldn't households already be sending their children there? A condition is a constraint on behavior. What good can come of adding a constraint to the household's optimization problem? Why not just make the transfer unconditionally?

Economists might think of at least two kinds of disadvantage associated with attaching conditions to cash transfers. First, some of the neediest households might find the conditions too costly to comply with (because the clinics are too far away or because their need for child help in harvesting a living from the land is too pressing), and may thus be deterred from taking up the benefit. Conditions thereby might exclude some of the people the program aims to reach. Second, those households that do opt for the benefit may incur a costly distortion to their own behavior for the sake of a little extra cash in the short run. Perhaps they know how bad the local school (or clinic) is. Perhaps it is wasteful for the children to spend time there, rather than learning how to tend the fields or how to weave a basket with their parents. By pushing poor households to do something that they would otherwise not be doing, CCTs might be imposing costly distractions on people who are trying to do the best thing for their families under conditions of severe scarcity.

Proponents of CCT programs should have good answers to questions and arguments such as those posed above. There are, in fact, a number of good reasons for attaching conditions to targeted cash transfers. This chapter reviews the case for conditioning, and briefly discusses some of the empirical evidence on how likely it is that circumstances that justify conditions are found in practice.

Cash Transfers: Arguments in Support and Against

The first question one might ask when considering whether a CCT makes sense is this: are cash transfers *in general* a good instrument in a particular country? That question is by no means rhetorical. Even if everyone accepts poverty reduction as a central policy objective, it does not follow immediately that the government should spend its scarce resources by transferring cash directly to poor people.

Broadly, one hears two arguments against such transfers: First, poverty is best reduced by economic growth, particularly in the poorest countries. In those same countries, fiscal efforts and administrative capacity both tend to be low, and governments should focus on providing basic infrastructure (which could include roads and ports as well as schools and clinics). In this view, cash transfers to a vast poor majority are seen as having a lower future payoff than investment in public capital, and as being harder to target and deliver. The second argument against cash transfers is that they provide the wrong incentives to recipients. For example, they may discourage labor supply or investment in a person's own human capital for future gainful employment. If the government provides the basic necessities of life, the thinking goes, why would people in low-productivity settings bother with very hard work that pays so little?

When combined, those arguments are not to be dismissed immediately. Direct investment in public infrastructure is likely to be a serious alternative use of public funds in very poor countries, and handouts of public cash can discourage self-reliance. But there also are many arguments *for* direct redistribution. First, in most developing countries, public expenditure on infrastructure and public services—of the kind just advocated—often fails to reach the very poor. In Nicaragua, only 10 percent of households in the bottom quintile of the expenditure distribution had access to electricity in 1998, compared with more than 90 percent of households in the top quintile (de Ferranti et al. 2004, p. 209). The sizable electricity subsidies that were in place in Mexico in 2000 also had a regressive incidence, as documented by Scott (2002). In fact, the proponents of the pioneering Oportunidades CCT program explicitly couched the initiative as an alternative to the electricity and tortilla subsidies, in a way that would be both more equitable (by reaching the poor) and more efficient (by eliminating the price distortions generated by the subsidies). In this context, if cash transfers can be shown to be targeted to the poor more effectively than other forms of public expenditure, they may contribute to poverty reduction in ways that direct public investment does not.

Second, markets seldom work perfectly in practice, and sometimes they fail in ways that prevent poor people from being as productive as they might otherwise be. If the root causes of some of these failures are too costly to correct, simple redistribution of current resources may be able to reduce the efficiency costs.[1] The classic example is that of credit-constrained families (in an economy with imperfect capital markets) that cannot make profitable investments in their children's education or in some other business project. A direct transfer of cash to these families might enable them to undertake an efficient project that would otherwise not have taken place. Once again, the transfer would be both equitable (by making a poor person better off) and efficient (by better allocating capital within the economy).

Similarly, insurance markets often are beyond the reach of many poor families. When incomes are volatile, reflecting a risky economic environment, cash transfers can smooth (some of) the fluctuations, raising household welfare. Fields et al. (2007) review evidence of substantial short-term income volatility in a number of countries in Latin America. If these fluctuations are sufficiently severe, they may affect demand for schooling or health investments, potentially with long-term consequences.[2] Once again, if fixing the insurance markets themselves is too costly or complicated, volatility can provide an additional argument for targeted cash transfer programs.

Finally, the fact that many of the inequalities one observes in the developing world are inherited from one's parents may make them ethically objectionable. Differences associated with circumstances over which individuals have no control (such as race, gender, or family background) often are regarded as "inequality of opportunity," which the state has a moral obligation to redress (see Roemer [1998] and Bourguignon, Ferreira, and Walton [2007]). Cash transfers might be suitable instruments for compensating families who suffer from inherited disadvantage.

In the face of arguments both for and against, it cannot be stated categorically that every country in the world should have a cash transfer program in place to help reduce poverty. But the case often can be made that *some* efficient redistribution of the kind just described can be achieved, as discussed in box 2.1. Chapter 5 of the *World Development Report 2006* (World Bank 2005) discusses other examples from across the developing world, both of market failures and of the resulting underinvestment.

CCT programs still may be justified in the absence of redistributive goals, as a means to improve incentives for households to invest in human capital. In the remainder of this report, however, it is assumed that policy makers have weighed the arguments for and against cash-based redistribution, and have reached a considered decision that there is some room for cash transfers in their policy arsenal against poverty.

This chapter next turns to the question of whether it makes sense to attach *conditions* to these cash transfers. The "theoretical default"

Box 2.1 Efficient Redistribution in the Presence of Market Failure

THERE ARE MANY SITUATIONS IN WHICH A market failure opens up the possibility of efficient redistribution. Under certain types of credit market imperfection, and if there are economies of scale, the poor may be unable to take advantage of profitable opportunities because they do not have access to the required scale. They thus may be trapped in a low-productivity sector of the economy, even as more productive opportunities go unexploited, because of an inability to commit to repayment in credit markets. Some amount of redistribution in cash from the rich to the poor may raise the ability of the latter to take advantage of these more profitable investments, thereby reducing both inequality and inefficiency.

This possibility was first modeled by Loury (1981), who introduced credit constraints into a model of intergenerational mobility. Galor and Zeira (1993) further noted the link between aggregate efficiency and reduced inequality under nonconvex production sets. Banerjee and Newman (1993) exploited long-term implications of the same basic type of mechanism by noting the effect of initial levels of inequality on patterns of occupational choice and subsequent inequality trajectories. All those papers demonstrate the theoretical plausibility that some redistribution may *increase efficiency*.

Empirical examples of aggregate underinvestment arising from the inability of the poor to access credit and insurance markets on equal terms now abound. In one striking case from Africa, Goldstein and Udry (1999) document the failure of many farmers to switch from a low-return maize and cassava intercrop to a much more profitable pineapple culture in southern Ghana. Despite an expected return of 1,200 percent, only 190 out of 1,070 plots in the study sample made the switch. When asked why, the modal answer was "I don't have the money." In Sri Lanka, de Mel, McKenzie, and Woodruff (2008) use a randomized experimental design to estimate the return on capital for microenterprises that generally are thought to be credit constrained. They find average monthly real rates of return of 5.7 percent—much higher than the market interest rate. The existence of investment projects (in preexisting firms) that are profitable at the prevailing market rate, but that do not take place (before the intervention) is *prima facie* evidence that the credit market is imperfect.

Until the underlying causes of failures in credit and insurance markets can be corrected, this kind of evidence suggests that targeted cash transfers can be useful not only in reducing inequality and current poverty, but also in reducing inefficiencies in the economywide allocation of resources.

position—with informed rational agents, benevolent governments, and functioning markets—should be to favor *unconditional* cash transfers. Standard revealed preference arguments establish that choice sets are larger for an unconditional cash transfer than if the same transfer is given in kind with a no-resale condition. Similar arguments also show that a consumer is at least as well-off under a cash transfer as when the same budget is used to subsidize a particular good. A transfer that is conditional on the purchase of a specific good (or the use of a particular service) is, of course, analogous to such a subsidy (even if the posttransfer price is negative).

There are three main conceptual arguments for conditioning a cash transfer. First, agents do not always behave exactly as one would expect fully informed, rational agents to behave. Private information about the nature of certain investments, or about their expected returns, may be imperfect and persistent. There is also a body of evidence from recent research in behavioral economics that suggests that people often suffer from self-control problems and excessive procrastination, in the sense that their day-to-day behavior is inconsistent with their own long-term attitude toward the future (for example, see O'Donoghue and Rabin [1999]). There also may be conflicts of interest within the household, either between the parents (who "pay" for education or health services today) and their children (who benefit tomorrow), or between the father and the mother. These conflicts of interest may result in "incomplete altruism": parental decisions that are not fully consistent with what the child would have chosen herself, if fully rational.

What imperfect information, myopia, and incomplete altruism have in common, for our purposes, is that they may cause a family's privately chosen level of investment in human capital to be too low, compared with its own "true" private optimal.[3] If they are pervasive, then these distortions in private decision making provide some contemporary support to the time-honored notion that governments may "know better" what is privately good for poor people than do the poor themselves, at least in some realms. The following section of this chapter therefore reviews these arguments under the general heading "Microfoundations of Paternalism."

The second main conceptual argument for conditioning a cash transfer is that governments typically do not behave like textbook benevolent dictators. Policy decisions generally result from decision-making processes that involve voting, lobbying, bureaucratic and interagency bargaining, and a variety of other forms of what one broadly might call political economy. Under some circumstances, conditioning cash transfers on "good behavior" may increase public support for them, making the program either feasible or better-endowed. The third section below briefly reviews this political economy argument.

A third set of justifications for making cash transfers conditional is that, even if the levels of human capital investment by the poor were privately optimal, they might not be *socially* optimal because of the presence of market failures, particularly, externalities. These justifications are considered in the fourth section, "Social Efficiency Arguments."

The Microfoundations of Paternalism

The idea that poor people need the push (or nudge) of government "incentives" to behave in ways that are "good for them" is a very old notion. It seems to imply that if left to their own devices, these agents somehow are not capable of choosing what is in their best interests. Although it is not a very fashionable notion among most mainstream economists today, paternalism (under different guises) has long been used to promote conditional forms of redistribution.

Consider, for instance, the idea that there are some specific goods that society sees as essential, as in Richard Musgrave's (1959) description of *merit goods* or merit wants. These might be goods that enter the social welfare function directly, implying that "society" derives utility from everyone being educated or from everyone having access to decent housing or health care—in addition to the benefits accruing to each individual from his or her own consumption of those goods. Another way to think about merit goods is that a "social planner" places greater welfare weight on consumption levels of certain specific goods than the individual himself would place on them (for example, see Besley [1988]). However it is modeled formally, this old idea of merit goods could be used as an argument in support of today's CCT programs: if society somehow places a value on every child being schooled or having access to health services that is greater than the value that individuals themselves place, then a CCT will provide an incentive toward that additional consumption of the merit good, as desired.[4,5]

Paternalism well may be justified if the individuals in question hold persistently erroneous beliefs; if they are not unitary agents, but households within which there may be conflicts of interest; or if they behave myopically. Recent developments in economic theory and recent empirical evidence both suggest that all three of those phenomena may be at work.[6]

The basic economics of these sources of private decision-making failure can be illustrated using a simple dynamic model of educational choice, outlined more formally in Ferreira (2008). The essence of the model is that individual welfare depends on consumption in two periods—childhood and adulthood. The link between the two periods is that children can contribute to household resources during childhood by working (some of the time) in the first period. But any time spent working comes at the expense of time spent studying (or otherwise investing in the child's human capital), and thus at the expense of earnings and consumption during adulthood. This trade-off between present and future welfare is at the heart of educational decisions made for or by children in developing countries, where child earnings (or contributions to family enterprises) often are not negligible.[7]

This simple framework sheds light on the consequences of each of the three kinds of distortion listed above for educational choice and for child welfare (under different assumptions about how the credit market works). In each case, the model tells us what we might expect from two kinds of policy response: unconditional cash transfers (UCTs) and conditional cash transfers.[8] When credit markets are missing, many of those insights can be illustrated by figure 2.1, where the household's choice of child time spent in school is plotted against the market wage rate for child labor.

The schooling investment function yields the household's demand for schooling, given the prevailing child wage rate (w_m) and a set of additional parameters, such as expected returns to schooling, the discount rate, the quality of the education expected from the school, and other incomes available to the family. When plotted against the wage rate, it slopes downward: the higher the opportunity cost of attending

Figure 2.1 Choice of Investment in Children with Missing Credit Markets

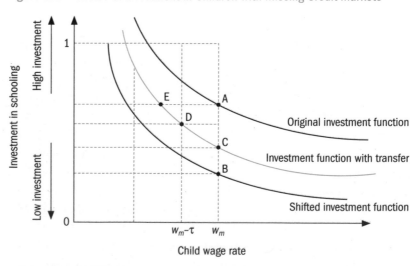

Source: Authors' illustration.
Note: w_m = child wage rate.

school, the lower the desired investment in education. Changes in the remaining arguments shift the function up or down in this space. For instance, a decline in the expected returns to (or quality of) education, a rise in the discount rate, or a reduction in the levels of other income sources available to the household would shift the investment function in figure 2.1 from a position such as that denoted "original" to one such as that denoted "shifted." This simple framework can be used to investigate the effects of the distortions mentioned above.

Misinformation or Persistently Misguided Beliefs

Suppose that, for some reason, potential beneficiaries are poorly informed about the future returns to education. Of course, if this is a simple information asymmetry with no mechanism causing the incorrect belief to persist, then the optimal policy intervention is to address the information problem—say through a publicity campaign. But processing information may be costly: Being convinced about the health benefits of greater schooling, for instance, may require time and effort to process the evidence. In addition, certain beliefs may be self-reinforcing so that when agents act on the basis of the beliefs, the outcomes confirm them, even if alternative beliefs would have led to superior outcomes.[9] It is possible that large groups of people may then believe that returns to education are lower than they really are. A possible example is that of poorer families believing that effort (perhaps in education) is less important than connections in generating upward mobility, whereas those who are better-off believe the opposite. These beliefs can lead to different actions and thus to different outcomes that appear to confirm the initial beliefs—even though the poor also would have benefited if they had put in greater effort.

It also is possible that people hold incorrect beliefs about how human capital itself accumulates (rather than about returns). They may believe that formal schooling requires very high levels of natural talent that are not to be found in their families. They may ignore the existence of links between formal schooling and parenting skills or health and hygiene outcomes. These inaccurate beliefs may result from the insufficient availability of information or from difficulties in processing the information that is available. If parents are poorly educated, it may limit their ability to process the information on education complementarities or on rates of return.[10]

In fact, there is some evidence that incorrect beliefs about education returns can persist in real populations. A practical way to test for such information problems is to compare expected returns to schooling (for example, by asking students or parents what they think) with the observed Mincerian returns from a household survey ("realized returns").[11] For example, Attanasio and Kaufmann (2008) compare expected and realized returns among 15–25-year-olds in Mexico and find that expected returns from additional schooling were lower than the realized returns, especially among children of fathers who have low education levels.

Similarly, Jensen (2006) finds that, in the Dominican Republic, eighth-grade students estimated the rate of return to secondary school to be only one quarter to one third of the rate derived from an income survey. When students were told of the real rate, those who underestimated it in the first place increased their secondary school graduation rate by 6 percentage points. Both studies provide evidence consistent with information failures resulting in inefficiently low investments in education. But the evidence is not conclusive, and testing for information failures in other types of investments in human capital is less straightforward.[12]

Also, investments in education may have positive impacts on health, and vice versa—another good reason why individuals may have a hard time adequately estimating returns. For instance, Jalan and Ravallion (2003a) show that piped water only improved health status when mothers were educated. Along similar lines, de Walque (2007) shows that an HIV/AIDS campaign in Uganda was most effective among educated households. Miguel and Kremer (2004) provide an example of how health investments (deworming) improve education outcomes.

As previously indicated, if the problem is *only* missing information, providing the information directly would seem to be the first-best intervention (rather than having a CCT). For example, Dupas (2007) shows how informing girls that HIV prevalence was higher among adult males and their partners than among teenage boys led girls to avoid the cross-generational partnerships that are riskier in terms of HIV infection rates.

However, there are at least two situations under which simply providing information may not do much. First, incorrect beliefs may be self-reinforcing, in which case merely providing the information will not help. Second, passively providing information may not be enough because, at least initially, people may not think they need the information and so may not respond to it. A transfer conditioned on attending relevant information sessions or activities thus may be a better option. One example is parenting interventions. There is a great deal of evidence that poor outcomes in early childhood can be a result of poor home environments, including inadequate parenting practices (some of this evidence for the United States is discussed in box 2.2). However, most people believe that they are not bad parents and, therefore, are unlikely to respond either to an information campaign or to home-visiting programs in which social workers teach them how to be better parents. Oportunidades and some other CCTs attempt to expose parents to new information and practices by conditioning transfers on participation in

---

Box 2.2 Investing Early in the Life Cycle

NOBEL-WINNING ECONOMIST JAMES HECKMAN and many others have argued recently for the importance of investments in early childhood (Heckman and Masterov 2007; Heckman 2008). This research makes a number of important points: (1) poor outcomes in early childhood have long-lasting implications for functioning in adulthood, including low earnings, increases in the likelihood of criminal activity, and poor parenting practices; (2) poor outcomes in early childhood are often a result of adverse home environments, including the absence of a stable family structure and nurturing relationships for children; (3) interventions in early childhood increase the productivity of interventions later in the life cycle ("learning begets learning"); (4) deficits in early childhood are much more costly to remedy later; and (5) investments in different dimensions of child well-being, such as those that lead to improvements in cognitive skills, behavioral outcomes, and child health, are interlinked in important ways. Improving outcomes in one dimension makes it more likely that children will be able to make up deficits in other dimensions.

Whereas the research by Heckman and his coauthors has focused on the United States, some of the conceptual underpinnings are relevant for the design of CCTs in developing countries. Unlike most other programs, CCTs seek to improve outcomes in various dimensions of child well-being, including education, health, and, through the *pláticas,* parenting practices (although *pláticas* are required in some but not all CCTs). Arguably, CCTs therefore implicitly attempt to exploit the synergies that Heckman and others have identified. In addition, CCTs seek to build the human capital of children throughout the life cycle, including at the earliest ages. Finally, CCTs transfer cash, and this can help alleviate the resource constraints that partly explain the adverse home environments and inadequate investments by parents in their children. That being said, CCT programs would benefit from more experimentation to see what combination of cash, conditions, social marketing, and information provision is most effective at ensuring that children do not fall behind at early ages—one of the main messages of this report.

pláticas; cumulative exposure of this sort may help do the trick, and the conditioned cash helps ensure that parents attend and participate in the talks (Schady 2006).

What might be the consequences of persistent misinformation? An underestimation of returns to schooling, for instance, could lead to an inefficiently low level of investment in education (or health), even under *perfect credit markets.* With lower expected returns, the demand for education depicted in figure 2.1 shifts downward and schooling investment falls from a high level in point A, to a low level in a point such as B. Since actual returns to schooling are higher than the household's expectation, point B is a (privately) inefficiently low level of schooling. Some form of intervention may be warranted—but what kind?

Because credit allows for a separation between investment and consumption decisions, a UCT would have *no* effect on investment under perfect credit markets. A UCT merely raises the overall level of permanent income. And when capital markets are perfect, investment in one's children, just like any other investment decision, is independent of one's income levels and depends only on expected returns and the interest rate.[13] A CCT, on the other hand, can help shift the investment level toward the optimal by reducing the opportunity cost of studying. It alters the expected returns to investment by affecting the *price* associated with the investment good, in addition to raising income levels. A CCT would move the agent along the shifted investment function, from point B upward and to the left.

On the other hand, if *credit markets are imperfect,* the effect of misguided beliefs is likely to be even greater, particularly for the poor. When credit is not available, those who are poor today may find it optimal to use child labor as a (very costly) consumption-smoothing mechanism: children may be sent out to increase the availability of consumption goods today, even at the expense of higher remuneration in the future. In this case, even a UCT would have some effect on present levels of investment in health and education. These effects correspond to the income effect of the transfer and reduce the effects of missing credit markets on educational investment. Nevertheless, a CCT generally will have a larger positive effect on investment than will an unconditional transfer of the same amount. This outcome simply follows from the fact that a CCT adds a substitution effect to the income effect of the UCT. If an underestimation of expected returns to education had shifted the household from point A to point B in figure 2.1, then a small UCT could shift it back upward to point C. A CCT of the same amount will move the household's choice to point D, entailing a higher level of investment in schooling. By remunerating school attendance, the CCT effectively lowers the opportunity cost of studying, relative to working.

Note that for the household's *welfare* (rather than simply its investment in schooling) at point D to be higher than at point C, it is critical that the household be operating under incorrect beliefs. That is why, as previously discussed, another imperfection (in addition to the credit market failure) is required to justify the condition. Credit constraints are relaxed by cash, not by conditions. If there were no additional imperfection and the only problem were a credit constraint, a UCT should be preferred. A CCT that provided the same income transfer would only inefficiently distort behavior (toward excessive schooling) through the condition.

The existence of the substitution effect discussed above has another important implication for program design: it is possible to set a CCT level too high, thus encouraging children to a rate of service use that is greater than optimal. This situation (which corresponds to points northwest of point E in figure 2.1) is evocative of anecdotes about children wasting valuable time in classrooms where they learn nothing instead of helping their parents in the field, or of children taken to unsanitary health facilities that act as disease contamination foci because parents have been bribed to take the risk. The upshot seems to be this: because CCTs impose a condition, they are more powerful instruments for inducing behavioral change than are UCTs. They are "higher-risk/higher-return" policy instruments. When private behavior is suboptimal, they correct it at a lower cost. When private behavior was fine to begin with, their misuse is likely to be costlier.

Principal–Agent Problems within the Household, or "Incomplete Parental Altruism"

Even if parents have a correct expectation of future returns to education, they may discount the future more heavily than is optimal from the point of view of the child. Basic models of schooling choice usually are written under the simplifying assumption of a unitary household. When that assumption is relaxed and the objectives of different household members are allowed to differ (say, by having different discount rates), then the ensuing conflict of interest within the household may provide another justification for CCTs: parents make the education decision for their children, but discount the future at a higher rate and, therefore, demand less schooling than the child's optimal. If policy makers take the view that the child is the principal in the matter of her own education, and that parents act as her agents, then a principal–agent problem is characterized.

A slightly different but equally plausible version of this problem is a conflict of interest between the parents themselves, as opposed or in addition to one between parents and children. One possibility is that mothers' objectives are more closely aligned with those of all her children. This closer alignment is mentioned often as a justification for handing the transfer to the mother (when there is one), as is common practice in most CCT programs, rather than to the father.

It turns out that differences in the discount rate do not affect the investment decision under perfect credit markets. Changing the discount rate will affect consumption choices—how much is consumed now versus how much is consumed in the future. Any adjustment will take place through borrowing or lending, with no effect on schooling or any other investment. As noted previously, investment and consumption decisions are separate.[14] But if credit markets are missing, then a higher parental discount rate affects the education decision in a way that is exactly analogous to a lower expected rate of return to education. The results described when discussing the effects of misguided beliefs do hold, with both a UCT and a CCT resulting in higher investments and welfare (for the child), but the conditional transfer does so at lower cost because of the induced substitution effect.

What is the empirical evidence on intrahousehold principal–agency problems? It is hard to test conclusively for the presence of "incomplete altruism".[15] Perhaps the most compelling evidence in that regard is the presence of gender differences in child human capital. The clearest case is in countries where girls' education lags significantly behind that of boys, even when the Mincerian rate of return to women's education is at least as high as that of men.[16] This kind of differential is *prima facie* evidence of inefficient underinvestment in girls' schooling and is most apparent in South Asia. Such differentials may be rational from the viewpoint of parents who are thinking of their own welfare (because girls are more costly in terms of dowries or boys are more likely to take care of their parents than are girls who move to their husbands' homes upon marrying), but they are most likely socially inefficient.

Somewhat more indirect evidence from countries outside South Asia has suggested that differential bargaining power between men and women affects the level of human capital investment in children. Indeed, there is a lengthy body of empirical literature showing that when mothers have greater control over resources, more resources are allocated to food and children's health and education (Thomas 1990; Hoddinott and Haddad 1995; Lundberg, Pollak, and Wales 1997; Quisumbing and Maluccio 2000; Attanasio and Lechene 2002; Rubalcava, Teruel, and Thomas 2004; Doss 2006; and Schady and Rosero 2008). That evidence provides a strong justification for making payments to mothers, as CCT programs do. At the same time, in circumstances in which women's power within the household is limited, attaching strings to the transfers by mandating specific human capital investments could strengthen the mother's bargaining position and reinforce her ability to shift household spending and time allocation decisions.[17]

Although the extent to which incomplete altruism can provide a blanket justification for the use of conditions is unclear, there is now a substantial body of evidence suggesting that parents (especially fathers) value their own utility more than that of their children. Girls, in particular, often are at a disadvantage. The implication is that schooling and health levels chosen on a child's behalf are likely to be too low relative to the child's optimal level, and that conditions attached to cash transfers can help drive the actual household choices toward that optimal.

A Political Economy Argument

The second class of arguments that may provide a justification for conditioning a cash transfer has to do with the political economy of funding redistribution. Transfers, whether conditional or unconditional, need to be financed, and budget allocation decisions are never really the choice of a benign social planner. Rather, they are the outcome of a (generally complex) political economy process. Most standard theories of the political determination of redistribution do not distinguish CCTs from UCTs. Voters are assumed to care only about their final welfare level, so they look at how much they receive in transfers and at how much they pay in taxes. If voters are not recipients of a targeted transfer, then, conditional on their tax bills, they should be indifferent to whether there are specific conditions attached to the transfers.

One implication of that kind of analysis is that transfer schemes narrowly targeted to the poor would tend to have limited support because a small share of the population benefit, whereas the costs are dispersed across all taxpayers. Gelbach and Pritchett (2002) have a model in which an increase in the degree of targeting actually can result in a reduction of both the equilibrium level of the transfer and the welfare of the poor. The implied vulnerability of targeted redistribution schemes to political change enjoys a measure of empirical support (see Subbarao et al. [1997] for examples from Colombia and Sri Lanka).

It is conceivable, however, that voters (or other decision makers) are not entirely self-regarding. It is possible, for instance, that taxpayers are more prepared to pay for transfers to those who are seen to be helping themselves than to other equally poor people who are seen to be lazy or careless. Some voters who object to unconditional "handouts" may be less averse to "rewards" to "deserving" poor people who are investing in the education or health of their children. (Box 2.3 contains a brief summary of evidence from the recent behavioral literature on fairness, which suggests that many people are routinely prepared to incur real financial losses to reward others whom they think are deserving or to punish those they feel have behaved unfairly.) If this view is commonly held, the introduction of conditions may result in an increase in the overall budget available for redistribution in the political equilibrium.

If none of the private inefficiencies discussed in the second section of this chapter existed, then attaching a condition to a cash transfer would be, of itself, suboptimal to beneficiaries (because it adds an additional constraint). But that cost *may* be offset by an increase in the overall size of the transfers that are funded, in which case the conditions will be justified for political economy reasons. The condition is justified by making redistribution more acceptable to taxpayers and voters—and possibly to many beneficiaries. Another way of seeing this is that, unlike a UCT, a CCT can be seen not as plain social assistance, but rather as part of a social contract whereby society (through the state) supports those poor households that are ready to make the effort to "improve their lives"—the *deserving poor.*

The notion that CCT programs constitute a new form of social contract between the state and beneficiaries has been manifested in the use of the term *co-responsibilities* (instead of conditions) in a majority of

Box 2.3 Fairness, Merit, and the "Deserving Poor"

PEOPLE OFTEN BEHAVE IN WAYS THAT ARE inconsistent with pure self-regarding preferences. In particular, there is now a substantial body of experimental evidence suggesting that large numbers of people are *altruistic rewarders* or *altruistic punishers* in the sense that they are prepared to incur personal losses to reward behavior they regard as socially fair or to punish behavior they regard as unfair (see Fehr and Schmidt [1999] for the basic theory; Fehr and Gächter [2000] for a review of the early evidence).

Some of the main results come from experiments in which subjects were asked to play what is known as an *ultimatum game* under experimental conditions. In the game, a first-mover proposes a split (of an exogenously given sum) between himself and the second player. If the second player accepts the proposal, the split is implemented. If he rejects it, both players earn zero. If people behaved as standard economic theories used to predict (that is, if preferences were purely self-regarding), then the outcome of this game—the so-called Nash equilibrium—would be "as little as possible for you, all the rest for me." Empirically, however, such an outcome is seldom observed. The modal offer is in the 30–60 percent range, depending on the cultural context.

And a sizable fraction of offers below that range is rejected outright even when the sums in play are nontrivial: people appear to be prepared to "pay" for the opportunity to punish a player whom they see as having behaved unfairly.

More interesting from the point of view of CCT programs, Hoffman et al. (1994) find that players in anonymous ultimatum games tend to be more tolerant of other players in positions of power when those positions are allocated on the basis of "merit" (that is, to those who score higher in a general knowledge quiz) than when they are allocated randomly. The accumulated evidence from the large body of literature on fairness suggests that people take considerations of "justice" into account when making decisions. The evidence from this particular study suggests that people's perceptions of what is a fair distribution may be affected by the perceived "merits" of the recipient.

Would a similar line of reasoning imply that taxpayers (or public officials) might be more willing to fund transfers to people who invest in the future of their children than to others who do not? Although some tentative suggestions in support of this conjecture are reported in the main text, more research is needed to address the question rigorously.

programs, at least in Latin America. This use is illustrated clearly in the words of the architects of the CCT program in Mexico:

> Poor families need help, but this should not suppress or undermine their role as protagonists in transforming their living conditions. Shared responsibility and respect are not only prerequisites for effectively combating poverty but are essential elements of a democratic society. Shared responsibility and respect inevitably imply a reciprocal effort by the poor families to link the benefits they receive to concrete actions on their part. Thus independently of technical considerations, in 1996

it was considered vital that PROGRESA benefits go directly to poor families and be conditioned on direct action by them to improve their own nutrition, health and education, and that such support complement but not substitute for their day-to-day efforts (Levy and Rodríguez 2004, p. 48).

A recent analysis of the treatment of the Bolsa Família program in the Brazilian media (Lindert and Vincensini 2008) provides additional support to the idea that conditions make transfer programs more politically palatable. There is little question that Bolsa Família is a popular program in Brazil. An Ipsos opinion poll taken in September 2007 found that the program tops the list of items mentioned in response to a question on what President Luiz Lula da Silva had done well in office. The authors of the study find that most media criticism of the program centered on the possibility that it would "generate dependency" and find that this criticism usually was coupled with reports that the conditions were not being monitored and enforced properly. Conversely, most of those people arguing the program was not *assistencialista* listed the existence of conditions as one of the top two reasons. Lindert and Vincensini (2008) conclude that the acceptance of conditions across the political spectrum—where the Left sees the conditions as merely restating citizen's rights, and the Right tends to see them as enforceable contracts—played an important role in generating broad-based support for the program in Brazil.

This perception of the condition as a mutually agreeable contract leads to an interesting apparent paradox: CCTs often are seen as less, not more, paternalistic than UCTs. Indeed, several authors have argued that CCT programs provide the basis for a less paternalistic (and possibly less clientelistic) form of social assistance (Cohen and Franco 2006; de la Brière and Rawlings 2006). Reconciling this view with the "paternalistic" arguments described in the second section of this chapter requires distinguishing between two very different justifications for conditioning. The first justification, which was discussed in the second section above, relies on imperfections in private decision making by the poor households themselves. They might be poorly informed, parents may not fully internalize the best interests of their children, and so on. Conditions then help, by inducing agents to do what is best for their children, individually.

The second view, which is being proposed here, is that when conditions are seen as co-responsibilities, they treat the recipient more as a "grown-up," capable of agency to resolve his or her own problems. The state is a partner in the process, not a nanny. This latter interpretation is particularly plausible when the counterfactual to a CCT is not an automatic, transparent, unconditional cash grant seen as a citizen's entitlement (which is close to the textbook concept of a UCT), but instead a myriad of ad hoc and mostly in-kind transfers, intermediated through various service providers, nongovernmental organizations, and local governments. Under those circumstances, conditioning the transfers on "good behavior" *may* be perceived as less paternalistic than the alternative of conditioning transfers on voting for a certain party or belonging to a given social organization.

Moreover, the fact that the conditions are focused on building the human capital of children (rather than simply supporting parents) adds to their political acceptability as an instrument to promote opportunities. After all, it is hard to "blame" children for being poor. In that sense, using public resources to support the human capital development of poor children makes CCT a "poverty reduction" rather than a "social assistance" program. Making payments to mothers also resonates with well-accepted beliefs (mostly supported by evidence, as shown above) that mothers tend to put funds to better use than men do.

This view of CCTs as an enabling instrument, which creates political viability for targeted redistribution that effectively reaches the poor, resonates in many of the Latin American countries that introduced CCT programs over the last decade. Social protection systems in the region have been characterized by "truncated welfare states" (de Ferranti et al. 2004) that channel significant public resources to subsidize social insurance schemes for the formal labor force and provide little, if any, redistribution (particularly in the form of cash) to the lower segments of the income distribution. As in other spheres (for example, service delivery [Fiszbein 2005]), political capture of state institutions and policies by elites meant an historical pattern of low social assistance. From that perspective, the introduction of CCT programs since the late 1990s can be seen as a break with history.

Take the case of Brazil, a country with extremely high inequality that long has subsidized social insurance programs (with limited reach to the poor). Public subsidies for (generally regressive) pension schemes alone represent more than 5 percent of GDP (Lindert, Skoufias, and Shapiro 2006). It was only in the late 1990s, with the introduction of a series of CCT-like programs such as the PETI, Bolsa Alimentação, and Bolsa

Escola, that cash-based social assistance programs became a significant federal public spending item, reaching approximately 0.5 percent of GDP in 2000.[18] And it is through the expanded and enhanced Bolsa Família program in more recent years that federal spending on social assistance reached the 1 percent of GDP mark (Lindert, Skoufias, and Shapiro 2006). The story is very similar for the case of Mexico: Oportunidades represented a major shift from broad price subsidies that benefited the poor only marginally to a cash-based redistribution to more than 5 million poor households. And, as discussed in chapter 1, Mexico's success appears to have influenced other countries in the region to follow a similar path.

The conclusion is that even in situations where a narrow technical assessment might suggest that a UCT is more appropriate than a CCT (say, because there is no evidence of imperfect information or incomplete altruism in poor families), CCTs might be justified because they lead to a "superior" political economy equilibrium. The political process may make significant cash transfers to the poor close to impossible unless those transfers are tied somehow to clear evidence of commitment and "positive behaviors" on the part of beneficiaries. Once again, the Latin American experience suggests that in the absence of dramatic political shifts, the increasing trend toward cash-based redistribution schemes has been associated with the use of some form of conditioned grants.

Social Efficiency Arguments

Attaching conditions to cash grants might make sense for political economy reasons or because distortions in individual behavior cause decision making in the household to be *privately* inefficient. We now turn to a third set of reasons for conditioning, namely, human capital externalities.

If investments in human capital generate positive externalities that parents do not take into account when making decisions, then the aggregate (market equilibrium) level of human capital in society will be inefficiently low. This is a standard argument for subsidizing provision of education or health care. Empirically, health investments have important external benefits. Although those benefits are well established in some cases (for example, immunization), the supporting evidence is rather new in other cases (such as deworming [Miguel and Kremer 2004] or insecticide-treated nets [Gimnig et al. 2003]).

In the case of education, externalities might arise if there are increasing returns to skilled labor in production, at the aggregate level. There is empirical support for the idea that more education can have spillover effects to other workers in the same plant (Moretti 2004b), in the same village (Foster and Rosenzweig 1995), or in the same city (Moretti 2004a). Possible spillovers also may be present if crime, violence, and related social ills decline with average schooling levels. There is solid evidence for the United States that education lowers crime—with perhaps the best evidence coming from the Perry Preschool program evaluation, which shows that children randomly assigned to the intervention have much lower incarceration rates as adults (Currie 2001; Schweinhart 2004).

How large these externalities are and whether (conditioned) cash transfers are the most effective instrument to correct for them, however, remains to be determined. In most countries, education and health services already are heavily subsidized. In many cases, they are publicly provided free of charge. To argue for an additional subsidy that compensates households for some of the indirect or opportunity costs of using these services, on the basis of the externality alone, would require showing that those externalities are quite large. If that were found to be true, then a CCT can be justified on that basis alone: it is effectively an additional component to a Pigouvian subsidy, which often already is implicit in the service fees.

Conclusion

Although market-driven economic growth is likely to be the main driver of poverty reduction in most countries, markets cannot do it alone. Public policy plays a central role in providing the institutional foundations within which markets operate, in providing public goods, and in correcting market failures. In addition to laying the groundwork for economic growth, policy also can supplement the effects of growth on poverty reduction, and one of the instruments that governments can use to that end is direct redistribution of resources to poor households. Although direct cash transfers have opportunity costs (in terms of forgone alternative public investments) and may have some perverse incentive effects on recipients, there is a growing body of evidence to suggest that some such transfers may be both equitable and efficient.

The cash transfer programs that have been growing most rapidly across the developing world over the last decade or so are CCTs, by which cash is paid to poor households on condition that they invest (in certain prespecified ways) in the human capital of their children. Because attaching a constraint on the behavior of those you are trying to help is an unorthodox idea for economists, this chapter has reviewed the conceptual arguments for making cash transfers conditionally.

Essentially, there are two broad sets of arguments for attaching conditions to cash transfers. The first argument applies if private investment in children's human capital is thought to be too low. The second argument applies if political economy reasons mean that there is little support for redistribution, unless it is seen to be conditioned on "good behavior" by the "deserving poor."

CCTs are not a panacea. If there is little evidence to suggest that private levels of investment in human capital are too low (in any of the senses previously discussed), and if the political economy can accommodate the desired levels of redistribution without appealing to co-responsibilities, then UCTs (or some completely different kind of public expenditure) may be preferable.

There also may be good arguments against conditioning if the same result can be achieved at a lower cost through the social policy equivalent of "moral suasion." Recent research has found evidence of "flypaper" or "labeling" effects, whereby the household expenditure shares of certain goods are higher out of transfers that are *notionally earmarked for* (but *not conditional on*) those goods, than out of other incomes.[19] Flypaper effects constitute a fairly fundamental violation of rationality in that they suggest households do not treat all their income sources as fully fungible. Like other departures from full rationality, flypaper effects certainly are plausible and, if ubiquitous, could have serious implications for the design of social protection, tipping the balance in favor of UCTs (which then would appear to have some of the benefits of conditions, without the costs). But much more research is needed before the evidence on these effects reaches critical mass.

CHAPTER THREE

Design and Implementation Features of CCT Programs

BEFORE DELVING DEEPLY INTO THE IMPACTS OF CCT PROGRAMS, IT is worth understanding some of the details of how the programs work. CCT programs require the same systems as other transfer programs: at minimum, a means to establish the eligibility of clients and enroll them in the program, a mechanism to pay their benefits, and preferably strong monitoring and evaluation systems. CCT programs further require a means to monitor compliance with co-responsibilities and to coordinate among the several institutions involved in operating the program.

In general, CCT programs have handled these systems rather well; in some cases, they have been leaders in modernizing social assistance practices. Of course, technical soundness is neither inherent to nor the exclusive domain of CCT programs. That fact should be understood fully by policy makers across the gamut of social policy so that those working on CCT programs make the deliberate choices required to continue the tradition of excellence, and those working on other sorts of programs adopt some of the practices that have led to success in the best of the CCT programs.

This chapter describes the nuts and bolts of the operation of CCT programs.[1] The chapter is divided into five sections, corresponding to targeting practices, benefit systems, conditions (including their definition, monitoring, and enforcement), monitoring and evaluation, and issues concerned with intersectoral and interinstitutional coordination.

Targeting in Practice

Almost all CCT programs established to date have tried to target their benefits rather narrowly to the poor.[2] Table 3.1 shows the targeting mechanisms used for a large number of programs, both established and nascent.

Table 3.1 Targeting Methods Used in CCT Programs, by Region

	Categorical		Household identification		
Region/Country/Program	Geographic	Other	Proxy means test	Means test	Community assessment
Africa					
Burkina Faso: Orphans and Vulnerable Children[a]	x		x		
Kenya: CT-OVC[a]	x	Orphan and vulnerable children incidence			x
Nigeria: COPE			x		x
East Asia and Pacific					
Cambodia: CESSP	x		x		
Cambodia: JFPR	x	Gender and ethnic minority	x		x
Indonesia: JPS	x[b]	Gender[c]			x
Indonesia: PKH	x		x		
Philippines: 4Ps	x		x		
Europe and Central Asia					
Turkey: SRMP			x		
Latin America and the Caribbean					
Argentina: Programa Familias	x	Beneficiaries of Jefes y Jefas program, with two or more children; head has not completed secondary school[d]			
Bolivia: Juancito Pinto	x[e]				
Brazil: Bolsa Alimentação	x			x	
Brazil: Bolsa Escola	x			x	
Brazil: Bolsa Família	x			x	
Brazil: PETI	x			x	
Chile: Chile Solidario			x		
Chile: SUF		Not part of social security system	x		
Colombia: Familias en Acción	x		x		
Colombia: SCAE-Bogotá			x		
Dominican Republic: Solidaridad	x		x		
Dominican Republic: TAE/ILAE	x				x
Ecuador: BDH			x		
El Salvador: Red Solidaria	x		x[f]		
Guatemala: Mi Familia Progresa	x		x		

Region/Country/Program	Categorical		Household identification		
	Geographic	Other	Proxy means test	Means test	Community assessment
Honduras: PRAF	x		x[g]		
Jamaica: PATH			x		
Mexico: Oportunidades	x		x		
Nicaragua: Atención a Crisis[a]	x		x		
Nicaragua: RPS	x		x		
Panama: Red de Oportunidades	x		x		
Paraguay: Tekoporã/PROPAIS II[h]	x		x		
Peru: Juntos	x				x
Middle East and North Africa					
Yemen: BEDP[a]	x	Gender			
South Asia					
Bangladesh: FSSAP	x	Gender			
Bangladesh: PESP	x[i]				x
Bangladesh: ROSC	x				x
India (Haryana): Apni Beti Apna Dhan	x	Gender	x		
Pakistan: CSP[a]		Beneficiary of food support program	x		
Pakistan: Participation in Education through Innovative Scheme for the Excluded Vulnerable	x				x
Pakistan: PESRP/Punjab Female School Stipend Program	x	Gender			

Source: Program profiles.

Note: BDH = Bono de Desarrollo Humano; BEDP = Basic Education Development Project; CESSP = Cambodia Education Sector Support Project; COPE = Care of the Poor; CSP = Child Support Program; CT-OVC = Cash Transfer for Orphans and Vulnerable Children; 4Ps = Pantawid Pamilyang Pilipino Program; FSSAP = Female Secondary School Assistance Program; JFPR = Japan Fund for Poverty Reduction; JPS = Jaring Pengamanan Sosial; PATH = Program of Advancement through Health and Education; PESP = Primary Education Stipend Program; PESRP = Punjab Education Sector Reform Program; PETI = Programa de Erradicação do Trabalho Infantil; PKH = Program Keluarga Harapan; PRAF = Programa de Asignación Familiar; ROSC = Reaching Out-of-School Children; RPS = Red de Protección Social; SCAE = Subsidio Condicionado a la Asistencia Escolar; SRMP = Social Risk Mitigation Project; SUF = Subsidio Unitario Familiar; TAE/ILAE = Tarjeta de Asistencia Escolar/Incentivo a la Asistencia Escolar.

a. Program at the pilot stage.

b. At both the national level (to identify the poorer districts) and the district level (to identify the poorer subdistricts/schools).

c. At least half of the scholarships at the school level were to be allocated to girls.

d. The Jefes y Jefas program started as a workfare program for unemployed heads of household.

e. Covers all children in public schools up to fourth grade.

f. Household targeting is only in the 68 less-poor municipalities. Targeting in the poorest 32 municipalities is geographic only.

g. Only households in the area covered by the Inter-American Development Bank project may participate.

h. PROPAIS II is a project, financed by the Inter-American Development Bank, that builds on the Tekoporã program and finances additional beneficiaries using similar procedures.

i. Only certain types of schools in rural areas may participate.

About two thirds of countries use geographic targeting; about two thirds use household targeting, mostly via proxy means testing; and many countries use both. Moreover, many programs use community-based targeting or community vetting of eligibility lists to increase transparency.

The methods of proxy means testing vary in their details. For example, in all cases, the formula for the proxy means test was derived from statistical analysis of a household survey data set; but, of course, there are differences in the quality and detail of that original data set, and differences in the statistical methods used and in the sophistication and rigor thereof. Significant variations also exist in how the implementation is done—whether households are visited; whether some variables are verified as part of the application process for all or for a sample of applicants; whether the staff members who help complete applications are permanent or contract workers and to which agency they report; and other such differences. Usually the proxy means testing system is led by a central agency (whether in the CCT program itself, independent, or in the ministry of planning), but the day-to-day staffing for it is delegated, often to municipalities, with considerable variability in independence and quality control.

In many cases, CCT programs have been the drivers for developing poverty maps or household targeting systems in their countries or for prompting upgrades to them. Indeed, it would not be an exaggeration to say that CCT programs have moved forward the state of the art and standards for targeted programs generally. Many countries first established proxy means tests when designing the CCT program (Cambodia, Jamaica, Kenya, Mexico, Pakistan, Panama, Turkey). Some countries with older proxy means tests have made significant reforms and improvements in their systems over time—if not because of, then certainly to the advantage of, their CCT programs (Chile, Colombia). Some of these are relatively low-income countries with limited administrative capacity, and they have made adaptations to accommodate that situation. Box 3.1 illustrates this for the case of Cambodia's scholarship program.

The household targeting systems used in some of the best-known CCT programs constitute major "institutional capital" for the country. The same system often is used to target many programs, sometimes with different thresholds or ancillary criteria. For example, in Chile (the first country to use proxy means tests extensively), the system is used not just for the recent Chile Solidario program, but also for much older child allowance and social pensions, for water price subsidies, for housing subsidies, and for other uses. Similarly, in Colombia, the same proxy means test (the SISBEN) used to determine eligibility for subsidized

Box 3.1 Proxy Means Testing Where Administrative Capacity Is Low: Cambodia's Scholarship Programs

BECAUSE CAMBODIA HAS RATHER LESS administrative capacity than the middle-income Latin American countries where proxy means testing originated, it has adapted the general practice of proxy means testing in a way that makes rigorous but simplified testing viable. The schools that participate in its scholarship program are subject to a prior round of geographic targeting, and applicants complete a proxy means test that is used to allocate scholarships among each selected school's students.

Cambodia's CESSP program dispenses with the cadre of field worker/social workers who often administer the instrument. Instead, students fill out the program application/proxy means test form in school. Then the teacher reads the information aloud and the classmates help verify/certify that it is correct. A local committee of school and community leaders score the forms by hand.[a] To assist in manual scoring, the formula uses only integers.

The ranking is done only within schools, rather than against a national standard as in most proxy means tests. In each school, the scored forms are arranged by score and the poorest children, up to the quota for that school, are selected for the scholarship. This process implies that recipients in poorer schools will be poorer, on average, than recipients in less-poor schools. It is thus less accurate than a ranking against a national standard, but eliminates the need for a national database and the information technology and communications networks that would be required to support it.

In a previous scholarship program, the formula was not very sound, so the committees were given leeway to deviate when they thought it appropriate; and when they did so, the students selected were, in fact, poor (as judged later by an evaluation survey). Subsequently the formula was based on statistical analysis of the same type used elsewhere, and the discretion of the local committees was reduced.

Source: CESSP Scholarship Team 2005.
a. In the first year of the CESSP program, an independent firm scored the forms centrally.

health insurance, hospital fee waivers, the public workfare program, a youth training program, and a social pension has been used to target the CCT program. Even in countries with a more recently established proxy means test, those tests can be used in multiple programs. Jamaica established its proxy means test expressly for the CCT program, but now uses it to grant fee waivers in the health system and for secondary education textbook rentals and school lunches. Such an investment will pay off sooner for programs that are generous in coverage or benefit levels and for countries that, at least eventually, will use the proxy means tests for multiple programs.

What have these procedures accomplished? It is difficult to measure targeting outcomes properly (see box 3.2), but we can approximate

Box 3.2   Who Benefits from CCT Programs?

TO KNOW HOW WELL A PROGRAM TARGETS, WE need to measure the welfare that a household would have if it did not receive the transfer and then to rank households according to that measure. Doing so would allow for any behavioral responses associated with the receipt (or removal) of the transfer, such as changes in the household's labor supply, savings, or receipt of remittances. These estimations are undertaken in chapter 4 for those programs for which consumption data are available for beneficiary (treatment) and nonbeneficiary (control) households before and after the start of the CCT program.

There are two possible "naïve" ways of determining where transfer recipients fall in the pre-intervention welfare distribution—measured consumption including the transfer and measured consumption minus the transfer. Using consumption including the transfer biases welfare upward, thus making households seem better-off than they would be without

the program. This will give the most conservative estimate of narrow targeting because a beneficiary who is poor even after receiving the transfer surely was poor beforehand. On the other hand, using consumption net of the full transfer value biases the estimate of initial welfare downward if behavioral responses offset the transfer in part. As will be discussed in chapter 4, there is little evidence of significant offsetting behavioral responses through private transfers and labor supply, at least in the early stages of such CCT programs as Mexico's Oportunidades and Nicaragua's Red de Protección Social.

To investigate how sensitive the targeting assessment is to the welfare measure used, we conducted comparative analysis using both naïve indicators, which will bracket the "true" but imprecisely known counterfactual. Figure 3B.1 shows the results for Jamaica and Mexico. As expected, the estimates net of transfer show the programs to be

Figure 3B.1   Coverage Using per Capita Expenditure Deciles Gross and Net of the CCT Transfer, 2004

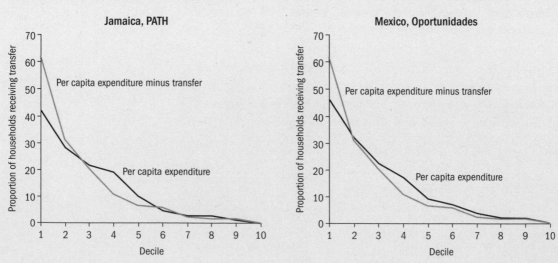

Source: Authors' calculations, using the 2004 Jamaica Survey of Living Conditions and the 2004 Mexico household survey (Encuesta Nacional de Ingreso-Gasto de los Hogares).

more progressive than do the estimates gross of transfer. The important thing is the magnitude of difference. For Jamaica's Program of Advancement through Health and Education (PATH), where the transfer is a small share of households' base consumption, the two curves are rather close together. In the case of Mexico's Oportunidades program, where the transfer is among the largest of any CCT program and, therefore, the sensitivity of results to method is the greatest, the curves diverge more; the estimated participation rate for the poorest decile drops from more than 60 percent (using consumption minus the transfer as the ranking variable) to less than 50 percent (using consumption including the transfer). However, the policy conclusion that the program concentrates resources at the bottom end of the distribution holds for both naïve estimators of the counterfactual.

outcomes for a number of programs, as shown in figure 3.1. Those estimates rank households on their observed per capita household consumption (or income, if a measure of consumption is not available) less the value of the transfer received. This is a naïve estimator that will exaggerate the accuracy of targeting if households change their behavior in ways that lower their autonomous, nontransfer income, perhaps through working less or receiving fewer private transfers. As we shall see in chapter 4, these behavioral responses to CCT programs appear to be modest. Moreover, the sensitivity analysis illustrated in box 3.2 gives some comfort that biases are not too large and do not affect greatly the conclusion that CCT programs largely have realized their intent to concentrate the benefits on the poorest households.

As figure 3.1 reveals, there is significant variation in coverage of the poor, depending on the size and budget of the programs—from about 1 percent of the poorest decile in Cambodia to more than 60 percent in Brazil, Ecuador, and Mexico.[3] The coverage rates in the larger CCT programs seem to compare well with international experience. In the Lindert, Skoufias, and Shapiro (2006) study of 40 targeted programs (including several CCT programs),[4] the mean coverage rate of the poorest quintile is 19 percent. In a study of Eastern Europe and Central Asia cash transfers, child allowances, and social pensions (Tesliuc et al. 2006), the mean coverage rate of the first quintile is 42 percent. A study reviewing experience in a small number of Organisation for Economic Co-operation and Development countries was able to model take-up more closely among eligible individuals, and concluded that take up rates typically are between 40 and 80 percent for social assistance and housing programs (Hernanz, Malherbet, and Pellizzari 2004).

Figure 3.1 Coverage of CCT Programs, by Decile, Various Years

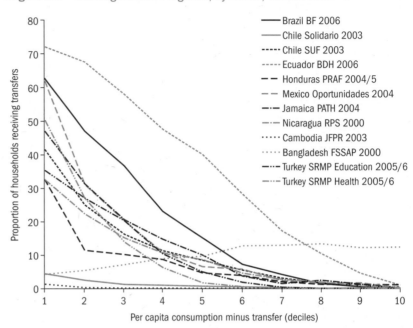

Sources: Authors' calculations, based on the following surveys: Ecuador's Encuesta de Condiciones de Vida 2006; Mexico's Encuesta Nacional de Ingreso-Gasto de los Hogares 2004; Brazil's Pesquisa Nacional por Amostra de Domicílios 2006; Jamaica's Survey of Living Conditions 2004; Chile's Encuesta de Caracterización Socioeconómica Nacional 2003; Honduras' Encuesta de Hogares de Propósitos Multiples 2004; Bangladesh's Household Income and Expenditure Survey 2000; and the Cambodia Japanese Fund for Poverty Reduction application form 2003. The numbers for Turkey are from Ahmed et al. (2007); for Nicaragua, the numbers are from the 2002 Mesoamerica Nutrition Program Targeting Study Group.

Note: BDH = Bono de Desarrollo Humano; BF = Bolsa Família; FSSAP = Female Secondary School Assistance Program; JFPR = Japanese Fund for Poverty Reduction; PATH = Program of Advancement through Health and Education; PRAF = Programa de Asignación Familiar; RPS = Red de Protección Social; SRMP = Social Risk Mitigation Project; SUF = Subsidio Unitario Familiar. For Brazil and Chile, the deciles are based on per capita income minus transfer per capita. For the remaining countries, the measure of welfare used is per capita expenditure net of the transfer per capita.

In thinking about coverage rates, it is important to distinguish the various reasons for low coverage. Some of these are likely to be benign, others problematic. The first and most obvious factor in low coverage is the size of the budget and the role a program is meant to play in broader social policy. Chile Solidario is meant to fill a defined and small niche in social policy, with other transfer and subsidy programs providing greater coverage and higher benefits. In Ecuador, by contrast, the BDH is meant to be the mainstay of social assistance for families. Its significant size contributes to this goal, as does the wide age range of children covered. Naturally, differences in the role of these programs lead to wide variations in the extent to which they cover the poor. Several of the smaller programs, however, clearly are constrained by budget and design. Cambodia and Honduras are targeted geographically, operating only in defined areas of the country, with the Cambodian program being only a very small pilot at the time of these results.

The second obvious factor involved in determining the share of the poorest people that a program can reach has to do with the range of ages and grades that the program covers. A program that covers all families with children aged 0–16 will help more of the poorest quintile than will one that covers families with girls in secondary school grades. (This theme is taken up in more detail in chapter 6.) Box 3.3 provides an in-depth analysis of the extent to which the proxy mean tests and the demographic composition of the households results in errors of exclusion in Brazil and Ecuador.

A third factor has to do with the requirements for service delivery (Nichols and Zeckhauser 1982; Das, Do, and Özler 2005). The essence of a CCT program is that families must make sure their children use health and education services. If those services are not available, then the families will be excluded from the program. Some programs, at least in their early years, aimed to cover poor areas as indicated by a poverty map, but they set up operations only in areas where services were deemed accessible and intentionally excluded all those poor people who lived in areas without minimum service capacity. For example, one of the preconditions for rural localities to be covered by Mexico's Oportunidades program was that they have a population between 50 and 2,500 individuals as well as a primary school situated within the locality and access to a paved road and a health center within a radius of 5 kilometers. Those conditions, by necessity, excluded a small share of very needy villages, although the requirement was relaxed in subsequent years. Similarly, for Colombia the program was targeted first by municipality—but only municipalities that offered the necessary services were allowed to join. Initially, 15 percent of municipalities containing 8 percent of the targeted beneficiaries thus were excluded (Lafaurie and Leiva 2004). More geographically dispersed versions of this problem will occur when households are allowed to participate, but some are more remote from services than others. For example, de Janvry and Sadoulet (2005) suggest that Oportunidades has little impact on children who live more than 4 kilometers from a secondary school; in

Box 3.3 Analyzing Errors of Exclusion of CCT Programs, Brazil and Ecuador

TO GET A PICTURE OF THE RELATIVE MAGNITUDE of some of the factors that lead to errors of exclusion, we look in detail at the Ecuadoran and Brazilian cases, focusing on those two countries because, for them, we are able to infer from the survey more accurately than usual which households are eligible for the programs. In Ecuador, the score from the proxy means test used to determine eligibility is available in the data set. In Brazil, the survey captures income, as does the means test. To make the analysis reasonably comparable between countries and pertinent to other countries, we define the target population as the poorest 20 percent of households. For those in the poorest quintile according to our survey-based measure of welfare (consumption net of transfer in Ecuador, income net of transfer in Brazil), we parse as best we can the reasons for errors of exclusion. These results are presented in table 3B.1.

In Ecuador, the proxy means test correctly predicts that 95 percent of households in the poorest quintile are eligible for the benefits, but it erroneously excludes 5 percent of them. Among those people in the poorest quintile who are eligible, we find that only 70 percent actually receive program

benefits—a finding that implies only 67 percent of the poor end up receiving benefits. In the Ecuadoran case, the budget covers about 40 percent of households (many more than this exercise considers), so there is no explicit rationing of slots other than the proxy means test. Thus one can infer that the less-than-full coverage of the lowest quintile stems not from a lack of offer by the program but from a lack of take-up by poor households. To understand the factors affecting exclusion from or nonparticipation in the program, we ran a probit analysis on the sample of poor households, looking for predictors of participation. The results show that the BDH has been successful in overcoming some problems endemic in transfer programs—indigenous, less-educated, and female-headed households are less likely than others to be excluded from the program, all else being equal. Thus, outreach has been sufficient to include groups who often face barriers to information and access. The role of self-selection would appear to be fairly strong because poorer households participate more often than do the less-poor; the same is true for those in rural areas where the effective value of the transfer is a little higher. There is a caveat: being located in the Oriente (the Amazonian part of Ecuador) does raise the probability of nonparticipation among poor and eligible people, probably a sign that transaction costs deter some of the residents because parts of this region are accessible only by air. That area may be an exception to the conclusion that nonparticipation generally is not too grave an issue in Ecuador.

In a parallel analysis for Brazil's Bolsa Família, we see that all households in the poorest quintile have incomes under the eligibility threshold of R\$100,[a] so errors of exclusion from the means test should be zero. That is a simplification because the implementation of the means test may be imperfect. But we would expect that self-declared income on the application would be underreported—if anything, the applicant would

Table 3B.1 Coverage of Poor Households, Brazil and Ecuador

Reason	Share of bottom quintile (%)	
	Brazil	Ecuador
Classified as eligible because of means or proxy means test	100	95
Eligible, receiving program benefits	55	67
Eligible, receiving program benefits with children ages 0–17	54	64

Source: Authors' calculations.

have an incentive not to reveal more than she or he had to reveal and the form itself may not fully elicit all income for those with irregular or in-kind income. Among those who are eligible by income, enrollment is shown at just 55 percent. In this case, a lack of offer from the program is probably a good deal of the cause. These figures are from 2006, when the program covered about 11 million families. But, of course, there may be other causes for exclusion and an element of self-selection. To understand that possibility, we again ran a probit model to predict the probability of participation based on the sample of poor and eligible households. Here, too, there is some good news relative to program outreach: For example, Afro-Brazilians were significantly less likely to be excluded, all else being equal. There seems to be an element of self-selection—those with more income and more education and those in urban areas were less likely to participate than were others. (The cost of living differentials are very large in Brazil, so the value of the benefit is implicitly lower in urban areas.) Therefore, outreach appeared to be quite good as early as 2006. The government has since expanded

the program and that expansion should reduce any issue of undercoverage substantially.

We return to table 3.2 to look at the potential impacts of the demographic restriction on the exclusion of poor households from the program. In Ecuador, 95 percent of the eligible participants have children aged 0–17. Thus, if the program were restricted to families with children, as is the case with most CCT programs, only a few percent more poor households would be excluded (a reduction of the eligible poor receiving benefits from 67 percent to 64 percent). In Brazil, the poorest families receive a transfer even if they have no children. If the age requirement of having children aged 0–17 were to be enforced, it would exclude only 1 percent of those who were in the program. This finding suggests that demographic restrictions are not an important factor for the exclusion of poor and eligible households from CCT programs with similar designs.

Source: Authors' calculations based on Brazil's Pesquisa Nacional por Amóstra de Domicílios 2006 and Ecuador's Encuesta de Condiciones de Vida 2006.

a. When this was written, in 2008, the eligibility threshold was R$120, but it was R$100 at the time of the survey in 2006.

Turkey, the qualitative evaluation suggests that the transfer is not sufficient for some households to pay for transportation or to compensate households for concerns over students having to travel outside the village (Adato et al. 2007). However, the fact that coverage is highest for the poorest decile indicates that the problems are not so widespread that they generally preclude coverage of the poorest people.

Another possible cause of errors of exclusion is that proxy means tests contain an element of statistical error in making their predictions of household welfare. In Panama, the ex ante assessment of the proxy means test is that with the eligibility threshold selected, a quarter of the extreme poor could be excluded from the program (World Bank 2006d). In Ecuador, such errors are lower, as we shall see below.

Errors of exclusion also may occur if outreach to potential beneficiaries to inform them of the benefits of the program and its application procedures is lacking and they never apply (see Atkinson 1996; Grosh et al. 2008, ch. 3). We do not have clear quantitative data on the extent of outreach in all CCT programs, but do have some indications that it has been good in a number of them. Castañeda and Lindert (2005) show that in Chile, Colombia, and Mexico as early as 2002–04, the proxy means testing systems already had registered more than the number of poor families in the countries. Of course, this finding does not mean that all of the poor necessarily were registered, but it does seem that the magnitude of outreach and the administrative mechanism to handle registration were of the right order of magnitude. Moreover, we know of a number of innovative or extensive examples of outreach. Several countries fielded teams to go door-to-door in poor areas to register households. All countries had information campaigns of one sort or another. In Ecuador, the mass media were used. In Cambodia, program rules carefully specify that information posters will be placed in all pertinent schools; on the commune council notice board; and in the health center, market, and pagoda. Furthermore, to ensure that out-of-school students hear of the program, school officials are directed to contact children who finished sixth grade in the last 2 years but did not go on to lower secondary school.

Even after outreach, some households will decide not to participate because of stigma or because the benefits do not seem worth the transaction costs implied. There is not much systematic evidence on stigma and CCT programs. Adato (2004) concludes from qualitative studies in Mexico and Nicaragua that the issue was not one of stigma for beneficiaries but one of envy of them by nonbeneficiaries. In Nicaragua, some communities even went so far as to provide school supplies to nonbeneficiary children because they felt stigmatized for not having what the programs provided. The general impression among many people in the CCT community is that stigma is not much of an issue, or at least is a lesser issue than it is for social assistance in, say, the United States or some European countries. It would seem that the notion of co-responsibilities helps households and the general public feel that the program beneficiaries are behaving in desirable ways and merit support.

As is true for other social programs, transaction costs are a concern—and more so where benefits are relatively small. Indeed, it is largely to minimize transaction costs to both participants and program budgets that many programs pay benefits only every two months when the logic of the program would imply that regular small flows of cash each month would be most helpful in supporting food expenditures, defraying the small regular costs of school attendance, and substituting for reduced child earnings. Despite that, we know that transaction costs can be high relative to the transfer for at least a subset of participants. In Ecuador, for example, residents of some isolated communities in Amazonia, *páramo,* or remote coastal areas can face very high costs for transportation (as high as $50–$480 by airplane, $10–$50 by motorboat or *panga;* or they require a walk of one or more days' duration). However, because beneficiaries allow transfers to accumulate before collecting them, and combine trips to program payment points with other activities they carry out in urban areas, the costs of collecting the transfer are generally much lower—perhaps as low as $0.25–$0.50 per month, on average, including in the Amazonia region (Carrillo and Ponce 2008).[5] In Bangladesh, the benefit level is very low, so many people fail to participate in the program.[6]

A comparison of the coverage of CCT-like programs in two countries, Bangladesh and Cambodia, helps illustrate the role that targeting practice can have in determining who is reached by a program. Both programs have several elements in common: They are in poor countries where administrative capacity is low, probably lower in Cambodia than in Bangladesh. Both programs have only education conditions and are limited to girls in secondary school. As such, both start with a challenge because base enrollment rates in upper primary grades are low among the poor. Nevertheless, because of careful geographic and proxy means targeting, Cambodia was able to concentrate transfers among the poor. Simple calculations suggest that approximately 70 percent of benefits reached households in the poorest quintile of per capita consumption (minus transfers), and less than 5 percent reached households in the richest quintile. In Bangladesh, the program operates nationally, except in the four largest cities, and is targeted only by gender. In practice, however, the incidence of the program has been regressive largely because the base enrollment is higher among the less poor. Simple calculations suggest that less than 10 percent of benefits reached households in the poorest quintile of per capita consumption (minus transfers), and approximately 35 percent reached households in the richest quintile.

It is important to recognize that targeting results seen to date are not inherent to the design of CCTs, but reflect the political will and technical effort made in the programs we examined. Although it is impossible to say whether that will continue over time, we note that a number of countries continue to refine and improve the implementation and use of their proxy means tests and poverty maps, the technical tools that drive the results. Several countries have carried out recertification processes to remove from the list of beneficiaries those who have prospered in the interim. We cannot quantify the effect of these changes because measures of comparable targeting outcomes over time are scarce. In many countries, the programs have been rolling out from year to year, covering areas of different inherent poverty characteristics, so measures across time would not be fully comparable. Even in countries with nationwide programs over several years, we would need information that straddles recertification periods. Deterioration of targeting outcomes could be expected within a single certification period, such as is observed but not statistically significant for Jamaica.

The Latin American CCT programs (which are the majority of the programs with known targeting results) have a fairly similar experience in using a combination of geographic targeting and proxy means testing and in devoting considerable effort to implementing these targeting systems well. Many of the countries with well-established programs have had time to improve and refine their targeting systems. In some of the countries with newer programs, improvements are likely to be needed. As the range of countries running CCT programs diversifies, we would expect their targeting mechanisms, and possibly the outcomes from them, to diversify as well. Some countries may choose universalism over targeting, as Bolivia has done in the Juancito Pinto program for all first-grade students. Eastern European countries that already have established means testing systems may use those; community-based targeting may play a larger role in Africa and Asia than in Latin America. Moreover, the results that reasonably can be achieved will vary, depending on such context and design features as the range of ages covered by the program.

Benefit Systems

Benefit systems have a number of aspects that can influence outcomes. Here we describe some of the main features of CCT programs, especially the structure and level of payments, the payee, and the payment mechanism.

Benefit Structures

CCT programs often differentiate payments by the number of children in the eligible age range, but otherwise have rather simple benefit structures—only two differentiate by poverty level, none by cost of living,[7] and few by age/grade or gender of the student. Those simple payment structures streamline administrative systems and greatly facilitate communication and community understanding of the programs. But they represent something of a missed opportunity in terms of fine-tuning the impact on poverty for a given budget and possibly on best leveraging changes in human capital (a theme taken up in chapter 6).

In most of the CCT programs, benefits depend directly on the number of children in the household. That is consistent with an underlying logic of the program that recognizes that each child needs to receive health and education services and that there are costs (explicit and implicit) in getting those services. However, a number of programs have capped the number of children who can be covered. Bolsa Família caps the benefit at R$45, equivalent to having three children in the program. Mexico caps the benefit at about $153, an amount that roughly corresponds with two children in primary school and one in high school. In the Dominican Republic, the maximum benefit amount is $19 for four or more children ($9 for one or two, $14 for three children).

A few programs, such as the ones in Ecuador, El Salvador, Panama, and Peru, pay a flat benefit per household, irrespective of the number of children. Paying such a flat benefit can be done as a way to ration benefits among families when the program budget cannot cover all who are poor, to counter any incentive to increased fertility,[8] or if the program logic is that households need an incentive to learn a new behavior but do not need one to practice it with each successive child.

Benefits also can be differentiated by grade or by gender. Oportunidades in Mexico, Familias en Acción in Colombia, the Social Risk Mitigation Project (SRMP) in Turkey, and recently Jamaica's Program of Advancement through Health and Education (PATH) pay higher amounts for children in secondary school than for children in primary school as a way of recognizing that the opportunity cost of the time of older students is higher than of younger students; often, explicit costs of secondary schooling are higher as well because schools are more distant and textbooks more expensive. Oportunidades and the SRMP pay higher benefits for girls in recognition that they have been disadvantaged in enrollment. The Bangladesh and Cambodia girls' scholarship programs originally were designed to benefit girls only, although Bangladesh is designing a reform to include poor boys and Cambodia now covers both sexes. Jamaica recently decided to make higher payments for boys in secondary school because boys have lower enrollment and schooling outcomes.

Many programs pay bimonthly or less often to economize on transaction costs for the program and for the beneficiary. Sometimes there are no payments for the months when school is not in session; in other cases, payments continue throughout the year; and in yet other instances, a payment is timed before the school year to enable households to pay for uniforms, shoes, textbooks, and any fees. Though lately there is much talk of moving to rewarding performance rather than attendance only, Bogotá's Subsidio Condicionado a la Asistencia Escolar (SCAE) program alone gives bonuses at the end of the school year.

Payee

In most of the programs, the payee is the parent rather than the student; exceptions are mostly in secondary scholarship programs, especially those in Asia and in the SCAE program in Bogotá. In nearly all programs where the adult is the payee, payments are made to the mother of the children, a feature that may be important, as we shall see in subsequent chapters.

Payment Systems

The range of payment systems used in CCT programs covers the full gamut of possibilities. In Brazil, payments are made on debit cards and cash can be withdrawn at banks, ATM machines, or lottery sales points. In Turkey, payments are made through the state bank, in cash, with clients going to tellers to withdraw funds. In Mexico, a fairly low-tech "Brinks truck" model is still the main payment modality, though payments through banks are being introduced in urban areas. Households are paid in cash at temporary pay points that use available infrastructure (such as community centers), with transportation and payment of the money contracted to the Mexican post and telegraph office. In Kenya, payments are made through the post office, but a pilot program being set up is considering paying via cell phone systems. And at the opposite end of the scale, a pilot program in Tanzania will disburse funds to community representatives who will make the payments.

There is diversity in how countries ensure that payments are made in full and understood by the client. Most of the Latin American programs work through the banking system, with the full panoply of audits that implies. Mexico gives each household pay statements that show details of payments for each different member/set of conditions and for whom any payments were suspended. Cambodia pays in cash, with payments made every quarter at ceremonies that celebrate and encourage the students' enrollment and academic status and bring an element of transparency and community monitoring to the payment system.

Payment Levels

One of the most important features of the payment structure is, of course, its level. Capturing this succinctly is complicated because of the differentiation of payments by number of children and other pertinent factors, differences in context, and the targeting of the programs. Data from household surveys enable us to summarize into a single number or two each program's level of generosity. Table 3.2 presents the share of recipient welfare that the transfers represent for the population of recipients. For a subset of the programs we also present the share of the transfer and for the poorer among them (defined in this exercise as those whose pre-transfer per capita expenditure is less than the 25 percentile of national distribution of the pre-transfer per capita expenditure or income). As table 3.2 reveals, there is significant variation in the generosity of CCT programs, from about 1 percent of pretransfer household expenditures in Bangladesh to 29 percent in Nicaragua. It is also encouraging that the generosity of the programs is slightly higher for the poorer beneficiaries—especially in the case of Mexico where the share of program transfer is estimated to be 33 percent of the pretransfer level of household consumption among households in the bottom quartile. As is documented in the next chapter, the combination of the generosity of the Oportunidades transfers and the program's high coverage of the poor resulted in a significant impact on poverty measures at the national level.

As a means of summarizing the extent to which CCT programs concentrate their benefits on the poorer segments of the population, figure 3.2 presents the proportion of various programs' transfer budgets received by

Table 3.2 Generosity of CCT Programs, Various Years

Country/Program/Year	Transfer as share of pretransfer consumption among all beneficiaries (%)[a]
Bangladesh: FSSAP, 2000[b]	0.6
Brazil: BF, 2006[b]	6.1
Colombia: Familias en Acción, 2002[c]	17.0
Ecuador: BDH, 2006[b]	6.0
Honduras: PRAF, 2000[c]	7.0
Jamaica: PATH, 2004[b]	8.2
Mexico: Oportunidades, 2004[b]	21.8
Nicaragua: RPS, 2000[c]	29.3

Country/Program/Year	Transfer as share of pretransfer consumption among poor[d] beneficiaries (%)
Bangladesh: FSSAP, 2000[b]	0.8
Brazil: BF, 2006[b]	11.7
Ecuador: BDH, 2006[b]	8.3
Jamaica: PATH, 2004[b]	10.7
Mexico: Oportunidades, 2004[b]	33.4

Source: Authors' calculations.

Note: BDH = Bono de Desarrollo Humano; BF = Bolsa Familia; FSSAP = Female Secondary School Assistance Program; PATH = Program of Advancement through Health and Education; PRAF = Programa de Asignacion Familiar; RPS = Red de Protección Social.

a. The transfer amounts as a proportion of per capita expenditures (or consumption) are not the same across all tables in the report because of differences in the surveys used, including their coverage and year.

b. The measure of welfare used for Brazil is pretransfer per capita income (PCI). For the remaining countries, the measure of welfare is pretransfer per capita expenditure (PCE). Pretransfer PCI or PCE is constructed by subtracting the value of the transfer per capita received from either PCE or PCI. The numbers reported are the median shares derived by first removing extreme outliers at both ends of the national distribution of PCE or PCI (that is, dropping households with PCE or PCI below the 1st percentile and above the 99th percentile of the national distribution).

c. The number reported is the share of consumption for the median control household.

d. A poor beneficiary is one whose pretransfer PCE is less than the 25th percentile of national distribution of the pretransfer PCE.

each decile of the welfare distribution. Except for Bangladesh, the CCT programs for which we have targeting outcomes have sharply progressive incidence, with much higher shares of benefits going to the poorest households than to the upper end of the distribution. Among the big, well-known programs, Mexico delivers more than 45 percent of benefits to the poorest decile. Next in line are Chile and Jamaica with approximately 35–40 percent of benefits to their poorest deciles.

Figure 3.2 Benefit Incidence of CCT Programs, Various Years

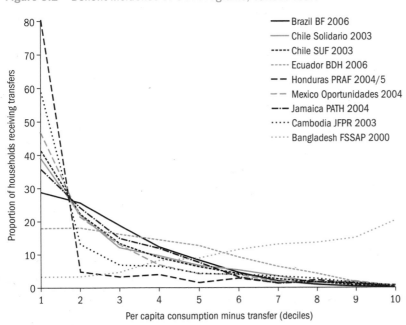

Source: Authors' calculations based on the following surveys: Ecuador's Encuesta de Condiciones de Vida 2006; Mexico's Encuesta Nacional de Ingreso-Gasto de los Hogares 2004; Brazil's Pesquisa Nacional por Amostra de Domicílios 2006; Jamaica's Survey of Living Conditions 2004; Chile's Encuesta de Caracterización Socioeconómica Nacional 2003; Honduras's Encuesta de Hogares de Propósitos Multiples 2004; Bangladesh's Household Income and Expenditure Survey 2000; and the Cambodia Japanese Fund for Poverty Reduction application form 2003.

Note: BDH = Bono de Desarrollo Humano; BF = Bolsa Família; FSSAP = Female Secondary School Assistance Program; JFPR = Japanese Fund for Poverty Reduction; PATH = Program of Advancement through Health and Education; PRAF = Programa de Asignación Familiar; SUF = Subsidio Unitario Familiar. For Brazil and Chile, the deciles are based on per capita income minus transfer per capita. For the remaining countries, the measure of welfare used is per capita expenditure net of the transfer per capita.

Therefore, it is not surprising that CCT programs have been recognized for their success in both reaching the poor and concentrating benefits among them. Although there are serious difficulties in properly measuring the incidence of transfers (see box 3.2), naïve comparisons of the Latin American CCT programs with other transfer programs suggest that CCT programs do a better job of concentrating benefits among the poorest (see Lindert, Skoufias, and Shapiro [2006], figure 11, p. 71).[9]

Looking forward, the agenda with respect to benefit systems will be more focused on benefit level and structure issues than on the payment mechanisms. Establishing payment mechanisms is a key effort, but one that countries generally have found easier to accomplish than developing sound targeting systems or monitoring beneficiaries' compliance with co-responsibilities. Refinements in payment mechanisms to reduce costs, increase convenience, or better ensure accountability will continue, but the basic issues already have been resolved in most countries. Where policy attention is focused is on the issues of how much to pay; whether to customize payments further by age, grade, household composition, poverty, and cost of living; and whether and how to pay for performance as well as attendance.

Conditions: Their Definition, Compliance Monitoring, and Enforcement

CCT programs vary somewhat with respect to the design of their conditions, and more so with respect to their enforcement of those conditions. Monitoring compliance with conditions is a complex task. It involves a variety of actors inside and outside the CCT program, requires the collection and processing of large amounts of information, and needs to happen in a timely manner for the conditions to have any meaningful link with the transfer payment the beneficiaries receive. Just as the role of the CCT program in social policy and its basic characteristics (such as targeting method, benefit amount, and payment system) differ from program to program, so do the mechanisms used to monitor beneficiaries' compliance with the conditions and the degree to which those conditions are enforced.

Definition of Conditions

Many programs condition the transfer both on enrollment and regular attendance of the households' children in school and on regular health center visits for the younger children and often the pregnant women. The conditions in programs that promote education can be defined for certain age brackets (Dominican Republic, Jamaica) or grades (Cambodia, El Salvador). Almost all CCTs require enrollment and attendance on 80 or 85 percent of school days; Bangladesh's FSSAP is the exception, requiring only 75 percent attendance. A few programs condition on some aspect of performance: Cambodia, for example, require passing grades; Turkey allows a grade to be repeated only once; and Nicaragua required grade promotion at year's end.

In programs defining conditions by the use of health services, conditions tend to apply to children aged 0 to 5 or 6 years, with the age set to allow continuous eligibility from birth to schooling, assuming "on-time" enrollment. In about half the cases with child health conditions, there also are conditions for pregnant women and/or lactating mothers. Less often are there conditions for adult health care more generally, although such conditions are present and well enforced in Mexico and are present albeit less enforced in Jamaica. Child health conditions are formulated in various ways, requiring children to have complete immunizations (Brazil) or to adhere to a schedule of regular health center visits for health checkups. In some countries, the kind of health services that mothers and children should receive are defined in great detail (Jamaica), but other countries mandate only that they regularly go to the health center (Honduras). Growth monitoring is required two to six times a year in most programs with child health conditions. Health and nutrition education sessions are a feature of many, but not all, Latin American programs and rarely are used elsewhere (for details, see the country at-a-glance tables in appendix A). Indeed, all Latin American programs have health conditions of some kind, whereas such conditions are much less common in active and planned programs in Africa and South Asia. Though malnutrition and immunization coverage are more problematic in those regions, services are more limited, so the programs have not focused on health conditions.

Some programs allow exceptions or exemptions to the conditions they impose. Most common is justification for absence during a specified reporting period on grounds of illness. Jamaica waives attendance requirements for children who are disabled and deemed unlikely to benefit from attending school (Mont 2006). Kenya waives attendance requirements for children who do not have access to schools or clinics (Government of Kenya 2006b).

Timing of Compliance Verification

The frequency of verifying compliance with conditions varies widely (see table 3.3). Frequency ranges from monthly (Turkey) to every four months (Honduras) or even once a year (Chile SUF). Verification frequency depends, in part, on the type of conditions a program imposes:

Table 3.3 Country and Program Variations in Monitoring and Penalties for Noncompliance with Conditions

Degree of monitoring	No penalties	Light penalties	Full penalties
No monitoring	Ecuador	None	None
Light monitoring (annually)	Pakistan: PESRP Chile: SUF	Bangladesh: FSSAP Cambodia: CESSP and JFPR	None
Full monitoring (monthly, bimonthly, or quarterly)	None	Brazil: Bolsa Alimentação, Bolsa Escola, Bolsa Família, and PETI Chile: Chile Solidario Honduras: PRAF Kenya: CT-OVC Pakistan: CSP	Colombia: Familias en Acción and SCAE-Bogotá El Salvador: Red Solidaria Jamaica: PATH Mexico: Oportunidades Nicaragua: Atención a Crisis and RPS Turkey: SRMP

Source: Authors' compilation.

Note: CESSP = Cambodia Education Sector Support Project; CSP = Child Support Program; CT-OVC = Cash Transfer for Orphans and Vulnerable Children; FSSAP = Female Secondary School Assistance Program; JFPR = Japan Fund for Poverty Reduction; PATH = Program of Advancement through Health and Education; PESRP = Punjab Education Sector Reform Program; PETI = Programa de Erradicação do Trabalho Infantil; PRAF = Programa de Asignación Familiar; RPS = Red de Protección Social; SCAE = Subsidio Condicionado a la Asistencia Escolar; SRMP = Social Risk Mitigation Project; SUF = Subsidio Unitario Familiar. Light penalties = warnings prior to penalties and/or delay or minor reduction in individual benefit and/or irregular application of reductions; full penalties = complete withdrawal of period's benefit for noncompliant person in payment period immediately following detection of noncompliance.

if beneficiaries are required to attend one training session a year, compliance verification can be determined only annually. Consequently, conditions related to health or awareness raising tend to be verified at longer intervals than do those for school attendance.

Another factor in determining the frequency of verification is capacity constraints. Given the amount of information and number of transactions involved, smaller-scale programs or programs in low-capacity settings may opt for longer intervals. Scholarship programs in Bangladesh and Cambodia have done so. But even if compliance verification is designed to be done more frequently, capacity constraints may yield delays in sanctioning noncompliance. Even in a high-capacity environment such as Mexico, the benefit amount paid in the period January/February reflects the beneficiary household's compliance or noncompliance in the period September/October of the preceding year. Such long lag times between the noncompliance and the reduction of benefit may weaken the positive quid pro quo effect of the program.

Sanctions and Enforcement

Although all CCT programs specify a schedule of sanctions in the case of noncompliance with the stated conditions, both the type of sanctions and the degree of enforcement vary quite substantially from one program to another. Most common is a temporary reduction of all or part of the benefit for the first instances of noncompliance, followed by an eventual termination of the benefit for repeated noncompliance. Such is the case, for example, in Colombia, Jamaica, and Mexico, where the benefit is reduced immediately for the period for which there was noncompliance and the reduction is reflected in the next payment.

Programs do not always take a hard line on compliance with the conditions they impose because CCT programs generally are targeted to the poorest and most vulnerable groups of the population—those people most in need of assistance. By design, some programs involve a social worker who, in the case of noncompliance, will reach out to the beneficiaries (El Salvador, Jamaica). Brazil even goes a step farther: the conditions fundamentally are viewed as *encouraging* beneficiaries to take up and exercise their right to free education and free health care, so noncompliance is taken to be a manifestation of some kind of obstacle that the family cannot overcome to access the service rather than an unwillingness to comply. A beneficiary who is noncompliant will receive a warning (written notice) of noncompliance for the first period and may be visited by a social worker to see if there is a noncash-related problem to be solved. Only on a third consecutive occasion of noncompliance will the benefit be "blocked" for 30 days, after which the full amount, including the amount accumulated during the blockage, will be paid out. Perhaps the ultimate "soft conditions" are those in Ecuador, where the program was announced as conditional, but effective systems of monitoring compliance and enforcing sanctions have yet to be developed.

In Brazil, El Salvador, and Mexico, compliance with education conditions has tended to be 90 percent or better among enrolled students; in Jamaica, compliance has improved over the years from 70 percent to 85 percent.[10] Compliance with health conditions (among those for whom compliance information is available) is in the same range or better for these countries.

Compliance Verification Mechanisms

The process of verifying beneficiaries' compliance with the conditions generally involves, at the very least, the providers of the services whose use is mandated, the program, the payment agency, and the beneficiaries themselves. Depending on the country context, not only one but various levels of government may be involved, as may be nongovernmental organizations (NGOs) or other community organizations helping with either the delivery of the services or the program itself.

Information is collected and processed by these various actors in many different ways. In most programs, the education or health service provider collects data on school enrollment and attendance or on health center visits. The provider gives the data either directly to the program or to a central unit in the provider's line ministry, which then compiles the data and passes them on to the program. In some programs, such as in Colombia, the beneficiaries are involved more heavily by having to get forms filled out and certified by each service provider and then to submit the forms to the program. Practices span anything from paper-and-pencil attendance lists kept by teachers and handed over to the program officials on a regular basis (Bangladesh, Cambodia) to optical-scan forms (Mexico) to experiments with different types of smart cards (Brazil).

Enforcement of sanctions for noncompliance demands the timely availability of reliable information, which may be especially problematic in the beginning phases of a program. Although about 93 percent of schools in Brazil reported information in 2006, only 55 percent did so in 2004; by 2006, information on compliance with health conditions was only available for about 33 percent of families. Jamaica was able to reduce the number of schools that did not return the beneficiary lists in time from about 10 percent of schools in 2003 to zero by the end of 2005. Mexico's Oportunidades, like some mature programs, now has timely information on compliance with all conditions for 96 percent of its beneficiaries (Castañeda 2006), but initially had problems with delays (IFPRI 2000).

Lack of information clearly precludes establishing a meaningful link between conditions and payments through the enforcement of sanctions. There are few studies that soundly address issues of the accuracy of compliance information. Although a qualitative study of Turkey suggested that education officials were hesitant to report absences, the bigger issue was getting them to fill in the forms at all (Kudat 2006). A series of operational audits of Jamaica's compliance monitoring has turned up no big discrepancies between attendance records kept in schools and clinics and the information submitted to the PATH program (Government of Jamaica 2006).

Unfortunately, little information is available on the costs of monitoring compliance with conditions, partly because some of the costs are borne by health or education sector employees or subsumed in other administrative costs and so are not easily accounted for. The only piece of comparative analysis of cost structures we are aware of is the study of Nicaragua (RPS pilot), Honduras (PRAF), and Mexico (Oportunidades) (Caldés, Coady, and Maluccio 2006). This study finds that the cost of verification can range from 2 percent to 24 percent of total program administrative costs (excluding transfers) in any given year. Those estimates have to be viewed with caution, however, because they very much depend on a program's stage of implementation (newly introduced versus mature) and on the associated shift in the relative shares of different project activities in the overall costs of the program.

Another way to estimate the costs of verifying compliance is to work backward. Grosh et al. (2008) compile administrative costs for 10 CCT programs, showing a range from 4 percent to 12 percent of total program costs. Those costs include running the systems for targeting and payments as well as monitoring compliance, plus all the support services of management, monitoring, and evaluation. If those functions each took the same share of administrative resources, monitoring compliance would be on the order of 1–3 percent of total program resources. It is interesting to note that the median administrative cost for CCT programs in the study is 8 percent; for other types of cash transfers it is 9 percent; and over the whole range of 54 social assistance programs, the median administrative cost is 10 percent (Grosh et al. 2008). Apparently the scale and generosity of the (mature) CCT programs has been sufficient to temper the extra administrative requirement imposed by monitoring compliance with conditions.

Monitoring and Evaluation

A number of CCT programs have had unusually proactive management based on cutting-edge technical systems, especially monitoring and evaluation systems. Two features inherent to CCTs programs—the number of actors involved and the need for extensive information management to verify compliance with conditions—may have interacted in ways that have spurred creative development of monitoring and management. This excellence in systems, the extensive documentation that has resulted from the amount of information available, and the degree of transparency about the information have contributed to the attractiveness of CCT programs, although such features are not inherent to them.

All CCT programs need to know how implementation is being carried out across diverse actors and processes, and they have developed various ways to elicit that information, some of which also add incentives for good performance. Colombia's Familias en Acción has used a system of sample-based site monitoring or "spot checks" as internal process evaluation. Interviews are conducted every six months in a sample of 20 municipalities; for participants, program officials, and local governments, interviewers use defined questionnaires that cover 400 indicators of various program aspects (including inscription processes, verification of compliance with conditions, payment systems, appeals, and quality of the health education component) (box 3.4). The results show which aspects of the program are working well; how much variability there is in program management across locations; and where changes in procedures, training, staffing, or other inputs are needed. The program has been good not only at collecting such information, but also in acting on it. Program managers detected problems with long queues for payments (including people waiting outdoors in the rain) and worked with banks to find various ways to reduce the queues. They found that some children were not being served continuously between the preschool and school portions of the program because of when their birthdays fell relative to enrollment, so they changed the specifications. And when they identified a number of areas where staff needed more training to carry out the program efficiently, they provided that training.

In Brazil, the Bolsa Família program depends to a great extent on work done by the municipalities. After an initial problem with the quality and timeliness of such work, the Bolsa implemented its "index of decentralized management," which captures the quality of functions performed by municipalities on the household registry, the monitoring of conditions, and all municipalities' social controls for the program. Municipalities receive support for their administrative

---

Box 3.4   Colombia's Familias en Acción
Sample-Based Site Monitoring, Selected Indicators

Knowledge
- Mother's knowledge of specific themes
- Clinic and school staffs' familiarity with their program guide

Use of materials
- Do mother leaders use materials?
- Do school and clinic staff consult their guides?

Compliance with operational procedures
- Do mother leaders report complaints?
- How many days do the banks allow for payments; what is the waiting time?

Infrastructure
- Do regional offices have necessary equipment?
- Do mothers stand in line at the bank, inside or outside?

Organization
- Percent of schools that require a written excuse for absence

Procedures
- Percent of complaints resolved at the Regional Coordination Unit
- Percent of municipalities that have lists of schools, clinics, and completed stickers

Source: Velásquez 2007.

---

costs, with the payments adjusted to their performance on the index.

From the early stages of program development, Oportunidades has put in place three structures to monitor program operations and results. The first structure, operating since 1998, generates a set of 64 monitoring and management indicators every two months (the Sistemas de Datos Personales de Oportunidades). A second structure, a survey of beneficiaries and program providers called *sentinel points,* was implemented in 2000 and produces information on perception of service quality twice a year. Third, external experts use monitoring and management data to make regular assessments of program operations. All the information and assessments are available to the public on the program Web site. In Mexico, compliance with conditions is certified on schedule in 96 percent of cases, payments are made on time in 98 percent of cases (Castañeda 2006), and overall administrative costs exclusive of payment transactions are 3 percent of total program costs (Gomez-Hermosillo 2006).

Of course, not all experiences are so positive. There are real logistic and institutional challenges in running CCT programs: Turkey's qualitative evaluation pointed to problems with the management information system in the first couple of years of operation (Ahmed et al. 2007), and Honduras sometimes is cited as a case where poor implementation has affected the expected impacts. Compliance monitoring has been a challenge in many countries. But the positive cases get more press and are setting new expectations for the administration of social assistance programs.

The evaluation culture around CCT programs is quite strong. It is present in a larger share of programs than is excellent monitoring, and it goes well beyond traditional practice in social policy. Many programs either have conducted or have plans to conduct impact evaluations with credible counterfactuals. Among those programs, a large share of countries have used experimental methods, at least initially. In several countries, the evaluations are neither simple nor one-off. There have been dozens of studies for Mexico's program, and there is a fairly diverse body of evaluation for Colombia and Nicaragua. Most evaluations have been conducted by agencies external to the program and often external to the government and international partners as well, a practice that enhances the credibility of the evaluation. In the great majority of cases, evaluations have been made public, often posted on program Web sites and/or published in respected academic journals. A number of those evaluations have had a real impact on policy. Evaluations showed, for example, that anemia was not declining as expected among Oportunidades beneficiaries. That finding led to a series of investigations of causes and the discovery that the bioavailability of iron in the original food supplement was low. Moreover, the supplement was shared among family members and thus the target child got less than the intended amount. The supplement was reformulated and the nutrition education component was strengthened (Neufeld 2006). In Jamaica, the increase in secondary enrollment was disappointing, so the government has decided to increase the benefits at the secondary level and to differentiate them by grade and gender.

This culture of evaluation is spreading not only from one CCT program to another, but also from CCT programs to other programs within the same countries. Mexico's decision to evaluate the early phases of Oportunidades in 1997 was, at the time, an unusually dramatic example of evaluation: it was motivated and paid for wholly by the program designers without external pressure, it used an experimental design, it was contracted to an independent third party, and the data collected were made publicly available so that scholars could replicate and extend the work. Since then, the notion of good evaluation has spread. Appendix B of this report provides a detailed discussion of the technical aspects of CCT impact evaluations.

In Mexico, a social development law, passed in 2004, requires that all new programs be evaluated, and established a National Council for the Evaluation of Social Development Policy. A separate transparency law mandates that evaluation results be made public. External evaluations are done and the summaries are passed to program managers, who annually must describe to Congress what they are doing in response to the evaluations (Hernández 2006). The Mexican Ministry of Social Development, which is responsible for Oportunidades and many other programs, has adopted a system of results-based monitoring. It plans to conduct evaluations of five national programs a year in each of three years and to have installed such a system in half its subnational agencies within six years (Rubio 2007). Chile and Colombia also have developed significant evaluation cultures, cited as "good practice" in global reviews (for example, Mackay 2007).

Meanwhile, the evaluation agenda remains vital among CCT programs. The large majority of new programs are planning credible evaluations, and several of those have included interesting dimensions not previously assessed (see box 3.5). For countries with programs that have reached their full intended coverage, a range of issues remains, although experimental design is no longer an option for many aspects of evaluation and so there are additional methodological challenges.

A noteworthy aspect of the experience of CCT programs has been the fact that lessons learned in one country often have been shared internationally. That sharing has happened to such an extent that an international community of practice has developed as a result (see box 3.6).

Box 3.5   Evaluation Remains Important in CCTs

DESPITE THE UNUSUAL QUANTITY AND QUALITY of impact evaluations of CCT programs to date, the agenda remains vital and there are quite a number of evaluations ongoing or planned. Those evaluations can be grouped into three types:

1. Relatively basic evaluations of new programs: Many of these will use experimental design. A significant subset is in new contexts, especially low-income countries (Bolivia, Kenya, Pakistan, Yemen), or has new twists on service delivery (community-driven development approaches being developed in Sierra Leone and Tanzania).

2. Evaluations that will help disentangle the role of different parts of the "classic" program in delivering impacts:
   - Pilot programs in Burkina Faso and Morocco have comparative treatment arms for conditional and unconditional transfers. The transfer will be discounted fully in the payment round that immediately follows noncompliance. Experiments already under way in Kenya and Pakistan test much softer versions of penalties: initial warnings to households rather than penalties, and final penalties amounting to only a small reduction in the transfer and occurring several months after noncompliance.
   - So far, virtually all CCT programs have paid the woman of the household. Doing so imposes no additional direct operational burden because a single person must represent the household in any case. However, the uniform payment to women has made it difficult to understand to what extent impacts have come from the release of the budget constraint via the transfer,

changes in behavior due to conditions, or changes in use of household resources due to the payment to women. Pilot programs in Burkina Faso, Morocco, and Yemen test treatment arms for delivering cash to men/fathers versus women/mothers.
   - The role of the health/nutrition education component in CCT programs has not been studied specifically. In Panama, the impact of adding community-based nutrition education (the Atención Integral de la Niñez en la Comunidad model) will be tested. In Indonesia, a less intense variant on providing health education to leaders of beneficiary groups will be tested.

3. Evaluations that propose to go beyond the use of services to look at final outcomes: Burkina Faso, Indonesia, Morocco, and Tanzania look at examination results or cognitive outcomes for school children. Nutritional status is measured in Burkina Faso, El Salvador, Indonesia, Panama, and Tanzania. Anemia is measured in Burkina Faso, El Salvador, and Panama.

There is still a large evaluation agenda on second-round and long-run impacts. Very little is known about how programs impact savings or investment, long-run autonomous incomes of beneficiary households, or spillover effects at the community level in any setting. Evidence on labor supply, on migration, and on remittances beyond the few settings in which these have been measured also would be useful, as would knowing what happens to families or children after they leave the program. Evaluations on those issues are under way for Chile and Mexico; are being considered in Colombia; and are pertinent in many other countries, especially those with programs that have operated for several years.

Box 3.6 The International CCT Community of Practice

CCT PROGRAMS HAVE ENGAGED INTENSIVELY in learning from each other—often directly, sometimes facilitated by international agencies—and using a full range of modalities:

- A series of three global conferences sponsored by international agencies and hosted by local governments have drawn together almost all countries that have had CCT programs active at the time of a conference: 2002 in Puebla, Mexico; 2004 in São Paulo, Brazil; and 2006 in Istanbul, Turkey. A series of smaller regional events has reinforced ties among program managers.
- There has been a series of study trips, often to the established Latin American programs.
- A video conference "learning circle," facilitated by the World Bank, has been formed by five of the established Latin American programs. Participants also have organized face-to-face sessions: January 2008 in

Cuernavaca, Mexico; September 2008 in Cartagena, Colombia.

- Extensive publication of evaluation results in academic journals has enabled a wider range of people to join in the learning.
- Several programs have very detailed public Web sites that publicize not only basic program information, but also operational manuals, monitoring statistics, evaluation results, program news, and the like.

Not only is the learning South-South, but it also has taken on South-North dimensions, with officials in London, New York City, and Sydney familiarizing themselves with the international CCT experience. The contacts have gone farther with Opportunity NYC: officials from the mayor's office and program management traveled to Mexico to visit Oportunidades, joined in some of the activities of the Latin American learning circle, and freely cited international experience as a justification for their pilot program.

Intersectoral and Interinstitutional Challenges

Poverty has been recognized as multidimensional for a long time, but most service provision is organized along unidimensional lines. CCT programs, especially in Latin America, often are at the heart of a move toward integrating policy and service delivery to achieve greater synergies among policies. The CCT programs sometimes are catalysts of such a move, and sometimes are forerunners in a larger explicit strategy to improve integration. That move toward coordination or integration has two facets—the increased coordination of actors and the integration of benefits.

CCTs inherently involve coordination among actors across several sectors (social assistance, health, education, planning, finance, auditing) and levels (federal, state, local, community). Many countries with a CCT program have at least national coordinating structures, and countries where service provision is local usually have some sort of local coordinating structures as well. For example, Mexico's national coordinating council, composed of senior policy makers, meets twice a year; the technical coordinating committee, comprising senior program managers, meets bimonthly, as do the state coordinating committees with local coordination around the 11,000 service centers (known as the *mesas de atención*). Those structures are concerned principally with operational details of ensuring that program beneficiaries meet conditions, that the information to monitor compliance flows appropriately, and that payments are made on time and correctly. But in handling those concerns, larger issues of the provision of at least health and education services arise. Because most countries with CCT programs also have taken simultaneous action to increase the quantity or quality of education and/ or health services, the points of contact on CCT operations can add a dimension of concrete management interface to such initiatives. (That will be discussed more fully in chapter 6.) Some CCT program managers feel that regularly presenting information about service availability (and the shortcomings thereof in specific locations) to local line staff and senior ministerial representatives exercises pressure for improved services, whether or not there is a comprehensive plan to do so.

In a number of cases, the CCT program has given the national government a new tool to affect the delivery of decentralized services. In Brazil, for example, the Ministry of Social Development signed a "joint management agreement" with each municipality that specifies who is responsible for what part of the Bolsa Família's administration. It also requires that states and municipalities give Bolsa participants priority in the wide range of locally run and funded programs. It thereby induces all these programs to share, at least partly, a targeting system and eligibility threshold. In Colombia, participating municipalities are required to appoint liaison officers who oversee all the functions the municipality is responsible for in the program and who communicate with the national and regional program offices. De facto, however, a good deal of what those municipal liaison officers do is coordinate among different social services supplied by the municipality. Moreover, the Familias en Acción program only works in municipalities that meet defined service standards for health and education. Initially, some target municipalities did not meet those standards but, over time, all did. Thus the national program has resulted in better coordination within municipal governments and has improved service delivery in some.

Financing is a potent tool. In El Salvador, the Red Solidaria has a budget to increase health services through contracting with NGOs. The national education budget goes to local schools on a capitated basis, so as local enrollments increase in response to the demand-side transfer, the supply-side budget will increase in step. Chile Solidario has an even stronger tool than most programs: the portion of the budget needed to provide priority services to its clients passes through the Ministry of Planning, which releases it only to the ministries in exchange for services.

Though hard to quantify or document, there is a sense in the CCT community that in at least a number of countries, the avenues of coordination established for the programs not only led to addressing the issues directly involved with the CCT program, but also have facilitated collaborative identification and solution of problems beyond that. Among the challenges currently felt in countries with mature and successful CCT programs are the needs to establish more clarity about the role of the CCT program versus other instruments and to pursue greater integration of social policy. In the countries with the most explicit instruments for meeting those challenges (Chile, Colombia, El Salvador), the leadership has come from a central agency under the presidency or ministry of planning rather than from within the CCT program itself.

One way of integrating benefits is geographic. In Panama, when the government developed the Red de Oportunidades, it also strengthened the Social Cabinet in the Ministry of Economy and Finance and created a multisector committee of the Red de Oportunidades to ensure that the supply of education and health prioritizes the areas where the Red will work. Similar approaches to giving priority in health and education improvements to areas in which CCT programs concentrate is not unusual. In some cases, the coordination has gone beyond the minimum level inherent in a CCT program. In El Salvador, for example, the Red Solidaria is focused on the poorest 100 municipalities. It includes the CCT program itself, a program to improve basic infrastructure services in the same municipalities, and a program to provide small-scale productive projects and microcredit. The Red then involves coordination on a greater range of subjects and from a wider range of actors, including those in agriculture, electricity, water, and sanitation.

Another place to integrate benefits is directly at the household level. As mentioned earlier, the household targeting systems used to select CCT beneficiaries often are used to target the benefits of other programs as well. This means that separate programs may reach the same households. In Jamaica, the beneficiaries of PATH are eligible not only for the cash transfer but also for fee waivers for hospital services and pharmaceuticals, for secondary school tuition, and for textbook rentals. In Brazil, Colombia, and Ecuador, the scope of programs that use the same household targeting system as the CCT program is much wider, encompassing other cash transfers, housing, school-to-work transition for youth, adult education, and so forth. In some countries, the integration goes beyond a common eligibility threshold in separately administered programs to specifically providing links or referrals. Several countries (Chile, Dominican Republic, and El Salvador, among them) help households get their birth, adoption, marriage, or identification papers in order—and that has spillover benefits in improving access to many other government programs, to voting rights, and sometimes to private banking services. In a decentralized context, Brazil's Bolsa Família has encouraged municipalities to use social workers to bring additional support and diagnostics to households where children fail to meet their co-responsibilities. Jamaica is beginning to set up a referral system (including a pilot program with one-stop shops) between PATH beneficiaries and a range of other programs, including skills and job-readiness training, job matching, business development, and caregiving support. The Chile Solidario program is focused on linking poor households into all pertinent branches of social policy. Colombia is rolling out a similar program, Juntos, that will link beneficiaries of Familias en Acción into a similarly large range of services.

One of the basic attractions of CCT programs is the potential synergy of getting health, education, and social assistance to the same families. Realizing such synergy at the operational level has been a basic challenge in all countries. The kernels of success often have motivated further waves of ambition toward more fully coordinating the actors in social policy and the benefits they can deliver to households. Thus, for the foreseeable future, coordination will remain a core issue of CCT work in the full range of countries, from those whose programs are nascent to those whose programs are mature.

Conclusion

CCT programs have been at the forefront of the modernization of social assistance. Many of the CCT programs have been ambitious and in some cases innovative in their mechanics. Most have chosen to focus narrowly on the poorest and have used (sometimes creating or refining) geographic and household targeting methods effectively to make possible a good record with respect to incidence. The larger programs also have a good record on coverage. Payment systems have been developed, and in most cases the systems function extremely well in getting payments reliably to the right people in the right amount at the right time. Also, there has been attention to keeping transaction costs reasonably low for participants. The banking sector or other payment agencies have been used to quite good effect in many countries. The monitoring of compliance with conditionalities has required the development of extensive and rapid information flows among numerous actors. Although monitoring compliance is still the least developed aspect of the programs in several countries, the mere fact (even the expectation) of routine exchange of large volumes of data is remarkable and a departure from common practice 10 years ago or in many other kinds of social programs today. CCT programs require the coordinating actions of many parties—the program itself, the providers of health and education services, the payment agency, and often subnational governments at one or more levels. This has reinforced the need for information sharing and led to wider discussions and actions on integrating different parts of social policy.

CCT programs have been very self-critical and open to learning. As a whole, they have a remarkable record for the extent and rigor of impact evaluation and public dissemination of findings. In most cases this is matched by extensive continuous monitoring systems that enable program managers to ensure that implementation is going as planned and to make adjustments as needed. There has been a great deal of exchange among programs as they seek to learn from each other how best to handle design issues and operational challenges.

The success of CCT programs documented in subsequent chapters could not have been achieved without the reliable implementation that their systems of targeting, payment, and monitoring and evaluation have delivered. However, none of these are inherent in, or limited to, CCT programs. Programs of other genres may learn from the implementation experience of CCTs. And CCT programs, both new and established, must be cognizant that success, or continued success, is not automatic, but dependent on excellence in their basic systems.

CHAPTER FOUR

The Impact of CCTs on Consumption Poverty and Employment

WE SAW IN CHAPTER 3 THAT CCT PROGRAMS GENERALLY HAVE DONE well in targeting their transfers to the poor. That does not mean, however, that they necessarily have a large impact on poverty. A number of factors, including behavioral and political economy responses to targeted programs, intervene in determining the ultimate impacts on poverty. For example, a study of China's Di Bao program—the largest cash transfer program in the developing world, though not a conventional CCT—found that the cities of China where the program was better targeted to the poor generally were not the ones where the scheme had the highest impact on poverty or where the program was the most cost effective in reducing poverty (Ravallion 2008).

This chapter directly assesses the performance of existing CCT programs in reducing consumption poverty. The chapter is divided into three sections and a conclusion. In the first section, we consider the impact of CCTs on short-term consumption and consumption poverty. This is done both for the target populations of CCT programs and, for a few countries, for the country population as a whole. We also discuss evidence showing that transfer income is used differently from other sources of income.

In principle, the impact of CCTs on poverty could be smaller than would be suggested by simple back-of-the-envelope calculations based on the size of the transfer because of both intended and unintended effects of the program. The second section of the chapter discusses the evidence on behavioral changes that could offset the impact of transfers. As will be shown in chapter 5, there is solid evidence that CCTs have increased school enrollment levels. If schooling and child work are substitutes, at least in part, then we would expect that CCTs might reduce child labor—and therefore reduce the contribution that children make to household income. We thus begin that section of the chapter with a discussion of CCT impacts on child labor. CCTs also could reduce adult labor supply for a variety of reasons: leisure is likely to be a normal good so households will tend to consume more of it as their incomes rise, and households could adjust their labor supply in an attempt to stay "poor enough" to continue being eligible for transfers. For that reason we next review the evidence on program effects on work by adults. Finally, we discuss whether CCTs appear to have crowded out transfers from other sources, had unintended impacts on fertility, or have had (local-level) general equilibrium effects.

If part of the transfer is invested, or if the transfer enables households to better smooth consumption, then CCT programs also can have impacts on consumption in the long run, above and beyond the changes arising from human capital accumulation. The third section of the chapter provides some evidence that this indeed has been the case. (Impacts on human capital accumulation will be discussed in chapter 5.)

Impact of CCTs on Household Consumption and Poverty

Impacts on Consumption among Program Beneficiaries

The impact of CCTs on immediate consumption is an important determinant of poverty alleviation in the short run, especially because most beneficiaries belong to the poorest part of the population. In this section we assess the impact of CCTs on short-term consumption or income for seven programs in which such data were collected as part of their evaluations and in which robust methods can be applied in the estimation of impact, namely, Bolsa Alimentação in Brazil,[1] Familias en Acción in Colombia, PRAF in Honduras, Oportunidades in Mexico, the RPS in Nicaragua, the BDH in Ecuador, and the CESSP scholarship program in Cambodia.[2] In all programs, consumption or income data were obtained through field surveys that interviewed both beneficiary and control households. Except for Brazil's Bolsa Alimentação, Mexico's Oportunidades, and the CESSP, all evaluations had baseline surveys that can be used to measure averages before the programs were implemented.[3]

Table 4.1 shows that preprogram median per capita consumption levels for the target population were low in all programs. This finding

Table 4.1 Impact of CCTs on per Capita Consumption, Various Years

Consumption	Brazil 2002	Cambodia 2007	Colombia 2002	Colombia 2006	Ecuador 2003	Ecuador 2005	Honduras 2000	Honduras 2002	Mexico 1998	Mexico Jun. 1999	Mexico Oct. 1999	Nicaragua 2000	Nicaragua 2001	Nicaragua 2002
Median daily per capita consumption of control households (current US$)	0.83	0.89	0.85	1.19	1.12	1.13	0.79	0.68	0.59	0.58	0.59	0.63	0.53	0.52
Daily per capita transfer (current US$)	0.06	0.02	0.12	0.13	0.08	0.08	0.06	0.06	0.12	0.14	0.13	0.16	0.15	0.15
Ratio of transfer to consumption (%)[a]	8	2–3	17	13	8	7	9	11	21	20	19	29	31	30
Impact on per capita consumption for the median household (%)	7.0**	B	A	10.0**	A	B	A	7.0*	B	7.8**	8.3**	A	29.3**	20.6**

Source: Authors' calculations for all countries in the table except Colombia. For Colombia, see Institute for Fiscal Studies, Econometría, and Sistemas Especializados de Información (2006).

Note: The estimated impacts presented here are not always equal to the unconditional double difference estimates because some regressions control for other correlates. The impact for Honduras was obtained from 2002 regression only. The impacts for Mexico are all for single equation cross-sectional regressions for each year. The lack of impact in 1998 is likely the result of the fact that this survey was carried out just a few months after the start of the program. Figures are in US$ obtained through the official exchange rates observed at the time of the surveys. In the case of Oportunidades in Mexico, the 1998 figures are for a few months after the start of the program. In the case of Bolsa Alimentação in Brazil, per capita consumption figures are for more than a year after the start of the program.

a. The transfer amounts as a proportion of per capita expenditures (or consumption) are not the same across all tables in the report because of differences in the surveys used, including their coverage and year.

A. Baseline, before households in CCT treatment group received transfers.

B. No significant impact on consumption.

* Significant at the 10 percent level.

** Significant at the 5 percent level.

corroborates the findings of chapter 3 that CCTs were well targeted. Per capita consumption varied between $0.52 per day in Nicaragua and $1.19 per day in Colombia.

Per capita transfers for the median household varied more widely across countries. They were as low as $0.02 per day in Cambodia, and as high as $0.16 per day in Nicaragua. This heterogeneity reflects the different weights that each program assigned to reducing short-term versus long-term poverty. Reducing current consumption poverty was a central objective of Oportunidades and the RPS. By contrast, the CESSP program had no redistributive or poverty alleviation goals.

Because the size of the transfer varies a great deal across countries, so does the ratio of the transfer to median consumption. This difference can be seen in the third row of the table: for households in Nicaragua, the transfer represented about 30 percent of consumption, whereas in Cambodia that number is only about 2 percent. Other programs fall somewhere in between, with Familias en Acción and Oportunidades making relatively large transfers, compared with the smaller transfers for the BDH program in Ecuador, PRAF in Honduras, Bolsa Alimentação in Brazil, and especially the CESSP program in Cambodia.

The fourth row of the table summarizes program effects on consumption. The largest impacts are found for the RPS, the program that made the largest transfers.

Other programs included in the table (including Familias en Acción in Colombia, Oportunidades in Mexico, PRAF in Honduras, and Bolsa Alimentação in Brazil) also had significant impacts on per capita consumption, ranging from 7 to 10 percent.[4] By contrast, neither the BDH program in Ecuador nor the CESSP program in Cambodia appears to have increased consumption levels. The results for the CESSP program are not unexpected, given the small size of the transfer and the fact that short-term poverty alleviation was not a program goal. The results for Ecuador are more surprising, and they appear to be related to the large reduction in child labor among BDH program beneficiaries (a point that we discuss in more detail below).

The estimated impact on consumption for the median households tells us very little about the potential distributional effects of CCTs. Therefore we next consider impacts on various poverty measures, including those that are distributionally sensitive.

The Impact of CCTs on Poverty at the Program Level

We estimate program impacts on three poverty measures of the Foster-Greer-Thorbecke (FGT) family: the headcount index, which is the number of people below the poverty line; the poverty gap, which measures the average distance between the consumption of poor people and the poverty line; and the squared poverty gap, which takes into account the distribution of resources among the poor. The analysis in this section focuses on Colombia, Honduras, Mexico, and Nicaragua. We exclude Cambodia and Ecuador; in those countries, the CCT did not have an effect on median consumption and, as would be expected, did not reduce poverty. We also exclude the Brazilian Bolsa Alimentação program because the evaluation sample is not representative of the program's target population, which makes the analysis of the impact on poverty less informative.

The results from these calculations are summarized in table 4.2. Consistent with table 4.1, programs that had large effects on consumption also had large effects on poverty. In Nicaragua, the RPS reduced the headcount index among beneficiaries by 5–7 percentage points, the poverty gap by 9–13 points, and the squared poverty gap by 9–12 points. In Colombia, Familias en Acción also had sizable effects on poverty, especially on the poverty gap, which was reduced by almost 7 percentage points. PRAF in Honduras and Oportunidades in Mexico had more modest impacts on poverty.[5]

Another way to measure the impact of CCTs on welfare is to compare the cumulative distribution of consumption per capita between the treatment and control populations. This method has the advantage of not relying on the selection of a poverty line, which can be somewhat arbitrary. If the cumulative distribution for treated households lies completely to the right of the distribution for control households—so-called first-order stochastic dominance—current welfare is improved unambiguously by CCTs. This is clearly the case for RPS beneficiaries in Nicaragua, as shown in panel A of figure 4.1. Panel B shows an improvement that is much smaller for Honduras, a result that is not surprising given the smaller magnitude of the transfer.

The Impact of CCTs on Poverty at the National Level

The welfare effects of CCT programs discussed so far are based on the sample of households in the impact evaluation surveys. That is, we have assessed impacts on those households and individuals directly

Table 4.2 Impact of CCTs on Poverty Measures, Various Years

Poverty measure		Colombia		Honduras		Mexico			Nicaragua		
		2002	2006	2000	2002	1998	Jun. 1999	Oct. 1999	2000	2001	2002
Headcount index	Control	0.95	0.90	0.88	0.91	0.89	0.93	0.94	0.84	0.91	0.90
	Impact	A	−0.03*	A	B	0.02**	−0.01**	0.00	A	−0.07**	−0.05**
Poverty gap	Control	0.58	0.54	0.49	0.54	0.47	0.55	0.56	0.43	0.50	0.50
	Impact	A	−0.07**	A	−0.02*	0.01*	−0.03**	−0.02**	A	−0.13**	−0.09**
Squared poverty gap	Control	0.53	0.43	0.30	0.36	0.28	0.35	0.36	0.26	0.32	0.32
	Impact	A	−0.02**	A	−0.02*	B	−0.03**	−0.03**	A	−0.12**	−0.09**

Source: Authors' calculations.

Note: We exclude Cambodia and Ecuador from this table because the CCT did not have an effect on median consumption in those countries and so it is not surprising that it did not reduce poverty. We also exclude the Brazilian Bolsa Alimentação program because the evaluation sample is not representative of the program's target population, which makes the analysis of the impact on poverty less informative. For Honduras, Mexico, and Nicaragua, calculations were done via regression of household level Foster-Greer-Thorbecke indicator on treatment dummy and other explanatory variables. Using the evaluation sample of each program, we compute $P(i,t,a) = (z − y(i,t) / z)a * \text{Poor}(i,t)$, for alpha = 0, 1, and 2; and for each household, where $y(i,t)$ is household i's level of consumption per capita at year t, z is the country-specific poverty line, and $\text{Poor}(i,t)$ is an indicator function that equals 1 if the household is poor and equals 0 otherwise. For Honduras, the poverty line used was Lps 24.6 per capita per day in 2000 lempiras. Expenditure values for 2002 were deflated to 2000 lempiras. For Nicaragua, we used C$13.87 per capita per day in 2000 córdobas. Expenditure values for 2001 and 2002 were deflated to 2000 córdobas. For Mexico, we used the value of the Canasta Básica of 1997, which was M$320 per capita per month. We inflated this value of the Canasta Básica for 1998 and 1999 using the Canasta Básica Price Index found at: http://www.banxico .org.mx/polmoneinflacion/estadisticas/indicesPrecios/indicesPreciosConsumidor.html. Therefore, for October 1998, we used M$320 × 1.134. For June 1999, we used M$320 × 1.280. For October 1999, we used M$320 × 1.314. For Colombia (see Institute for Fiscal Studies, Econometría, and Sistemas Especializados de Información 2006), the estimated impacts presented here are not equal to the unconditional double difference estimates because regressions control for other correlates. The impact for Honduras was obtained from 2002 regression only. The impacts for Mexico are all for single equation cross-sectional regressions for each year.

A. Baseline, before households in CCT treatment group received transfers.

B. No significant impact on poverty measure.

* Significant at the 10 percent level.

** Significant at the 5 percent level.

Figure 4.1 Impact of CCTs on the Distribution of Consumption, Nicaragua and Honduras, 2002

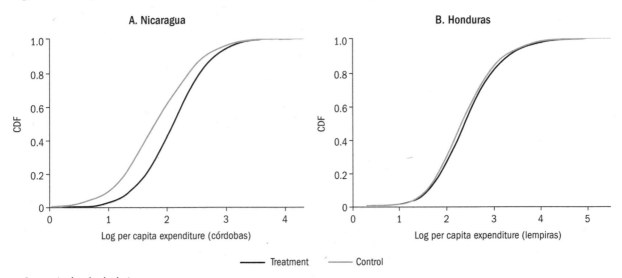

Source: Authors' calculations.

Note: CDF = cumulative distribution function.

affected by the programs at a given stage of each program's implementation. Given that the evaluation samples were derived either from the pilot stages of a program (as in Honduras and Nicaragua) or from the early phases of expansion of the program (as in the Bolsa Alimentação program in Brazil and the Oportunidades program in Mexico), these estimates may not be representative of the impacts of CCTs on the population of beneficiaries after coverage has been expanded to the national level. In this section, we investigate the poverty impacts of some relatively large CCT programs, using nationally representative household surveys in four countries: Brazil, Ecuador, Jamaica, and Mexico.[6] The welfare measure used is household consumption per capita (except for Brazil, where we use household income per capita because consumption data were not available). The poverty line is set in each country at the 25th percentile of the pretransfer distribution of consumption or income.

To approximate pretransfer income or consumption for CCT beneficiaries, we simply subtract the full value of the transfer from income or consumption reported in the survey. This approach has important shortcomings: it amounts to ruling out behavioral changes, such as reductions in labor supply or remittances arising from the receipt of transfers, *by assumption*. Furthermore, and unlike the evaluations

109

discussed in the previous section, these calculations may be biased by purposeful program placement or self-selection.[7] Nevertheless, and keeping these important caveats in mind, the results are useful because they enable us to approximate the impact of large-scale CCT programs on measures of poverty at the national level.

Table 4.3 suggests that CCTs generally helped reduce national poverty. In Mexico there are large effects on poverty, especially for the poverty gap and squared poverty gap measures. For example, the estimates in table 4.3 suggest that Oportunidades decreased the squared poverty gap by approximately 29 percent. In Jamaica, PATH reduced the squared poverty gap index by 13 percent from its pretransfer value. In Brazil, the impacts of the Bolsa Família program on the headcount index and the poverty gap are modest; however, the program reduces the squared poverty gap by a substantial amount, 15 percent. This finding is consistent with the findings of Paes de Barros, Foguel, and Ulyssea (2006), who suggest there is a strong link between the introduction of CCTs and the fall in inequality in Brazil.

The most puzzling findings correspond to the BDH program in Ecuador because the results in tables 4.2 and 4.3 are very different. It is likely that this difference arises, at least in part, because the estimates in

Table 4.3 Impact of CCT Programs on Poverty Indexes at the National Level, Various Years

Country	Headcount		Poverty gap		Squared poverty gap		Size of the transfer (% of PCE)[a]
	Pre-transfer	Post-transfer	Pre-transfer	Post-transfer	Pre-transfer	Post-transfer	
Brazil	0.2421	0.2369	0.0980	0.0901	0.0553	0.0471	11.7
Ecuador	0.2439	0.2242	0.0703	0.0607	0.0289	0.0235	8.3
Jamaica	0.2439	0.2329	0.0659	0.0602	0.0258	0.0224	10.7
Mexico	0.2406	0.2222	0.0847	0.0683	0.0422	0.0298	33.4

Source: Authors' calculations.

Note: PCE = per capita expenditure. The poverty line used in each country is the 25th percentile of the pretransfer national distribution (prior to the symmetrical trimming of the distribution for extreme outliers; that is, values of less than the 1st percentile and above the 99th percentile of the distribution). For Brazil, the measure of welfare used is per capita income (PCI). In the other three countries, the measure of welfare is PCE. Pretransfer welfare is derived by subtracting the full value of the per capita cash transfer reported by a beneficiary household in each country from its welfare measure, inclusive of the transfer (PCE or PCI in Brazil). For Brazil, we use the Pesquisa Nacional por Amostra de Domicilios 2006. For Ecuador, we use the Encuesta de Condiciones de Vida 2006. For Jamaica, we use the Survey of Living Conditions 2004. For Mexico, we use the Encuesta Nacional de Ingresos y Gastos de los Hogares 2004.

a. The transfer amounts as a proportion of per capita expenditures (or consumption) are not the same across all tables in the report because of differences in the surveys used, including their coverage and year.

table 4.3 disregard the very large reduction in child labor, which offsets the impact of the transfer (Edmonds and Schady 2008). In addition, differences in the coverages of the surveys may be important: the survey used for table 4.3 is nationally representative, whereas the data collected for the impact evaluation of the BDH was limited to four provinces and to poor households within those provinces.[8]

Impacts on the Composition of Consumption

In addition to impacts on aggregate consumption, CCTs may affect disproportionately the consumption of particular items, such as food. This is of interest for a variety of reasons, including the link between food consumption and such measures of nutritional status as height-for-age and weight-for-height in children and body mass index for adults.[9] Also, in analyzing consumption patterns among CCT recipients, it is possible to test whether households use transfer income differently from other sources of income. This could happen for a variety of reasons. Transfers are made to women, and there is a large body of evidence suggesting that women have different preferences over consumption than do men (Thomas 1990; Hoddinott and Haddad 1995; Lundberg, Pollak, and Wales 1997; Doss 2006; Ward-Batts 2008); that the conditions attached to transfers or the social marketing of programs may affect how transfer income is used;[10] and that transfer income may be perceived as temporary, in which case households may save rather than consume the bulk of it (as suggested by the permanent income hypothesis).

A number of authors have analyzed CCT effects on the food Engel curve—the share of consumption that is devoted to food at various levels of total consumption. The intuition behind this is as follows: CCTs transfer cash, which increases total consumption, as shown above. If households perceive CCTs as any other source of income, we would expect that transfers move them *along* the food Engel curve. On the other hand, if transfer income is treated differently from other sources of income, CCTs may result in *shifts* of the food (and other) Engel curves.

To see whether that is the case, figure 4.2 graphs food Engel curves for treated and control households in Ecuador and Nicaragua. The figure shows that Engel curves in both countries have the familiar downward-sloping shape, with the share of food decreasing as total expenditures rise. This phenomenon is known as "Engel's law." However, both panels of the figure show that, at the time of follow-up,

Figure 4.2   Impact of CCTs on Food Shares in Ecuador and Nicaragua

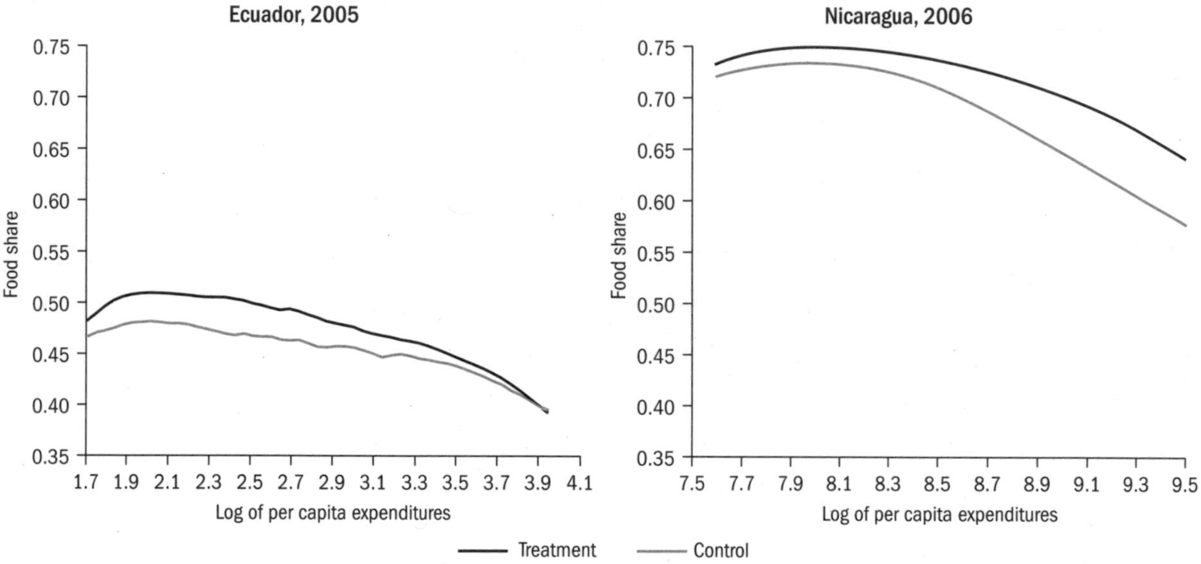

Sources: For Ecuador, Schady and Rosero (2008); for Nicaragua, Macours, Schady, and Vakis (2008).

the food Engel curves of CCT beneficiaries are everywhere above those for control households—clear evidence that transfer income was used differently from other sources of income.

Similar results are reported elsewhere. Using nonexperimental data for the Familias en Acción program in Colombia and the urban Oportunidades program in Mexico, Attanasio, Battistin, and Mesnard (2008) and Angelucci and Attanasio (2008) report upward shifts of the food Engel curves among program beneficiaries. The regression results presented in table 4.4 also corroborate these findings. Food share regression results indicate that for a given level of total household expenditure, treated households tend to consume a larger proportion of food. For example, the food share is about 4 percentage points higher among program beneficiaries in Colombia, Ecuador, and Nicaragua than among non-beneficiaries. Moreover, insofar as CCT programs affect total consumption, the effect on the *level* of food expenditures (as opposed to the share, measured by the Engel curve) can be considerable. In Mexico, for example, the median value of food consumption was 11 percent higher for beneficiary households than for comparable control households, and the median caloric consumption had increased by 8 percent (Hoddinott, Skoufias, and Washburn 2000).

Table 4.4 Impact of CCTs on Food Shares

| | | Brazil | Colombia | | Ecuador | Honduras | | Nicaragua | | |
		2002	2002	2006	2005	2000	2002	2000	2001	2002
Daily per capita food consumption	Control	0.45	0.6	0.65	0.73	0.53	0.47	0.44	0.35	0.35
	Impact (%)	12**	A	6**	B	A	B		38**	31**
Food shares	Control (%)	60	74	56	54	71	72	73	69	68
	Impact (percentage points)	0.02**	A	0.04**	0.04**	A	B		0.04**	0.04**

Sources: For Brazil, Ecuador, Honduras, and Nicaragua, authors' calculations. For Colombia, see Institute for Fiscal Studies, Econometría, and Sistemas Especializados de Información (2006).

Note: Daily per capita food consumption is presented in US$ converted by the official current exchange rates at the time of the surveys. Food share is the percentage of total per capita consumption dedicated to food. The estimated impacts presented here are not always equal to the unconditional double-difference estimates because some regressions control for other correlates. In the case of Honduras, impacts were estimated with 2002 data only (via cross-sectional regression).

A. Baseline, before households in CCT treatment group received transfers.

B. No significant impact on poverty measure.

** Significant at the 5 percent level.

The increase in expenditures on food generally is directed toward increasing quality. Households that benefited from Familias en Acción in Colombia significantly increased items rich in protein, such as milk, meat, and eggs (Attanasio and Mesnard 2006); and the increases in food expenditures in Mexico and Nicaragua were driven largely by increased consumption of meat, fruits, and vegetables (Hoddinott, Skoufias, and Washburn 2000; Maluccio and Flores 2005). Oportunidades also increased caloric diversity as measured by the number of different food-stuffs consumed. At similar overall food expenditure levels in Nicaragua, Macours, Schady, and Vakis (2008) show that households that receive transfers from the Atención a Crisis program spend significantly less on staples (primarily rice, beans, and tortillas) and significantly more on animal protein (chicken, meat, milk, and eggs), as well as on fruits and vegetables. Angelucci and Attanasio (2008) report similar results using data for urban Oportunidades in Mexico. Not only did households diversify their diets; they also shifted toward higher-quality sources of calories.

What causes these Engel curve shifts? Schady and Rosero (2007, 2008) hypothesize that CCTs increase the bargaining power of women within the household, and that this results in increased food expenditures. They use data on the BDH program in Ecuador to test that hypothesis. Specifically, they argue that if changes in bargaining power are important, one would expect to see program effects on the food Engel curve among households that included prime-age men and prime-age women at baseline (where bargaining between males and females is an issue), but not among households with only prime-age women (where there is no bargaining of this sort). The results of their analysis are consistent with this prediction.

Analyzing Offsetting Behavioral Responses to CCTs

The size of the transfer and the fraction of poor households that receive it are major determinants of CCT impacts on consumption poverty. However, table 4.1 shows that, for most countries, the *impact* of the transfer is generally somewhat smaller than the *magnitude* of the transfer (when both are normalized as a fraction of the consumption or income of households in the control group).[11] The difference between these two values may be a result of behavioral changes by CCT beneficiaries, which partly offset the value of the transfer itself. We now turn to a discussion of the evidence on these possible offsetting effects, focusing on impacts on child labor, adult labor, remittances, fertility, and spillovers and other general equilibrium effects.

Child Labor

Whether CCT programs help reduce the prevalence and amount of child work is of interest not only because of the resulting difference between the amount of the transfer and the change in household consumption. Rather, a reduction in child work is often seen as a good in its own right: working under poor conditions can adversely affect both the physical and mental health of children, and income-generating activities for children often take place at the cost of reductions in educational attainment and future earnings.

There are two main channels through which CCTs could reduce the prevalence and amount of work among school-age children. The first channel works though the conditional nature of the programs. Given the requirement of school enrollment and regular attendance, children have less time available for participation in income-generating activities.

Conditions also may increase parents' awareness of the importance of schooling and thereby decrease child work. The second channel is a pure income effect: households that receive the transfer are less likely to be dependent on the income of their children, and therefore may reduce child work, as suggested by a number of theoretical models (Basu and Van 1998; Baland and Robinson 2000).

Several CCTs have been successful in reducing child work. Frequently, these impacts have been concentrated among older children. Table 4.5 shows that Oportunidades reduced child work among older children, aged 12–17, especially among boys (for whom baseline levels of child work also were substantially higher). Skoufias and Parker (2001) also show that domestic work decreased substantially, especially for girls.

In Ecuador, Edmonds and Schady (2008) show that the Bono de Desarrollo Humano program had very large effects on child work among those children most vulnerable to transitioning from schooling to work. Those effects are concentrated in work for pay away from the child's home. On the other hand, BDH transfers had small effects on child time allocation at peak school attendance ages and among children already out of school at baseline. In Cambodia, the CESSP program, which gives transfers to children in transition from primary to lower-secondary school, reduced work for pay by 11 percentage points (Filmer and Schady 2009c).

Table 4.5 Impact of Oportunidades on the Probability of Children Working

Age group	Pre-program level	November 1999	
		Coefficient	t-statistic
Boys			
8–11 years	0.0620	−0.011	−1.3
12–17 years	0.3775	−0.047	−2.1
Girls			
8–11 years	0.0353	0.000	−0.5
12–17 years	0.1317	−0.023	−1.8

Source: Skoufias and Parker 2001, table 5.

Other CCT programs also appear to have reduced child work. In Nicaragua, the RPS reduced child work by 3–5 percentage points among children aged 7–13 (Maluccio and Flores 2005). Furthermore, the fraction of children who only studied (as opposed to worked and studied, only worked, or neither worked nor studied) increased significantly (from 59 percent to 84 percent) as a result of the RPS (Maluccio 2005). Yap, Sedlacek, and Orazem (2008) estimate the effects of the Brazilian PETI, another precursor of the Bolsa Família program. PETI gave out conditional transfers to secondary school-age children enrolled in school. Stipends were given directly to students, not to the families, conditional on school attendance and participation in special training workshops. PETI beneficiaries reduced substantially their probability of working. Attanasio et al. (2006), however, find no effect of the Familias en Acción program on child work in Colombia (although the program does appear to have reduced the amount of time dedicated to domestic chores); and Glewwe and Olinto (2004) find no effects of the PRAF program on child work in Honduras.

Two recent papers consider the impact of CCTs on child work when the transfer is conditional on school attendance for only one child in the household, and that child has siblings. Potentially, programs of this nature could have positive or negative spillovers for other siblings—positive if the income effect reduces child work for all children, if transfers increase the bargaining capacity of women within the household, or if the social marketing by the program leads parents to reduce child work even for children whose school attendance is not monitored; negative if parents compensate for the reduction in work of one child by increasing the work of other siblings. Barrera-Osorio et al. (2008) analyze Subsidio Condicionado a la Asistencia Escolar, a pilot CCT program in Bogotá, Colombia. This program randomized assignment to individual children rather than households, and made transfers directly to students rather than to their parents.[12] Barrera-Osorio et al. show that, within the same household, a student selected into the program is 2 percentage points more likely to attend school and works about 1 hour less than a sibling who has not been selected. However, the beneficiary's sibling (particularly if this sibling is a girl) is less likely to attend school than are children in households that received no cash transfer at all. On the other hand, Filmer and Schady (2009c) find that the CESSP program in Cambodia had no effect on the school enrollment of a beneficiary's ineligible siblings. More research is needed to understand this difference between the two programs, especially if the number of CCTs that attempt to target individual children increases. (For a discussion of time spent in school as a substitute for child labor, see box 4.1.)

Adult Labor Supply

Of greater concern than changes in the amount of child labor are any possible reductions in adult work that result from CCTs. Such reductions could happen for a variety of reasons. If leisure is a normal good, then the income effect associated with the transfer might result in more leisure and less work. There also may be a price effect: beneficiaries of CCTs may believe (correctly or incorrectly) that they need to supply less labor to become or continue to be "poor" and eligible for a means-tested program. Adults also may have to take time away from work—for instance, to take children to school or health clinics. All of these could result in a reduction in adult work effort. Indeed, concern with possible work disincentives was one of the main reasons for the reform of transfer and other welfare programs in the United States in the 1990s (see box 4.2).

In practice, CCTs appear to have had, at most, modest disincentives for adult work. Two studies (Parker and Skoufias 2000; Skoufias and

---

Box 4.1   Is Time Spent in School a Perfect Substitute for Time Working?

AN IMPORTANT QUESTION IS WHETHER TIME spent in school and time spent at work are fully substitutable. The answer seems to be rarely so. In Colombia, Attanasio et al. (2006) provide evidence of partial substitution between school and work, with at most 25 percent of each extra hour spent on schooling coming from time otherwise spent at work. Because most of the substitution arises from a decrease in hours of domestic work activities, time spent on income-generating activities largely is unaffected and leisure is somewhat reduced. The substitution effects are largest among the children ages 10 to 13 in rural areas and ages 14 to 17 in urban areas.

In their analysis of the FFE program in Bangladesh, Ravallion and Wodon (2000) show that the decrease in the prevalence of child work for boys was only about a quarter of the increase in the percentage of boys enrolled in school. For girls, it was only about one eighth of the increase in enrollment.

On the other hand, using data from Oportunidades and a broad definition of work (including market, farm, and domestic work), Skoufias and Parker (2001) show that the reduction in time spent at work largely equals the increase in schooling for boys, but not for girls. Rather, leisure time is reduced significantly for girls. The pattern also varied by gender in other ways, with boys reducing both market and domestic work and girls reducing mainly domestic work.

Box 4.2   Work Disincentive Effects of Social Assistance Programs in Developed Countries

THE LITERATURE ON WORK DISINCENTIVE effects of social assistance programs in developed countries is vast (for surveys, see Atkinson 1987; Krueger and Meyer 2002; Moffitt 2002). Moffitt, for instance, finds that because of its implicit tax on income, the U.S. federal assistance program, Aid to Families with Dependent Children (AFDC), reduced labor force participation of beneficiaries by 10 to 50 percent, when compared with similar nonbeneficiary households.[a]

To address the issue of a strong built-in disincentive to work, in 1996 the U.S. government replaced AFDC with a new program, Temporary Assistance for Needy Families (TANF). TANF is different from AFDC in many ways. First, there is no entitlement. The fact that a household's income is below a certain level does not entitle it to a transfer. Second, TANF introduced time limits. Individuals cannot receive cash benefits for more than five years (with few exceptions); and after two years in the program, recipients must work at least 30 hours per week to continue to be eligible for the transfers. Third, at least 50 percent of single-mother recipients and 90 percent of two-parent families must be working or in a job training program offered by the state. Finally, states now may decide on their program's benefit reduction rates (or implicit tax on income). That is, instead of being required to reduce the benefits by one dollar for each dollar earned, states can decide

whether this implicit tax rate will be zero to one, one to one, or any other rate in between.

A study by Grogger (2003) indicates that up to 12 percent of the welfare caseload decline observed between 1993 and 1999 (from 33 percent to 15 percent), and up to 7 percent of the observed increase in employment rates of families headed by single mothers (from 69 percent to 83 percent) during the same period were the result of time limits introduced by TANF. The study finds no effects of time limits on hours worked by recipient single mothers. Bloom and Michalopoulos (2001) show results from randomized experiments that indicate time limits seem to increase employment of welfare recipients by 4–11 percentage points (from a base that varied from 40 percent to 55 percent employment rates).

According to the research surveyed by Blank (2002) and Moffitt (2002), however, the marginal tax rate changes embodied in TANF do not seem to have had any effect on work effort. It seems that most of the changes in labor supply induced by TANF came from its time limits and work requirement.

a. Between 1935 and 1996, the main government cash transfer program in the United States was AFDC. Federal law required that the AFDC grant to an individual be reduced by one dollar for each dollar earned as income. This requirement represented a 100 percent implicit tax on income, and many policy makers and academics alike worried that such design features created strong work disincentives.

di Maro 2006) examine the effects of Oportunidades on adult labor supply; neither finds evidence of disincentive effects. The data used by Edmonds and Schady (2008) suggest that the BDH program in Ecuador had no effects on adult labor supply; in a similar vein, Filmer and Schady (2009c) report that adult labor supply was largely unaffected by the CESSP program in Cambodia. Only in Nicaragua is there some evidence of significant negative effects on adult work: Maluccio and Flores (2005) show that the RPS resulted in a significant reduction

In hours worked by adult men in the preceding week (by about 6 hours), with no effect among adult women.

Why did CCT programs not lead to larger reductions in adult labor supply, as had been a concern of many policy makers and academics? There are various possible explanations. First, the beneficiaries of CCT programs generally are very poor, and the income elasticity of leisure may be quite low for households that are this poor. Moreover, for some households the reduction in income from child work and the increase in school expenditures associated with the additional school enrollment offset the amount of the transfer. Obviously, that is particularly true for programs that made small transfers but had large effects on school enrollment and child work, as with the CESSP program in Cambodia; but Edmonds and Schady (2008) show that it was also the case for beneficiaries of the BDH program in Ecuador. Under these circumstances, increasing adult labor supply (or at least not reducing it) is one way to keep income and consumption at a level comparable with what it would have been had a household not taken up the program. Not coincidentally, perhaps, disincentive effects on adult labor supply are found only for the program that made the most generous transfers, the RPS in Nicaragua.

There are other reasons that might help explain why there have not been large disincentives to adult labor associated with CCTs. First, there are issues of timing. If households perceive transfers to be "temporary" rather than a permanent new "entitlement," they would treat them as a windfall, and generally would not change the labor supply of adults. Moreover, the data used to estimate the CCT impacts on labor supply generally reflect household responses shortly after they have become eligible for the program for the first time. In the longer run, as households have more time to adjust their behavior, disincentive effects on adult labor may become more of an issue. Nevertheless, recent research on the South African old-age pension (OAP) scheme, which makes transfers that dwarf those of even the most generous CCTs and which is likely to be seen as "permanent" by beneficiaries, is encouraging. As box 4.3 shows, the OAP does not appear to have reduced work effort by prime-age adults.

Crowding-Out of Remittances and Transfers

The impact of CCTs on consumption poverty also could be offset if they crowd out transfers from other sources, such as remittances. That could happen if senders of remittances or other private transfers target

Box 4.3   Do Transfers Reduce the Supply of Adult Labor?
Evidence from the South African Pension Scheme

THE SOUTH AFRICAN OAP SCHEME PROVIDES A generous benefit to retirees in that country. The value of the transfer is more than twice median per capita income for African (black) households. In principle, the program is means tested. In practice, however, all households that do not have a private pension are eligible. The program was made available to black families after the end of apartheid in 1994. By now, it is likely that the program is seen as an "entitlement" by most beneficiary households.

Early research on the OAP suggested that it had substantial negative effects on adult labor supply (Bertrand, Mullainathan, and Miller 2003). More recent research (Ardington, Case, and Hosegood 2008) disputes those findings. These new results are

based on better data—specifically, panel data rather than a single cross-section, which allows the authors to control for time-invariant differences between pension recipients and nonrecipients; and data on nonresident (migrant) household members, which are important because migrant status is correlated with pension receipt. The preferred specification in Ardington, Case, and Hosegood (2008) suggests that the OAP had a *positive* effect on adult labor supply—the probability that prime-age adults are employed is approximately 3 percentage points higher in households with at least one pension recipient. Those authors argue that the OAP relieves financial and child care constraints, which can be short-run impediments to migrating, even when the medium-run returns to migrating are positive.

a fixed level of income for recipient households or seek to equate marginal utility across donors and recipients. When part of the transfer is crowded out, this fraction will accrue to households outside the target group, and program recipients will benefit less than intended. However, the implied mistargeting of program resources also means that there is a positive effect of the program beyond that measured by evaluation surveys in the treatment areas.

Empirical evidence on the crowding-out effects of CCTs shows mixed results. For Mexico, Albarran and Attanasio (2003) show some indication of crowding out for Oportunidades, using one round of ex post evaluation data. However, Teruel and Davis (2000) reject the crowding-out impact of Oportunidades on private transfers, using more rounds of evaluation data. Their result holds for both monetary and in-kind transfers.

More recently, Nielsen and Olinto (2008) provide evidence on crowding-out effects of the Honduran and Nicaraguan CCT programs. They find that both the prevalence and the amount of remittances in the two countries were unaffected by the programs. That finding is comforting because remittances constitute a major source of foreign currency for many countries in Central America. However, the evidence in Nielsen and Olinto (2008) points toward some crowding out of private food transfers and money and food transfers from NGOs in Nicaragua, which could be a concern if it represents a change in informal insurance schemes. The PRAF in Honduras does not seem to crowd out any of these private transfers, most likely because of the modest size of CCT payments in that program.

Fertility and Family Composition

Transfers made by CCT programs are often a function, in part, of the number of children, sometimes with a cap on the total amount of transfers for which a household can be eligible (see the discussion in chapter 3). One concern is that CCTs could provide incentives for increased fertility, which could result in eventual reductions in household (and national) welfare.

In practice, any effects on fertility appear to have been modest. A recent paper (Stecklov et al. 2006) finds no effects on the total fertility rate among beneficiaries of Oportunidades in Mexico or the RPS in Nicaragua; however, it appears that PRAF increased fertility among eligible households in Honduras by 2–4 percentage points. The authors argue that these differences can be explained by differences in program design: In Mexico, the transfer to households with preschool children was a lump sum, regardless of the number of children; and (in the first three years of the program) poor, childless households could not become eligible for transfers if they had children after the first wave of inscriptions. In Nicaragua, the transfer was also a lump sum, although some households became eligible for transfers once they had children. In Honduras, finally, new households could be registered if they gave birth to children, and the amount of the transfer depended on the number of young children. If borne out by results from other countries, the evidence in Stecklov et al. (2006) would suggest that the details of program design are important because they can provide incentives that result in unintended outcomes.[13]

Spillovers and General Equilibrium Effects

CCT programs often are targeted geographically to poor and remote rural areas. In some cases, transfers are substantial and a large proportion of the population in a community receives them. Potentially, this could result in general equilibrium and spillover effects in the local economy. For instance, CCTs could increase the prices of consumption goods through higher demand, or could increase prevailing local wages because of the reduction in the labor supply of children.

To assess whether such spillover effects occurred in Mexico, Angelucci and de Giorgi (2008) analyze the evaluation data of Oportunidades for both beneficiaries and ineligible households living in treatment communities. They find that there was no indirect negative effect on labor earnings, prices, and the receipt of other welfare payments. In fact, they observe that the real incomes of ineligible households living in treatment communities seem to have been affected positively by the program. They show that ineligible households in treatment villages consumed more by receiving more private transfers, by borrowing more (almost exclusively from family, friends, or informal moneylenders), and by reducing their stocks of grains and animals. In addition, they show that the indirect program effects on consumption and loans are larger for households hit by a negative shock.

The lack of impact on wages and prices of consumer goods is not surprising. In most countries in which CCTs have been evaluated, labor and goods markets are sufficiently developed so that both labor and goods are largely tradable. CCTs may induce larger local demand for goods and lower local supply of labor, and, in the short run, prices may change to reflect these imbalances; in the long run, however, prices should return to their initial equilibrium.

Another kind of spillover effect is related to changes in access to and use of the formal banking sector. A number of CCT programs, including Bolsa Família in Brazil and the BDH in Ecuador, directly deposit benefits in bank accounts created for beneficiaries, who then can withdraw cash using an automated teller machine (ATM) card. That payment system appears to have reduced transaction costs (such as standing in line to receive transfers), and is likely to have reduced any stigma attached to the program. In addition, creating a bank account for CCT beneficiaries and giving them ATM cards may make it more likely that they use the formal banking sector in other capacities—potentially, a very important benefit of CCT programs and one that has not been evaluated to date.

Long-Term Impacts of CCTs on Consumption

As we have shown, many CCT programs have had substantial effects on consumption and poverty in the short run. A natural question is whether those positive impacts are likely to remain, at least in part, once households are no longer eligible for the CCT or the program ceases to exist altogether. Positive effects could be maintained, for example, if part of the transfer is saved and invested in productive assets, or if the stable income stream of the transfer allowed households to gain access to credit and overcome liquidity constraints. It also is possible that the transfer enables households to smooth consumption when they face negative shocks. If CCT programs do have a long-term impact on household consumption, then the estimates of program impact on short-term consumption and poverty reported above will underestimate the true (medium- and long-run) impact of CCTs on poverty.

Looking first at the investment of transfers, Gertler, Martínez, and Rubio-Codina (2006) provide extensive evidence on the Mexican experience. They find that the program had a substantial positive impact on investment in productive activities such as microenterprises and agriculture (animals and land). On average, 12 percent of transfers were invested, and households that received more transfers from Oportunidades also invested more. It seems that the CCT helped alleviate two market failures. First, the increased income allowed households to overcome credit constraints. Second, the stable stream of income may have made households willing to undertake more risky (and profitable) investments.

Another study (Maluccio 2008) assesses the impact of the RPS program in Nicaragua on various types of investments. The author finds only limited evidence that the program led to an increase in investment for agricultural equipment. His findings do not imply that the program had no long-term effects—it almost certainly did in terms of investment in child health and education, which should continue to lead to benefits for many years to come. In contrast to Mexico, however, there was only weak (albeit positive) evidence that RPS improved investment activities, possibly because of an economic downturn during the period, the strong program orientation toward increased food expenditures, and the limited opportunities in the impoverished rural areas where the program operated.

CCTs also may help households smooth their consumption and protect them from adverse shocks. If that is true, treated households may

123

be relatively more willing to undertake risky investments and less likely to sell assets or discontinue their children's school enrollment during an economic downturn.

The ability of the RPS to function as a social safety net during the so-called coffee crisis provides empirical evidence that CCTs can protect households from adverse shocks. For Nicaragua during 2000 and 2001, the crisis consisted of a drop in coffee prices to a 30-year low (or a 100-year low, adjusting for inflation) due to a worldwide oversupply of coffee (Varangis et al. 2003). The fall in prices hurt farmers and laborers socially and financially. By comparing coffee-growing and non-coffee–growing areas and treatment and control households, one can measure how well the RPS performed as a social safety net. Maluccio (2005) finds that the RPS enabled beneficiary households to maintain per capita expenditures during the crisis and helped reduce labor supply increases in coffee-growing areas. The effect was larger for those who were most affected by the fall in coffee prices.

It is important to make clear that the protection of income during a shock was achieved even if the RPS in no way was designed to respond to shocks. A similar result holds for Mexico, where Oportunidades helped beneficiary households smooth their consumption in the face of income fluctuations (Skoufias 2002). Skoufias also finds that Oportunidades provided that protection without replacing existing informal insurance schemes.

Conclusion

This chapter has reviewed the impacts of CCTs on household consumption, poverty, the composition of consumption, behavioral responses that might offset the effect of transfers, and long-term welfare. We focus on CCT programs for which there are robust evaluation data.

Policy makers and academics alike long have been concerned with the disincentive and general equilibrium effects of government cash transfers to the poor. That fear stems from hypothesized disincentives to work, crowding out of private transfers, effects on fertility and family composition, and effects on local wages and prices. The evidence reviewed in this chapter, however, suggests that these offsetting effects generally have been modest.

First, by and large, programs have had positive impacts on consumption, especially when the transfer amount is generous (as with the RPS program in Nicaragua). In and of itself, those positive impacts on consumption are indirect evidence that the offsetting behavioral responses are unlikely to be large, and that the marginal propensity to consume out of transfer income is high. Moreover, because transfers generally are well targeted to the poor, the effects on consumption have translated into impacts on poverty.

Second, the evidence suggests that CCTs generally do not have large disincentive effects on the labor supply of adults. More research is needed to see whether those patterns are maintained as programs mature and beneficiaries have more time to adjust their behavior. However, the results to date indicate that the popular view that cash transfers encourage indolence is not supported by the evidence.

Third, unlike most social assistance programs in the developed world, CCTs do not seem to crowd out private transfers. Although there is some evidence that CCTs crowd out intracommunity transfers of in-kind goods, these usually are transfers among the poor and therefore have very little redistributional impact. Also, CCTs do not appear to have had large effects on fertility.

Fourth, CCTs seem to have no significant negative effects on local wages, local prices, and the receipt of other welfare payments. In fact, contrary to expectations, there is some evidence that the real incomes of ineligible households living in program communities have been affected positively by CCTs. In Mexico, nonpoor households in treatment villages received more private transfers, borrowed more, and reduced their stocks of grains and animals; they also consumed more.

Finally, although the evidence suggests that, as intended, CCTs do have significant impacts in reducing child labor, the resulting income losses generally are not large enough to offset the impact of transfers on per capita consumption. (Cambodia and especially Ecuador appear to be exceptions to this general pattern.)

In sum, the main conclusion of this chapter is that redistribution via direct cash transfers seems to have worked well. Most programs, especially those making sizable transfers, have had substantial impacts on consumption and on poverty. The offsetting effects that were a source of concern when CCT programs were created do not appear to have occurred on a scale large enough to offset the bulk of the transfer.

CCTs do not seem to reduce the labor supply of adults or to crowd out private transfers. They do reduce the supply of child labor, but this reduction seems to have only a modest impact on household income and consumption. Moreover, some CCTs seem to increase productive investment, which boosts the impact on poverty even farther.

CHAPTER FIVE

The Impact of CCT Programs
on the Accumulation
of Human Capital

IN ADDITION TO THE OBJECTIVE OF REDUCING CURRENT POVERTY, as discussed in the previous chapter, CCT programs try to encourage households to invest in the human capital of their children. This chapter turns to the evidence of program impacts on education, health, and nutrition. As in chapter 4, the evidence provided in this chapter relies on rigorous impact evaluations (described in appendix B) and on calculations done for the purpose of this report.

The first section presents evidence of CCT program effects on the use of education and health services. We show that, by and large, CCTs have had significant and, in some cases, large effects on school enrollment and attendance. There is also some evidence of increases in the use of preventive health services, although that is not as clear. The second section of the chapter presents evidence of CCT program effects on "final" outcomes in education and health—for example, years of schooling completed, test scores, child height for age, and infant mortality. We show that there are many fewer evaluations to draw on, with a disproportionate amount of the evidence coming from a single country (Mexico). Importantly, the evidence on the impact of CCTs on these "final" outcomes is somewhat mixed. Thus CCTs appear to have had a modest impact on years of schooling completed by adults; they reduced the incidence of low child height for age only in some countries and only among some populations; and they resulted in modest improvements in cognitive development among very young children, but had no discernible effect on learning outcomes for children who benefited from CCT programs while they were of school age. The third section of the chapter then considers the extent to which CCT program effects on human capital appear to be a result of the "income" effect associated with the transfer, the "price" effect that results from the condition, or both.

CCT Program Effects on the Use of Education and Health Services

CCTs transfer cash and require that households make regular use of education and health services. In this section, we review evidence of the impact of CCT programs on the use of those services, focusing first on education and then on health.

Table 5.1 Impact of CCTs on School Enrollment and Attendance, Various Years

Country	Program	Age/Gender/ Grade	Baseline enrollment (%)	Impact[a]	Transfer (% of PCE)[b]	Evaluation method	Reference
Latin American and Caribbean countries							
Chile	Chile Solidario	Ages 6–15	60.7	7.5*** (3.0)	7	RDD	Galasso (2006)
Colombia	Familias en Acción	Ages 8–13	91.7	2.1** (1.0)	17	PSM, DD	Attanasio, Fitzsimmons, and Gómez (2005)
		Ages 14–17	63.2	5.6*** (1.8)			
Ecuador	Bono de Desarrollo Humano	Ages 6–17	75.2	10.3** (4.8)	10	IV, randomized	Schady and Araujo (2008)
Honduras	Programa de Asignación Familiar	Ages 6–13	66.4	3.3*** (0.3)	9	Randomized	Glewwe and Olinto (2004)
Jamaica	Program of Advancement through Health and Education	Ages 7–17	18 days[c]	0.5** (0.2)	10	RDD	Levy and Ohls (2007)
Mexico	Oportunidades	Grades 0–5	94.0	1.9 (25.0)	20	Randomized	Schultz (2004)
		Grade 6	45.0	8.7*** (0.4)			
		Grades 7–9	42.5	0.6 (56.4)			
Nicaragua	Atención a Crisis	Ages 7–15	90.5	6.6*** (0.9)	18	Randomized	Macours and Vakis (2008)
Nicaragua	Red de Protección Social	Ages 7–13	72.0	12.8*** (4.3)	27	Randomized	Maluccio and Flores (2005)

Effects on School Enrollment and Attendance

Overall Program Effects   A large number of evaluations estimate the effect of CCTs on school enrollment and attendance. Table 5.1 shows that virtually every program that has had a credible evaluation has found a positive effect on school enrollment, although those effects sometimes are found among some age groups and not others.

Table 5.1   continued

Country	Program	Age/Gender/ Grade	Baseline enrollment (%)	Impact[a]	Transfer (% of PCE)[b]	Evaluation method	Reference
Non–Latin American and Caribbean countries							
Bangladesh	Female Secondary School Assistance Program	Ages 11–18 (girls)	44.1	12.0** (5.1)	0.6	FE	Khandker, Pitt, and Fuwa (2003)
Cambodia	Japan Fund for Poverty Reduction	Grades 7–9 (girls)	65.0	31.3*** (2.3)	2–3	DD	Filmer and Schady (2008)
Cambodia	Cambodia Education Sector Support Project	Grades 7–9	65.0	21.4*** (4.0)	2–3	RDD	Filmer and Schady (2009c)
Pakistan	Punjab Education Sector Reform Program	Ages 10–14 (girls)	29.0	11.1*** (3.8)	3	DDD	Chaudhury and Parajuli (2008)
Turkey	Social Risk Mitigation Project	Primary school	87.9	–3.0* n.a.	6	RDD	Ahmed et al. (2007)
		Secondary school	39.2	5.2 n.a.			

Source: Authors' compilation.

Note: DD = difference-in-differences; DDD = difference-in-difference-in-differences; FE = fixed effects; IV = instrumental variables; n.a. = not available; PCE = per capita expenditure; PSM = propensity score matching; RDD = regression discontinuity design. This table contains unweighted means for the coefficients for Colombia ages 8–13 and 14–17, Chile ages 4–5 and 6–15, and Mexico grades 0–5 and 7–9. The standard errors in each case are the square roots of the averaged variances of these estimates.

a. The column for "impact" reports the coefficient and standard error (in parentheses); the unit is percentage points, with the exception of the Jamaican PATH program, where the unit is days.

b. The transfer amounts as a proportion of per capita expenditures (or consumption) are not the same across all tables in the report because of differences in the surveys used, including their coverage and year.

c. Impacts were measured in Jamaica only for student attendance over a 20-day reference period. The baseline enrollment rate prior to PATH was 96 percent.

* Significant at the 10 percent level.

** Significant at the 5 percent level.

*** Significant at the 1 percent level.

In Latin America and the Caribbean, there are evaluations for programs in Chile, Colombia, Ecuador, Honduras, Jamaica, Mexico, and Nicaragua. Five of those evaluations identify program effects on the basis of random assignment. In Mexico, the impact of Oportunidades in rural areas is significant for children making the transition from primary to secondary school, a point to which we return below (Schultz 2004; Behrman, Sengupta, and Todd 2005; de Janvry and Sadoulet 2006). Oportunidades also appears to have had positive spillover effects—school enrollment increased even among children above the cut-off point of the proxy means who were ineligible for transfers. Bobonis and Finan (2008) argue that the increase was a result of peer effects—barely ineligible children in Oportunidades communities were more likely to enroll because their eligible peers were in school. In Nicaragua, the RPS program was targeted at children aged 7–13 who had not yet completed the fourth grade of primary school. The evaluation results show that the RPS had large effects on school enrollment—13 percentage points (Maluccio and Flores 2005). In Honduras, the PRAF also had a positive effect on school enrollment, although the impact was much smaller—on the order of 3 percentage points (Glewwe and Olinto 2004).

Other evaluations have used quasi-experimental methods. Schady and Araujo (2008) use instrumental variables to estimate an impact of approximately 10 percentage points on enrollment for the BDH program in Ecuador. Galasso (2006) analyzes the impact of the Chile Solidario program on a variety of outcomes, including preschool and school enrollment. Using regression discontinuity techniques, she estimates program effects of 4–5 percentage points on preschool enrollment and of approximately 7 percentage points on the probability that all children aged 6–14 are enrolled in school. In Colombia, Fitzsimmons and Gomez (2005) use differences-in-differences to compare changes in villages where the Familias en Acción program was operational with a comparison group of villages. Their results suggest that the program had impacts of 2 percentage points for children aged 8–13 at baseline and 6 percentage points for those aged 14–17 at baseline. Finally, an evaluation of PATH in Jamaica indicates that the program increased school attendance by approximately 0.5 days per month (Levy and Ohls 2007).

As we showed in chapter 1, CCTs have been most popular in Latin America, but they have gradually spread to a number of countries in other regions. In those countries, programs often are referred to as "scholarship" or "stipend" programs. In practice, however, they work much like CCTs. Two programs in South Asia target girls. Khandker, Pitt, and Fuwa (2003) assess the impact of the FSSAP program on enrollment in Bangladesh. They use data from a panel of households to show that the probability that a girl enrolls in school increased more in villages that participated in the FSSAP program earlier than in villages that participated later. On the basis of those comparisons, they estimate that every year of program exposure increased the female enrollment rate by 12 percentage points.[1] Chaudhury and Parajuli (2008) consider the impact of the Punjab Education Sector Reform Program in Pakistan. They use regression discontinuity and triple-differencing techniques, and conclude that the program increased enrollment by approximately 11 percentage points.

In Cambodia, Filmer and Schady (2008) evaluate the impact of the JFPR program, which is targeted at girls making the transition from elementary to lower-secondary school. Their differences-in-differences estimates suggest a very large program impact—approximately 31 percentage points. A follow-on program, the CESSP scholarship, was made available to boys as well as girls. An evaluation of that program using regression discontinuity techniques finds a program effect of 21 percentage points (Filmer and Schady 2009c). In Turkey, finally, the CCT program had an impact on secondary school enrollment, but not on the enrollment of children in primary school (Ahmed et al. 2007).

Heterogeneity by Baseline Enrollment   Whereas table 5.1 shows that virtually all of the programs that have been evaluated have had positive effects on school enrollment, those effects appear to vary considerably across countries and across population groups within countries. One dimension of heterogeneity is by baseline enrollment, with generally higher impacts found in settings where school enrollments prior to the CCT program were low. This pattern is apparent when making comparisons across countries—for example, the impact among children of primary school–age is substantially larger in Nicaragua than in Mexico or Colombia. It is also apparent when making comparisons within countries—for example, the results reported in Ahmed et al. (2007) suggest that the CCT in Turkey had no effect on enrollment in primary school and among boys in secondary school; however, among girls of secondary school–age, for whom baseline enrollment rates were very low (38.2 percent), the impact of the program on enrollment was approximately 11 percentage points.

To some extent, the fact that CCT impacts are larger when enrollment is lower is purely mechanical because net enrollment rates cannot exceed 100 percent. However, this pattern also may be driven at least partly by differences in the expected rate of return to schooling. A number of authors have argued that there may be heterogeneity in these returns (Card 1999; Heckman and Carneiro 2003). If children or their parents select into school at least in part on the basis of expected returns (so-called Roy selection), the children who can expect to benefit the most from schooling generally will enroll first. In this case, the rate of return for the marginal unenrolled child may be higher when overall schooling levels are low. Also, in countries where overall school enrollment rates are low, educated workers will be relatively scarce and generally able to command a higher premium in the labor market. Higher rates of return to education should make households more responsive to a transfer that is conditional on schooling.

Heterogeneity by Transfer Size and Timing of Payments   All else being equal, we would expect programs that make larger transfers to have larger effects on school enrollment (among other outcomes). However, the evidence presented in table 5.1 suggests that, at current transfer sizes, larger transfers are not consistently associated with larger program effects on school enrollment. Within Latin America, the program that makes the largest transfers, RPS, had the largest effects on enrollment. However, other programs that made large transfers, including Oportunidades in Mexico and Familias en Acción in Colombia, had much smaller impacts on enrollment. Meanwhile, some programs that made more modest transfers, including the BDH in Ecuador and Chile Solidario, produced substantial impacts on enrollment. Furthermore, by far the biggest program effects on enrollment are found among programs in Bangladesh, Cambodia, and Pakistan, all of which make very modest transfers (between 1 and 3 percent of the expenditures of the median recipient household).

The issue of how transfer size affects enrollment is addressed explicitly in a recent paper by Filmer and Schady (2009a), who exploit the fact that the CESSP scholarship program in Cambodia made payments of different magnitudes: within any school, the poorest 25 students were offered scholarships of $60, and the next-poorest 25 students were offered scholarships of $45. Figure 5.1 shows a clear jump in the probability that a child who was offered a $45 scholarship was attending school on the day of an unannounced visit, relative to those who were offered no scholarship at all. By contrast, the effect of the additional $15 was small—on average, students who were offered a $60 scholarship were only 4 percentage points more likely to be attending school than those who were offered a $45 scholarship. In per dollar terms, every dollar of the first $45 had more than twice as large an impact on attendance as every dollar of the additional $15.

What can we learn from these results? Ultimately, the effect of transfer size on enrollment outcomes is likely to be highly context specific and will depend on a variety of other factors. However, one would expect there to be diminishing marginal returns to transfer size. Figure 5.1 and the differences across countries in impacts summarized in table 5.1 suggest that, at current transfer levels, the marginal effect of larger transfers on school enrollment may be modest.

Figure 5.1 Impact of Transfers of Different Magnitude on School Attendance in Cambodia, 2005–06

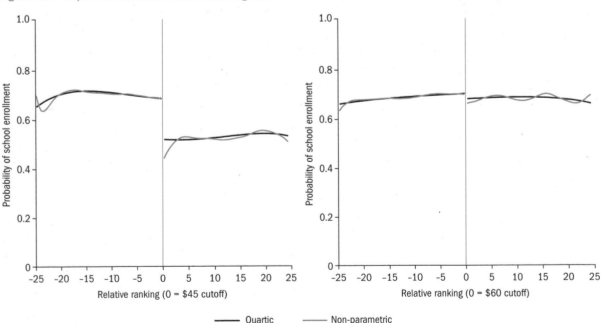

Source: Filmer and Schady 2009a.

Note: Intent-to-treat effects. The left-hand panel compares the enrollment effect of receiving a $45 scholarship versus no scholarship, whereas the right-hand panel compares the effect of receiving a $60 scholarship versus a $45 scholarship.

Timing of payments is another potentially important design feature. CCT programs have adopted different schemes. For example, Brazil's Bolsa Família pays on a monthly basis, Colombia's Familias en Acción pays bimonthly, and Cambodia's JFPR and CESSP pay quarterly. The driving force behind these design choices has been operational in nature, balancing convenience for beneficiaries with costs for the program. Even so, the timing (and frequency) of payments may affect program impacts. That possibility is illustrated in the case of Bogotá's Subsidio Condicionado a la Asistencia Escolar, in which beneficiaries were assigned randomly to different payment structures: a regular bimonthly payment, a smaller bimonthly payment supplemented by an end-of-year bonus, and the same smaller bimonthly payment supplemented by a larger bonus at school graduation. Barrera-Osorio et al. (2008) find that reducing the monthly payment and adding an end-of-year bonus does not reduce impacts (a finding the authors interpret as indicative that "short-term" liquidity constrains are low), whereas the lump-sum payment upon graduation has positive effects on attendance. The latter result, in particular, suggests that some payment schedules may augment incentives for behavioral change. To date, however, few programs have experimented in that direction.

Heterogeneity by School Grade or Child Age We next turn to a discussion of differences in enrollment effects by school grade. Figure 5.2 shows the enrollment trajectories of Oportunidades recipients and nonrecipients in Mexico. Each line corresponds to the probability of being enrolled in a school grade, conditional on having completed the grade before (the "continuation rate"). The figure shows that in Mexico this probability is highly nonlinear—the bulk of dropouts occur in the transitions from primary school to lower-secondary school (6th to 7th grade) and from lower-secondary to upper-secondary school (9th to 10th grade). The impact of Oportunidades transfers on school enrollment is given by the vertical distance between the two lines. That distance is clearly largest for children entering the first grade of secondary school—indeed, the results in Schultz (2004) show that Oportunidades effects on enrollment are significant *only* for children enrolled in grade 6 at baseline. Schady and Araujo (2008) find that the BDH program in Ecuador also had the largest program effects among children in transition grades. Note also that table 5.1 shows that the largest impacts on enrollment observed for *any* CCT program are those found among

Figure 5.2 Oportunidades Impacts on School Enrollment, by Grade, 1998

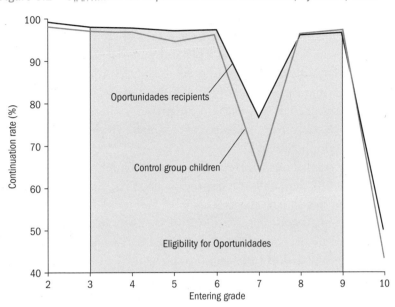

Source: de Janvry and Sadoulet 2006.

recipients of the JFPR and CESSP programs in Cambodia. Both of those programs focus on children making the transition from primary to lower-secondary school.

Heterogeneity by Socioeconomic Status   A final dimension of hetero-geneity concerns differences in program effects by the socioeconomic status of households at baseline. *A priori,* there are several reasons why one might expect that the impact of a CCT program would be larger for the poorest households. Those households have worse education outcomes at baseline, so there is more margin for improvement; they may be more credit constrained in ways that affect their schooling choices; the cost of forgoing transfers if children do not comply with the program conditions may be higher for the poor, either because the transfer is a higher fraction of household income or because of the diminishing marginal utility of income; and finally, if there is heterogeneity in the returns to schooling, as discussed above, the expected returns to schooling for the marginal unenrolled child may be higher among the poorest children because their baseline enrollment rates are lower.

135

In practice, numerous studies have shown larger CCT program effects among households that are poorer at baseline. That point is made in figure 5.3, which presents the results of an impact evaluation of the RPS in Nicaragua. The left-hand panel of the figure focuses on school enrollment among children aged 7–13, and the right-hand panel focuses on the fraction of children aged newborn to 3 years who have been weighed at least once in the previous 6 months. The figure clearly shows that program effects on both outcomes were largest among extremely poor households.

Similar results are reported elsewhere. In Cambodia, Filmer and Schady (2008) show that the impact of the JFPR program on enrollment is approximately 50 percentage points for girls in the poorest two deciles of a composite measure of socioeconomic status, compared with 15 percentage points for girls in the richest two deciles. As a result of the larger program impacts among the poorest households, the JFPR eliminated the "gradient" between poverty and school enrollment among beneficiaries. In Honduras, Glewwe and Olinto (2004) also find significantly larger program effects on enrollment among households with lower per capita expenditures. In Mexico, Behrman, Sengupta, and Todd (2005) argue that Oportunidades program effects are largest for children with the lowest propensities to enroll in school at baseline. Finally, Oosterbeek, Ponce, and Schady (2008) show that the BDH program in Ecuador had a significant effect on enrollment for children around the 20th percentile of the proxy means, but no effect among children around the 40th percentile.[2,3]

Figure 5.3 Heterogeneity of Impacts by Socioeconomic Status, Nicaragua, 2000

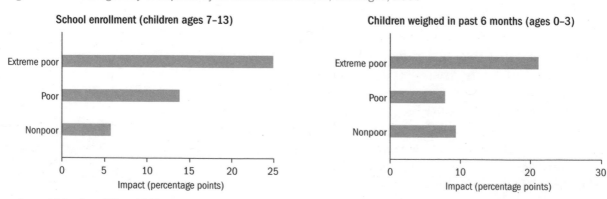

Source: Maluccio and Flores 2005.

Effects on the Utilization of Preventive Health Services

Regular use of preventive health care services is a requirement of many CCT programs, and we next turn to a discussion of program effects on utilization rates. As with education, there is a reasonably large number of evaluations that assess the impact of CCT programs on the use of preventive health services. With one exception (an evaluation of the CCT program in Turkey), however, all evaluations are of Latin American programs. Some evaluations have found that program beneficiaries make more use of health services than they would have made in the absence of the intervention, but that is apparent only for some outcomes (such as growth monitoring for children) and generally not for others (such as immunization rates).

Table 5.2 summarizes results from various evaluations that estimate the effects of CCT programs on preventive health checkups for children. Most of these evaluations suggest there were positive program effects on growth and development monitoring visits to health centers by children. For Nicaragua's RPS, for example, Maluccio and Flores (2005) report a borderline-significant impact of 13 percentage points on the probability that a child aged 0–3 had been taken to a health center and weighed in the last 6 months. Macours, Schady, and

Table 5.2 Impact of CCTs on Health Center Visits by Children, Various Years

Country	Program	Outcome	Age range (years)	Baseline level (%)[a]	Impact[b]	Transfer (% of PCE)[c]	Evaluation method	Reference
Chile	Chile Solidario	Regular checkups	0–6	17.6	2.4 (2.7)	7	RDD	Galasso (2006)
Colombia	Familias en Acción	Child taken to growth and development monitoring	0–1	n.a.	22.8*** (6.7)	17	PSM, DD	Attanasio et al. (2005)
			2–4	n.a.	33.2*** (11.5)			
			4+	n.a.	1.5* (0.8)			
Ecuador	Bono de Desarrollo Humano	Child had growth control in last 6 months	3–7	n.a.	2.7 (3.8)	10	R	Paxson and Schady (2008)

continued

Table 5.2 continued

Country	Program	Outcome	Age range (years)	Baseline level (%)[a]	Impact[b]	Transfer (% of PCE)[c]	Evaluation method	Reference
Honduras	Programa de Asignación Familiar	Child taken to health center at least once in past month	0–3	44.0	20.2*** (4.7)	9	R	Morris, Flores, et al. (2004)
Jamaica	Program of Advancement through Health and Education	Number of visits to health center for preventive reasons in past 6 months	0–6	0.205	0.278*** (0.085)	10	RDD	Levy and Ohls (2007)
Mexico	Oportunidades	Number of visits to all health facilities in past month	0–2	0.219	−0.032 (0.037)	20	R	Gertler (2000)
			3–5	0.221	0.027 (0.019)			
Nicaragua	Atención a Crisis	Child weighed in last 6 months	0–6	70.5	6.3*** (2.0)	18	R	Macours, Schady, and Vakis (2008)
Nicaragua	Red de Protección Social	Child taken to health center at least once in past 6 months	0–3	69.8	8.4 (5.9)	27	R	Maluccio and Flores (2005)
		Child taken to health center and weighed in past 6 months	0–3	55.4	13.1* (7.5)			

Source: Authors' calculations.

Note: DD = difference-in-differences; n.a. = not available; PCE = per capita expenditure; PSM = propensity score matching; R = randomized; RDD = regression discontinuity design. This table contains weighted means for the coefficients for Chile, combining rural and urban estimates. The standard error in this case is the square root of the averaged variances of these estimates.

a. The unit for baseline level corresponds to the proportion of children who have been taken to the health center, with the exception of Jamaica and Mexico, where the unit corresponds to the number of visits.

b. The column for "impact" reports the coefficient and standard error (in parentheses); the units are percentage points, with the exception of Jamaica, where the unit is the number of visits to the health center in the past six months, and Mexico, where the unit is the number of visits to the health center in the past month.

c. The transfer amounts as a proportion of per capita expenditures (or consumption) are not the same across all tables in the report because of differences in the surveys used, including their coverage and year.

* Significant at the 10 percent level.

*** Significant at the 1 percent level.

Vakis (2008) report a significant increase of 6 percentage points in the probability that a child aged 0–6 had been weighed in the last 6 months (among beneficiaries of the Atención a Crisis program). Even larger effects are reported by Attanasio et al. (2005) for the Familias en Acción program in Colombia, and by Morris, Flores et al. (2004) for PRAF in Honduras. In Jamaica, Levy and Ohls (2007) also report significant effects of PATH on the number of preventive health care visits by children under the age of 6. On the other hand, there do not appear to be significant effects on preventive health care visits by children for the Chile Solidario program (Galasso 2006), for the Ecuador BDH program (Paxson and Schady 2008), or for beneficiaries of Oportunidades (Gertler 2000).

Table 5.3 presents comparable evidence on the effects of CCT programs on immunization coverage. The effects are mixed. Barham (2005b) uses the randomized design in Oportunidades to estimate program effects on the coverage of tuberculosis and measles immunization rates. The program effects she estimates are small and not significant—something she attributes to the high immunization rates (around 90 percent) at baseline. In Colombia, Attanasio et al. (2005) find positive program effects for Familias en Acción on immunization rates, although the effects generally are not significant. In Honduras, PRAF appears to have increased coverage of immunization for diphtheria/pertussis/tetanus, but not for measles. Barham and Maluccio (2008) find large impacts of the RPS on full vaccination coverage in Nicaragua. In Turkey, too, the CCT program increased vaccination coverage significantly: the fraction of children under the age of 6 who have all required immunizations is 14 percentage points higher among those who participated in the CCT program.

To conclude this section, we briefly discuss the evidence on changes in the use of preventive health care services by adults. In Honduras, Morris, Flores et al. (2004) use a differences-in-differences strategy to show that the fraction of women who reported five or more antenatal visits increased by 19 percentage points more in the randomly assigned PRAF treatment group than in the control group.[4] On the other hand, PATH in Jamaica appears to have had no effect on the use of preventive health care services by the elderly. The Oportunidades program effects in Mexico are small and not significant at conventional levels, whereas the impact of the Chile Solidario program on checkups by the elderly is not consistent with a positive program impact.

Table 5.3   Impact of CCTs on Vaccination and Immunization Rates, Various Years

Country	Program	Outcome	Age range	Baseline level[a]	Impact[b]	Transfer (% of PCE)[c]	Evaluation method	Reference
Colombia	Familias en Acción	Compliance with DPT vaccination	<24 months	n.a.	8.9* (4.7)	17	PSM, DD	Attanasio et al. (2005)
			24–48 months	n.a.	3.5 (2.6)			
			>48 months	n.a.	3.2 (3.9)			
Honduras	Programa de Asignación Familiar	Child vaccinated with DPT	<3 years	73.2	6.9*** (3.0)	9	R	Morris, Flores et al. (2004)
		Child vaccinated for tetanus	<3 years	59.6	4.2 (7.1)			
		Child vaccinated for measles	<3 years	82.2	−0.2 (4.7)			
Mexico	Oportunidades	Child vaccinated for tuberculosis	<12 months	88.0	1.6 (2.4)	20	R	Barham (2005b)
		Child vaccinated for measles	12–23 months	92.0	2.8 (2.8)			
Nicaragua	Red de Protección Social	Full vaccination coverage (household data)	<3 years	54.0	13.0 (9.0)	27	R	Barham and Maluccio (2008)
		Full vaccination coverage (administrative data)		60.0	18.0*** (5.0)			
Turkey	Social Risk Mitigation Project	Full immunization	<6 years	43.8	13.6*** (4.2)	6	RDD	Ahmed et al. (2007)

Source: Authors' compilation.

Note: DD = differences-in-differences; DPT = diphtheria/pertussis/tetanus; n.a. = not available; PCE = per capita expenditure; PSM = propensity score matching; R = randomized; RDD = regression discontinuity design. Figures for Mexico and Nicaragua are after 2 years of their respective programs.

a. The unit for the baseline level corresponds to the proportion of children who have received a given vaccination.

b. The column for "impact" reports the coefficient and standard error (in parentheses). The unit is percentage points.

c. The transfer amounts as a proportion of per capita expenditures (or consumption) are not the same across all tables in the report because of differences in the surveys used, including their coverage and year.

* Significant at the 10 percent level.
*** Significant at the 1 percent level.

Impact of CCTs on "Final" Outcomes in Education and Health

As we have shown above, CCTs generally have increased the use of education and (some) health services. However, service utilization is arguably only an "intermediate" outcome. School enrollment is of interest primarily insofar as the children who are enrolled as a result of the CCT ultimately complete more years of schooling, learn more, and earn higher wages as adults. Similarly, increases in the use of health services are of interest primarily insofar as they help improve the health status of children and adults and reduce mortality. For those reasons, we now turn to a discussion of the evidence of CCT program effects on arguably final measures of education and health status.

Effects on Learning Outcomes and Completed Schooling

We begin by discussing CCT impacts on learning outcomes. It is useful to start by considering carefully the problem of selection—particularly in evaluations that give tests to children in school. Many CCT programs have resulted in increases in school enrollment. The children who are brought into school by the transfer tend to be poorer, on average, than children who already are enrolled in school. Furthermore, even among the poor, there may be heterogeneity in the expected returns to schooling, as discussed above. If there is selection on expected returns, then poor children who already are enrolled in school will have higher average returns to schooling than will other poor children. For those reasons, a simple comparison of test scores among children *in school* in the CCT "treatment" and "control" groups is not appropriate, even if the comparison is limited to similarly poor children. Indeed, that comparison might misleadingly suggest that CCT programs have a negative effect on achievement, even if that were not the case. Note also that a convincing identification strategy to evaluate the CCT effects *on enrollment* will not take care of this problem.

Two evaluations use in-classroom tests to assess the impact of CCT programs on test scores in language and mathematics. Behrman, Sengupta, and Todd (2000) use the random assignment in the rollout of Oportunidades. They correct for differences in age and gender between Oportunidades-treated and control children, but difficulties merging data that make it impossible for them to control for other observable characteristics somewhat limit the appeal of their evaluation. Ponce and Bedi (2008) use a regression discontinuity approach to evaluate the impact of the BDH in Ecuador on test performance among second-grade students around the 40th percentile of the proxy means that is meant to determine eligibility for transfers They argue that sample selection is unlikely to be a problem for their estimates, given the absence of a program effect on enrollment for children in that sample (see the study by Oosterbeek, Ponce, and Schady [2008] discussed above).

Methodological considerations aside, the results of the evaluations for Ecuador and Mexico are similar: In neither case is there a significant effect of the CCT program on test scores. How should one interpret these findings? One interpretation would be that this is grounds for guarded optimism: The marginal (additional) children brought into school by a CCT appear to learn *no less than* other children learn. However, one also could take a more negative view: Despite a transfer of (in some cases) considerable magnitude, which could have resulted in increases in spending on various inputs to learning such as food, books, or school supplies, CCT-treated children learn *no more than* other children who go to school without the transfer.

A more convincing approach to assessing the impact of CCTs on learning is not to condition on school enrollment because that avoids the problem of nonrandom selection. This approach generally involves applying tests at home rather than in school, and there are two evaluations that do that. In Mexico, Behrman, Parker, and Todd (2005) analyze the impact of two additional years of Oportunidades exposure on performance on the language and mathematics batteries of the Woodcock-Johnson tests. They find that young adults who benefited from the program for two more years when they were children do no better on these tests than do those who received transfers for a shorter period of time—despite the fact that the children who started receiving the transfers earlier have more years of schooling, on average.

In Cambodia, Filmer and Schady (2009b) apply a Khmer translation of the Peabody Picture Vocabulary Test to test language attainment, and a 20-item problem-solving test that focuses on basic competencies in mathematics. By construction, all children in their sample were enrolled in sixth grade at baseline because that was a prerequisite for program eligibility. Two years later, approximately one in five children offered the CESSP scholarship had completed one more year of schooling (seventh grade) than they would have completed in the absence of the program. Nevertheless, despite those large changes in enrollment and school attainment, Filmer and Schady (2009b) show that CESSP beneficiaries do no better on either the mathematics or the language tests than do children in the control group.

There are various possible explanations for these disappointing results. It could be that the tests used in both studies are inappropriate or are very noisy measures of skills or knowledge. That explanation is unlikely to be fully satisfying, however, because scores on those tests are correlated with other variables in the expected ways. For example, Filmer and Schady (2009b) show that among students in the control group, years of schooling for both children and their parents are significant predictors of test performance. An alternative explanation is that schools particularly fail the disadvantaged children who are induced to enroll by a CCT, perhaps because the curricula and pedagogical methods used are geared toward relatively more advanced students (as suggested by Banerjee et al. [2007] for a different set of school-based interventions in India). It also may be that there are other household constraints—nutrition, parenting quality, the value placed on education—that particularly affect the poorest households, are not resolved by a cash transfer, and limit the amount of learning that takes place in school by CCT beneficiaries.

These findings suggest that policy experimentation and innovation is important to increase the impact of CCTs on learning outcomes. Experimentation would be valuable on a number of fronts, such as different bundles of interventions—for example, CCT plus reforms to improve the quality of the supply of services, or CCT plus programs that seek to improve the home environment. In addition, serious thought should be given to the possibility of paying parents not only for school enrollment, but also for their children's performance on standardized tests. As box 5.1 describes, that approach has been the focus of a number of recent innovations in the United States that seek to incentivize student behavior. (We return to this topic in chapter 6.)

Even if the additional enrollment that results from CCTs does not translate into more learning, CCTs could result in higher wages—for example, if there are "sheepskin" or "diploma" effects in schooling. Students could develop important noncognitive skills, like discipline, responsibility, and motivation, and those skills may have large payoffs in the labor market (Heckman and Carneiro 2003). More years of schooling also could have other positive effects, including delayed marriage and childbearing and better health practices.

Box 5.1   Monetary Incentives to Students: Evidence from the United States

A NUMBER OF RECENT PROGRAMS IN THE UNITED States seek to improve the outcomes of students from disadvantaged backgrounds by giving monetary incentives. These programs include Opportunity NYC and Spark programs in New York and the Capital Gains program in Washington, DC.

Opportunity NYC and Spark make payments to parents and students if they comply with a series of conditions, including school attendance by students, attendance by parents at parent-teacher association meetings, and performance on standardized tests. The Spark program also will experiment with group incentives, in addition to individual incentives, to investigate whether group rewards provide an impetus for collaborative learning and tutoring across different achievement levels. Washington, DC's Capital Gains is innovative because it is being implemented in tandem with a series of city-based initiatives to

improve teacher performance, including performance-based pay. All of these pilot projects place a heavy emphasis on evaluation, including random assignment to treatment and control groups for the study period.

Opportunity NYC was modeled explicitly on Mexico's Oportunidades. Staff from the office of Mayor Michael Bloomberg and a number of city agencies traveled to Mexico to learn about the program. Numerous learning meetings also were facilitated by the World Bank so that policy makers designing Opportunity NYC could learn from the experience in developing countries—an example of the North learning from the South. Administrators of CCT programs in the developing world now could benefit from the experimentation in U.S. programs paying students for learning outcomes, including performance on standardized tests.

Ideally, to evaluate the effects of CCTs on these outcomes, one would have a measure of program effects on the years of schooling completed by adults.[5] However, the bulk of program evaluations of CCT effects on enrollment and grade attainment has focused on short-run effects. This is not surprising—many CCT programs are relatively recent; and even for those programs that were created a number of years ago, program administrators generally are more interested in evaluating the program "as it is now" than in evaluating some earlier incarnation of the program that perhaps was run by a previous administration. There also are practical difficulties in revisiting CCT-treated and control households many years after collection of the baseline data. In particular, attrition rates may be unacceptably high, and the potential for estimation biases is serious.

For all of those reasons, there is only one evaluation that has attempted to estimate the impact of a CCT program on completed school attainment. Behrman, Parker, and Todd (2005) conclude that children in the random sample that received Oportunidades transfers for two more years as a result of the staggered program rollout attain an average of one fifth more of a year of schooling. They argue that these comparisons are likely to provide an approximation to the final impact on school attainment of the additional exposure to Oportunidades.

Some crude calculations are helpful to put the magnitude of these impacts in perspective. Suppose that the Mincerian return to every year of schooling is 10 percent, a reasonable figure for developing-country settings. The results on school attainment in Behrman, Parker, and Todd (2005) then suggest that children exposed to the Oportunidades program for two more years will earn wages that are about 2 percent higher than the wages earned by other children. More intuitively, perhaps, because schooling grades are completed in full years (rather than in fractions of years), every fifth child who received program benefits for two more years would have earnings that are 10 percent higher than he or she would have had if randomly assigned to the control group.[6] Of course, that assumes that the return to schooling for this sample of beneficiaries will be reasonably similar to the return found in the population at large, despite the fact that the evaluation by Behrman, Parker, and Todd (2005) fails to find an impact on learning outcomes.

Should one regard these effects as "large" or "small"? There is no easy way to answer that question. An average 1 percent increase in lifetime earnings for every year of program exposure is obviously a good thing. But these simple back-of-the-envelope calculations also make clear that Oportunidades likely will be able to make only a small dent in poverty in the next generation, at least through its effects on schooling and wages in Mexico. In countries such as Bangladesh, Cambodia, or Pakistan, where enrollment rates are low (in some cases, especially among girls), CCTs may have larger effects on current schooling levels, and the aggregate effects on poverty in the next generation may be of a greater magnitude.[7]

Effects on Nutrition, Health Status, and Cognitive Development in Early Childhood

In much the same way that school enrollment is an input into learning, the use of preventive health services is an input into health status. This section now turns to the evidence of CCT program effects on "final" outcomes in health and nutrition.

Impacts on Child Height and Anemia   Child height for age and weight for height are among the two most-used measures of child health. In a number of Latin American countries, where CCTs have been implemented most extensively, malnutrition (particularly low height for age) remains stubbornly high. CCT programs were designed in part with the expectation that they could help improve child nutritional status through the combination of income transfers, which should enable households to purchase more (and more nutritious) foods, and the requirement that children be taken for regular health checkups.

Table 5.4 summarizes the results from a number of evaluations of the impact of CCTs on child height. Where possible, we disaggregate the results by the baseline age of the child because there is a reasonable consensus in the nutrition literature that height deficits are hard to make up after approximately 2 years of age (Martorell 1995; Shrimpton et al. 2001).

Table 5.4 Impact of CCTs on Child Growth Indicators

Country	Program	Outcome	Age range (months)	Baseline level[a]	Impact[b]	Transfer (% of PCE)[c]	Evaluation method	Reference
Brazil	Bolsa Alimentação	Height-for-age Z score	<24	−0.90	−0.110 (0.130)	9	R	Morris, Olinto et al. (2004)
			24–48		−0.190 (0.110)			
			49–83		−0.040 (0.090)			
Colombia	Familias en Acción	Height-for-age Z score	<24	n.a.	0.161* (0.085)	17	PSM, DD	Attanasio et al. (2005)
			24–48		0.011 (0.055)			
			>48		0.012 (0.033)			
Ecuador	Bono de Desarrollo Humano	Height-for-age Z score	0–23	−1.07	−0.030 (0.090)	10	R	Paxson and Schady (2008)
			24–47	−1.12	−0.060 (0.090)			
			48–71	−1.23	0.080 (0.090)			
Honduras	Programa de Asignación Familiar	Height-for-age Z score	0–60	−2.05	−0.02 n.a.	9	R	IFPRI (2003)

Country	Program	Outcome	Age range (months)	Baseline level[a]	Impact[b]	Transfer (% of PCE)[c]	Evaluation method	Reference
Mexico	Oportunidades	Height (cm)	12–36	n.a.	0.959*** (0.334)	20	R	Gertler (2004)
Mexico	Oportunidades	Change in height (cm)	4–12	–1.76	0.503 (0.524)	20	R	Behrman and Hoddinott (2000, 2005)
			12–36		1.016** (0.398)			
			36–48		–0.349 (0.529)			
Mexico	Oportunidades	Change in height (cm)	<6	–0.36	1.1** (0.550)	20	R	Rivera et al. (2004)[d]
			6–12	–1.04	–0.6 n.a.			
Nicaragua	Atención a Crisis	Height-for-age Z score	0–23	–0.76	–0.140 (0.130)	15	R	Macours, Schady, and Vakis (2008)
			24–47	–1.41	–0.120 0.140			
			48–71	–1.56	–0.030 (0.140)			
Nicaragua	Red de Protección Social	Height-for-age Z score	<60	–1.79	0.17** (0.080)	27	R	Maluccio and Flores (2005)

Source: Authors' compilation.

Note: DD = differences-in-differences; n.a. = not available; PCE = per capita expenditure; PSM = propensity score matching; R = randomized. For Atención a Crisis and Bono de Desarrollo Humano, authors' calculations are based on the data used by Paxson and Schady (2008) and Macours, Schady, and Vakis (2008), disaggregated by child age; impact regressions include single-month age dummies and a dummy for child gender. Gertler and Behrman (2000) and Hoddinott (2005) refer to ages at follow-up, whereas the Rivera et al. (2004) paper refers to ages at baseline. Authors' calculation of the standard error from Gertler (2000) and Rivera et al. (2004) are done using the *p*-values reported by the authors.

a. The baseline Z score for Brazil is an average for all children ages 0–83 months; for the Behrman and Hoddinott study (2005) for Mexico, the baseline Z score is an average for all children ages 4–48 months.

b. The column for "impact" reports the coefficient and standard error (in parentheses); the units are Z-score points for all evaluations except the three evaluations of the Mexico Oportunidades program, where the units are centimeters.

c. The transfer amounts as a proportion of per capita expenditures (or consumption) are not the same across all tables in the report because of differences in the surveys used, including their coverage and year.

d. The estimates reported from Rivera et al. are based on children below the 50th percentile of the distribution of their measure of socioeconomic status. The authors compare children in households that have received Oportunidades for two years with children in households that have received transfers for only one year.

* Significant at the 10 percent level.

** Significant at the 5 percent level.

*** Significant at the 1 percent level.

Three studies focus on the short-term impact of Oportunidades: Gertler (2004), Rivera et al. (2004), and Behrman and Hoddinott (2005). All three papers have some limitations related to data problems (box 5.2), but all report an estimated program impact on child height of approximately 1 centimeter for some children. In the case of the papers by Gertler (2004) and Behrman and Hoddinott (2005), that impact is found among children aged 12–36 months at follow-up, which roughly corresponds to children younger than 2 years of age at baseline; Rivera et al. (2004), however, find significant effects only for children who were younger than 6 months at baseline and who lived in households with below-median wealth.

As with the results on schooling outcomes, it is useful to consider the magnitude of these effects. Thomas and Strauss (1997) use data on Brazil to estimate that a 1 percent increase in height is associated with a 2.4 percent increase in lifetime earnings. Assuming that each year of exposure to Oportunidades increases child height by 1 centimeter for children under the age of 2, an increase in height of 1 centimeter represents a change of 0.66 percent for an adult of 150 centimeters. That (extremely simple) calculation suggests that, if one can apply the results from Brazil to Mexico and if the associations between height and wages reported by Thomas and Strauss have a causal interpretation, every year of Oportunidades exposure in early childhood results in wages that are approximately 1.6 percent higher in adulthood (0.66*2.4).[8]

That is likely to be an upper bound on the long-term effects of Oportunidades on child height, however, because it is not clear whether the estimated program impacts are sustained over time. A paper by Neufeld et al. (2005) uses a 2003 survey to compare the heights of children in the original Oportunidades treatment and control samples. As a result of the randomized assignment, children approximately 5 years of age in 2003 would have received transfers in their first year of life if they were in the original treatment group but not if they were in the original control group. Remember that the program effects estimated by Gertler (2004), Rivera et al. (2004), and Behrman and Hoddinott (2005) were apparent only among the youngest children in 1999. Therefore, one might expect that the height differences between children in the original treatment and control groups would persist because children in the original control group would have received transfers only after their first year of life, when transfers no longer appear to affect height. However, Neufeld et al. (2005) show that, in 2003, there are no differences in

Box 5.2   Impact of Oportunidades Transfers on Child Height in the Short Run

CHILD HEIGHT AND WEIGHT DATA HAVE BEEN collected in some Oportunidades surveys since 1998, and data on hemoglobin status has been gathered since 1999, although these data generally have been collected for a relatively small subsample of children from the full evaluation sample. Gertler (2004) compares child height among 1,552 Oportunidades-eligible children in the original treatment and control villages, using a 1999 survey. His sample is limited to children ages 12–36 months at the time of the follow-up. Gertler estimates that children exposed to the program are 0.96 centimeters taller than other children. Those estimates are based on comparisons between treatment and control groups at follow-up. However, when he matches children in the 1999 survey to a 1997 socioeconomic survey, which did not collect information on child height, he finds significant differences between the treatment and control households in two of the 11 sociodemographic characteristics he analyzes. That difference is more than one would have expected by chance, and it could be a source of concern.

Behrman and Hoddinott (2005) use the same 1999 survey as Gertler uses. To construct a pre-intervention baseline, the authors attempt to match children from that survey to a 1998 survey that collected data on child height. But matching children across surveys appears to have been a serious problem—the sample of children ages 12–36 months in the Behrman and Hoddinott paper is only one fifth the size reported in Gertler. Like Gertler, Behrman and Hoddinott first focus on comparisons between children who were *offered* the Oportunidades treatment and other children—the so-called intent-to-treat effects. The implied program effects in those estimates are not significant; are just as likely to be positive as negative, depending on whether the dependent variable is child height at follow-up or changes in child height; and are sensitive to the inclusion of controls—all of which suggests that random assignment did not equate characteristics of the treatment and control groups in this smaller sample. Behrman and Hoddinott next turn to regressions that

compare height outcomes between children who actually *participated* in Oportunidades and other children. That comparison is much more likely to be biased by selection into the program. To address possible endogeneity concerns, the authors run regressions in first differences. The identifying assumption therefore is that children who participated in Oportunidades did not have different growth trajectories than did other children in the sample. On the basis of those regressions, the authors conclude that Oportunidades resulted in height gains of 1.02 centimeters for children ages 12–36 months at follow-up, and insignificant effects for children ages 4–12 months and 36–48 months.

Rivera et al. (2004) analyze changes in child height between 1998 and 2000 for children randomly assigned to Oportunidades treatment and control communities. They limit their sample to children ages 0–12 months in 1998, and focus on program effects by the age of the child and by the socioeconomic status of the household. The authors present results based on regressions of changes in height on a main effect in Oportunidades treatment eligibility, as well as on interactions between eligibility and a dummy variable for children ages 6 months or younger; eligibility and a dummy variable for households with below-median socioeconomic status (SES); and a three-way interaction between treatment eligibility, age, and SES. The SES composite is based on a variety of household characteristics and assets, aggregated by principal components; one shortcoming of this composite is that it is based on data from 1999 and 2000. Given the size of the transfers made by the program, the measure of SES is itself likely to be endogenous. At the time of the 2000 follow-up survey, one group had been eligible for Oportunidades for two years whereas the other group had been eligible for one year only. Rivera et al. conclude that there are only significant program effects among children aged less than 6 months at baseline in households with below-median SES; those children grew 1.1 centimeters more if they were eligible for two years than if they were eligible for only one year. There are no significant program effects for older children or for relatively better-off children.

height whatsoever between the two groups, thus suggesting that whatever advantage early incorporation into the program had conferred on children in terms of height had vanished over time.

Turning to CCT programs in other countries, the evidence of short-term program effects on child height is somewhat mixed. In Nicaragua, Maluccio and Flores (2005) find that the RPS increased by about 0.17 points the height-for-age Z score for children younger than 5 years of age, but Macours, Schady, and Vakis (2008) find no effect of the Atención a Crisis program on child height among children of any age group. In Honduras, Hoddinott (2008) finds PRAF had no effect on child height. He argues that the small size of the transfers made by PRAF accounts for the lack of a program effect on nutrition.[9] In Ecuador, the BDH program does not appear to have improved child height among children of any age group (Paxson and Schady 2008). Attanasio et al. (2005), evaluating the impact of Familias en Acción on nutritional outcomes in Colombia, find that the Z scores of treated children younger than 2 years of age improved by 0.16 points, implying a 7–percentage point reduction in the probability of stunting; there are no program effects on child height for children aged 3–7 years at baseline.[10]

A final study included in table 5.4 is the evaluation of the effect of the Brazilian Bolsa Alimentação CCT program on child height and weight (Morris, Olinto et al. 2004). Theirs is an ingenious identification strategy: Because of a series of administrative errors, some potential beneficiaries inadvertently were excluded from program benefits. Specifically, entire batches of beneficiaries were lost when files were transferred from participating municipalities to a central data-processing unit in Brasilia, and the data-processing software initially rejected applications with names having nonstandard characters (such as é, ç, or ô). Morris, Olinto et al. (2004) argue that this source of variation is as good as random, and therefore is uncorrelated with potential outcomes. They show that Bolsa Alimentação appears to have had a significant *negative* impact on weight for age and a borderline-significant *negative* effect on height for age. Those negative program effects occurred despite the fact that the program appears to have increased the availability of nutritious foods in the household. The authors discuss a number of possible explanations for this puzzling finding, and conclude that it may be a result of perverse incentives: Because an earlier program (Incentivo para o Combate de Carencias Nutricionais) made powdered milk available to mothers if their children were underweight, beneficiaries of Bolsa Alimentação may have believed that their children needed to be underweight to qualify for transfers. That explanation is plausible, although corroborating evidence (for example, qualitative information gathered from children's mothers) would have made it more convincing. In any event, the findings from the evaluation of Bolsa Alimentação show that it is important to consider incentive effects seriously when designing the conditions in CCT programs.

There also are several papers that estimate CCT impacts on child hemoglobin levels and anemia. Gertler (2004) estimates that children exposed to the Oportunidades program were 26 percent less likely to be anemic after the first year than were children not exposed to it. Paxson and Schady (2008) conclude that the BDH program had a large effect on the hemoglobin levels of the poorest children in rural areas in Ecuador, corresponding to an improvement of approximately 0.3 standard deviations; however, the BDH program had no effect on hemoglobin levels among somewhat-less-poor children. Neither the RPS in Nicaragua nor PRAF in Honduras had a significant effect on the prevalence of anemia (Maluccio and Flores 2005; Hoddinott 2008). The lack of a significant program effect on anemia in Nicaragua is particularly surprising because the program included provision of iron supplements, and Maluccio and Flores (2005) show that mothers in the treatment group were twice as likely to have received iron supplements as those in the control group. It is possible that children actually did not ingest the tablets, or that deficiencies in other micronutrients limited the effectiveness of iron supplementation in Nicaragua.

In sum, the evaluations of the impact of CCT programs on child height and hemoglobin status present a mixed picture. Some find program effects among younger children, but many do not. It is not clear whether these differences in results reflect differences in the data and estimation choices, or underlying differences in population characteristics and program design or implementation. Only one study has attempted to investigate the somewhat longer-term effects of transfers on child height, and it finds no evidence that the positive impacts that had been observed initially were sustained over time (Neufeld et al. 2005). Given the very high rates of chronic malnutrition in many of the Latin American countries where CCT programs have been implemented, the impact of CCTs on child nutritional status should be an important area for future policy experimentation and evaluation.

Impacts on Infant Mortality and Child and Adult Health Status   In addition to their presumed effect on nutrition, CCTs were expected to reduce mortality and improve child and adult health. Barham (2005a) analyzes the impact of Oportunidades on infant mortality. She concludes that a rural municipality that enrolled every household in the program could expect to see an infant mortality rate that is 2 deaths per 1,000 live births lower than a comparable municipality that enrolled no one. That corresponds to a reduction in infant mortality of approximately 11 percent. Using a different estimation strategy, Hernández et al. (2005) also conclude that Oportunidades reduced both infant and maternal mortality.

Gertler (2004) uses the randomized Oportunidades design to estimate program effects on child illness. He shows that approximately two years after program implementation, newborns in the treatment group were 25 percentage points less likely to be reported as having been ill in the preceding four weeks; children aged 0–35 months at baseline were 22 percentage points less likely to have been ill. In Colombia, Attanasio et al. (2005) find that Familias en Acción resulted in a lower incidence of diarrhea among children aged 48 months or less in rural areas. However, the program did not have significant effects on the incidence of diarrhea among older children in rural areas or among children of any age group in urban areas; nor did it have significant effects on the incidence of respiratory infections among children of any age group in urban or rural areas. Finally, the evaluation of PATH in Jamaica assesses the impact of the program on the health status of children, as reported by their mothers (Levy and Ohls 2007). The authors conclude there is no evidence of improvements in child health status among PATH beneficiaries.

Turning to estimates of CCT program effects on adult health status, Gertler (2000) uses the original experimental evaluation design to analyze Oportunidades program effects on a variety of adult health measures. He finds significant effects mainly for adults aged 51 and older: adults in this age group who received transfers report fewer days of difficulty performing daily tasks, fewer days incapacitated by illness, and fewer days bedridden, and they report being able to walk longer distances.[11] More recently, Fernald, Gertler, and Olaiz (2005) analyze the impact of Oportunidades on obesity and chronic illness. They suggest that the program reduced the incidence of obesity by 6 percentage points, hypertension by 7 percentage points, and diabetes by 4 percentage points.[12] Gutiérrez et al. (2005) consider the effects of Oportunidades on adolescent behavior. Adolescents in households in Oportunidades-eligible communities are less likely to smoke (by 13–15 percentage points), and less likely to consume alcohol (by 11–13 percentage points) than are those in a sample of comparison communities. However, those results probably should be seen as only suggestive. To identify program effects, both Fernald, Gertler, and Olaiz (2005) and Gutiérrez et al. (2005) match communities that benefited from Oportunidades with a set of comparison communities on the basis of "retrospective" baseline data. It is not clear how well such procedures work: Chen, Mu, and Ravallion (2006) present evidence from China that suggests they can perform very poorly in practice.

Impacts on Child Cognitive Development   An extensive body of research stresses that there are large payoffs to interventions that improve cognitive development in early childhood (for example, Heckman [2006a, 2006b]; Knudsen et al. [2006]; Grantham-McGregor et al. [2007]; Walker et al. [2007]). In poor countries, early cognitive development is a strong predictor of school attainment in Brazil, Guatemala, Jamaica, the Philippines, and South Africa, even after controlling for wealth and maternal education (Grantham-McGregor et al. 2007).

We close this section by discussing two recent studies of the effect of CCT programs on child cognitive development. Both studies are based on random assignment, and both collect unusually rich data on a variety of child development measures. The main results on CCT program effects on child cognitive development from both papers are presented in table 5.5.[13]

Looking at rural areas of Ecuador, Paxson and Schady (2008) evaluate the impact of the BDH program on child cognitive development for children between 3 and 6 years of age. Their data include children in approximately the first four deciles of the national PCE distribution. The authors first show that the relationship between cognitive outcomes and household socioeconomic status tends to be highly nonlinear: in the absence of the program, there are large differences in outcomes between children in the first (poorest) decile of the PCE distribution and other children, but much smaller differences between children in the second, third, and fourth deciles. Paxson and Schady (2008) therefore separately analyze the BDH program effects for children in the poorest decile and those for children in the other three deciles. They show that the BDH

Table 5.5 Effect of CCTs on Child Cognitive Development, Ecuador (2004–05) and Nicaragua (2005–06)

Indicator	Ecuador (poorest 40%)	Ecuador (poorest 10%)	Nicaragua
Language (TVIP)	0.005 (0.098)	0.137 (0.129)	0.228*** (0.084)
Language (Denver)	n.a.	n.a.	0.189*** (0.065)
Short-term memory	−0.019 (0.100)	0.079 (0.143)	0.070 (0.058)
Long-term memory	0.141 (0.092)	0.173* (0.097)	n.a.
Visual integration-executive function	0.054 (0.095)	0.256 (0.160)	n.a.
Behavioral Problems Index	0.066 (0.091)	0.240 (0.147)	0.037 (0.064)
Personal-behavioral skills	n.a.	n.a.	0.135** (0.066)
Average effect on cognitive outcomes	**0.049 (0.066)**	**0.177* (0.094)**	**0.132*** (0.040)**

Source: Authors' calculations, based on Paxson and Schady (2008) for Ecuador; and on Macours, Schady, and Vakis (2008) for Nicaragua.

Note: n.a. = not available; TVIP = Test de Vocabulario en Imágenes Peabody. The table reports coefficients on the CCT treatment variable, and standard errors (in parentheses). All regressions adjust for clustering at the village level. Average effects are calculated by seemingly unrelated regressions. All measures have been standardized so they have mean 0 and a standard deviation of 1. The coefficients therefore can be interpreted as changes in standard deviation units. All regressions include single month-of-age dummy variables and a dummy variable for gender. In both countries, the sample is limited to children aged 36–83 months, for comparability.

* Significant at the 10 percent level.
** Significant at the 5 percent level.
*** Significant at the 1 percent level.

transfers improved cognitive outcomes by 0.18 standard deviations for the poorest children. However, there are no significant program effects on any outcome for children who were somewhat better-off.

Macours, Schady, and Vakis (2008) study the effect of the Atención a Crisis program on child cognitive development in Nicaragua. Theirs, too, is a very rich data set, including measures of child language development, gross and fine motor skills, personal-behavioral skills, and the incidence of behavior problems. After only nine months, children who received the Atención a Crisis transfers had significantly better language skills (improvements of 0.19–0.23 standard deviations) and significantly better personal (or emotional) skills (an improvement of 0.14 standard deviations). Macours, Schady, and Vakis (2008) also show that the CCT impacts are found for the entire sample, not just the poorest children—unlike the Ecuador results in Paxson and Schady (2008). However, households in the evaluation sample in Nicaragua appear to be noticeably poorer than those in the Ecuador sample, which may account for some of the differences.[14]

The results of the evaluations of CCT impacts in Ecuador and Nicaragua are reasonably encouraging. It also is worth noting the contrast between evaluations that do not find evidence of learning outcomes among children who benefited from CCT when they were of *school age* (Behrman, Parker, and Todd [2005] on Mexico; Filmer and Schady [2009b] on Cambodia) and those evaluations that show significant improvements in cognitive and learning outcomes among children who benefited from similar programs *before they entered school* (Paxson and Schady [2008] on Ecuador; Macours, Schady, and Vakis [2008] on Nicaragua). These patterns suggest that, insofar as CCTs seek to improve learning outcomes, the payoffs to early investments in a child's life may be substantially larger than those that focus on children who already have entered the school cycle. That is an important topic for the design of effective programs. (We return to it in chapter 6.)

Cash, Behavioral Changes, and Outcomes

CCTs provide households with an income transfer that is conditional on certain behaviors. In principle, therefore, the impact of CCT programs on schooling and health outcomes could be a result of the income effects associated with the transfers, the price changes implicit in the conditions, or both. It also could be a result of the fact that transfers are made to women, who are generally believed to devote to children a larger share of the income they control than do men.[15] Finally, even when conditions are not strictly monitored, the social marketing surrounding programs could affect how transfer resources are used.[16] These issues are of more than academic interest; they have important implications for program design, including the optimal size of the transfer that should be given and the extent (if any) to which conditions should be monitored and noncompliers penalized.

Ideally, to disentangle the effect of conditions from the income effect inherent in the transfer, an experiment would be designed whereby a first group of households or villages receives a UCT, a second group receives a CCT, and a third group serves as a control group. That experiment has not yet been conducted anywhere. As a result, the evidence that exists on this issue generally has drawn on a variety of sources—comparisons across programs or countries, accidental glitches in program implementation, or structural models of household behavior. Individually, none of those approaches is a definitive test of the relative importance of the cash and conditions. Taken together, however, they provide some evidence that suggests that CCT impacts on service use are larger than would have been the case if the programs had not included explicit conditions, or had not made an effort to launch social marketing campaigns that stressed the importance of household investments in children.

We first look at the evidence regarding education outcomes. In two countries, Mexico and Ecuador, there were implementation glitches whereby some households believed transfers were conditional and others did not. In Mexico, when Oportunidades was first launched, a fraction of eligible households that received transfers were never given the forms that were required to monitor school conditions. de Brauw and Hoddinott (2008) compare the impact on school enrollment between households that did and did not receive the forms. Using propensity score matching to control for a variety of observable characteristics, they estimate that children in households that did not receive the forms were 5 percentage points less likely to enroll in school than those who received them. For children enrolled in sixth grade (who are most likely to drop out of school in the absence of an intervention), those who received the forms were 17 percentage points more likely to be enrolled in school. Moreover, de Brauw and Hoddinott (2008) find that the effect is larger in households with illiterate heads—arguably, those households among whom one would expect the lack of information about the benefits of education to be the most serious.[17]

In Ecuador, policy makers initially intended to make the BDH conditional. As a result, there was an information campaign that stressed the program's human capital goals.[18] In practice, because of administrative constraints, the BDH did not monitor the schooling "condition," and did not penalize households whose children were not attending school. Nevertheless, the BDH information campaign had an effect: In various surveys, a fraction (approximately one quarter) of respondents state that they believe that sending children to school is a BDH program requirement. Schady and Araujo (2008) compare the impact of the program among "conditioned" households (those telling enumerators that school enrollment was a BDH requirement) and "unconditioned" households (those telling enumerators that there was no enrollment requirement attached to transfers). They show that program effects on enrollment are much larger and are significant only among "conditioned" households. Because exposure to the information campaign was not assigned randomly, those comparisons are not experimental. However, Schady and Araujo (2008) use various matching, trimming, and double-differencing techniques to make conditioned and unconditioned households more closely comparable. None of these estimation choices has an appreciable effect on their results, so they conclude that the larger program effect among conditioned households most likely has a causal interpretation.

Filmer and Schady (2009c) analyze the effects of the CESSP program on school enrollment and employment in Cambodia. To be eligible for the CESSP, households had to have at least one child enrolled in sixth grade at baseline before the program was implemented. Transfers were then made conditional on the enrollment of these children in lower-secondary school. No requirements were made on the school enrollment of children in other grades, even though most recipient households had more than one child. As a result, the transfer was *conditional* for children who were in sixth grade at baseline, but *unconditional* for their siblings. Filmer and Schady (2009c) exploit this feature of the program to tease out the income and substitution effects of the transfer. They show that the CESSP had very large effects on the school enrollment of children who were in sixth grade when the program started, but had no effect on the enrollment of their siblings. The authors therefore conclude that the observed changes in enrollment can be explained by the substitution effect (because this affects only children who were in sixth grade to begin with) rather than the income effect (because this affects all children in the household).

Simulation methods and structural modeling also have been used to estimate the relative importance of income and price effects associated with transfers in Brazil (Bourguignon, Ferreira, and Leite 2003) and Mexico (Todd and Wolpin 2006a).[19] In such an approach, child wages are used to approximate the opportunity cost of going to school and to model the effects of schooling subsidies on the schooling and work choices made by children. The analysis for Mexico has an additional virtue: the results from the randomized evaluation of Oportunidades can be used to check the estimated parameters. The models then can be used to estimate the effects of various policy experiments. The papers for both Brazil and Mexico suggest that replacing a CCT with an unconditional program would reduce the schooling effects substantially: in Brazil, the UCT essentially has no impact on school enrollment (which is surprising), whereas in Mexico, the impact of the unconditional program on schooling attained is only 20 percent as large as the impact of the CCT.

Somewhat less evidence is available on the relative importance of the income and price effects in explaining changes in the use of health services or in final health outcomes. A number of authors have used quasi-experimental methods to argue that *unconditional* transfers have had positive effects on health outcomes in South Africa. Those authors include Agüero, Carter, and Woolard (2007), who evaluate the impact of the Child Support Grant program; and Duflo (2003), who considers the effects of the old-age pension program. Both studies report positive program effects; for example, Duflo shows that girls whose grandmothers receive transfers have large improvements (about 1.2 standard deviations) in weight and height. But transfers made by these programs are very large—especially in the case of the OAP, which amounts to more than twice the median per capita income for African (black) households.

In Latin America, Paxson and Schady (2008) and Macours, Schady, and Vakis (2008) argue that the impact of CCT programs on child cognitive outcomes (and, in the case of the Paxson and Schady (2008) study on Ecuador, child physical health and fine motor control) is larger than would be expected if transfers were used like other sources of income. Ironically, neither of the two programs studied— the BDH program in Ecuador and the Atención a Crisis program in Nicaragua—monitored the condition that required children of preschool age to be taken for regular checkups at health centers. Nevertheless, both programs involved a social marketing campaign that stressed the importance of investments in early childhood. Paxson and Schady (2008) show that the improvements they observe ning children in the poorest decile cannot be explained fully by movements along the curves that relate child cognitive development and health to PCE; rather, there are upward shifts in these curves—outcomes for children randomly assigned to the BDH treatment group are above those for children assigned to the control group at any given level of expenditures. Macours, Schady, and Vakis (2008) find that households that received transfers altered their spending and behavior patterns, spending less on food staples and more on animal protein, fruits, and vegetables even after accounting for the income effect of the transfer. Figure 5.4 shows that at every level of overall

Figure 5.4 Impact of Transfers Made by the Atención a Crisis Program on Stimulation in Early Childhood, 2005–06

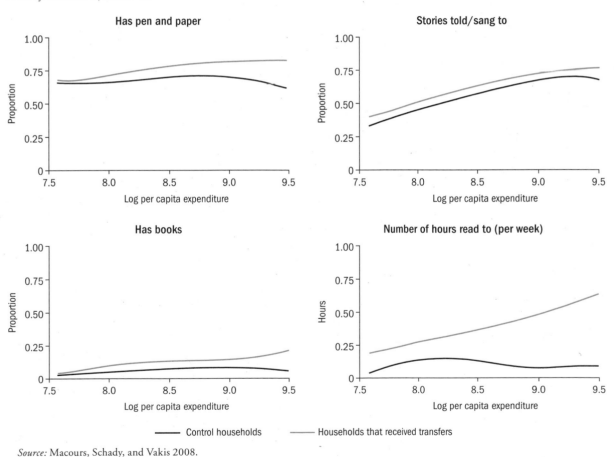

Source: Macours, Schady, and Vakis 2008.

expenditures, households receiving the Atención a Crisis transfers also were more likely to read, tell stories, and sing to their children, and to have books, paper, and pencils for them to use at home. Both papers conclude that the observed improvements in child cognitive outcomes are inconsistent with a simple explanation whereby "a dollar is always a dollar," no matter where it comes from and who in the household receives it. They also stress, however, that they cannot identify whether the larger-than-expected program impacts are a result of the social marketing of the programs or the fact that transfers were made to women.

Conclusion

Although the goals of individual programs vary, most CCTs were created with the expectation that they would help reduce consumption poverty, increase the utilization of health and education services, and result in improvements in final outcomes in schooling, nutrition, and health. We conclude this chapter by summarizing its main messages on the evidence of CCT effects on the accumulation of human capital in its various dimensions.

First, in country after country, CCTs have led to significant and sometimes substantial increases in the use of services. School enrollment rates have increased among program beneficiaries, especially among those who had low enrollment rates at the outset. These impacts are found in both the middle-income countries where CCT programs first were implemented (for example, Mexico), in lower-income countries in Latin America (Honduras, Nicaragua), and in low-income countries in other regions (Bangladesh, Cambodia, Pakistan). CCT programs also have had a positive effect on the use of preventive health services, although the evidence is less clear than with school enrollment. Finally, CCTs may have helped protect human capital investments during economic downturns in some countries (box 5.3).

Second, because CCT program effects on utilization are concentrated among households least likely to use services in the absence of the intervention, CCTs have contributed to substantial reductions in preexisting disparities in access to education and health care. In Bangladesh, Pakistan, and Turkey, where school enrollment rates among girls were lower than among boys, CCTs have helped reduce this gender gap. In

Box 5.3   Do CCTs Help Protect Human Capital Investments during Economic Shocks?

BECAUSE CCTS TRANSFER CASH, THEY MAY HELP cushion the impact of systemic or idiosyncratic shocks, including any possible effects that these may have on the accumulation of human capital by children. This is an important question because it often is argued that sharp deteriorations in income can have potentially irreversible effects on education and child nutritional status—and that, in turn, may be one of the mechanisms whereby poverty is transmitted across generations.

We briefly discuss the evidence that CCTs protect human capital investments during economic downturns, using results from Nicaragua, Mexico, and Indonesia. Maluccio (2005) considers patterns of occupational choice, employment, consumption, school enrollment, and child nutritional status in the 2000–02 period in Nicaragua. The data cover communities randomly assigned to the RPS treatment and control groups, and households in coffee-growing and non-coffee–growing areas, which are found in both the RPS treatment and control communities. The 2000–02 period saw a sharp downturn in the price of coffee. Maluccio begins by analyzing patterns in control communities. He shows that in those communities that did not receive RPS transfers over the period, household PCE fell by 18 percent. Nevertheless, school enrollment of children aged 7–12 increased—particularly in coffee-growing areas. Among boys, for example, school enrollment increased by 15 percentage points, which suggests that the opportunity cost of going to school fell sharply.[a] Turning next to a comparison of changes in enrollment in RPS treatment and control communities, Maluccio shows that increases in school enrollment were larger in RPS communities than in the control communities, and even larger in RPS communities that also were in coffee-growing areas. But it would not be accurate to conclude that the

RPS "protected" school enrollment during a downturn because school enrollment increased during the period in control communities, especially in coffee-growing areas.

Maluccio next analyzes changes in nutritional status over the period. He shows that height for age deteriorated in control communities between 2000 and 2002, but did not do so in RPS communities. However, the positive impact of the RPS on child nutritional status was larger in non-coffee–growing areas than in areas where coffee is grown—a finding that suggests, if anything, that the RPS was better able to improve child nutritional status in areas in which household incomes were stable than in areas affected by the economic downturn.

de Janvry et al. (2006) combine the randomized assignment in Oportunidades with data on systemic shocks (drought, natural disaster) and idiosyncratic shocks (unemployment or illness of the household head, illness of preschool-age children) to compare household responses to shocks in treatment and control villages.[b] They show that shocks generally reduced school enrollment in the sample, but that those effects were offset partially or fully by Oportunidades (in particular, with systemic shocks such as droughts and other natural disasters).

During the Indonesian crisis of 1997–98, the government made children in poor households eligible for a "scholarship" program. It is not surprising, given the crisis context, that little attention was paid to a possible evaluation of the effect of the program. Using regression and matching techniques, Cameron (2002) concludes that the program reduced dropout levels in lower-secondary school by about 3 percentage points. Sparrow (2007) runs ordinary least squares regressions that suggest a larger effect on enrollment for children aged 10–12 (about 7.6 percentage points).[c]

continued

Box 5.3 continued

In their study of Oportunidades, de Janvry et al. (2006) conclude that "beneficiaries of conditional transfers can be effectively protected from the risk of shocks that would induce them to take their children out of school" (p. 372). In practice, shocks are likely to have very different effects on different dimensions of human capital, and the impact will depend critically on whether shocks are idiosyncratic or systemic (see Ferreira and Schady [2008]). In many developing countries, child health and nutritional status deteriorates during crises (see, for example, Cutler et al. [2002]; Paxson and Schady [2005]; Baird, Friedman, and Schady [2007]). The effects on schooling are less uniform. For example, Jensen (2000) finds that negative weather shocks have large negative effects on school enrollment in Côte D'Ivoire; and Thomas et al. (2004) find that the Indonesian financial crisis of 1998 had a negative effect on school enrollment, although the magnitude of the effect is very small. On the other hand, schooling may increase during downturns if the decrease in the opportunity cost of going to school is large enough to offset the negative income effect for credit-constrained households. This appears to have been the case in Nicaragua; it also has been observed in Peru during the deep recession of the late 1980s (Schady 2004), in Mexico in the 1990s (Mckenzie 2003), and in the United States during the Great Depression of the 1930s (Goldin 1999).

In conclusion, CCTs may be one of the policy instruments that enable households to better weather crises, but this effect is likely to vary a great deal by country, by the nature of the economic shock, and by the outcome that is considered. As we discuss in chapter 6, however, CCTs arguably are not the *best* instrument to respond to idiosyncratic or systemic shocks to household income for various reasons: they have no provisions whereby new households easily can be added to the roster of eligible beneficiaries, and they have no mechanisms whereby payment levels increase for households that see a temporary downturn in their economic circumstances.

a. These numbers are based on changes over the 2000–02 period. In Maluccio's words: "It would seem that the downturn did not adversely affect enrollment and, if anything, had negative effects on the incidence of child labor for young children, possibly because of reduced labor demand" (p. 25).

b. Information on shocks was collected only in later survey rounds, after Oportunidades had been implemented; and the specifications used by de Janvry et al. (2006) include child fixed effects. As a result, they are able to recover only the parameter on differential school enrollment responses by Oportunidades beneficiaries and nonbeneficiaries during shocks, not the parameter on average responses to the program.

c. Sparrow also uses "mistargeting" that resulted from outdated poverty data as an instrument for receipt of the scholarship program. On the basis of these calculations, he estimates a larger program effect on enrollment (about 10 percentage points) for children aged 10–12. However, the identifying assumption—in effect, that enrollment decisions respond to current but not lagged poverty levels—is not trivial. Despite their limitations, the ordinary least squares results reported by both Sparrow and Cameron perhaps are less likely to be biased than are these instrumental variable regressions.

Cambodia, the JFPR scholarship program eliminated sharp socioeconomic gradients in enrollment among eligible households, although the coverage of the program was quite small. As Amartya Sen and other authors have noted, poverty takes many forms, including an inability to develop basic "capabilities" in education and health (Sen 1985; 1999). Providing all citizens in a country with an equality of opportunities, if not of outcomes, is an important policy goal; and CCTs have helped level the playing field between rich and poor, more favored and less favored (World Bank 2005).

Third, although there is limited evidence on exactly which feature of CCT programs matters most—the cash, the conditions, the social marketing of the program, the fact that transfers are made to women—it does not appear that the cash alone can explain the observed changes in outcomes. More research on this topic would have very large payoffs because it could inform the design of CCT programs so as to maximize their impacts.

Fourth, the evidence on the impact of CCTs on "final" outcomes in education and health is mixed. A number of evaluations (but by no means all) have suggested that CCTs contributed to improvements in child height among some population groups; there is also some evidence that program beneficiaries have somewhat better health status. In Mexico, the only country in which a study of the long-term effects of CCTs has been conducted, adults with more exposure to the program have completed more years of schooling; however, the likely increase in wages associated with that added schooling is small. More discouragingly, a number of evaluations have failed to find effects of transfers on learning, even after accounting for selection into school. This pattern of program effects—increases in enrollment without attendant improvements in learning outcomes—is not particular to CCTs (see box 5.4), but it is sobering because it suggests that the potential for CCTs *on their own* to improve learning may be limited. The evidence is somewhat more encouraging regarding the impact of CCT programs on cognitive development in early childhood. It suggests that very early intervention might have larger payoffs than one would conclude, for example, by looking at the pattern of program effects on school enrollment by age or school grade.

There are numerous reasons why CCTs may have had only modest effects on final outcomes in education and health. One possibility is that there are important constraints at the household level that are not addressed by CCTs as currently designed, perhaps including poor parenting practices, inadequate information, or other inputs into the production of education and health. Another possibility is that the quality of services is so low, perhaps especially for the poor, that increased use of them does not yield large benefits in and of itself. More research

Box 5.4   Increasing School Enrollment without Improving Learning Outcomes

A NUMBER OF EDUCATION PROGRAMS HAVE been shown to increase school enrollment (in some cases dramatically so) without improvements in learning outcomes.

A well-known study by Miguel and Kremer (2004) shows that the provision of deworming drugs reduced student absenteeism by about one quarter in a sample of schools in Kenya. However, despite the increase in attendance, students in treated schools score no better on tests than do those in control schools. In a separate study, Glewwe, Kremer, and Moulin (2008) show that a program that distributed textbooks in Kenya did not raise average test scores. Banerjee et al. (2005) find similarly discouraging results from a program that provided additional teachers in rural Rajasthan.

Some evaluations have found that interventions in education, such as those described above, result in better learning outcomes only among relatively better-off students or when the quality of the supply is adequate. For example, Glewwe, Kremer, and Moulin (2008) show that, although textbook distribution had no effects on learning for the *average* student, it did impact learning positively for students who had the highest test scores at baseline. The authors suggest that a centralized curriculum and a language of instruction (English) that is the second or third language for most children are particularly detrimental for low-performing students. That suggestion has led to calls for inputs that are targeted toward low-

performing students, such as tutors or early tracking of students—which in theory could help ensure that teaching is appropriate for low-performing students. Banerjee et al. (2007) find evidence that a tutoring program was effective at raising the scores of low-performing students in India; Duflo, Dupas, and Kremer (2008) find evidence suggesting that tracking benefits all students, including low-performing ones, in Kenya. Other authors have found that it is the quality of the supply that determines whether programs that increase school attendance also improve learning outcomes. For example, Vermeersch and Kremer (2004) conclude that a Kenyan program that provides school meals raises test scores—but only in schools where the teacher was relatively experienced prior to the program.

The results from these evaluations present particular challenges for CCTs. Conditional cash transfers frequently are targeted geographically. Because they work in especially poor areas, the quality of the supply of education (and health) services is low. In addition, CCTs use proxy means to identify poor households. The evaluations discussed above generally suggest that raising the achievement of these disadvantaged students is particularly difficult—even when they have been brought into school. For this reason (and as we discuss in chapter 6), carefully evaluated pilot tests of interventions that attempt to combine CCTs with improvements in the supply of services would be particularly valuable.

clearly is needed to understand these findings. However, these results also suggest that it may be important to experiment with different bundles of interventions—CCTs together with other programs to address household-level constraints, or CCTs together with interventions to improve the quality of service delivery.

CHAPTER SIX

CCTs: Policy and Design Options

IN PREVIOUS CHAPTERS WE REVIEWED THE PERFORMANCE OF CCT programs in terms of their impacts on poverty (chapter 4) and human development outcomes (chapter 5). Overall, the evidence supports the view that CCT programs have generated positive results. From the point of view of a policy maker, however, knowing that CCT programs have performed well is not enough. When is a CCT the right policy instrument? How does one determine the right design features of a CCT program needed to generate the desired impact? Are there complementary policy actions that are needed? Those are the questions addressed in this chapter.

The chapter starts with a discussion of the conditions under which CCT programs are the right policy instrument. Building on the discussion in chapter 2, a simple decision-making framework is offered, as are some illustrations of how the framework can be used. Next, assuming that a decision has been made to have a CCT, the second section of the chapter considers the key design features that can be used to make the program an efficient instrument: the selection of beneficiaries, the nature and enforcement of conditions, and the level of benefits. However, CCT programs cannot be thought of in isolation from other social policies. In particular, achieving the human capital accumulation goals sought by these programs typically will require some (often major) adaptation of the supply of social services. And CCT programs alone seldom will be sufficient to provide assistance to all categories of poor households and individuals. Thus they should be considered as components of broader social protection systems. The third and fourth sections of the chapter discuss complementary actions required on both fronts. The final section concludes the chapter and identifies research challenges for the future.

When Is a CCT Program the Right Policy Instrument?

CCTs are quite complex programs, given that they seek to affect poverty both in the short run (by redistributing income to poor households) and in the long run (by building the human capital of poor children). Their multidimensionality actually may be a key reason why they have become so popular: it is not often that government programs can "kill several birds with one stone"—and do it effectively. At the same time, using one instrument to address more than one policy goal implies that decisions on when or whether to use it also will be complex and will need to consider a combination of factors.

Chapter 2 considered a range of factors and concluded that when there is a strong rationale to redistribute income, a CCT can be justified under two broad sets of conditions: first, when private investment in human capital (among the poor) is suboptimal from a social point of view and, second, when conditions are necessary for political economy reasons (that is, redistribution is politically feasible only when conditioned on "good behavior").[1]

Here we extend that discussion by presenting a simple framework that identifies critical questions that can guide the decision to have a CCT program and the type of information that can support such decisions. We also seek to provide a sense of the trade-offs or costs involved in those decisions. Figure 6.1 graphically presents the overall decision framework.

A logical starting point in our framework is the justification for using tax revenues to transfer income to the poor. As noted in chapter 2, there are both efficiency and distributional considerations that, in theory, provide the justification for redistribution. Such considerations are not specific to CCT programs and should precede the discussion of whether a CCT should be used. Here we briefly mention two sets of conditions that should be considered: First, standard measures of poverty and inequality provide a good starting point to assessing the *need* for redistribution from an equity perspective. In that sense, it is not surprising that the CCT wave started (and became so popular) in Latin America, a region widely characterized by high levels of both poverty and inequality (de Ferranti et al. 2004). Second, whether and how income transfers will affect efficiency should be considered before a decision is made to redistribute. One key aspect to consider is the potential for income transfers to affect labor supply. If the disincentive effects associated with

Figure 6.1   Decision Tree Approach to Identifying CCT Programs as the Right Policy Instrument

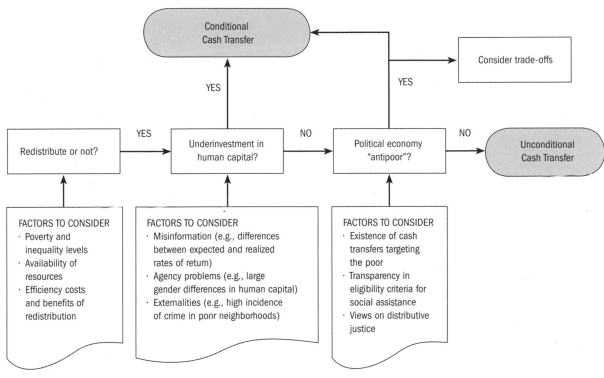

Source: Authors' illustration.

transfers are small (as suggested by the evidence presented in chapter 4), then the case for redistribution is much stronger. Moreover, the presence of low-productivity traps, particularly in some sectors or regions, may indicate that redistribution actually may increase efficiency (see World Bank 2006d, ch. 5). Evidence of such effects typically is difficult to gather but, when available, could provide a more solid basis for deciding whether to go ahead with a cash transfer (and possibly could provide a *prima facie* case for determining beneficiaries). Ultimately, the decision on whether (or how much) redistribution is acceptable is one that each polity must make (a point we return to later in the chapter).

The next step in our decision-making framework is to establish the presence of distortions that make the human capital investment decisions of (poor) households inefficiently low from a social point of view. Low levels of human capital investments are not, per se, enough to justify the use of conditions; household decisions not to accumulate more human capital could be rational and efficient (even from a social point of view). That would be the case, for example, if the expected returns to schooling (given the quality of schools available and the learning ability of the child) are lower than the returns to alternative uses of the child's time. What is needed is an indication of the presence of distortions that would yield socially inefficient investments in human capital by the poor unless household behaviors are modified. In other words, the use of a CCT is predicated on the assumption that the pure income effect is insufficient and thus conditions are required to generate a further substitution effect in favor of investments in child health or education.

Chapter 2 identified different types of distortions: misinformation, agency problems, and externalities. Under what contexts should we expect such distortions to be present? And how could we identify the likelihood of socially inefficient decisions being the reason for observed low levels of human capital investment? While there are no straightforward means of testing for the presence of such inefficiencies, there are a number of indicators that can be used for that purpose.

Comparisons of expected and realized rates of returns provide an indication of possible information problems. In the case of investments in education, this comparison can be done relatively easily by asking students or parents how much they think people with more education earn in the labor market and comparing the implied returns with the Mincerian returns from a household survey (for example, see Jensen 2006; Attanasio and Kaufmann 2008; Nguyen 2007). Small-scale experiments can help establish whether the sole provision of information is sufficient to address such problems, or whether conditions attached to the transfer are needed.

The presence of gender differences in child human capital is a signal of potential agency problems, particularly when rates of return to human capital investments (for example, schooling) are not different (see Behrman and Deolalikar 1995; Alderman and King 1998).[2] In-depth, qualitative studies can be helpful in identifying the extent to which power relationships within the household generate biases against investments in the human capital of all or some specific group of children.

Identifying the presence of specific externalities associated with low investments in human capital by poor households is a more complex endeavor. In some cases, existing research in-country can provide solid evidence of such externalities (for example, Miguel and Kremer [2004] on deworming or Gimnig et al. [2003] on insecticide-treated nets), and thus can provide the basis for considering whether the use of a CCT is justified.[3] More generally, however, policy makers may need to rely on more indirect evidence. For example, the observation of a high incidence of crime in poor neighborhoods, particularly among out-of-school youth, can be used as the basis to argue for a CCT program to increase school participation, under the expectation that higher levels of schooling will reduce crime both in the short term and in the future. Naturally, such hypotheses can and should be tested empirically when the CCT program is pilot-tested and/or implemented.

In the absence of significant distortions leading to under-investment in human capital by poor households, conditions are most likely redundant. Even worse, they could be inefficient, to the extent that they may lead some households to "over-invest" in human capital. In those circumstances, there is a *prima facie* case for a UCT: its redistributive impact most likely would be larger (because take-up rates should be larger), and the reliance on just the income effect limits the danger that the added human capital accumulation will be inefficient.

Whereas a technical assessment may indicate that a UCT is more appropriate than a CCT, the political process may make significant cash transfers to the poor close to impossible unless those transfers are tied somehow to clear evidence of beneficiaries' commitment and "positive behaviors." As argued in chapter 2, satisfying the conditions in a CCT makes the transfer less of a "handout" and more of a reward for effort. That perception might make redistribution more acceptable to taxpayers and voters—and possibly to many beneficiaries as well. Determining ex ante how important those factors are typically will require an analysis of the extent to which the prevailing political economy favors redistribution to the poor. The lack (or small size) of cash transfers targeting the poor is a strong indication that the political process has not been supportive of such redistribution. As was shown in chapter 2, political economy considerations were an important motivation for launching the PROGRESA program in Mexico as a conditional rather than unconditional cash transfer. More generally, assessing the extent to which political economy factors demand the use of conditions even in the absence of distortions in household behaviors vis-à-vis the accumulation of human capital requires an understanding of prevailing views on distributive justice. Developing such an understanding can be done in various ways, including opinion polls or, more indirectly, through media analyses, as illustrated by Lindert and Vincensini (2008) in the case of Brazil.

Ultimately, the decision on whether to adopt a CCT or a UCT (assuming that the latter is politically feasible) should be based on an assessment of their respective costs and benefits. Quite often, the factors justifying the use of a CCT will apply to some, but not all, poor households with children—the potential target for a CCT. Even assuming that it is feasible to identify correctly which poor households are inefficiently under-investing in the human capital of their children and which are not, setting up a CCT for the former and a UCT for the latter could involve both administrative and political costs.

Figure 6.2 presents a simple way of considering the trade-offs associated with adopting a CCT. It distinguishes among four groups of poor households with children:

- Group A comprises households in which children are already attending school and receiving proper medical and nutrition care; there is no under-investing in the human capital of children. For this group, a CCT would be a de facto UCT, given that the conditions would be redundant.
- Group B comprises households that are under-investing in the human capital of their children.[4] This is the group for whom a CCT is the right instrument.
- Groups C and D are poor households whose children are experiencing low levels of human capital; these households, however,

Figure 6.2   Types of Households with Children

Poor Households with Children

| GROUP A Children in school without conditions; CCT = UCT | GROUP B Low schooling reflecting inefficient under-investment in children's schooling. | GROUP C Efficiently low schooling; take up program. |
| | | GROUP D Efficiently low schooling; no take-up of program. |

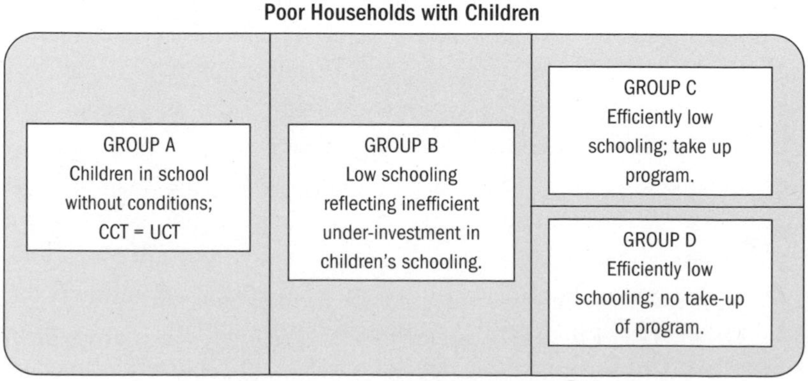

Source: Authors' illustration.

are making efficient decisions, given other factors. For example, the quality of schools available and/or the learning ability of children may make the returns to further schooling low. These are the groups for whom, in principle, a UCT would be a better option. Group C comprises those households that would take up the CCT if it were offered. As a result, they would be better-off with a CCT than without a transfer (after all, take-up is voluntary so that the added cash must be making them better-off), but worse off than under a UCT (because the condition is making them over-invest in human capital). Group D, on the other hand, does not take up the CCT (because the transfer is not large enough to compensate for the cost of complying with the conditions). For them, the cost of having a CCT instead of a UCT is the amount of the (lost) transfer.

The case for a CCT, rather than a UCT, will depend on the relative size of the various groups and on the cost of the excess (shortage of) investment in human capital by group C (group D). The possible combinations are many, but consider the following cases:

- A large share of the poor households with children are inefficiently under-investing in human capital (group B is large). There are large take-up rates among eligible households (group D is small). Satisfying conditions is not too costly to a majority of participating households. This is a high-impact CCT.
- A large share of poor households with children are not under-investing in human capital (group A is large). Although small, a group of households is heavily and inefficiently under-investing in human capital with high social costs (the benefits of conditioning transfers to group B are large). In this case, conditions are unnecessary (but harmless) for a majority, but are needed for a minority. A CCT is still the right instrument.
- A large fraction of poor households with children have low levels of human capital investment, but that is an efficient decision based on the low quality of schools and health clinics (groups C and D are large). Moreover, given the level of benefit the government can afford from a fiscal perspective, a large part of those households would not take up such a costly program (group D is large). This is a case in which a CCT is an inefficient program: its opportunity costs may be too high to justify a CCT, even on political economy grounds.

171

The answer to the question of whether a CCT is the right policy instrument will be country specific. Assessing the extent and nature of human capital under-investment among poor households is of critical importance. As suggested in figure 6.1, such assessment can draw on quantitative indicators as well as on more qualitative information (including beneficiary assessments).

The previous discussion highlights the importance of considering the initial conditions to determine not only whether a CCT is the right instrument but also to identify the right target population, the ensuing conditions (and degree of enforcement), and the payment levels. In the next section, we discuss these in more detail.

Designing an Efficient CCT Program

Given that a CCT is to be put in place, how should it be designed? To answer this question, we focus on cases where the CCT seeks both to redistribute income and build the human capital of poor children. For some cases, these objectives may be in conflict, so we discuss the possible tradeoffs.

Selecting the Target Population

Defining the target population is the first issue any policy maker considering a CCT must address. It follows from the definitions above that, in theory, a CCT should be designed to target poor households (for whom there is a stronger rationale to redistribute) that under-invest in the human capital of their children. Applying such general definitions in specific countries, though, will typically imply setting very different targets, depending on the initial conditions in terms of the prevailing distribution of both income and human capital.

Selecting the target population for a CCT first implies defining the criteria for eligibility based on poverty. As discussed in chapter 3, CCT programs have been characterized by their use of some type of means test to establish eligibility, and this often has contributed to their poverty-targeting success. The challenges of selecting the "right" targeting method and setting cut-off points for program eligibility (that is, deciding who qualifies as poor) are similar to those faced in designing any kind of social assistance program that seeks to maximize its poverty alleviation impact for a given budget (see Grosh et al. [2008]). There is, however, one important twist to this general theme. As reviewed in chapter 5, there is growing evidence that CCT impacts on human capital outcomes are larger among poorer households. The implication is that, in addition to any considerations regarding the optimal targeting to achieve redistributive goals, tighter poverty targeting also may contribute to maximizing the CCT impact on human capital accumulation. In other words, if in the case of Nicaragua's RPS (see Maluccio and Flores [2005]) the average impact of the program on enrollment for 7–13-year-old children in first to fourth grades was 25 percentage points for the extremely poor and 14 percentage points for the poor, we could expect that a program targeting the extremely poor would have a larger average effect on enrollment.[5]

Identifying households that under-invest in their children's human capital is more complicated in practice. From a conceptual point of view, this could be done by first identifying poor households based on some means test and then proceeding to identify the particular ways in which those households are under-investing in the human capital of their children. To some extent, that is the approach followed by the Chile Solidario program. Eligible households in extreme poverty are identified using a standard proxy means test. Beneficiaries then must agree with a government-appointed social worker on a set of minimal critical conditions (including many related to the well-being of their children) that constitute the basis of the "contract" for program participation (Galasso 2006). This approach, however, requires intensive interaction between social workers and families not only in the diagnosis phase but also in terms of monitoring. Clearly, that interaction is seen as a critical aspect of program design in the case of Chile (and probably is feasible because of the combination of a relatively small target group and the country's high administrative capacity). Chile Solidario may serve as a model for other middle-income countries with persistent pockets of poverty, but may not be affordable for many developing countries.

It thus is not surprising that a majority of countries implementing CCT programs have complemented poverty targeting with some form of demographic targeting as a proxy for human capital underinvestment. Doing so typically implies defining eligibility on the basis of the age (and sometimes gender) of the children, and linking it to the human capital investments most relevant for their ages (that is, growth monitoring and feeding for younger children, school attendance for older ones). In simple terms, when they qualify based on some poverty-targeting criteria, households will receive the transfer as long as they have children of the "right" age and send them to school and/or take them to the clinic.

In other words, households and children are typically not targeted based on the actual observation of a human capital gap, but on the presumption of one. Seen from the perspective of the human capital goals of CCT programs, this targeting method is bound to have errors of inclusion because some households eligible to receive the payments already may be making the desired investments in the absence of the program. So, for example, programs that define eligibility on the basis of the presence of children of a certain age conditioned on attending school will include households that would have sent their children to school even without a transfer. Similarly, not all young children receiving a transfer based on evidence of visits to health clinics for growth monitoring will be malnourished. One way in which such errors of inclusion can be minimized is to adopt "narrow demographic targeting"—that is, to target those demographic subgroups among the poor who experience the largest human capital gaps and to define the conditions so that they are relevant (binding) for that group. Doing that may imply targeting poor households with children transitioning from primary to secondary school in some countries; in other countries it may imply targeting poor households with young children in regions with high rates of malnutrition.

The importance of considering initial conditions is illustrated in figure 6.3, which shows grade survival rates among the poor in two countries. In the case of Mexico, the almost-universal primary school enrollment among the poor implies that the CCT's impact on schooling is bound to be low when targeted to poor households with younger children. Such a program still may be justified for its redistributive effects if alternative means of providing cash assistance to those families are not feasible. But those households are not, in principle, the primary target for a CCT. Narrower targeting thus could be justified in two ways. First, by targeting households with children transitioning to secondary school, the CCT would be helping remove the kink in the curve—clearly the most efficient way to achieve increases in enrollment (see de Janvry and Sadoulet [2006]). Attanasio et al. (2005), for example, estimate that eliminating the transfers to children in sixth grade and below, and using those resources to increase the size of the

Figure 6.3 Grade Survival Profile, Ages 10–19, Poorest Quintile, Cambodia and Mexico

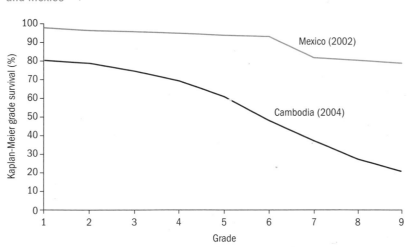

Source: Based on analysis of IHS-WDR07 data, which can be found at http://econ.worldbank. org/projects/edattain.

Note: Survival rates represent the portion of 10–19-year-olds who attain each grade level.

transfer to children in seventh grade and beyond, almost would double school participation among the older children, with no effect on school participation by the younger ones.

Second, reaching out to the relatively small number of poor households with children not attending primary schools may require more specific eligibility criteria developed by using good predictors of non-attendance. For the case of Mexico, de Janvry and Sadoulet (2006) identify factors such as being indigenous or having illiterate parents as examples of such predictors. Gender targeting (as in the scholarship programs in South Asia) may play a similar role. At the same time, when human capital under-investment is concentrated in a small group of socially excluded households (see box 6.1), the additional cost of a social worker (as in Chile Solidario) who is better able to determine eligibility on the basis of a more detailed assessment of family conditions may be justified.

Such retargeting, however, would come at a cost. In the Mexico case, the number of poor households not covered by the program would increase because those families with children in primary school no longer would qualify, and that would create a conflict with the program's redistributive goals. It could be argued that a UCT (like the one those

Box 6.1 CCTs As an Instrument to Fight Social Exclusion

COUNTRIES IN CENTRAL AND EASTERN EUROPE tend to have high rates of use of education and health services and well-established safety nets. However, there are sometimes socially excluded groups for whom low levels of human capital remain a serious bottleneck. For example, in many countries in Central and Eastern Europe, the educational attainment of the Roma minority lags far behind that of the majority population. This point is made apparent in figure 6B.1, which shows educational attainment of poor and nonpoor adults between the ages of 20 and 28 in Bulgaria, and of ethnic Bulgarians, Turks, and Roma in that same age group. The figure shows that only roughly 60 percent of young Roma adults have completed primary school, compared with almost

100 percent for the majority Bulgarian population. Differences become more pronounced at higher education levels: Approximately 95 percent of the majority Bulgarian population has completed at least nine years of schooling, compared with approximately 10 percent of the Roma minority. Taken together with a variety of other disadvantages, the Roma's low educational attainment dramatically increases the probability that they will have limited options in the labor market and low earning potential. CCT programs could potentially provide the necessary incentives to increase schooling among young Roma.

Sources: Andrews and Ringold 1999; World Bank 2008c.

Figure 6B.1 Education Attainment, Bulgaria, 2007

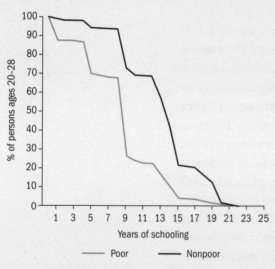

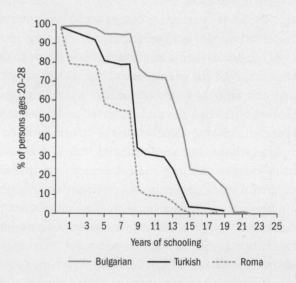

Source: 2007 Bulgaria Multi-Topic Household Survey data.

families are receiving de facto) is exactly what is required to redistribute income to those households. Under these circumstances, the decision on whether to have two separate transfer programs or a single one with "broad demographic targeting" is really one about administrative efficiency and political feasibility, as discussed above.

In Cambodia, dropping out of school starts much earlier (as early as in the transition from second to third grade) and increases gradually with every grade. As a result, low school enrollment among children from poor households is less sharply concentrated among a specific age group than it is in Mexico. A CCT targeting seventh graders would flatten out the end-tail of the distribution but leave schooling in the earlier grades untouched, at least in the short run; in the long run, it is possible that households also will keep young children in school longer, knowing that they may have access to transfers when those children reach seventh grade. On the other hand, a CCT targeting younger children would shift the entire curve up, over time, because the increased enrollment rates in the lower grades would push up enrollment in higher grades even if dropout rates at that level remain unchanged. Cambodia provides a different example of how initial conditions matter for the choice of targeting criteria—perhaps one in which trade-offs between redistributive and human capital goals are less serious and, as a result, retargeting could be seen as a win-win solution. Retargeting to cover earlier grades may be good both in terms of poverty (because the proportion of poor households covered likely would increase) and in terms of impact on total enrollment, given that increasing the number of children enrolling in the earlier grades is a precondition to expanding coverage at the secondary level. Moreover, because the opportunity cost of schooling is probably lower for younger children, a smaller benefit level may be sufficient to incentivize the desired change in behavior, enabling a further expansion in coverage without increasing program costs.

The two cases discussed above illustrate that the trade-offs between redistributive and human capital goals resulting from alternative targeting approaches are likely to differ across countries. In a setting in which a large share of the poor experience significant and similar human capital gaps (as in Cambodia), trade-offs are likely to be small. However, when the human capital gaps that justify the need for a CCT are highly concentrated on a relatively small proportion of the poor, designing a CCT to maximize impact on human capital accumulation may limit its ability to act as a redistributive mechanism. As indicated before, other safety net instruments may be better suited for that purpose. But when, for whatever reasons, other instruments are not feasible, a less "efficient" selection of beneficiaries in terms of the expected impact on human capital accumulation actually may be desirable.

Selecting Conditions and Enforcement Levels

The impact of CCT programs on human capital outcomes is linked directly to the programs' ability to affect the behaviors of beneficiary households. The right conditions would be different in each case and would require different means of enforcement. The evidence reviewed in chapter 5 suggests that conditions can be important in terms of increasing service use—particularly if the income elasticity of demand for those services among the target population is low. Thus, when increasing service use is a goal in itself (for example, widening the use of immunization), defining the condition becomes mostly a question of detail (how often? where?).

More generally, however, service use is a means to an end. Thus, the first step in selecting the "right" condition(s) is a review of the evidence on links between "service use" and the desired outcomes. Is getting children into health facilities the most effective way to improve their nutrition and health more broadly? Or is it more effective to give mothers information and training on nutrition and parenting? In the case of Mexico, for example, there is evidence suggesting that the *pláticas* may have contributed to the improved health outcomes by encouraging better diets (Hoddinott and Skoufias 2004) and by improving knowledge on a variety of health issues (Duarte Gómez et al. 2004).[6] In that sense, conditioning on "training" may be more effective than conditioning on actual health service use. This critical first step can be challenging because the right instrument to achieve the desired outcome may fall outside the sectoral realm of those involved in the design of the program. In some settings, for example, improved child health may be better pursued through the elimination of open-air defecation, and that would require using a different type of condition (that is, targeting communities rather than individuals).

The previous discussion also suggests that a narrower definition of the behaviors the program is seeking to affect could be helpful in designing the specific incentives required. For example, monetary incentives have been found to be efficient in improving abstinence and treatment adherence for drug and alcohol abuse (Petry 2002; Petry and Bohn 2003). This finding has led to the use of so-called contingency management approaches that use incentives to reinforce behavioral change. In designing such approaches, clinical researchers have focused on considerations that apply very closely to CCT programs: the choice of target behavior and target population; and the type, magnitude, frequency, timing, and duration of the incentive (Petry 2000). Payments are seen as a mechanism to reinforce the specific clinical treatment. In other words, when the objective is to change behaviors that are unlikely to be income elastic, the use of CCTs ought to be tailored to the specific behaviors and population to generate efficient incentives.

Conditioning the transfer on the achievement of outcomes themselves is another possibility, particularly when links between specific behaviors (such as service use) and outcomes are unknown or complex, and outcomes are mostly within the control of beneficiaries. Some health outcomes may be amenable to that approach, which would imply, for example, conditioning payment to young people on evidence that they are free from sexually transmitted diseases. In the case of education, it would imply moving away from conditioning on school attendance and moving to school completion and perhaps to evidence of actual learning (as measured through tests), although the latter approach may be problematic unless practical ways are found to also control for teacher effort.

As was shown in box 5.1, in the United States there is some experience with programs that pay for final outcomes rather than for service use. Given the concerns about whether CCT programs in developing countries are succeeding in improving final outcomes (for example, learning outcomes), experimentation with alternative incentive schemes (perhaps through small-scale pilot programs) is justified. A practical way to do that is to structure such incentives as additional to the basic benefits qualifying households receive for satisfying attendance conditions (that is, as performance bonuses).

More generally, though, the choice of conditions ought to be informed by the evidence of expected returns from alternative types of investment in human capital. Returns, of course, will vary across countries and social groups. However, the accumulated evidence regarding returns to investments in the human capital of young children is consistently strong. Moreover, life-cycle skill formation is believed to be a dynamic process in which early inputs affect the productivity of inputs later in life; and thus investments in young (particularly disadvantaged) children are not only good from an equity point of view but also are highly efficient (Heckman 2006a, 2006b).

The review in chapter 5 found no evidence of CCT impacts on learning outcomes among school-age children, but did find significant (albeit modest) improvements among younger children. That evidence suggests that the payoffs of CCT programs may be higher when focused on development at early ages in life. Figure 6.4 illustrates that point, drawing on information from Ecuador. Paxson and Schady (2007) use the Spanish version of the Peabody Picture Vocabulary Test (that is, the Test de Vocabulario en Imágenes Peabody) to measure cognitive development among young children. They find that between the ages of 3 and 6, the poorest children go from scoring 90 on the normalized scale (the equivalent of being about two thirds of a standard deviation behind where they should be) to scoring below 70. That decline implies that the median child in this group (corresponding approximately to the poorest quintile of the national wealth distribution) is 2.5–3.0 standard deviations behind the reference population. By the time they start school, these children are severely handicapped in terms of their cognitive development. The implication is clear: it is hard to see how a CCT by itself, or even in combination with "high-quality" schools, can remedy such disadvantages. Using CCT programs to support earlier investments in children may be a more effective approach.

Figure 6.4 Cognitive Development by Wealth Decile in Ecuador, 2003–04

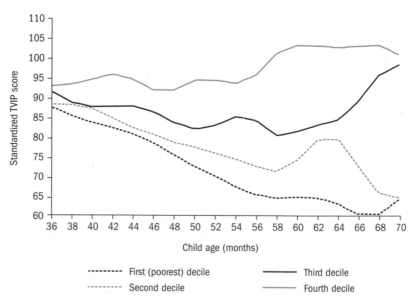

Source: Paxson and Schady 2007.

Note: TVIP = Test de Vocabulario en Imágenes Peabody. Each line corresponds to one decile from the national distribution of wealth, from the first (poorest) decile, to the fourth. The test is coded so that a score of 100 corresponds to the average performance in a reference population, and the standard deviation is 15.

Seen from that perspective, the emphasis of many CCT programs on secondary education rather than early childhood development may appear paradoxical. In fact, several countries are considering adapting their CCT programs to focus also on expanding participation in early childhood development programs among low-income households (for example, Colombia and Mexico). Such changes also may require improvements in the availability and quality of nutrition and parenting interventions.

In practice, it is not just about which conditions are selected, but also about how they are monitored and enforced.[7] Do programs that enforce conditions strictly get better results than others that are more lenient? Unfortunately, very little is known about how important the degree of monitoring and enforcement is in explaining results; and no country, so far, has experimented with different approaches in that regard. There is, however, some evidence suggesting that the sole announcement of the intended purpose of a cash transfer may have an effect on how resources actually are used. Two well-known examples from developed countries are Kooreman (2000) and Fraker, Martini, and Ohls (1995). Kooreman analyzes the case of a child benefit in the Netherlands and finds that the marginal propensity to spend on child clothing out of the benefits is much larger than out of other sources of income. He argues that this may be the result of a "labeling effect": parents consider the benefit a benchmark that tells them how much they should spend on their child. Fraker, Martini, and Ohls examine estimates of the effect on household food expenditures of converting food stamps into a cash transfer in the United States. Their estimates imply that households spend more on food out of food stamps that have been monetized than out of other sources of income.

There is also some suggestive evidence from CCT programs. As discussed in chapter 5, evidence from Ecuador shows that the sole announcement that beneficiaries of the BDH were expected to send children to school had that effect without the conditions ever being monitored or enforced (Schady and Araujo 2008). In the CCT component of the Atención a Crisis program in Nicaragua, the anticipated increase in health service supply did not occur because of implementation problems, and children's visits to the health centers were not monitored during the study period. During program enrollment and on paydays, however, the program included repeated information and communications about the importance of varied diets, health, and education. Macours, Schady, and Vakis (2008) find significant positive effects on early childhood development outcomes and changes in the composition of food consumption (toward more nutritious food). Moreover, the size of those effects is too large to be the result of the cash transfer alone: there appears to be a change in behavior despite the fact that the conditions for children of preschool age were not monitored or enforced.

Those cases illustrate the possibility that less than full enforcement of conditions may be sufficient—although our understanding of what influences the seriousness with which parents take the program's stated goals remains limited. The fact that transfers typically have been paid to mothers raises the question of whether the observed results are associated with mothers' preferences for investing in children's nutrition (see box 6.2 on whether it matters who receives the payment).

Overall, these are areas on which the existing evidence from evaluations of CCT programs is mostly silent and thus will require further research and experimentation in the future.

Selecting Payment Levels

The setting of benefit levels and structure is a critical design aspect in CCT programs. Budget availability obviously is an important factor influencing benefit levels. And when a CCT replaces preexisting programs, there are strong pressures to set benefit levels to avoid the perception of benefit cuts. In the case of Mexico, for example, the amount of monthly assistance under Oportunidades' food component was estimated to be greater than the previous subsidies received in 90 percent of the cases (Levy and Rodríguez 2004). In Brazil, where Bolsa Família replaced a series of existing transfer programs, the payment level was set to prevent eligible beneficiaries of the prereform programs from losing as a result of the reform. Moreover, an "extraordinary benefit" was established to compensate losers from the reform (Lindert et al. 2007).

In terms of the human capital goals of a program, however, the key parameter in setting benefit levels is the size of the elasticity of the relevant outcomes to the benefit level. In other words, the benefit level ought to be set in relation to the desired impacts. That is what several programs have attempted to do (ex ante) in a variety of ways. For example, the size of the education grant for Oportunidades was set to cover the opportunity costs for students, estimated on the basis of observed

Box 6.2   Does It Matter Who Receives the Cash?

A MAJORITY OF CCT PROGRAMS HAVE TARGETED payments to mothers. The justification for doing so has been that mothers have a stronger preference for investing in children than do fathers. (Chapters 4 and 5 discuss the relevant evidence.) At the same time, a number of studies suggest that women and men may value boys and girls differently. For example, Thomas (1994), using data from Brazil, Ghana, and the United States, finds that fathers and mothers invest different amounts of resources in the human capital of their children, with mothers allocating more to daughters and fathers allocating more to sons. In Duflo's (2003) study of the South Africa OAP, the positive effect on child nutrition associated with pension receipt by a female is observed only if the child is a girl. Rangel (2006) analyzes the extension of alimony rights to couples in consensual unions in Brazil (an act that arguably increased the bargaining power of women), and he finds an increase in attendance rates among oldest daughters. The implication is that if mothers really do have a preference for girls, targeting payments to mothers would result in some form of discrimination against boys. Depending on the context, that discrimination may help or hurt the achievement of human development outcomes.

How about targeting payments to children? Very few programs do it, and the reasons are understandable. In those cases that do (Bangladesh's Female Secondary School Assistance Program, Bogotá's Subsidio Condicionado a la Asistencia Escolar), the transfer actually is a deposit in a bank account that the student can use at a later time. Although evaluations are available for those programs, they don't consider the differential impact of making payments to the students versus to their parents. The Education Maintenance Allowance (EMA) in the United Kingdom provides a cash subsidy to young people aged 16–19 from poor households to encourage them to remain in education after the end of compulsory schooling. During that program's pilot phase, different implementation variants were tried. In one variant of the program, the payment was made to the young people themselves; in another variant, parents received the transfer. An impact evaluation found that the impact on education participation was twice as large where EMA was paid to the young person (Ashworth et al. 2002). That finding suggests that the alternative of paying at least some part of the transfer (perhaps as a savings deposit) to young people, perhaps those attending secondary school, may be worth considering.

children's incomes (Levy and Rodríguez 2004); and in Honduras it was set to cover both the opportunity and direct costs, the latter including the costs for books, uniforms, and the like (IFPRI 2000).

Overall, however, there is little evidence available from impact evaluations to inform decisions about payment levels. An exception is the Cambodia evaluation (Filmer and Schady 2009a), which found positive but diminishing marginal returns to transfer size. These questions also have been analyzed using structural models that explore the effects of different program choices on education outcomes (see box 6.3).

Taking into account heterogeneity among beneficiaries further complicates the process of setting optimal benefit levels. For example,

Box 6.3   Using Behavioral Models to Simulate the Effects of CCT Design Changes

HOW LARGE SHOULD A CCT BE? SHOULD TRANSFER amounts differ with the child's age or grade level? Answers to questions such as these might be helpful to policy makers charged with designing a new—or reforming an existing—CCT program. An ideal way to seek those answers would be to launch pilot programs of various alternative designs, with randomized assignment and a control group. An ex post impact evaluation of the various pilot programs would teach us much about how each alternative design performs in practice.

Such detailed experimentation takes time, however, and can be expensive. The number of alternative designs is a combination of different values for various program parameters (the value of the transfer, the level of the means test, plus grade and gender variations, for instance), leading to an experiment that is demanding and complex. That is why simulating program impacts on the basis of an economic model of household behavior can be useful.

Model-based simulation exercises (also known as "ex ante program evaluations") typically consist of a structural model of the aspects of economic behavior that are most relevant for the program at hand. For CCTs, those aspects tend to focus on the child's occupational choice between staying in school and dropping out. More complex models also can consider the effects of the transfer on adult labor supply, or even on fertility. Models are written to yield estimable equations, which then are taken to the data. The models are estimated on data that predates the program—typically, but not always, a household survey. When the parameters of the model have been estimated, the equations that contain policy parameters can be used to simulate (counterfactual) outcomes under various scenarios. Comparing those outcomes and their simulated costs can be informative for policy makers—at least in selecting which parameter combinations to pilot-test in an actual experiment.

Two examples of structural models applied to simulating CCT impacts are Attanasio, Meghir, and Santiago (2005) and Todd and Wolpin (2006a). Those models are estimated on preprogram (baseline) Oportunidades survey data. Attanasio, Meghir, and Santiago (2005) use a school participation model to predict the impact of the program when the distribution of transfers is shifted toward later grades. Specifically, they increase the grant for children above grade six and eliminate the transfer for children in lower grades.

Todd and Wolpin (2006a) use a detailed intertemporal structural model to predict the impact of Oportunidades on school enrollment, wages, and fertility. The predicted changes in enrollment rates derived from the model closely match the actual changes measured in the ex post evaluation of the program. The authors also simulate the relative impact and costs of alternative program designs, including various cash transfer levels, cash transfers restricted to the sixth grade and beyond, and a bonus for completing ninth grade. The results of these simulations suggest that the original Oportunidades subsidy or a cash transfer solely targeted to those students in sixth grade and above is the most cost-effective means of increasing student enrollment, a finding similar to that in Attanasio, Meghir, and Santiago (2005).

Bourguignon, Ferreira, and Leite (2003) and Todd and Wolpin (2006b) offer simpler models of the impact of CCTs on educational attainment, which trade some structural complexity for added flexibility. Using preprogram household survey data from Brazil, Bourguignon, Ferreira, and Leite (2003) estimate an occupational choice model for children that enables the authors to simulate the impacts of various alternative designs on school attendance and child labor. The policy alternatives they consider include changing the size of the transfer, the maximum transfer per household, and the eligibility cut-off point for households; and making Bolsa Escola transfers unconditional. The authors estimate that doubling the size of the Bolsa Escola transfer in Brazil would have reduced by half the percentage of children in poor households not attending school, and a further doubling of the transfer would reduce nonattendance among the poor to one third. As a corollary to the prediction of the impact on school enrollment and child labor, the authors examine the relative changes in program design as it affects per capita income, inequality, and income poverty. Although the authors find that school enrollment is rather elastic to the size of the transfer, at least when it is conditional, they find very little effect on income and poverty variables, except when the transfer is quadrupled.

Todd and Wolpin (2006b) use propensity score matching based on pre-Oportunidades data to match households having a specified income level and child wage rate with households who would have that level of income and child wage rate after the transfer. The central assumption of their matching model is that those households that receive the transfer will behave in the same manner as those that have the specified income level before the program. Todd and Wolpin (2006) use this model to test multiple transfer sizes. Like Bourguignon, Ferreira, and Leite (2003), Todd and Wolpin (2006b) find that enrollment responds sharply to the size of the conditional transfer.

All of these studies acknowledge that these simulations or "predictions" of alternative scenarios are only as good as the models (and data) on which they are based. Of course, when a decision on program design is made and implemented, the predictions of the ex ante simulation should be tested against an actual, ex post evaluation of the program. (See Bourguignon and Ferreira [2003] for a general discussion.)

smaller transfers may be needed for children of primary school age than for those of secondary school age because the latter may incur a higher opportunity cost for attending school. The elasticity of some human development outcomes to the transfer level could vary according to the child's gender—either because the child's opportunity costs differ or because of parental preferences. In Mexico, for example, the design of the program recognized those factors and, as a result, pays more for secondary school–age children and for girls. Achieving similar improvements in outcomes may require different payment levels in rural and urban areas because of various factors, including differences in relative prices.

In theory, the efficacy of a CCT program in terms of its expected impact on human capital accumulation could be improved by calibrating the size of the transfer to the relevant characteristics of beneficiaries. In other words, ideally the CCT could be designed to recognize the fact that the cost of achieving a given improvement in child health or an increase in school attendance may vary significantly, even among the eligible population. In practice, of course, doing so not only requires a wealth of information on the different effect sizes, but also demands that the criteria to be used for such calibration be feasible to implement from both administrative and political points of view. Moreover, the more complicated the system is, the more likely it is that households will try to game it—for example, by manipulating the observable characteristics (such as ownership of specific assets) that influence eligibility.

So far, we have considered benefit levels and structure as means of improving the design of CCT programs to achieve human capital outcomes, but they are equally relevant to achieve redistributive goals. Say, for example, that a small transfer (that is, small as a proportion of the poverty gap) is sufficient to generate improved nutrition or school attendance, but insufficient to have a significant effect on consumption poverty. As long as redistributive goals are an important aspect of the program, setting benefit levels above the minimum necessary for the human capital goals will be justified. That could be done by adding a fixed amount per household or by raising the per-child benefit.

Heterogeneity among beneficiaries is also an important factor when considering the structure of payments from the point of view of the program's redistributive goals. Particularly in large programs that, by design, target several deciles of the income distribution (such as Brazil's Bolsa Família or Ecuador's BDH), the question of whether higher benefit levels should be set for the poorest beneficiaries is very relevant. In the Bolsa Família program, Brazil has adopted a benefit structure whereby the extreme poor (defined on the basis of per capita income) get a base benefit that is supplemented by a per-child benefit (Lindert et al. 2007). The (less) poor beneficiaries get only the per-child benefit. This is a practical way to pursue the program's redistributive goals without altering the overall structure of the program as it relates to its human capital goals.[8]

Adapting the Supply of Social Services

CCT programs cannot be thought of in isolation from other social policies. In particular, achieving the human capital accumulation goals sought by CCT programs typically will require adapting the supply of social services, including expanding coverage and improving quality. Moreover, in many cases it will require going beyond improvements in the provision of traditional health and education services and involving social work activities to affect promoting and other "within-household" practices.

Although it is conceivable that a CCT could be implemented in conditions where the supply of education and health services is perfectly adequate (and, as a result, no complementary actions would be required), in practice that is highly unlikely in most developing countries where the delivery of education and health services typically is dysfunctional (World Bank 2003). Poor infrastructure, absenteeism, and lack of adequate supplies are not unusual problems in schools and health centers in most developing countries—including those that have ongoing CCT programs. Indeed, there is some evidence that weaknesses in the supply of services are a limiting factor to the effectiveness of CCT programs. In their comparison of program effects for children randomly assigned to two more years of Oportunidades intervention in rural areas, Behrman, Parker, and Todd (2005) show that program impacts on enrollment were larger when children had access to general or technical schools than when they had access only to the long-distance, satellite-based *telesecundaria* schools.[9] Program impacts also are larger for students in areas where, prior to implementation of the program, student-teacher ratios were low (fewer than 20 students per teacher). Both of those results suggest that in assessing whether to send their children to school in response to the CCT, parents took account of the quality of local schools, and were more likely to enroll their children if quality was higher.

In that sense, actions oriented to improving the adequacy of the relevant services typically will be needed to complement a CCT. Of course, CCT programs also may be competing with other supply-side actions, at least in terms of funding, and decisions on the right size of CCT programs ought to be based on their "productivity" relative to such supply-side interventions. At the same time, those decisions also ought to be based on the marginal social value of both CCT programs and health and education services relative to other categories of public spending. (See box 6.4 on the cost–benefit analysis of CCT programs.) However, no matter how one answers the question of what is the right budget allocation to the CCT, the need for complementary actions to improve the supply of services most likely will remain central in most countries.

A review of the experience of those countries that have implemented CCT programs confirms the latter point. Governments have often

Box 6.4 Cost–Benefit Analysis of a CCT: The Case of Familias en Acción

MEASURING THE COST AND BENEFIT OF CCT programs can be a daunting task, given the multidimensionality of such programs. A detailed cost–benefit analysis of the Colombian program Familias en Acción was undertaken jointly by the Institute for Fiscal Studies, Econometría, and Sistemas Especializados de Información (2006).

Their analysis values the benefits of Familias en Acción in terms of the increased future earnings that result from (1) lowered incidence of underweight infants, (2) lowered incidence of malnutrition and child morbidity among children aged 0–6 years, and (3) increased years of secondary schooling. The effects of Familias en Acción on those outcomes are derived from an impact evaluation, and then are monetized using evidence from a combination of sources (for example, a net additional year of secondary school education is assumed to increase future income by 8 percent, based on estimates of Mincerian rates of return; an increase of 0.4 kilograms in birth weight is assumed to increase future income by 5 percent, based on international evidence). When those monetized benefits are discounted, the total net present value of benefits is calculated to be $259.4 million.

Costs are summed to $163 million, and they consist of (1) program costs for both the nutrition and the education components, (2) the private costs incurred by the household for additional food and education expenditure, (3) private household costs of collecting transfers, (4) infrastructure and input costs of additional school and health center supply, and (5) the public cost generated to finance the CCT.

Comparing the benefit and cost figures, the authors estimate a ratio of benefits to costs of 1.59, which is high by traditional cost–benefit ratio standards and suggests that the CCT is worth its cost. The ratio also means that even if the assumptions used in this model are imperfect, costs would need to increase 59 percent relative to benefits to reach a point where the benefits do not justify the costs. It should be noted that this analysis does not consider other benefits, including the increased household consumption (other than through child nutrition and birth weight).

Source: Institute for Fiscal Studies, Econometría, and Sistemas Especializados de Información 2006.

undertaken actions (in parallel, in coordination, or as an integral part of the CCT program) to improve the supply of those services that beneficiaries are expected to use. It is fair to say that the policy dilemma is not *whether* such actions are needed, but *how* they should be carried out. Table 6.1 illustrates the range of complementary actions that countries have taken to improve the adequacy of education and health services. The table also shows the diversity of cases in terms of the approaches being followed, and whether these are schemes specifically targeting CCT beneficiaries or part of broader efforts to improve the supply of services.

At one extreme across the possible range of cases, all that really is required to improve the adequacy of services is ensuring that

Table 6.1 Examples of Supply-Side Interventions Complementary to a CCT

Country	Supply-side intervention, education	Targeting only CCT communities?	Supply-side intervention, health and nutrition	Targeting only CCT communities?
Bangladesh	(1) Government school and classroom construction; (2) nonformal and religious school expansion	Both stipend and school expansion were national; madrassa expansion was influenced by secondary school stipend; NGO-managed schools did not participate in early years of the primary school stipend	No health component in CCT	No health component in CCT
Cambodia	New classroom construction for lower-secondary school	Some overlap, but not full coverage	No health component in CCT	No health component in CCT
El Salvador	School-based management (Redes Escolares Efectivas)	No, covers a wide set of communities, including those in Red Solidaria	NGO contracts and mobile brigades for the delivery of basic health package (including community-based nutrition component)	No, program covers a wide set of communities, including those in Red Solidaria.
Honduras	(1) School construction; (2) transfer payments to parent-teacher associations	(1) No, national coverage; (2) yes, intervention piloted with CCT, but discontinued	Construction of health centers	Yes, intervention piloted with CCT, but discontinued
Jamaica	Provision of textbooks, teaching materials, and library resources; new school construction	National coverage	Established health education sessions in response to low health center attendance	Yes, education sessions were designed specifically for PATH recipients
Mexico	Rehabilitation of primary schools and construction of secondary schools; incentive grants for teacher performance	Yes	Mobile health teams	National coverage

continued

189

Table 6.1 continued

Country	Supply-side intervention, education	Targeting only CCT communities?	Supply-side intervention, health and nutrition	Targeting only CCT communities?
Nicaragua (RPS)	Cash transfer for teachers	Yes	Basic health package (including nutrition) supplied by NGOs and mobile institutional brigades	Yes, intervention was based on preexisting model covering non-CCT communities, but implementation was adapted for CCT communities
Panama	Nonformal preschools and home-based early childhood education	Yes, Educational Development Project and the Second Basic Education Project were adapted to meet the supply needs of Red de Oportunidades	Basic health package plus community-based nutrition	Yes, program existed prior to CCT, but nutrition component was added to the basic health package of services for indigenous and remote rural villages

Source: Authors' compilation.

Note: NGO = nongovernmental organization; PATH = Program of Advancement through Health and Education; RPS = Red de Protección Social.

beneficiaries know and understand the services available and that service providers have the outreach capabilities to attract them. That is most likely to be the case in countries with relatively well-functioning services and where CCT programs are targeting a relatively small group of beneficiaries. Chile provides a good example: The Chile Solidario program seeks to cover the 225,000 poorest households in the country. Because Chile has a broad and rather sophisticated network of education and health service providers, no major investments were needed to expand or change the supply of services. Nevertheless, Chile Solidario also works on the supply side to ensure coordination with providers. The social workers that give psychosocial support to the beneficiaries are trained on how to collaborate with the municipalities (which are responsible for schools and primary health centers in Chile) to make sure that beneficiaries are not excluded from existing services. As a result of that interaction, over time municipalities have introduced new social services to meet the needs of the Chile Solidario beneficiaries.

At the other extreme of the range of cases, supply is so inadequate that the proper functioning of the program requires major adjustments, including providing services where none existed before. Several countries have implemented initiatives to expand public sector capacity to supply services in parallel with the CCT, often relying on existing programs rather than establishing new ones. For example, in tandem with Oportunidades, the government of Mexico took steps to improve the supply of schooling through a combination of interventions: rural primary schools and *telesecundarias* were rehabilitated in Oportunidades communities; grants were offered to parent associations to pay for minor classroom maintenance and repairs; and in some communities, secondary schools were constructed to help meet the supply requirements in line with Oportunidades (Levy and Rodríguez 2004).[10] Efforts also were undertaken through the Programa de Ampliación de Cobertura to expand access to basic health services in rural areas (González-Pier et al. 2006). Similar efforts are found in other countries as well. Just to mention a few: In Bangladesh, starting in the 1980s, government spending on education almost doubled as a proportion of social sector spending, allowing for a significant expansion in the capacity of the schooling system (Hossain 2004); in Cambodia, the CESSP, which finances the scholarships that effectively function as a CCT, also finances the construction of new lower-secondary classrooms in communes with high poverty rates (communities also targeted for the scholarships).

Other countries have decided to use nongovernmental providers instead. For example, seeking to keep costs down and avoiding the inefficiencies experienced by public providers, several countries in Central America have contracted out basic health and nutrition services to NGOs and community groups.[11] Although these programs typically were implemented independently of the CCT programs at first,[12] in most cases they became the instrument used to deliver services to CCT beneficiaries.

Implementation of such efforts has involved both financial and administrative resources and coordination among different institutions (for example, between the agencies in charge of the CCT program and health and education ministries, and between them and local governments). Whereas those efforts resulted in important achievements in some countries (for example, more than 50,000 Mexican schools were rehabilitated), serious implementation difficulties impaired success in

191

others countries. In the Nicaraguan program Atención a Crisis, the anticipated increase in the supply of services by public clinics didn't materialize and, as mentioned earlier, resulted in a lack of monitoring of health conditions.[13] Similarly in Honduras, PRAF contemplated a health service package that involved the transfer of resources to the community to finance an annual work plan. The package was not implemented in accordance with protocol because no legal means could be identified to transfer resources from the central government to community-based teams. Thus only 17 percent of one year's transfers were disbursed (with central procurement), and only introductory training in quality assurance methods was given (Morris, Olinto et al. 2004). The pilot program was later discontinued.

Clearly, expanding the supply of health and education services in many countries is an important aspect of the efforts needed to implement a CCT. But, more generally, many countries face the challenge of improving the quality of services, particularly to respond to the needs of beneficiaries from the CCT programs themselves. In part, the efforts described above have sought to address issues of quality—for example, through more and better inputs or the training of providers. In a few cases, however, CCT programs also have introduced explicit monetary incentives to providers seeking to improve the quality of services. In Nicaragua, beneficiary households in the RPS were given an additional quantity of money, called the *bono a la oferta,* to be paid to the teacher by the child or parents. Oportunidades also included incentive grants to teachers (equivalent to a 29 percent increase in the average teacher salary) tied to attendance and participation in extracurricular activities with students and parents. In Bangladesh, the FSSAP II program incorporated incentive awards for school performance and improvement.

Whether or not the CCT programs become a vehicle to introduce innovations in service delivery, their success in promoting human capital accumulation among poor children is bound to be affected by other government efforts to reform service delivery. In some Central American countries (El Salvador, formerly in Nicaragua), children benefiting from CCT programs may attend schools that follow school-based management practices, or they may receive health services from nongovernmental providers who operate under "pay-for-performance" contracts. In Colombia, the existence of demand-side financing in health enables CCT beneficiaries to use both public and private health providers (see box 6.5). And

Box 6.5   Private Sector Delivery and CCT Programs

ALTHOUGH A MAJORITY OF THE EXISTING CCT programs have structured conditions around the use of government-managed facilities (schools, clinics), CCT programs can be (and have been) designed in a more pluralistic fashion, combining their demand-side incentives to change household behavior with both public and private provision of health and education services. It is assumed sometimes that the need to monitor conditions restricts CCT beneficiaries to using public facilities. But that is not the case. In Bangladesh, FSSAP recipients are permitted to attend their choice of government, secular-private, or religious schools. In addition to the regular reporting of enrollment and attendance by schools, the program is introducing audits as well as random checks by an independent third-party survey firm. In Colombia's Familias en Acción, mothers are required to ask doctors or nurses to verify their and their children's attendance at the health clinic, regardless of whether the clinic is public or private. And in the Chile Solidario program, education conditions are met through enrollment at the school (or preschool) that is nearest to the residence of the family. CCT recipients thus may enroll their children at public schools/preschools or at subsidized private

schools/preschools that accept government vouchers. Monitoring the conditions is the same in all cases: school enrollment is verified by the social worker assigned to a given family.

If the regulatory environment is flexible enough, the private sector (both for and not for profit) can help by responding, over time, to the increased demand enabled by CCT programs. The experience of Bangladesh appears to be relevant in this regard: A large share of the increase in school enrollments that took place starting in the 1990s was enabled by the expansion in the private supply of schools. BRAC (Bangladesh Rural Advancement Committee), the largest Bangladeshi NGO, offers a clear example: Starting with 22 single-room, one-teacher schools in 1985, it had 35,000 schools serving more than 1.1 million students by 1999 (Nath, Sylva, and Grimes 1999; Ahmed and Nath 2003). The government push to modernize schools (including making primary school attendance legally compulsory) led many madrassas, or religious schools, to open their doors to female students and to reformulate their curricula. As a result, enrollment in reformed madrassas increased by 62 percent between 1990 and 2003 (Niaz Asadullah and Chaudhury 2007).

in countries as diverse as Brazil and Pakistan (Punjab), CCT programs operate in the context of decentralized provision of education services. Whether and how local governments respond in terms of adapting the supply of services is critical in those cases, and this is an important area for future research.[14]

To date, there is little robust evidence to assess the effectiveness of different means of adapting the supply of services to the needs of poor households (such as those households benefiting from CCT programs).[15] One thus should not simply assume that shifting resources to provide more or different health or education inputs will generate better results (as argued, for example, by Reimers, Da Silva, and Trevino 2006). Moreover, the evidence base is still thin on the joint effects of supply and demand actions like the ones discussed above. Maluccio, Murphy, and Regalía (2006), for example, find that the effectiveness of the Nicaraguan RPS was larger in areas in which schools were autonomous than in areas where they were not, suggesting that school-based management reforms may be an important complement to a CCT program. But it is hard to make more general assessments without evidence from other settings.

The trend toward systematic impact evaluation first seen for CCT programs now is observed for the case of initiatives seeking to improve the delivery of social services, particularly in education (World Bank 2007). As results of such evaluations become available, it will be easier to answer the many remaining questions regarding how to design much needed supply-side complementary actions to CCT programs.

Chapter 5 showed that CCT programs to date have had only modest effects on "final" outcomes in education and health. The poor quality of services, particularly those to which poor people have access, may mean that increased utilization alone does not lead to better outcomes in the form of increased learning or reduced mortality. Thus it is important when considering complementary actions to improve the quality (and not just the quantity) of education and health (including nutrition) services. As illustrated in table 6.1, several countries already are seeking to do exactly that in various ways.

Another possible explanation for the apparently weak effects on final outcomes is the important constraints at the household level that are not addressed by the CCT programs, at least as currently designed. Those constraints could include poor parenting practices, inadequate information, or other inputs into the household production of education and health. More research is needed in this area, but two implications of this line of thought should be noted: First, as discussed above, simply conditioning the transfers on service use (regardless of the quality of the service) may not be sufficient to achieve the desired outcomes. In some cases, rethinking the nature of conditions may be needed. Second, a more proactive approach to outreach and support to households may be necessary. In other words, if household constraints really are a serious impediment to improving final outcomes, the cash/condition combination may not be sufficient, and social work interventions may be necessary. That is what Chile has been doing through Chile Solidario, and what other countries (Colombia, El Salvador, Panama) are pilot-testing or starting to implement more generally.

CCT Programs As Components of Social Protection Systems

As we have discussed at various points throughout this report, CCT programs are only one option within the arsenal of social assistance programs that can be used to redistribute income to poor households. The logical implication is that CCT programs should not be seen in isolation, but rather must be considered as part of a broader social protection system.

Why is that so? First, CCT programs *cannot* be the right instrument for all poor households. Because of their focus on building the human capital of poor children, CCT programs are not a feasible option for some groups among the poor, such as the elderly poor, poor households without children, or households with children outside the age range covered by the CCT. Redistribution to those groups is better handled through other means. In the case of the elderly poor, the potential labor supply disincentives from cash transfers are likely to be low, and the justification for further investments in human capital is questionable. As a result, UCT programs in the form of social or noncontributory pensions often are the instrument preferred by both developed and developing countries to provide assistance to that group.[16] As discussed in chapter 5, the evaluations of some social pension schemes (most notably in South Africa) show that some of the benefits of such redistribution accrue to other family members, including children.

The potential complementarities between CCTs and social pensions have not escaped policy makers. Eligibility rules for participation in a CCT program can be expanded to include the elderly simply by exempting them from the accompanying human capital conditions (and thereby effectively making the program into a UCT for that subpopulation). That approach was suggested by Camargo and Ferreira (2001) in their policy paper proposing the consolidation of Brazil's disparate social protection initiatives into a more coherent program. The proposal was implemented as part of Brazil's Bolsa Família; this approach also has been taken in Jamaica's PATH, Ecuador's BDH, and Chile Solidario. Although the costs of reforming existing programs need to be assessed, the administrative synergies of running the two components from the same agency and using the same beneficiary database may provide an argument for including the elderly poor in a CCT (rather than setting up a separate program), particularly in countries where no social pension exists.

Even among those poor households that potentially are eligible for a CCT, countries face different options, including UCTs or workfare programs. The choice among instruments needs to give serious consideration to their respective costs and benefits (as considered in the first section of this chapter). Rapid appraisals of the type suggested by Ravallion (1999) for workfare programs conceivably can be applied to CCT and UCT programs and can serve as inputs for decision making. For example, Murgai and Ravallion (2005) conduct such an exercise to compare workfare and a universal UCT for the case of India. They find that a budget-neutral, untargeted transfer has greater impact on poverty than does workfare, unless wages paid are extremely low and there is full recovery of nonwage costs.

Because of their emphasis on long-term human capital accumulation and on administrative targeting, CCT programs are better suited as instruments for structural poverty than as responses to episodes of transient poverty. Whether and how CCT programs can play a role as an insurance mechanism in the face of income shocks remain open questions—ones that have acquired increased importance in the face of the recent global economic slowdown (see box 6.6).

The previous discussion illustrates the overall message that in most country contexts, conditional and other cash transfer programs are likely to coexist, and should be seen as complementary rather than as substitutes—addressing different household characteristics and the nature of poverty those households experience. Thus it is not surprising that policy makers and program managers for CCT programs in Latin

---

Box 6.6   CCT Programs and the Financial Crisis

IT IS WIDELY BELIEVED THAT THE FINANCIAL CRISIS of 2008 in the United States and other industrial countries, and the ensuing global economic slowdown, could have dire consequences for the well-being of people in the developing world. Poverty may increase dramatically in countries where a sizable share of the population already lives in desperate circumstances. If families cut back on investments in the education, health, and nutrition of their children, this could have serious long-term consequences for the opportunities these children have as adults. The possibility of sharp reductions in living standards rightly has focused the minds of policy makers and academics on finding tools to mitigate the costs of the crisis for the world's poorest households. Can CCTs be part of the solution?

CCTs transfer cash and, as we have shown elsewhere in this report, that cash can help poor households weather systemic shocks like an economywide crisis, or idiosyncratic shocks like unemployment, illness, or the death of the main breadwinner. Moreover, the requirements that young children be taken to health centers for growth monitoring and that older children be enrolled in school and attend regularly may ensure that households do not cut back on critical investments in childhood.

That being said, CCTs by their nature primarily are instruments to address long-term, structural poverty rather than sudden income shocks, particularly if those shocks are expected to be short-term ones. A number of the properties of CCT programs are inconsistent with the type of flexible social insurance instrument required to manage social risk. First, CCTs are not countercyclical in nature. The administrative targeting methods they use are such that it is hard to add new beneficiaries in the short term and hard to remove them from the program rosters when a crisis has passed. Second, households that already are receiving transfers from a CCT program may not be those worst hit by an aggregate economic shock. Third, CCTs ask that households make "lumpy" investments in child education and health—investments that only make sense with a longer-term horizon. And finally, as described in box 5.3, it is not clear that households always will disinvest in child human capital during systemic shocks, especially in the middle-income countries in Latin America where CCTs are most widespread.

For all of these reasons, CCTs are not an ideal instrument for dealing with transient poverty. Transfer programs that do not involve long-term commitments (such as those implicit in CCT conditions), that are self-targeted (and thus do not involve complex administrative decisions for program entry or exit), and that involve the participation of beneficiaries in activities that can help address the source of the shock (for example, job-related activities) appear to be better suited than are CCTs to act as risk management instruments. Those characteristics tend to make workfare a better instrument in this regard. There is also plenty of empirical evidence on how workfare programs operate (for example, see Drèze and Sen 1991; Ravallion, Datt, and Chaudhuri 1993; Datt and Ravallion 1994; Ravallion and Datt 1995; Jalan and Ravallion 2003b).

Nevertheless, having a CCT in place clearly is better when there is a crisis than is not having any large-scale social assistance program at all. Several Latin American countries (including Chile, Ecuador, and Mexico) temporarily have increased the level of payments to CCT beneficiaries. These additional payments have been presented (or labeled) clearly as supplemental payments made on an exceptional basis. The intent behind this labeling is to give policy makers room to scale back payments to their precrisis levels in the future. Numerous programs also have accelerated the expansion in coverage they originally had planned for a longer period of time (World Bank 2008b).

CCT programs have a role to play in the context of a "permanent safety net" (as discussed in Ravallion 2009). Some experimentation with design features that make them more nimble in responding to sudden changes in aggregate economic circumstances may be useful. And some features of CCT programs—including the high technical quality of staff, the transparency in the processing of information, the absence of political interference, and an emphasis on monitoring and evaluation—could (and should) be replicated by other social assistance programs, including those whose primary goal is helping poor households cope with income volatility and risk. However, CCTs should continue to be policy tools whose main goals are reducing structural poverty and increasing investments in child human capital, especially where these investment levels are low.

America—the region where such programs have the longest tradition and the most established status—increasingly are emphasizing the importance of casting CCTs not as isolated poverty reduction programs (no matter how effective they may be), but as part of a broader system of social protection (World Bank 2008b).

What does it mean, in practice, for a CCT program to be part of a social protection system? The answer could vary significantly depending on the country. In particular, the broader social protection system is bound to take very different shapes in advanced, highly urbanized, middle-income countries with relatively well-developed institutions and in low-income countries with a large share of their population residing in rural areas and with relatively weak institutions.

That having been said, there are some common elements. First, as explored in some detail earlier in the chapter, the target population for a CCT program must be defined in a comprehensive way by considering the nature of poverty experienced by different groups and the availability of alternative instruments for income redistribution. Second, the specific design features of CCT programs must be compatible with the design features of other cash transfers (that is, the transfer size cannot be set in isolation but must be relative to other cash transfers) both to limit distortions and to ensure horizontal equity—if for no other reason than political sustainability.[17]

Third, it implies having clear and transparent eligibility rules and procedures for admission into the program in order to avoid confusion among potential beneficiaries and close the door to potential manipulation and abuse on the part of government officials and program administrators.

Entry and exit rules also are important in terms of their incentive effects, particularly those related to labor force participation. Until now, CCTs have used a proxy means rather than an income threshold to target benefits, and so the correspondence between program eligibility and labor supply is weaker than in many welfare programs in developed countries. However, the better a proxy means is at distinguishing "poor" from "nonpoor" households, the more highly it will be correlated with income and consumption—and the more likely it is to provide disincentives for adult labor market participation. Also, the roster of households eligible for transfers, based on the proxy means, is updated only infrequently in most countries, so recipient households have no incentive (other than the income effect, which would push them toward consuming more leisure) to reduce labor supply. However, many programs (including Oportunidades in Mexico, Familias en Acción in Colombia, and the BDH in Ecuador) have updated their proxy means or are in the process of doing so. Therefore it is possible that as CCT programs mature, any disincentive effects will become more apparent. Potential solutions to such effects include the use of time limits on benefits (as in Chile or under TANF in the United States), or the adoption of graduated benefits (where benefits are reduced only partially after recertification shows households have ceased to be eligible under the original criteria) to avoid "cliffs" and the associated negative incentives on labor supply.

Fourth, the potential administrative synergies across cash transfer programs are large. Using common systems for administrative targeting as well as systems to make payments to beneficiaries (for instance, by setting up an electronic card system) may be the most obvious example of such synergies. But more generally, as illustrated in chapter 3, setting up a common outreach and service platform (one-stop shops) through which beneficiaries of *all* social protection programs can access benefits and interact with program administrators is an innovation that several countries are either considering or experimenting with at present.

Although the challenges of inter-institutional coordination often are recognized in terms of the relationship between CCT programs and education and health ministries in charge of service delivery, it is equally important to recognize the challenges in terms of coordination among social protection programs. CCT programs are housed in and managed by a variety of agencies and ministries, depending on the countries in which they operate. It is often the case that other cash transfer programs are managed separately—for example, through ministries of labor or social security agencies. Making CCT programs part of a broader social protection system thus will require some coordination mechanism. Ministries of finance or planning can play and have played that role.

In many developing countries, however, subnational governments increasingly are playing an important part in social protection. Brazil, where CCT programs were local before they became national, is perhaps an extreme example. But in even smaller and nonfederal countries, subnational governments are a relevant actor not only in the implementation of CCT programs, but also by running their own social protection programs. That adds another complex dimension to the challenges of coordination. Challenges, however, often present opportunities for change and reform—a point we come back to below.

Conclusion

As noted in the introduction to this report, CCT programs have been seen in both extremely positive (a "magic bullet in development") and extremely negative ("superfluous, pernicious, atrocious, and abominable") terms.

Our review of the CCT experience so far confirms that they have been effective in reducing short-term poverty and increasing the use of education and health services. These achievements cannot and should not be dismissed or minimized because they represent powerful proof that well-designed public programs can have significant effects on critical social indicators.

At the same time, the review provides ample reasons to be cautious and to avoid transforming their obvious virtues into a blind advocacy campaign for CCT programs. The programs are not the right policy instrument for all poor households or in all circumstances. In particular, whether conditions are needed and what types of conditions are appropriate remain critical questions that countries planning to initiate a new or reform an existing CCT must consider seriously. The evidence on their impact on final outcomes in education and health is mixed. And it should be remembered that CCT programs typically will require a set of complementary actions, in terms of both other social protection programs and the adaptation of the supply of social services. Improving their impact on learning and health outcomes may require a combination of stronger services, a different set of conditions, and more decisive actions to target children at the right time in the life cycle. Deciding on when (or for whom) to have a CCT program, and how to design it, requires careful consideration of local conditions. Moreover, CCT programs run the risk of becoming less effective when their mandate is expanded to address challenges for which they may be less well suited.

Thanks to the extremely valuable efforts of policy makers and managers of CCT programs around the world to invest in data collection and include evaluation modules as a routine aspect of program management, we now have more rigorous evidence on CCTs than on practically any other development program. As noted throughout the report, however, many important questions regarding the design of CCT programs remain unanswered and require further research.

From the point of view of the generation of global public goods, the returns to additional evaluations of relatively standard CCTs are likely to be small (even if these evaluations help build the evidence base for specific countries, and perhaps help build political support). However, there are three broad areas where additional research would be extremely valuable.

The first of those research areas is unpackaging the overall CCT impact. How important are the magnitude of the transfer, the gender of the recipient, the choice of conditions, and the degree to which conditions are monitored and households penalized for noncompliance? For what outcomes do these choices matter most? Answering those questions is important for program design, and will help governments make CCT programs more efficient in the future.

The second critical research area involves the interactions between CCTs and other programs. Are CCT effects on health and education outcomes larger when they come hand-in-hand with efforts to improve the quality of the supply? Is the sum of the effects larger than the sum of the parts (which would suggest that there are important synergies)? Are there particular programs that target households, such as parenting interventions, amenable to being combined with CCTs? Under what circumstances would those programs work? The answers to all of those questions are critical to understanding how best to coordinate CCT programs with other investments.

The third area where further research is important relates to the impact of CCTs in very different settings or on outcomes that have not yet been studied. Although there is some encouraging evidence of the impact of CCTs in low-income countries, including Bangladesh, Cambodia, and Nicaragua, the bulk of the evidence on CCTs comes from the middle-income countries in Latin America. There would be high returns to evaluations of CCT-like programs in sub-Saharan Africa where institutional capacity may be weaker, poverty is more widespread, and human capital deficits are deeper. It also is important to assess whether the CCTs currently in place have impacts on outcomes about which we know little or nothing—for example, long-term poverty, or interactions with the formal banking sector in the middle-income countries of Latin America—and to assess whether CCTs are useful tools for improving outcomes in other settings—for example, if they can be used to prevent HIV infection in Africa. All of those questions will require experimentation and careful evaluation. Many also involve following households for longer time horizons than traditionally has been the case in standard CCT and other program evaluations, which itself poses important methodological challenges.

In concluding, it is important to recognize that the multidimensionality of a CCT program is a source of both strength and complexity. CCT programs cannot and should not be seen as only education or health interventions. After all, they are cash transfers and should be considered and analyzed as social protection interventions. In that sense, experience indicates that CCT programs have been very successful in reforming social assistance policies by replacing badly targeted and ineffective subsidies and in creating the political conditions for expanding income support to the poor. Moreover, where they have been implemented, CCT programs have brought an enhanced attention to the behavioral consequences of social policies. That, by itself, is important.

Experience so far suggests that CCT programs also have had positive institutional externalities. Most notably, through their emphasis on monitoring and evaluation they are helping strengthen a results culture within the public sector—at least within social policies. The emphasis on monitoring and evaluation appears to have transcended international borders, and new CCT programs have emulated older, more established ones in this important regard—clearly a legacy worth sustaining.

Equally important are the potential institutional externalities affecting health and education systems. Supporting human capital accumulation among children from poor households cannot be addressed solely by a CCT program. Clearly, a supply of health and education services of adequate quality must be developed. Thus it is important to consider the question of whether these tasks should be tackled sequentially or must be solved all at once. Particularly in countries or regions where the supply of such services is insufficient or of low quality, policy makers must consider such questions with care. Cash transfers may be the right policy instrument to alleviate poverty in the short run, but their contribution to longer-term poverty reduction also will depend on what happens on the supply side.

That question is closely associated with the debates in development economics concerning the tension between balanced and unbalanced growth.[18] As Albert Hirschman (1958) argued, development is a "chain of disequilibria" whereby the expansion of one sector creates backward or forward pressures and *can* thus provide the necessary stimulus for the expansion of another sector that is yet underdeveloped. Such links operate not only through the standard motivation for profit, but also by building political pressure for government action. Seen from that perspective, by increasing poor households' demand for human capital, CCT programs have the potential to unleash a broader process of transformation in the development of adequate-quality health and education services to which children from poor households have access. Whether such a process materializes depends on how permeable the political system is to such pressures. Responses on the supply side can take many different forms, including through the development of an enabling environment for the expansion of service provision by the private sector. But those responses are likely to be thwarted unless there is some political receptivity to the demand-side pressures. As Hirschman (1990) argued, "getting stuck" is the risk of a sequential approach, particularly when "a one thing at a time" approach operates as an excuse for political paralysis on other, equally important fronts.

We cannot tell at this time whether the current wave of CCT programs will be successful in unleashing a sustainable transformation in both the provision of health and education services and the broader design of social protection policies we discussed above. Although it may be too early to tell, the experience so far provides room for hope.

Summary Tables

Country Programs (by region)

Sub-Saharan Africa

Burkina Faso	Orphans and Vulnerable Children
Kenya	Cash Transfer for Orphans and Vulnerable Children
Nigeria	Care of the Poor

East Asia and Pacific

Cambodia	Cambodia Education Sector Support Project; Japan Fund for Poverty Reduction Girls Scholarship Program
Indonesia	Jaring Pengamanan Sosial; Program Keluarga Harapan
Philippines	Pantawid Pamilyang Pilipino Program

Europe and Central Asia

Turkey	Social Risk Mitigation Project

Latin America and Caribbean

Argentina	Programa Familias
Bolivia	Juancito Pinto
Brazil	Bolsa Alimentação; Bolsa Escola; Bolsa Família; Programa de Eradicacão do Trabalho Infantil
Chile	Chile Solidario; Subsidio Unitario Familiar
Colombia	Familias en Acción; Subsidio Condicionado a la Asistencia Escolar–Bogotá
Dominican Republic	Solidaridad; Tarjeta de Asistencia Escolar
Ecuador	Bono de Desarrollo Humano
El Salvador	Red Solidaria
Guatemala	Mi Familia Progresa
Honduras	Programa de Asignación Familiar
Jamaica	Program of Advancement through Health and Education
Mexico	Oportunidades (formerly PROGRESA)
Nicaragua	Atención a Crisis; Red de Protección Social
Panama	Red de Oportunidades
Paraguay	Tekoporã/PROPAIS II
Peru	Juntos

Middle East and North Africa

Yemen, Republic of	Basic Education Development Project

South Asia

Bangladesh	Female Secondary School Assistance Program; Primary Education Stipend Program; Reaching Out-of-School Children
India	Apni Beti Apna Dhan
Pakistan	Child Support Program; Participation in Education through Innovative Scheme for the Excluded Vulnerable; Punjab Education Sector Reform Program/Punjab Female School Stipend Program

		Categorical	Household identification		
Region/Country/Program	Geographic	Other	Proxy means test	Means test	Community assessment
Africa					
Burkina Faso: Orphans and Vulnerable Children[a]	x		x		
Kenya: CT-OVC[a]	x	Orphan and vulnerable children incidence			x
Nigeria: COPE			x		x
East Asia and Pacific					
Cambodia: CESSP	x	Gender and ethnic minority	x		
Cambodia: JFPR	x	Gender			x
Indonesia: JPS	x[b]	Gender[c]			x
Indonesia: PKH	x		x		
Philippines: 4Ps	x		x		
Europe and Central Asia					
Turkey: SRMP			x		
Latin America and the Caribbean					
Argentina: Programa Familias	x	Beneficiaries of Jefes y Jefas program, with two or more children, head has not completed secondary school[d]			
Bolivia: Juancito Pinto		x[e]			
Brazil: Bolsa Alimentação	x			x	
Brazil: Bolsa Escola	x			x	
Brazil: Bolsa Família	x			x	
Brazil: PETI	x			x	
Chile: Chile Solidario			x		
Chile: SUF		Not part of social security system	x		
Colombia: Familias en Acción	x		x		
Colombia: SCAE-Bogotá			x		
Dominican Republic: Solidaridad	x		x		
Dominican Republic: TAE/ILAE	x				x
Ecuador: BDH			x		
El Salvador: Red Solidaria	x		x[f]		
Guatemala: Mi Familia Progresa	x		x		
Honduras: PRAF	x		x[g]		

Region/Country/Program	Categorical		Household identification		
	Geographic	Other	Proxy means test	Means test	Community assessment
Jamaica: PATH			x		
Mexico: Oportunidades	x		x		
Nicaragua: Atención a Crisis[a]	x		x		
Nicaragua: RPS	x		x		
Panama: Red de Oportunidades	x		x		
Paraguay: Tekoporã/PROPAIS II[h]	x		x		
Peru: Juntos	x				x
Middle East and North Africa					
Yemen, Republic of: BEDP[a]	x	Gender			
South Asia					
Bangladesh: FSSAP	x	Gender			
Bangladesh: PESP	x[i]				x
Bangladesh: ROSC	x				x
India (Haryana): Apni Beti Apna Dhan	x	Gender	x		
Pakistan: CSP[a]		Beneficiary of food support program	x		
Pakistan: Participation in Education through Innovative Scheme for the Excluded Vulnerable	x				x
Pakistan: PESRP/Punjab Female School Stipend Program	x	Gender			

Source: Program profiles.

Note: BDH = Bono de Desarrollo Humano; BEDP = Basic Education Development Project; CESSP = Cambodia Education Sector Support Project; COPE = Care of the Poor; CSP = Child Support Program; CT-OVC = Cash Transfer for Orphans and Vulnerable Children; 4Ps = Pantawid Pamilyang Pilipino Program; FSSAP = Female Secondary School Assistance Program; JFPR = Japan Fund for Poverty Reduction Girls Scholarship Program; JPS = Jaring Pengamanan Sosial; PATH = Program of Advancement through Health and Education; PESP = Primary Education Stipend Program; PESRP = Punjab Education Sector Reform Program; PETI = Programa de Erradicação do Trabalho Infantil; PKH = Program Keluarga Harapan; PRAF = Programa de Asignación Familiar; ROSC = Reaching Out-of-School Children; RPS = Red de Protección Social; SCAE = Subsidio Condicionado a la Asistencia Escolar; SRMP = Social Risk Mitigation Project; SUF = Subsidio Unitario Familiar; TAE/ILAE = Tarjeta de Asistencia Escolar/Incentivo a la Asistencia Escolar.

a. Program at the pilot stage.

b. Is at both the national level (to identify the poorer districts) and the district level (to identify the poorer subdistricts/schools).

c. At least half of the scholarships at school level were to be allocated to girls.

d. The Jefes y Jefas program started in the crisis as a workfare program for unemployed heads of household.

e. Covers all children in public schools up to fourth grade.

f. Targeting is only in the 68 less-poor municipalities. Targeting in the poorest 32 municipalities is geographic only.

g. Only households in the area covered by the Inter-American Development Bank project may participate.

h. PROPAIS II is a project financed by the Inter-American Development Bank, that builds on the Tekoporã program and finances additional beneficiaries using similar procedures.

i. Only certain types of schools in rural areas may participate.

Table A.2 Targeting Structure in CCT Programs

Region/Country/Program	Household income	Household structure			Age/grade of children	Gender	Length of time in program
		Number of children	Cap	Other household members			
Africa							
Burkina Faso: Orphans and Vulnerable Children[a]		x			x		
Kenya: CT-OVC[a]		x					
Nigeria: COPE		x					x
East Asia and Pacific							
Cambodia: CESSP	x[b]		No				
Cambodia: JFPR			No			x	
Indonesia: JPS		x	No		x		
Indonesia: PKH		x	Yes	x	x		
Philippines: 4Ps	x	x	Max = 3[c]		x		x
Europe and Central Asia							
Turkey: SRMP		x	Yes[d]	x[e]	x	x	
Latin America and the Caribbean							
Argentina: Programa Familias		x	Max = 6				
Bolivia: Juancito Pinto	x[f]		No				
Brazil: Bolsa Alimentação		x	Max = 3	x[g]			
Brazil: Bolsa Escola		x	Max = 3				
Brazil: Bolsa Família	x[h]	x	Max = 3		x		
Brazil: PETI		x	Yes[i]				
Chile: Chile Solidario							x
Chile: SUF[j]		x					
Colombia: Familias en Acción		x			x[k]		
Colombia: SCAE-Bogotá		x	No				
Dominican Republic: Solidaridad		x	Yes[l]				

Region/Country/Program	Household income	Basis of benefit variation					
		Household structure			Age/grade of children	Gender	Length of time in program
		Number of children	Cap	Other household members			
Dominican Republic: TAE/ILAE[m]							
Ecuador: BDH				x[n]			
El Salvador: Red Solidaria					x[o]		
Guatemala: Mi Familia Progresa					x		
Honduras: PRAF		x	x[p]	x[q]	x		
Jamaica: PATH		x	Max = 20	x[r]	x[s]	x	
Mexico: Oportunidades		x	Yes	x	x	x	x
Nicaragua: Atención a Crisis[a]		x[t]					
Nicaragua: RPS		x[u]			x		
Panama: Red de Oportunidades[v]					x		
Paraguay: Tekoporã/PROPAIS II		x	Max = 4	x			
Peru: Juntos[w]							
Middle East and North Africa							
Yemen, Republic of: BEDP[a]			Max = 3		x	x	
South Asia							
Bangladesh: FSSAP		x	No		x[x]		
Bangladesh: PESP		x	Yes[y]				
Bangladesh: ROSC		x			x		
India (Haryana): Apni Beti Apna Dhan		x	Max = 3				x
Pakistan: CSP[a]		x	Yes[z]				
Pakistan: Participation in Education through Innovative Scheme for the Excluded Vulnerable		x	No				
Pakistan: PESRP/Punjab Female School Stipend Program		x					

Source: Program profiles.

Note: BDH = Bono de Desarrollo Humano; BEDP = Basic Education Development Project; CESSP = Cambodia Education Sector Support Project; COPE = Care of the Poor; CSP = Child Support Program; CT-OVC = Cash Transfer for Orphans and Vulnerable Children; 4Ps = Pantawid Pamilyang Pilipino Program; FSSAP = Female Secondary School Assistance Program; JFPR = Japan Fund for Poverty Reduction Girls Scholarship Program; JPS = Jaring Pengamanan Sosial; max = maximum; PATH = Program of Advancement through Health and Education; PESP = Primary Education Stipend Program; PESRP = Punjab Education Sector Reform Program; PETI = Programa de Erradicação do Trabalho Infantil; PKH = Program Keluarga Harapan; PRAF = Programa de Asignación Familiar; ROSC = Reaching Out-of-School Children; RPS = Red de Protección Social; SCAE = Subsidio Condicionado a la Asistencia Escolar; SRMP = Social Risk Mitigation Project; SUF = Subsidio Unitario Familiar; TAE/ILAE = Tarjeta de Asistencia Escolar/Incentivo a la Asistencia Escolar.

a. Program at the pilot stage.

b. Children with the highest poverty ranking in each local management committee will receive the higher amount of the scholarship.

c. Cap applies only to education grant.

d. The health support part of the transfer is a flat benefit independent of the number of eligible children in the household. The education support part of the transfer is paid per eligible child.

e. Health benefit for pregnant and lactating women, as well as additional payment for delivery in a health clinic.

f. Benefit was per child for all children in public schools up to fifth grade in 2006 and sixth grade in 2007.

g. Pregnant or lactating women in the household also are eligible.

h. If the household's monthly per capita income is below R$60, the household receives a flat benefit as well as a variable benefit that depends on the number of eligible children in the household; if income is between R$61 and R$120, the household receives only the variable benefit.

i. Varies across states.

j. If there are two qualifying children, the mother would get two SUF benefits. Subsidy to mother also is paid where the mother is qualified.

k. Benefit varies both with grade/age of children attending school (different amounts for primary and secondary school) and with the age of other minors in the household (because of the nutrition subsidy paid for minors aged 0–7 years). There is no limit on the number of beneficiaries. Benefit also varies by location because it is different in large urban areas where they are pilot-testing different structures of subsidies for secondary school and eliminating the subsidy for primary education in some cities. For those locations, the program also extends the nutrition subsidy to older children in some cases to avoid "dropping" the family if the only subsidy it would have received is for primary school attendance.

l. There is a flat benefit for the "Comer es Primero" component; and an education benefit that ranges from $9 for one to two children, to $14 for three children, to $19 for four or more children.

m. Transfers were independent of the size of the household.

n. There is a flat benefit, but different amounts if the head of household is disabled or elderly.

o. There is a flat benefit for both education and health ($15); there is a different amount if the household has children whose ages qualify them for both benefits ($20).

p. Health incentive has a maximum of two children; education incentive has a maximum of three children.

q. There is an additional payment for delivery in a public facility.

r. Starting October 1, 2008, a new benefit scheme took effect. Benefits for secondary grades were increased by 50 percent, relative to the base benefit level; and benefits for upper-secondary grades were increased by 75 percent. PATH students who complete high school and move to a tertiary institution receive a one-off bonus of J$15,000 to assist with that transition.

s. Starting October 2008, boys receive a benefit that is 10 percent higher than the benefit that girls receive at their respective grade.

t. In addition to the traditional CCT component, this pilot program also included an occupational training component and a business grant component. Those components were allocated randomly across eligible households. In the program's final design, beneficiary households were allocated one of the following three interventions: (1) CCT component, (2) CCT plus occupational training, or (3) CCT plus a business grant component.

u. Only the school material support payment and teacher incentive are paid per child; the rest of the benefit is paid per household. The benefits are for children aged 7–13 who have not completed the fourth grade of primary school. The second phase of the RPS varied slightly in terms of benefit amounts and structure.

v. This is a flat benefit.

w. This is a flat benefit.

x. Both the stipend paid to the beneficiary and the tuition paid directly to the school by the program are increasing for each grade of the five years of secondary school.

y. Tk 100 per household per month, Tk 125 per household each month if there is more than one student in the household.

z. Each beneficiary family is entitled to receive PRs 200 a month for one child and PRs 350 a month if there are two or more children in the family.

Table A.3 Payment Schedules

Region/Country/Program	Payee	Frequency of payments	Payment system
Africa			
Burkina Faso: Orphans and Vulnerable Children[a]	Parent/guardian	Quarterly	Through the village committee against HIV/AIDS
Kenya: CT-OVC[a]	Parent/guardian	Bimonthly	In 30 of the 37 districts, through the existing government structure via district treasuries; in the remaining 7 districts, through post offices[b]
Nigeria: COPE	Mother and designated household member	Monthly	Through microfinance agencies and local community banks
East Asia and Pacific			
Cambodia: CESSP	Parent/guardian	Three installments[c]	Cash handed out at ceremonies in the school
Cambodia: JFPR	Parent/guardian	Three installments	Cash handed out at ceremonies in the school
Indonesia: JPS	Directly to the students (or their families)	Monthly	Cash paid through local post offices[d]
Indonesia: PKH	Mother or woman who takes care of the children in family	Quarterly	Cash paid through local post offices
Philippines: 4Ps	Mother	Monthly	Land Bank of the Philippines
Europe and Central Asia			
Turkey: SRMP	Mother	Bimonthly[e]	Through a banking institution; where the bank has no branches, through the postal service
Latin America and the Caribbean			
Argentina: Programa Familias	Mother	Monthly	Through debit cards with the Banco de la Nacion Argentina
Bolivia: Juancito Pinto	Child (accompanied by parent or guardian)	Annually	Army distributes cash payments at school sites
Brazil: Bolsa Alimentação	Mother	Monthly	Transfers were credited to a magnetic card that could be used to withdraw cash at offices of a federally owned bank; in very isolated municipalities, at lottery agents or shops

continued

Table A.3 continued

Region/Country/Program	Payee	Frequency of payments	Payment system
Brazil: Bolsa Escola	Mother	Monthly	Transfers credited to a magnetic card that could be used to withdraw cash at offices of a federally owned bank; in very isolated municipalities, at lottery agents or shops
Brazil: Bolsa Família	Mother	Monthly	Transfers credited to a debit card distributed to beneficiaries
Brazil: PETI	Mother	Monthly	Deposited into a beneficiary's bank account
Chile: Chile Solidario	Mother	Monthly	Through National Social Security Institute service centers or payment points
Chile: SUF	Mother	Monthly	Through National Social Security Institute service centers or payment points
Colombia: Familias en Acción	Mother	Bimonthly	Through the banking system
Colombia: SCAE-Bogotá	Student	Bimonthly[f]	Through beneficiary's bank account with associated debit card
Dominican Republic: Solidaridad	Head of household	Bimonthly[g]	Through debit cards that can be used only in certain stores for certain products (food and education supplies)
Dominican Republic: TAE/ILAE	Mother	Bimonthly	By checks distributed through the schools
Ecuador: BDH	Women	Monthly	Collected at any branch office from the largest network of private banks (Banred) or from the National Agricultural Bank
El Salvador: Red Solidaria	Mother	Bimonthly	In cash at payment posts; payments are outsourced to a commercial bank
Guatemala: Mi Familia Progresa	Mother	Bimonthly	Through a government-owned bank (BanRural)
Honduras: PRAF	Mother	Every six months	Vouchers cashed at branch offices of BANHCAFE
Jamaica: PATH	Family representative or his/her agent	Bimonthly	Checks disbursed through post offices; prepaid cash cards
Mexico: Oportunidades	Mother	Bimonthly	Cash at payment points and payments through beneficiary's savings account with BANSEFI
Nicaragua: Atención a Crisis[a]	Child's caregiver	Bimonthly	Cash at payment points
Nicaragua: RPS	Child's caregiver	Bimonthly	Cash at payment points
Panama: Red de Oportunidades	Mother	Bimonthly	At post offices and commercial banks
Paraguay: Tekoporã/PROPAIS II	Mother	Bimonthly	Mobile cashier
Peru: Juntos	Mother	Monthly	Through beneficiary's bank account at the Banco de la Nacion and associated debit card

Region/Country/Program	Payee	Frequency of payments	Payment system
Middle East and North Africa			
Yemen, Republic of: BEDP[a]	Mother for some schools; father in others	Quarterly	Cash handed out at parent meetings in school
South Asia			
Bangladesh: FSSAP	Female student	Twice yearly	Through direct deposit to a bank account in the girl's name
Bangladesh: PESP	Beneficiary's guardian	Quarterly	By direct transfer to beneficiary's bank account
Bangladesh: ROSC	Mother/guardian	Twice yearly[h]	By direct transfer to beneficiary's bank account
India (Haryana): Apni Beti Apna Dhan	Girls	Once	Savings bond that matures when beneficiary turns 18 years of age
Pakistan: CSP[a]	Parent/guardian	Quarterly	At post offices
Pakistan: Participation in Education through Innovative Scheme for the Excluded Vulnerable	Student's household	Quarterly	Direct transfer via postal money order
Pakistan: PESRP/Punjab Female School Stipend Program	Student's household	Quarterly	Through direct transfer via postal money order from the education district office

Source: Program profiles.

Note: BANHCAFE = Banco Hondureño del Café; BANSEFI = Banco del Ahorro Nacional y Servicios Financieros; BDH = Bono de Desarrollo Humano; BEDP = Basic Education Development Project; CESSP = Cambodia Education Sector Support Project; COPE = Care of the Poor; CSP = Child Support Program; CT-OVC = Cash Transfer for Orphans and Vulnerable Children; 4Ps = Pantawid Pamilyang Pilipino Program; FSSAP = Female Secondary School Assistance Program; JFPR = Japan Fund for Poverty Reduction Girls Scholarship Program; JPS = Jaring Pengamanan Sosial; PATH = Program of Advancement through Health and Education; PESP = Primary Education Stipend Program; PESRP = Punjab Education Sector Reform Program; PETI = Programa de Erradicação do Trabalho Infantil; PKH = Program Keluarga Harapan; PRAF = Programa de Asignación Familiar; ROSC = Reaching Out-of-School Children; RPS = Red de Protección Social; SCAE = Subsidio Condicionado a la Asistencia Escolar; SRMP = Social Risk Mitigation Project; SUF = Subsidio Unitario Familiar; TAE/ILAE = Tarjeta de Asistencia Escolar/Incentivo a la Asistencia Escolar.

a. Program at the pilot stage.

b. Other payment modalities will be tested and evaluated in the upcoming second phase of the program.

c. October, January, and April.

d. This later changed to the schools collecting the funds directly "on behalf of the parents."

e. Bimonthly for the education grant, monthly for the pregnancy grant, one-time grant for birth at a clinic.

f. The pilot program comprises three types of interventions with different payment schedules: (1) bimonthly payments; (2) bimonthly payments of a partial benefit, the rest being accumulated and made available at the beginning of the school year (December); and (3) bimonthly payments, an additional payment being made upon graduation and enrollment in higher education.

g. The Comer es Primero component is paid monthly, and the ILAE component is paid bimonthly.

h. March/April and September/October.

Table A.4 CCT Programs at a Glance

Region/Country	Program	Evaluation
Africa		
Burkina Faso	Orphans and Vulnerable Children[a]	
Kenya	CT-OVC[a]	
Nigeria	COPE	
East Asia and Pacific		
Cambodia	CESSP	x
	JFPR Girls Scholarship Program	x
Indonesia	JPS	x
	PKH[a]	
Philippines	4Ps	
Europe and Central Asia		
Turkey	SRMP	x
Latin America and the Caribbean		
Argentina	Programa Familias	
Bolivia	Juancito Pinto	
Brazil	Bolsa Alimentação	x
	Bolsa Escola	x
	Bolsa Familia	x
	PETI	x
Chile	Chile Solidario	x
	SUF	
Colombia	Familias en Acción	x
	SCAE-Bogotá[a]	x
Dominican Republic	Solidaridad	
	ILAE (formerly TAE)	
Ecuador	BDH	x
El Salvador	Red Solidaria	
Guatemala	Mi Familia Progresa	
Honduras	PRAF	x

Region/Country	Program	Evaluation
Jamaica	PATH	x
Mexico	Oportunidades (formerly PROGRESA)	x
Nicaragua	Atención a Crisis	
	RPS	x
Panama	Red de Oportunidades	
Paraguay	Tekoporã/PROPAIS II	
Peru	Juntos	
Middle East and North Africa		
Yemen, Republic of	BEDP[a]	
South Asia		
Bangladesh	FSSAP	x
	PESP	
	ROSC	x
India (Haryana)	Apni Beti Apna Dhan (Our Daughter, Our Wealth)	
Pakistan	CSP[a]	
	Participation in Education through Innovative Scheme for the Excluded Vulnerable	
	PESRP/Punjab Female School Stipend Program	x

Source: Program profiles.

Note: BDH = Bono de Desarrollo Humano; BEDP = Basic Education Development Project; CESSP = Cambodia Education Sector Support Project; COPE = Care of the Poor; CSP = Child Support Program; CT-OVC = Cash Transfer for Orphans and Vulnerable Children; 4Ps = Pantawid Pamilyang Pilipino Program; FSSAP = Female Secondary School Assistance Program; JFPR = Japan Fund for Poverty Reduction Girls Scholarship Program; JPS = Jaring Pengamanan Sosial; PATH = Program of Advancement through Health and Education; PESP = Primary Education Stipend Program; PESRP = Punjab Education Sector Reform Program; PETI = Programa de Erradicação do Trabalho Infantil; PKH = Program Keluarga Harapan; PRAF = Programa de Asignación Familiar; ROSC = Reaching Out-of-School Children; RPS = Red de Protección Social; SCAE = Subsidio Condicionado a la Asistencia Escolar; SRMP = Social Risk Mitigation Project; SUF = Subsidio Unitario Familiar; TAE/ILAE = Tarjeta de Asistencia Escolar/Incentivo a la Asistencia Escolar.

a. Program at the pilot stage.

Burkina Faso

Program: Orphans and Vulnerable Children

Year started	2008 (October)
Status	Active

Targeting

Target population	Poor households of OVC with HIV/AIDS in villages of the Nahouri region; the program in the Sanmatenga Province has not yet been launched
Targeting method	Geographic targeting and proxy means testing
Coverage	3,250 households
Incidence	Not available

Household Benefits

Benefit structure	• Children aged 0–6: CFAF 1,000/quarter or CFAF 4,000/year • Children aged 7–10: CFAF 2,000/quarter or CFAF 8,000/year • Children aged 11–15: CFAF 4,000/quarter or CFAF 16,000/year • In villages with CCTs, payments are made as described below under "conditions." In villages with UCTs, payments are made without conditions.
Payee	Parent/guardian
Payment method	Through the village committee against HIV/AIDS
Payment frequency	Quarterly
Duration	2 years
Additional benefits	Health and education

Conditions

Health	Children aged 0–6 regularly attend a health center; this is confirmed by a health care provider
Education	At least 90% school attendance in a 3-month cycle
Other	None
Verification of compliance–method	Beneficiaries receive forms/booklets on which their compliance with conditions is confirmed by health and education service providers; beneficiaries provide these forms to the local program office on a regular basis
Verification of compliance–frequency	Quarterly
Compliance statistics	Not yet recorded

Program Administration

Institutional arrangement	Le Conseil national de lutte contre le VIH/SIDA et les IST
Program costs	Budget: $1.4 million (program and impact evaluation)

Source: World Development Indicators database 2008.
Note: OVC = orphans and vulnerable children; PPP = purchasing power parity.

General

Population (total)	14.8 million (2006)
GDP per capita (PPP, 2006 $)	$1,120 (2007)
Poverty headcount ratio at $2/day	Not available

Education

Net enrollment in primary level	47.8% total (2006) 42.9% for girls, 52.5% for boys
Net enrollment in secondary level	12% total (2006) 10% for girls, 14% for boys

Health

Prevalence of child malnutrition (stunting)	35% (2006)
Births attended by skilled health staff	53.5% (2006)

Kenya

Program: Cash Transfer for Orphans and Vulnerable Children

Year started	2004
Status	Active

Targeting

Target population	Poor households fostering OVC aged 0–17
Targeting method	Geographic targeting and community assessment
Coverage	12,500 OVC in 37 districts (the program aims to target 100,000 households at full scale, reaching an estimated 300,000 OVC)
Incidence	Not available

Household Benefits

Benefit structure	K Sh 1,000 ($13.70) for 1–2 OVC, K Sh 2,000 ($20.50) for 3–4 OVC, and K Sh 3,000 ($27.40) for 5 or more OVC aged 0–17
Payee	Parent/guardian
Payment method	Through district treasuries and post offices[a]
Payment frequency	Bimonthly
Duration	As long as eligible, or maximum of 5 years in the program
Additional benefits	Referral to other programs for anti-retroviral treatment for beneficiaries who voluntarily declared themselves to be HIV/AIDS positive[b]

Conditions

Health	• Health facility visits for immunizations for children aged 0–1 six times per year • Health facility visits for growth monitoring and vitamin A supplement for children aged 1–5 twice a year
Education	• School attendance of at least 80% at basic school institutions for children aged 6–17 • Attendance at awareness sessions for adult members once a year
Other	None
Verification of compliance–method	• District children's office provides forms to the health and education service providers responsible for recording attendance of beneficiary children • Volunteer children's officers collect forms and deliver them to the district children's office where the information is entered into the management information system
Verification of compliance–frequency	• Every 2 months for children aged 0–1 • Every 6 months for children aged 1–5 • Every 2 months for children aged 6–17 • Every 12 months for adult awareness sessions
Compliance statistics	Not available

Program Administration

Institutional arrangement	Department of Children's Services in the Ministry of Home Affairs
Program costs	• Total cost: $2.2 million, reaching 3,000 households (FY2006). Full-scale program is estimated to cost $31.6 million, reaching 100,000 households (FY2011).
	• Administrative costs[c] (as percent of transfers): 183.5% (FY2006). At full scale, the administrative costs are estimated to decrease to 13.9%.

Sources: Government of Kenya 2006b, 2007; Pearson and Alviar 2006; country context: *World Development Indicators* database 2008.

Note: OVC = orphans and vulnerable children; PPP = purchasing power parity.

a. Other payment modalities are under discussion as program is being scaled up.

b. The link with these programs is still under discussion.

c. The administrative costs do not include costs of design, targeting, enrollment, and capacity building.

Country Context

General

Population (total)	36.5 million (2006)
GDP per capita (PPP, 2005 $)	$1,421 (2006)
Poverty headcount ratio at $2/day	58.3% (1997)

Education

Net enrollment in primary level	75.8% total (2005) 76.1% for girls, 75.5% for boys
Net enrollment in secondary level	41.5% total (2005) 41.8% for girls, 41.3% for boys

Health

Prevalence of child malnutrition (stunting)	35.8% (2003)
Births attended by skilled health staff	41.6% (2003)

Nigeria

Program: Care of the Poor

Year started	2008
Status	Active

Targeting

Target population	• Female-headed households • Aged parent–headed households • Physically challenged people–headed households (for example, leprosy patients) • Transient-poor–headed households (for example, seasonal farmers) • VVF (Vesico vaginal fistula) patients, HIV-affected households
Targeting method	Community targeting with proxy means testing
Coverage	3,000 households each in 12 pilot states by end of 2009
Incidence	

Household Benefits

Benefit structure	Cash transfer (the Basic Income Guarantee) based on number of children per household: 1 child, ₦1,500; 2–3 children, ₦3,000; 4 or more children, ₦5,000. A compulsory saving of ₦7,000 monthly in favor of the participants to be disbursed as a lump sum after a year for the establishment of viable microenterprises after undergoing training.
Payee	Mother and designated household member
Payment method	Through microfinance agencies and local community banks
Payment frequency	Monthly
Duration	As long as eligible
Additional benefits	None

Conditions

Health	Pregnant women within benefiting households must attend and show evidence of antenatal care.
Education	Beneficiaries must ensure school enrolment of school-age children up to basic education level (that is, primary to junior secondary education). At least 80% monthly school attendance is necessary to access transfer.
Other	Trainable member of the benefiting household must attend training in life and vocational skills, basic health, and sanitation as available to the community.
Verification of compliance–method	Beneficiaries receive forms on which their compliance with conditions is confirmed by health and education service providers; they provide these forms to the local program office on a regular basis.
Verification of compliance–frequency	Monthly
Compliance statistics	Not available

Program Administration

Institutional arrangement	National Poverty Eradication Program office at federal and state levels; state agencies for CCT, local government office
Program costs	Not available

Sources: Bank staff and *World Development Indicators* database 2008.
Note: PPP = purchasing power parity.

Country Context

General	
Population (total)	148 million (2007)
GDP per capita (PPP, 2005 $)	$1,731
Poverty headcount ratio at $2/day	54.4% (2004)
Education	
Net enrollment in primary level	63% total (2006) 58% for girls, 68% for boys
Net enrollment in secondary level	Not available
Health	
Prevalence of child malnutrition (stunting)	27% (2003)
Births attended by skilled health staff	36% (2003)

Cambodia

Program: Cambodia Education Sector Support Project

Year started	2005
Status	Ongoing

Targeting

Target population	Children who have completed grade 6
Targeting method	Geographic targeting of schools, then "scoring" of application forms in each school by the LMCs
Coverage	100 secondary schools located in the poorest communes across the country, with each small school (less than 200 students) receiving 30 new scholarships a year, and each large school (more than 200 students) receiving 50 new scholarships a year; about 3,850 new scholarship recipients in each year, in approximately 14% of lower-secondary schools
Incidence	32% to the poorest quintile

Household Benefits

Benefit structure	"Poorest" (according to the proxy means score) half of the scholarship students within each school receive a scholarship of $60; the less-poor half receive $45.
Payee	Parent/guardian (usually mother)
Payment method	Cash handed out at ceremonies in the school
Payment frequency	3 installments
Duration	3 years of lower-secondary school

Conditions

Health	None
Education	• Enrollment in school • Regular school attendance (no more than 10 days of absence in a year without "good reason") • Maintaining a passing grade
Other	Agreement to use scholarship funds toward education (not verified)
Verification of compliance–method	School monitors enrollment, attendance, and grade progression; provides information to the LMCs as needed
Verification of compliance–frequency	• Attendance: ongoing • Progression: at end of school year
Compliance statistics	Not available

Program Administration

Institutional arrangement	Directorate General of Education at the central level; LMCs located at school level, supported by the provincial and district education offices
Program costs	Overall budget: $5 million over 5 years

Sources: Royal Government of Cambodia 2005; country context: *World Development Indicators* database 2008.
Note: LMC = local management committee; PPP = purchasing power parity.

Country Context

General	
Population (total)	14.19 million (2006)
GDP per capita (PPP, 2005 $)	$1,569 (2006)
Poverty headcount ratio at $2/day	77.7% (1997)

Education	
Net enrollment in primary level	89.9% total (2006) 89.0% for girls, 90.9% for boys
Net enrollment in secondary level	23.9% total (2005) 21.9% for girls, 26.0% for boys

Health	
Prevalence of child malnutrition (stunting)	43.7% (2006)
Births attended by skilled health staff	43.8% (2005)

Cambodia

Program: Japan Fund for Poverty Reduction Girls Scholarship Program

Year started	2002
Status	Closed (but continued in modified form under CESSP)

Targeting

Target population	Girls starting grade 7
Targeting method	Geographic targeting of schools, then "scoring" of application forms in each school by the LMCs, with additional subjective assessment by LMCs
Coverage	93 secondary schools located in the poorest communes across the country, with each school receiving 45 scholarships for poor girls to go into grade 7 (that is about 4,185 girls and 15% of lower-secondary schools)
Incidence	

Household Benefits

Benefit structure	Flat benefit of $45/girl
Payee	Parent/guardian (usually mother)
Payment method	Cash handed out at ceremonies in the school
Payment frequency	3 installments
Duration	3 years of lower-secondary school

Conditions

Health	None
Education	• Enrollment in school • Regular school attendance (no more than 10 days of absence in a year without "good reason") • Maintaining a passing grade
Other	Agreement to use scholarship funds toward education (not verified)
Verification of compliance–method	School monitors enrollment, attendance, and grade progression; provides information to the LMCs as needed
Verification of compliance–frequency	• Attendance: ongoing • Progression: at end of school year
Compliance statistics	Not available

Program Administration

Institutional arrangement	Directorate General of Education at the central level; LMCs located at school level, supported by the provincial and district education offices
Program costs	Overall budget: $3 million over 3 years

Sources: Collins 2006; Filmer and Schady 2006; country context: *World Development Indicators* database 2008.
Note: CESSP = Cambodia Education Sector Support Project; LMC = local management committee; PPP = purchasing power parity.

Country Context

General	
Population (total)	14.19 million (2006)
GDP per capita (PPP, 2005 $)	$1,569 (2006)
Poverty headcount ratio at $2/day	77.7% (1997)

Education	
Net enrollment in primary level	89.9% total (2006) 89.0% for girls, 90.9% for boys
Net enrollment in secondary level	23.9% total (2005) 21.9% for girls, 26.0% for boys

Health	
Prevalence of child malnutrition (stunting)	43.7% (2006)
Births attended by skilled health staff	43.8% (2005)

Indonesia

Program: Jaring Pengamanan Sosial

Year started	1998
Status	Closed

Targeting

Target population	6% of enrolled students at primary schools, 17% at junior secondary schools, and 10% at senior secondary schools
Targeting method	Geographic targeting to poorest districts, then community assessment by district committees to identify schools and by school committees to identify students[a]
Coverage	• Between 1.2 and 1.6 million scholarships (1998/99 academic year) • 9.5% (2001), 5.9% (2002), and 7.6% (2003) of households with children attending primary to senior high schools (with higher coverage in poorer regions) • 14.9% (2001), 9.4% (2002), and 12.1% (2003) of poorest quintile
Incidence	39.3% to poorest quintile (2004)

Household Benefits

Benefit structure	• Rp 10,000 a month for students in primary school • Rp 20,000 a month for students in junior secondary school • Rp 25,000 a month for students in senior secondary school
Payee	Directly to the students (or their families)
Payment method	Cash paid through local post offices[b]
Payment frequency	Monthly
Duration	As long as eligible
Additional benefits	Block grant to schools

Conditions

Health	None
Education	Remain enrolled in school
Other	None
Verification of compliance–method	Not available
Verification of compliance–frequency	Not available
Compliance statistics	Not available

Program Administration

Institutional arrangement	
Program costs	$114 million for the first year (1998/99 academic year), $350 million over 3 years[c]

Sources: Cameron 2002; Pritchett, Sumarto, and Suryahadia 2003; World Bank 2006c; Sparrow 2007; country context: *World Development Indicators* database 2008.

Note: PPP = purchasing power parity.

a. A minimum of 50 percent of scholarships were to be allocated to girls, if at all possible.

b. This later changed to the schools collecting the funds directly "on behalf of the parents."

c. Rp 2.7 trillion in 2003; the program was expanded in 2005 to Rp 6.3 trillion, approximately Rp 5.1 trillion of which is allocated to block grants to schools, and only about Rp 272 billion goes to scholarships for students in senior secondary schools.

General	
Population (total)	223 million (2006)
GDP per capita (PPP, 2005 $)	$3,347 (2006)
Poverty headcount ratio at $2/day	52.4% (2002)
Education	
Net enrollment in primary level	94.5% total (2005) 92.8% for girls, 96.2% for boys
Net enrollment in secondary level	57.4% total (2005) 57.1% for girls, 57.7% for boys
Health	
Prevalence of child malnutrition (stunting)	28.6% (2004)
Births attended by skilled health staff	71.5% (2004)

Indonesia

Program: Program Keluarga Harapan

Year started	2007
Status	Ongoing

Targeting

Target population	Poorest households
Targeting method	Proxy means testing
Coverage	• In 2007: 348 subdistricts in 49 districts, 7 provinces; includes 387,928 poorest households (target in 2007 is 500,000 poorest households) • In 2008: figure in 2007 above plus new locations (292 subdistrict, 22 districts, 6 provinces); includes new members numbering approximately 245,371 poorest households
Incidence	No data yet

Household Benefits

Benefit structure	Minimum Rp 600,000; maximum Rp 2,200,000
Payee	Directly to mother or woman who takes care of the children in the family
Payment method	Cash paid through local post offices
Payment frequency	Quarterly
Duration	As long as eligible during 6 years. Recertification will be made twice (for example, after 3 and 6 years of implementations). Members will be excluded if the first recertification (after 3 years) confirms they are not eligible in terms of poverty. Members will be excluded regardless of the second recertification results (after 6 years). Exit strategies will be developed for those who are still in poverty.
Additional benefits	Members automatically are eligible for both *AskesKin* (health insurance for the poor) and *Bantuan Opersional Sekolah* (school fee waiver and transportation assistance) programs.

Conditions

Health	• Children aged 0–6 visit health clinics to use health services as outlined in the Department of Health protocols. • Pregnant (and lactating) women attend health clinics to receive antenatal (and postnatal) examinations, according to the Department of Health protocols
Education	• Children aged 7–15 enroll and attend a minimum of 85% of school days • Children aged 15–18 who have not completed 9 years of basic education enroll in an education program to complete the equivalent of 9 years of basic education
Other	None
Verification of compliance–method	Still sporadic; management information system is under construction
Verification of compliance–frequency	Every 3 months
Compliance statistics	No data yet

Program Administration	
Institutional arrangement	The National Development Planning Board (design), the Central Statistics Agency (targeting), Ministry of Social Welfare (implementation), PT Post Indonesia (payment), Coordinating Ministry of Social Welfare (control and coordination)
Program costs	Rp 1 trillion

Sources: Government of Indonesia 2007a, 2007b, 2007c, 2007d; country context: *World Development Indicators* database 2008.
Note: PPP = purchasing power parity.

Country Context

General	
Population (total)	223 million (2006)
GDP per capita (PPP, 2005 $)	$3,347 (2006)
Poverty headcount ratio at $2/day	52.4% (2002)
Education	
Net enrollment in primary level	94.5% total (2005) 92.8% for girls, 96.2% for boys
Net enrollment in secondary level	57.4% total (2005) 57.1% for girls, 57.7% for boys
Health	
Prevalence of child malnutrition (stunting)	28.6% (2004)
Births attended by skilled health staff	71.5% (2004)

Philippines

Program: Pantawid Pamilyang Pilipino Program

Year started	2008
Status	Active

Targeting

Target population	• For health grant: Poor households with children less than 5 years old and/or pregnant women • For education grant: Poor households with children aged 6–14 • Total beneficiaries: approximately 380,000 households
Targeting method	National household targeting system based on proxy means testing
Coverage	Poor households in 140 of the poorest municipalities and 10 cities
Incidence	Not measured yet

Household Benefits

Benefit structure	• Health transfer currently set at ₱500 ($11)[a] per household per month (for a period of 12 months per year), regardless of the number of children • Education transfer is ₱300 (US$7)[a] per month (for a period of 10 months per year), up to a maximum of 3 children
Payee	Mother
Payment method	Land Bank of the Philippines (cash cards and payroll)
Payment frequency	Monthly
Duration	2008 (prepilot); currently targeted total beneficiaries to be covered for 5 years (2009–13)
Additional benefits	Nutrition, breastfeeding seminars, family planning sessions for mothers and parents

Conditions

Health	Children and pregnant women attend health centers and posts to get regular preventive health checkups and immunizations, according to the Department of Health's protocol
Education	Children enroll in schools and attend more than 85% of school classes
Other	None
Verification of compliance–method	Schools and health centers report monthly nonattendance of beneficiaries to the municipal link; information is processed at municipal or regional level to update central database and make payments accordingly
Verification of compliance–frequency	Quarterly
Compliance statistics	Not available

Program Administration	
Institutional arrangement	Department of Social Welfare and Development acting as executing agency, in partnership with Departments of Health and Education
Program costs	$471 million over 5-year period (2009–13)

Sources: Bank staff; for population: National Statistics Office; for GDP per capita: *World Development Indicators 2008;* for headcount ratio: World Bank; for country context/education: Philippines Department of Education; for country context/health: *World Development Indicators 2008*, National Statistical Coordination Board.

a. $1 = ₱45.

Country Context

General	
Population (total)	88.6 million (August 2007)
GDP per capita (PPP, 2005 $)	2,956
Poverty headcount ratio at $2/day	56.1%
Education	
Net enrollment in primary level	83.2% (2007)
Net enrollment in secondary level	58.6% (2007)
Health	
Prevalence of child malnutrition (stunting)	34% (2003)
Births attended by skilled health staff	70.4% (2006)

Turkey

Program: Social Risk Mitigation Project

Year started	2001
Status	Active

Targeting

Target population	Poor families with children aged 0–6 or in primary or secondary school, and pregnant mothers (poorest 6% of the population)
Targeting method	Proxy means testing
Coverage	855,906 households; that is, about 2.5 million beneficiaries or 2.8% of population (end 2006)
Incidence	Not available

Household Benefits

Benefit structure	• Education grant per month: primary—$13 per boy, $16 per girl; secondary—$23 per boy, $30 per girl • Health grant: $12.50 a month per child aged 0–6, over 12 months • Pregnancy grant: $13 per month during pregnancy and a 2-month lactating period • Delivery at a health clinic: one-time payment of $41
Payee	Mother
Payment method	Through a banking institution and the postal service (for areas in which the bank does not have any branches)
Payment frequency	Bimonthly (education grant), monthly (pregnancy grant), and one time (institutional delivery grant)
Duration	As long as eligible
Additional benefits	• In addition to health grant, mothers are informed/trained about child care, nutrition, and other relevant medical information at the health clinics when they bring their children for regular medical examination • Services for adults: the local initiative component of the SRMP, and other project supports of the Directorate General, allow for support to needy citizens (or parents of CCT beneficiaries) for employability training, temporary employment, or income-generating projects

Conditions

Health	Health grant and pregnancy grant: visit the clinic regularly, according to the table given by the Ministry of Health[a]
Education	• School attendance of at least 80% of the total education days each month • Not to repeat the same grade more than once
Other	None[b]
Verification of compliance–method	Local social assistance offices send follow-up forms to the schools and health clinics that CCT beneficiaries attend; offices receive completed forms in return. Local offices enter the data in Web-based software; payment amounts for each beneficiary are calculated automatically on the basis of that data.
Verification of compliance–frequency	Monthly
Compliance statistics	Not available

Program Administration

Institutional arrangement	Project Coordination Unit of the Directorate General of Social Assistance and Solidarity of the Turkish Prime Ministry, local offices of the Directorate General
Program costs	Budget: $360 million (0.14% of GNP; May 2006)

Sources: Ahmed, Gilligan et al. 2006; Kudat 2006; Adato et al. 2007; country context: *World Development Indicators* database 2008.
Note: PPP = purchasing power parity; SRMP = Social Risk Mitigation Program.

a. In the health grant, health follow-up periods are (1) children aged 0–6 months require regular checkups every month, (2) children aged 7–18 months require regular checkups every 2 months, and (3) children aged 19–72 months require regular checkups every 6 months. For the pregnancy grant, follow-up periods are (1) regular checkups are required every month until the birth, (2) birth will be given in a hospital, and (3) postpartum checkups are required following the birth.

b. Implicitly, it is to obtain documentation, because beneficiaries must present birth and marriage certificates to be able to apply for the benefit.

Country Context

General

Population (total)	70.5 million (2007)
GDP per capita (PPP, 2005 $)	$8,157 (2006)
Poverty headcount ratio at $2/day	18.7% (2003)

Education

Net enrollment in primary level	97.4% total (2005) 96.1% for girls, 98.5% for boys
Net enrollment in secondary level	58.6% total (2005) 58.8% for girls, 61.2% for boys

Health

Prevalence of child malnutrition (stunting)	16% (2004)
Births attended by skilled health staff	83% (2003)

233

Argentina

Program: Programa Familias

Year started	2002
Status	Active

Targeting

Target population	Families with a current beneficiary of the Jefes y Jefas de Hogar Desocupados[a] program, who have at least 2 children to take care of and who have not completed secondary school[b]
Targeting method	Categorical; criteria are heads of household (self-declared), pregnant (or with pregnant spouse), children below 18 or disabled, not included in any federal records
Coverage	504,784 families (August 2007)
Incidence	Not available

Household Benefits

Benefit structure	Arg$155–305 a month per child aged 5–19, depending on the number of children (minimum 2, maximum 6)
Payee	Mother
Payment method	Through debit cards with the Banco de la Nacion Argentina
Payment frequency	Monthly
Duration	As long as eligible
Additional benefits	• Monthly benefit of Arg$50 for youth and adults in the family who want to complete their education or vocational training • Activities to encourage and support completion of education, literacy campaigns, training, community development

Conditions

Health	• Compliance with the National Immunization Plan for children under 19 years • Bimonthly checkups for pregnant women
Education	• School enrollment • Regular school attendance by each child aged 5–19, or completion of the secondary level or "polimodal"
Other	None
Verification of compliance–method	Beneficiaries must provide proof of compliance with conditions at the local program office
Verification of compliance–frequency	Twice a year
Compliance statistics	Not available

Program Administration	
Institutional arrangement	Ministry of Social Development, local program offices
Program costs	Budget: $853.3 million in phase I (IADB loan amount)

Sources: Program Web site: http://www.desarrollosocial.gov.ar/planes/pf/default.asp; country context: *World Development Indicators* database 2008.

Note: IADB = Inter-American Development Bank; PPP = purchasing power parity.

a. Transfer program for unemployed heads of household.

b. Beneficiaries of the Jefes program migrate to the Programa Familias on a voluntary basis. It is not in addition to the Jefes benefit. Up to 10 percent of beneficiaries may come in through proxy means testing rather than through Jefes.

Country Context

General	
Population (total)	39.1 million (2006)
GDP per capita (PPP, 2005 $)	$11,615 (2006)
Poverty headcount ratio at $2/day	17.4% (2004)
Education	
Net enrollment in primary level	98.8% total (2003) 98.4% for girls, 99.2% for boys
Net enrollment in secondary level	78.9% total (2004) 82.5% for girls, 75.5% for boys
Health	
Prevalence of child malnutrition (stunting)	8.2% (2005)
Births attended by skilled health staff	99.1% (2005)

Bolivia

Program: Juancito Pinto

Year started	2006
Status	Ongoing

Targeting

Target population	Public school children up to grade 6
Targeting method	Categorical (universal coverage offered to children)
Coverage	1.2 million children
Incidence	Not available

Household Benefits

Benefit structure	Bs 200 ($25) per child per year
Payee	Child accompanied by parent or guardian
Payment method	Army distributes cash payments at school ceremony
Payment frequency	Annually
Duration	As long as eligible
Additional benefits	None

Conditions

Health	Not available
Education	Attend class at least 75% of the school year
Other	Not available
Verification of compliance–method	Schools required to present their enrollment records to the district government office
Verification of compliance–frequency	Annually
Compliance statistics	Not available

Program Administration

Institutional arrangement	Ministry of Education
Program costs	$30 million per year

Sources: World Bank 2007; country context: *World Development Indicators* database 2008.
Note: PPP = purchasing power parity.

Country Context

General	
Population (total)	9.4 million (2006)
GDP per capita (PPP, 2005 $)	$3,815 (2006)
Poverty headcount ratio at $2/day	42.2% (2002)

Education	
Net enrollment in primary level	94.9% total (2006) 95.3% for girls, 94.5% for boys
Net enrollment in secondary level	70.9% total (2004) 70.0% for girls, 71.7% for boys

Health	
Prevalence of child malnutrition (stunting)	32.5% (2004)
Births attended by skilled health staff	66.8% (2003)

Brazil

Program: Bolsa Alimentação

Year started	2001
Status	Stopped (integrated into Bolsa Família starting end of 2003)

Targeting

Target population	Poor families with pregnant and lactating women and young children aged 0–6, and with a monthly PCI below R$90.21
Targeting method	Geographic targeting and means testing
Coverage	1.5 million beneficiaries in 2003 (24,175 families in December 2005)
Incidence	Not available

Household Benefits

Benefit structure	R$15 per child per month, for a maximum of 3 children
Payee	Mother
Payment method	Transfers were credited to a magnetic card that could be used to withdraw cash at offices of a federally owned bank, or in very isolated municipalities with lottery agents
Payment frequency	Monthly
Duration	6 months initially, and after verification of compliance, additional 6-month periods
Additional benefits	None

Conditions

Health	• Complying with a minimum schedule of visits for prenatal and postnatal care • Monitoring the growth of children • Keeping their vaccinations up-to-date • Participating in nutritional education seminars
Education	None
Other	None
Verification of compliance–method	The health ministry of each municipality verified the attendance of each beneficiary at clinics, and informed the federal authorities by sending a list of complying beneficiaries every 6 months.
Verification of compliance–frequency	Varied across municipalities; reporting to federal authorities every 6 months
Compliance statistics	Not available

Program Administration

Institutional arrangement	Ministry of Health
Program costs	• Budget: R$8.3 million (2005) • Administrative cost: 3.42% of program cost[a] (2003)

Sources: Government of Brazil 2004; Morris, Olinto et al. 2004; country context: *World Development Indicators* database 2008.
Note: PCI = per capita income; PPP = purchasing power parity.
a. This is the ratio of administrative costs to transfers.

General	
Population (total)	189.3 million (2006)
GDP per capita (PPP, 2005 $)	$8,673 (2006)
Poverty headcount ratio at $2/day	21.2% (2004)

Education	
Net enrollment in primary level	94.7% total (2004) 95.2% for girls, 94.2% for boys
Net enrollment in secondary level	77.7% total (2004) 81.3% for girls, 74.2% for boys

Health	
Prevalence of child malnutrition (stunting)	10.5% (1996)
Births attended by skilled health staff	96.6% (2003)

Brazil

Program: Bolsa Escola[a]

Year started	2001
Status	Stopped (integrated into Bolsa Família starting end of 2003)

Targeting

Target population	Families with children ages 6–15 and monthly PCI no greater than R$90 ($43)
Targeting method	Geographic targeting and means testing
Coverage	8.2 million children in 4.8 million families (end 2001), 1.9 million families in December 2005
Incidence	40% to poorest quintile (2003)

Household Benefits

Benefit structure	R$15 ($7) per month per child for a maximum of 3 children[b]
Payee	Mother
Payment method	Transfers credited to a magnetic card; benefits could be withdrawn at Caixa Econômica Federal branch offices or in very isolated municipalities with lottery agents
Payment frequency	Monthly
Duration	As long as eligible
Additional benefits	None

Conditions

Health	None
Education	School attendance at least 85% of school days
Other	None
Verification of compliance–method	School directors sent attendance data to municipal secretary of education, who entered them in Ministry of Education system (Internet or CD-ROM)
Verification of compliance–frequency	Bimonthly
Compliance statistics	19% of schools reporting attendance information

Program Administration

Institutional arrangement	Ministry of Education
Program costs	• Budget: R$626 million (less than 0.2% of GDP; 2005) • Administrative cost: 5.3% of program costs (2002)

Sources: World Bank 2001a; de Janvry et al. 2005; country context: *World Development Indicators* database 2008.

Note: PCI = per capita income; PPP = purchasing power parity.

a. This refers to the federal Bolsa Escola program. Before its creation, a number of similar programs operated in many municipalities.

b. School attendance is only monitored for these three children, but not for the rest of the school-age children in the family.

Country Context

General	
Population (total)	189.3 million (2006)
GDP per capita (PPP, 2005 $)	$8,673 (2006)
Poverty headcount ratio at $2/day	21.2% (2004)
Education	
Net enrollment in primary level	94.7% total (2004) 95.2% for girls, 94.2% for boys
Net enrollment in secondary level	77.7% total (2004) 81.3% for girls, 74.2% for boys
Health	
Prevalence of child malnutrition (stunting)	10.5% (1996)
Births attended by skilled health staff	96.6% (2003)

Brazil

Program: Bolsa Família[a]

Year started	2003
Status	Active

Targeting

Target population	Poor and extremely poor families: • Poor families: monthly PCI from R$60.01 to R$120.00[b] • Extremely poor families: monthly PCI up to R$60.00
Targeting method	Geographic targeting and means testing (self-declared)
Coverage	11.1 million families (June 2006)
Incidence	73.7% to poorest quintile, 94% to poorest 40% (2006)

Household Benefits

Benefit structure	• Basic benefit (R$62) for extremely poor families • Variable benefit (R$15) per child (maximum 3[c] less than 15 years of age) for both extremely poor and poor families • Variable benefit (R$30) per youth (maximum 2[d] aged 15–17) for both extremely and poor families
Payee	Mother
Payment method	Through a debit card distributed to the beneficiaries
Payment frequency	Monthly
Duration	As long as eligible, with recertification every 2 years
Additional benefits	The adult literacy and education program (Brazil Alfabetizado) targets Bolsa Família beneficiaries who have less than 4 years of schooling. The government of Brazil is developing a national training program targeted to adult members of Bolsa Família households (one member per family) to improve their skills and provide employment opportunities through the Programa de Aceleracao do Crescimento strategy (a federal civil works program). Some municipalities either are topping up the benefit or are targeting the beneficiaries with other services, such as social worker accompaniment, professional training and other active labor market programs, and microcredit.

Conditions

Health	• Children aged 0–6: vaccine schedules, regular health checkups, and growth monitoring • Pregnant and lactating women: prenatal and postnatal checkups, and participation in educational health and nutrition seminars offered by local health teams[e]
Education	• School enrollment of all children aged 6–15 and youth aged 15–17 • Daily school attendance of at least 85% each month for all school-age children • Participation in parent-teacher meetings
Other	None

Verification of compliance–method	• Education: municipalities consolidate attendance information; Caixa Econômica Federal consolidates and passes to the Ministry of Education and the Bolsa Família program in the Ministry of Social Development • Health: health service providers at the municipal level enter information into a national health information system; municipality consolidates information for the Bolsa Família beneficiaries and passes it on to the Ministry of Health twice a year; Ministry of Health provides consolidated information to the program
Verification of compliance–frequency	• Education: bimonthly • Health: twice a year
Compliance statistics	• Education: 4.6% of students did not comply with the attendance requirement in May/July 2006 (information available for 71% of Bolsa Família students) • Health: 99.5% of families were in compliance in the first semester of 2006 (information available for 38.3% of families)

Program Administration

Institutional arrangement	Ministry of Social Development, in cooperation with the ministries of health and education, the Caixa Econômica Federal, the municipalities, state governments, and control agencies
Program costs	• Budget: R$10.4 billion ($5 billion) in 2005 (0.36% of GDP) • Administrative cost: 4% of program budget

Sources: Lindert et al. 2007; program Web site: http://www.mds.gov.br/bolsafamilia/; country context: *World Development Indicators* database 2008.

Note: PCI = per capita income; PPP = purchasing power parity.

a. The Bolsa Família program resulted from a merger of the following prereform cash transfer programs: Bolsa Escola, Bolsa Alimentação, Auxílio Gás, and Cartao Alimentação. In 2006, the cash transfers paid under the Child Labor Eradication Program (PETI) also were merged into the Bolsa Família program.

b. Originally, these income ceilings were set at R$50 for the extremely poor, and R$100 for the poor. They were increased in 2006 to account for increases in the cost of living.

c. Education and health conditionalities apply to all the children in the family, not only the three for which the variable benefit is paid.

d. Conditionalities apply only to the individual youth for whom the benefit is paid.

e. Participation in these seminars is not monitored by the federal government.

See page 245 for Country Context table.

Brazil

Program: Programa de Eradicacão do Trabalho Infantil

Year started	1996
Status	Stopped (integrated into Bolsa Família in 2006[a])

Targeting

Target population	Poor households with PCI below one-half the minimum wage (roughly equal to $65/month) and children aged 7–14 involved in the worst forms of child labor[b]
Targeting method	Geographic targeting and means testing
Coverage	400,000 students (2000), 1,010,057 children (2005), 3.3 million beneficiaries (2002)
Incidence	66% to poorest quintile (2003)

Household Benefits

Benefit structure	• Urban areas (capitals, metropolitan regions, and municipalities with more than 250,000 habitants): monthly transfer of R$40 per child (to family) • Rural areas: R$25 per month (to family) for each child registered • For after-school activities: R$10 (urban areas) and R$20 (rural areas) to schools for each child or adolescent enrolled • For 15-year-olds at extreme risk: transfer of R$65 per month and of R$220 per year for school activities
Payee	Mother
Payment method	Through bank accounts
Payment frequency	Monthly
Duration	As long as eligible
Additional benefits	None

Conditions

Health	None
Education	• School attendance of at least 80% • Attendance at after-school sessions (*jornada ampliada*) that roughly doubled the length of the school day
Other	Households need to sign a contract stipulating that their child would not work
Verification of compliance–method	Not available
Verification of compliance–frequency	Not available
Compliance statistics	Not available

Program Administration

Institutional arrangement	Ministry of Social Development and municipalities
Program costs	R$535 million in 2005

Sources: World Bank 2001b; country context: *World Development Indicators* database 2008.
Note: PCI = per capita income; PPP = purchasing power parity.
a. Only the cash transfer part was incorporated into Bolsa Família, not the *jornada ampliada*.
b. Not all such children in the family had to be enrolled.

Country Context

General	
Population (total)	189.3 million (2006)
GDP per capita (PPP, 2005 $)	$8,673 (2006)
Poverty headcount ratio at $2/day	21.2% (2004)

Education	
Net enrollment in primary level	94.7% total (2004) 95.2% for girls, 94.2% for boys
Net enrollment in secondary level	77.7% total (2004) 81.3% for girls, 74.2% for boys

Health	
Prevalence of child malnutrition (stunting)	10.5% (1996)
Births attended by skilled health staff	96.6% (2003)

Chile

Program: Chile Solidario

Year started	2002
Status	Active

Targeting

Target population	268,000 households (the estimated number of indigent households in the country)
Targeting method	Proxy means testing
Coverage	256,000
Incidence	56% to poorest quintile (2003)

Household Benefits

Benefit structure	• Decreasing monthly benefits for the first 24 months: $21 per month for the first 6 months, $16 per month for the second 6 months of the program, $11 per month for the third 6 months, and finally $8 for the last 6 months, an amount equivalent to the family allowance (SUF) adjusted yearly for inflation; these amounts are for 2006[a] • After 24 months, "exit grant" equivalent to a monthly SUF for 3 years
Payee	Mother
Payment method	Through National Social Security Institute service centers or payment points
Payment frequency	Monthly
Duration	5 years[b]
Additional benefits	• Psychosocial support in the form of intensive social worker accompaniment for the first 2 years • Preferential access to other social programs for which the household is eligible

Conditions

Health Education Other	Signature and compliance with a contract committing to participate in the activities identified, together with personalized assistance in 7 areas (health, education, employment, housing, income, family life, and legal documentation)
Verification of compliance–method	Regular meetings with the social worker to monitor progress toward unmet goals
Verification of compliance–frequency	• In the first 6 months: once a week for 2 months, twice a month for 2 months, and once a month for 2 months[c] • In the next 6 months: every 2 months • In the final 12 months: every 3 months
Compliance statistics	15,972 (6%) families "interrupted" (2006)[d]

Institutional arrangement	Ministry of Planning and Cooperation, and Fondo de Solidaridad e Inversión Social, in cooperation with the municipalities
Program costs	• Budget: 0.3% of social protection spending (0.08% of GDP; 2005) • Administrative cost: 20% of program costs, half of that being the cost of the social worker accompaniment[e]

Sources: Galasso 2006; program Web site: http://www.chilesolidario.gov.cl/; country context: *World Development Indicators* database 2008.

Note: PPP = purchasing power parity; SUF = Subsidio Unitario Familiar.

a. This amount is equivalent to the amount paid by the SUF, the basic social assistance program.

b. Psychosocial support covers the first two years only. The cash transfer is graduated over five years, as described under benefit structure.

c. This can be extended or reduced, depending on the family's progress on their contract.

d. This means it was decided that they did not satisfy the overall requirements to continue their participation and were dropped by the program.

e. "The direct cost per family to access the Chile Solidario System (via the Puente Program) is estimated to be around $330, of which $275 (about 80%) correspond to the transfer itself. The social worker accounts for about 10% of the direct cost."

Country Context

General	
Population (total)	16.4 million (2006)
GDP per capita (PPP, 2005 $)	$12,627 (2006)
Poverty headcount ratio at $2/day	5.6% (2003)
Education	
Net enrollment in primary level	Not available
Net enrollment in secondary level	Not available
Health	
Prevalence of child malnutrition (stunting)	1.4% (2004)
Births attended by skilled health staff	99.8% (2003)

Chile

Program: Subsidio Unitario Familiar

Year started	1981
Status	Active

Targeting

Target population	Poor households (in the bottom 40% of the income distribution) with pregnant women, school-age children, or disabled members
Targeting method	Proxy means testing
Coverage	1.2 million individuals[a]
Incidence	60% to poorest quintile (2003)

Household Benefits

Benefit structure	Ch$5,393 ($10) per month (2007)[b]
Payee	Mother
Payment method	Through National Social Security Institute service centers or payment points
Payment frequency	Monthly
Duration	As long as eligible
Additional benefits	None

Conditions

Health	Regular medical controls for children less than 6 years
Education	Regular school attendance for children aged 6–18
Other	None
Verification of compliance–method	Not available
Verification of compliance–frequency	Once a year
Compliance statistics	Not available

Program Administration

Institutional arrangement	Ministry of Planning and Cooperation
Program costs	Budget: $70 million in 1998

Sources: Program Web site: http://www.mideplan.cl/final/categoria.php?secid=49&catid=126; country context: *World Development Indicators* database 2008.

Note: PPP = purchasing power parity; SUF = Subsidio Unitario Familiar.

a. This is the estimate for 2007 and represents an expansion of the program.

b. In the case of disabled members of the household, it is double this amount—that is Ch$10,786 ($20). In the case of an expectant mother, the so-called maternity benefit in the amount of Ch$53,930 ($100.20) for the whole pregnancy applies. After the child's birth, the family will receive the SUF.

General	
Population (total)	16.4 million (2006)
GDP per capita (PPP, 2005 $)	$12,627 (2006)
Poverty headcount ratio at $2/day	5.6% (2003)

Education	
Net enrollment in primary level	Not available
Net enrollment in secondary level	Not available

Health	
Prevalence of child malnutrition (stunting)	1.4% (2004)
Births attended by skilled health staff	99.8% (2003)

Colombia

Program: Familias en Acción

Year started	2001
Status	Active

Targeting

Target population	Extremely poor families[a] with minors aged 0–6 not participating in other programs (health subsidy), and/or minors aged 7–17 enrolled in school (education subsidy)
Targeting method	Geographic targeting and proxy means testing
Coverage	1.7 million households by end of 2007
Incidence	Not available

Household Benefits

Benefit structure	• Education subsidy: in elementary school, Col$15,000 per month (approximately $8) for each minor attending grades 2–5;[b] in high school, Col$25,000–60,000 per month (approximately $14–33) per minor attending grades 6–11[c] • Health subsidy: Col$50,000 per month (approximately $3,028) per family with members aged less than 7 years[d]
Payee	Mother
Payment method	Through the banking system
Payment frequency	Bimonthly
Duration	As long as eligible
Additional benefits	Health and nutrition education and empowerment of mothers through their organization in groups

Conditions

Health	Meet the growth control and development checkups scheduled every 2 months for children aged 0–1, 3 times a year for children up to 2 years, and 2 times a year thereafter up to 7 years
Education	At least 80% school attendance in a 2-month cycle (maximum of 8 unjustified absences in a 2-month period)
Other	None
Verification of compliance–method	Beneficiaries receive forms on which their compliance with conditions is confirmed by health and education service providers; they provide these forms to the local program office on a regular basis[e]
Verification of compliance–frequency	Bimonthly
Compliance statistics	90% for health and education

Program Administration	
Institutional arrangement	Presidential Agency for Social Action and International Cooperation, local program offices
Program costs	• Budget: $200 per month (0.2% of GDP; 2007) • Administrative cost: 5.0% of program budget (1.0% is for materials related to verification of compliance), plus 3.4% in banking commissions

Sources: Attanasio, Battistin et al. 2005; Attanasio, Fitzsimmons, and Gómez 2005; Attanasio, Gómez et al. 2005; Institute for Fiscal Studies, Econometría, and Sistemas Especializados de Información 2006; program Web site: http://www.accionsocial.gov.co/contenido/contenido. aspx?catID=204&conID=157; country context: *World Development Indicators* database 2008.

Note: PPP = purchasing power parity.

a. Sistema de Identificación de Beneficiarios level 1, or part of Sole Registry for Displaced Populations.

b. In 12 cities, including Bogotá, no education subsidy is paid for grades 2–5.

c. The education subsidy is paid for 10 months per year, and amounts vary according to geographic area.

d. The health subsidy is paid for 12 months per year. In the 12 cities, including Bogotá, where no education subsidy is paid for grades 2–5, if families have only minors aged 7–11, they are paid a nutrition subsidy of Col$20,000 (approximately $11).

e. The process of verification of conditions is changing because the program is further expanding and needs to adapt accordingly.

Country Context

General	
Population (total)	45.6 million (2006)
GDP per capita (PPP, 2005 $)	$6,181 (2006)
Poverty headcount ratio at $2/day	17.8% (2003)
Education	
Net enrollment in primary level	88.5% total (2006) 88.4% for girls, 88.6% for boys
Net enrollment in secondary level	64.9% total (2006) 68.5% for girls, 61.5% for boys
Health	
Prevalence of child malnutrition (stunting)	12% (2005)
Births attended by skilled health staff	86.4% (2000)

Colombia

Program: Subsidio Condicionado a la Asistencia Escolar–Bogotá

Year started	2005 (pilot program)
Status	Active

Targeting

Target population	Poor students in grades 6–11
Targeting method	Proxy means testing
Coverage	10,000 beneficiaries
Incidence	Not available

Household Benefits

Benefit structure	3 types of transfers:[a] • $15 per month conditional on attendance • $10 per month to the household and approximately $50 ($5 a month for 10 months) at the end of the academic year • $10 per month and $240 at the end of secondary school, conditional on completion[b]
Payee	Student
Payment method	Through beneficiary's bank account with associated debit card
Payment frequency	Bimonthly
Duration	As long as eligible
Additional benefits	None

Conditions

Health	None
Education	School attendance and/or completion, depending on the type of transfer tested (see benefit structure)
Other	None
Verification of compliance–method	Students' principals report attendance/completion information to the Secretary of Education for the city of Bogotá
Verification of compliance–frequency	Bimonthly
Compliance statistics	Not available

Program Administration

Institutional arrangement	Secretary of Education for the City of Bogotá
Program costs	Not available

Sources: Barrera-Osorio et al. 2008; program Web site: http://www.sedbogota.edu.co/secretaria/export/SED/svirtuales/subsidios_condicio-nados.html; country context: *World Development Indicators* database 2008.

Note: PPP = purchasing power parity.

a. Transfer only paid during the academic year.

b. The city decided in favor of the first type of transfer.

General	
Population (total)	45.6 million (2006)
GDP per capita (PPP, 2005 $)	$6,181 (2006)
Poverty headcount ratio at $2/day	17.8% (2003)

Education	
Net enrollment in primary level	88.5% total (2006) 88.4% for girls, 88.6% for boys
Net enrollment in secondary level	64.9% total (2006) 68.5% for girls, 61.5% for boys

Health	
Prevalence of child malnutrition (stunting)	12% (2005)
Births attended by skilled health staff	86.4% (2000)

Dominican Republic

Program: Solidaridad[a]

Year started	2005
Status	Active

Targeting

Target population	Families living in extreme or moderate poverty with children aged 0–16 or adults 16+ lacking identification
Targeting method	Geographic targeting and proxy means testing
Coverage	• 461,446 families (December 2008) • 10% of total population (2006)
Incidence	Not available

Household Benefits

Benefit structure	• Education (ILAE): RD$300 ($9) for 1 or 2 children, RD$450 ($14) for 3 children, and RD$600 ($19) for 4 or more children aged 6–16 per month • Food income component (Comer es Primero): RD$700 ($20) per month • Identification component: covers the fees to obtain the birth certificate and/or identification card for children and adults in Solidaridad families
Payee	Head of household
Payment method	Through debit cards that can be used only in certain stores (*colmados*) for certain products (food and education supplies)
Payment frequency	Monthly (Comer es Primero) and bimonthly (ILAE)
Duration	3 years, with recertification and possible continuation for another 3 years
Additional benefits	Bonogas: subsidy ($6.5/month) for the purchase of domestic gas. Unconditional transfer ($8.6/month) for beneficiary households with members ages 65 or older and without a job or pension.

Conditions

Health	Regular visits to health center for examinations, growth and development monitoring, and immunizations, for children aged 0–12 months (every 2 months) and children aged 1–5 years (every 4 months)
Education	• School enrollment • School attendance on at least 85% of actual school days for children aged 6–16
Other	• Attendance at capacity-building sessions for household head and spouse (every 4 months) • Obtaining identity documents (birth certificate, identification card) for family members who lack them
Verification of compliance–method	• Health: program liaison staff at the community level collects the forms with compliance information at the health centers (similar process for documentation and capacity-building conditions) • Education: school directors send attendance information on a regular basis through the education sector to the State Secretariat for Education • Social Subsidy Administration agency compiles the information and links it to the transfer payments

Verification of compliance—frequency	Every 4 months
Compliance statistics	Health 56.6%; training 94.9%; documentation 69%
Program Administration	
Institutional arrangement	Coordination of the Cabinet for Social Policies
Program costs	Budget: $124,944,407 in 2008

Sources: Regalía and Robles 2005; program Web site: http://www.gabsocial.gov.do/solidaridad/; country context: *World Development Indicators* database 2008.

Note: ILAE = Incentivo a la Asistencia Escolar ; PPP = purchasing power parity.

a. In September 2005, the government established by presidential decree the Solidarity Program as an amalgamation of two existing CCT programs, Comer es Primero and Incentivo a la Asistencia Escolar.

Country Context

General	
Population (total)	9.6 million (2006)
GDP per capita (PPP, 2005 $)	$5,684 (2006)
Poverty headcount ratio at $2/day	16.2% (2004)
Education	
Net enrollment in primary level	77.5% total (2006) 78.5% for girls, 76.5% for boys
Net enrollment in secondary level	52.1% total (2006) 57.4% for girls, 46.9% for boys
Health	
Prevalence of child malnutrition (stunting)	9.8% (2007)
Births attended by skilled health staff	97.8% (2008)

Dominican Republic

Program: Tarjeta de Asistencia Escolar[a]

Year started	2001
Status	Stopped (replaced by ILAE[b] and then integrated into Solidaridad)

Targeting

Target population	Poor households with children aged 5–15 enrolled in school[c]
Targeting method	• Geographic targeting of municipalities, and of schools with less than 300 students; identification of eligible mothers through parents' school committee and other community organizations • In second stage of expansion, poverty map was not used when identifying schools with 750 or more students in urban marginal areas; socioeconomic information was gathered for identifying eligible mothers[d]
Coverage	• 88 SEE districts, 2,115 schools, and 29 provinces, benefiting approximately 100,000 households (2003) • 4.1% of households (2004)
Incidence	59.1% to poorest 40% (2004)

Household Benefits

Benefit structure	RD$300 per eligible household (flat benefit)
Payee	Mother
Payment method	Payments made by checks distributed through the schools
Payment frequency	Bimonthly
Duration	As long as eligible
Additional benefits	None

Conditions

Health	None
Education	• School enrollment • School assistance at least 85% of school days • Satisfying school performance (also was supposed to be monitored)
Other	None
Verification of compliance–method	No structure in place
Verification of compliance–frequency	No structure in place
Compliance statistics	No structure in place

Program Administration	
Institutional arrangement	SEE, through its Planning Office
Program costs	RD$236.6 million ($5.7 million) in 2004[e]

Sources: Regalía and Robles 2005; World Bank 2006a; country context: *World Development Indicators* database 2008.

Note: ILAE = Incentivo a la Asistencia Escolar; PPP = purchasing power parity; SEE = State Secretariat of Education; TAE = Tarjeta de Asistencia Escolar.

a. The design of a plan to strengthen TAE's operations started at the end of 2003. In late 2004, the restructuring plan for the TAE program began to be implemented under a new name (Incentivo a la Asistencia Escolar) and with a new team of about 15 people in the SEE.

b. A proxy means test began to be implemented, and payments began being made to students rather than to households.

c. Since the very beginning, a prerequisite for mother's enrollment was possession of a valid personal identification document. This prerequisite caused the exclusion of one out of five mothers deemed eligible.

d. According to the program's rule, the criteria that should have been used to identify eligible mothers were (1) women heads of household, and (2) families whose parents were unemployed or under-employed but not self-employed. These criteria made the beneficiary selection mechanism problematic. An initial revision of specific cases, during January–September 2004, caused 3,700 mothers to be taken off the roster of beneficiaries because they did not have any children or did not meet other eligibility criteria.

e. Amount of transfers executed in 2004.

Country Context

General	
Population (total)	9.6 million (2006)
GDP per capita (PPP, 2005 $)	$5,684 (2006)
Poverty headcount ratio at $2/day	16.2% (2004)
Education	
Net enrollment in primary level	77.5% total (2006) 78.5% for girls, 76.5% for boys
Net enrollment in secondary level	52.1% total (2006) 57.4% for girls, 46.9% for boys
Health	
Prevalence of child malnutrition (stunting)	11.7% (2002)
Births attended by skilled health staff	95.5% (2002)

257

Ecuador

Program: Bono de Desarrollo Humano[a]

Year started	2003
Status	Active

Targeting

Target population	Households with children aged 0–16 in the poorest 2 quintiles, and poor households with elderly and/or disabled members
Targeting method	Proxy means testing
Coverage	• 1,060,416 households (January 2006) (approximately 5 million people) • 40% of population
Incidence	33% to poorest quintile (2004)

Household Benefits

Benefit structure	• $15 per month per family • Senior and disabled heads of household: $11.50 per month
Payee	Women
Payment method	Can be collected at any branch office from the largest network of private banks (Banred) or from the National Agricultural Bank
Payment frequency	Monthly
Duration	As long as eligible
Additional benefits	None

Conditions

Health	Children aged 0–5: bimonthly visits to health posts for growth and development checkups and immunizations
Education	• School enrollment for children aged 6–15 • School attendance at least 90% of school days • Must be enrolled in school and have attendance at basic education classes of at least 80% (including both justified and unjustified absences)
Other	None
Verification of compliance–method	No verification of compliance with conditions
Verification of compliance–frequency	No verification of compliance with conditions
Compliance statistics	No verification of compliance with conditions

Program Administration	
Institutional arrangement	Social Protection Programme under the Ministry of Social Welfare
Program costs	• Budget: $194 million in 2005 (0.6% of GDP, 2.25% of total nonfinancial public expenditure) • Administrative cost: $8 million[b]

Sources: Paxson and Schady 2008; Ponce and Bedi 2008; Schady and Araujo 2008; Schady and Rosero 2008; program Web site: http://www.mbs.gov.ec/MBS/index.htm; country context: _World Development Indicators_ database 2008.

Note: BDH = Bono de Desarrollo Humano; PPP = purchasing power parity.

a. In 2004, the BDH was created by integrating the Bono Solidario, a cash transfer originally designed to compensate the poor for the removal of electricity and gas subsidies, and the Beca Escolar, a CCT program providing a small cash transfer to families whose school-age children were enrolled and regularly attending school.

b. From country program profiles for the Third International Conference on Conditional Cash Transfers, Istanbul, 2006 (http://www.virtualcct.net).

Country Context

General	
Population (total)	13.2 million (2006)
GDP per capita (PPP, 2005 $)	$6,925 (2006)
Poverty headcount ratio at $2/day	40.8% (2004)
Education	
Net enrollment in primary level	97.3% total (2005) 97.8% for girls, 96.8% for boys
Net enrollment in secondary level	55.4% total (2005) 56.0% for girls, 54.7% for boys
Health	
Prevalence of child malnutrition (stunting)	29% (2004)
Births attended by skilled health staff	74.7% (2004)

El Salvador

Program: Red Solidaria

Year started	2005
Status	Active

Targeting

Target population	Families living in extreme poverty with children aged 0–15 in rural El Salvador
Targeting method	Geographic targeting and proxy means testing
Coverage	77 municipalities in 2008
Incidence	• 24,106 families in 32 municipalities in 2006 • 89,000 households in 77 municipalities by 2008 • Expected 100,000 households (roughly 800,000 population) in the 100 poorest municipalities by the end of 2009

Household Benefits

Benefit structure	• Education: $15 per month per household with children aged 6–15 • Health: $15 per month per household with children aged 0–5 and/or pregnant women • Health and education: $20 per month per household for households that qualify for both health and education benefits
Payee	Mother
Payment method	In cash at payment posts; payments are outsourced to a commercial bank
Payment frequency	Bimonthly
Duration	3 years
Additional benefits	Program has two additional components: (1) a supply-side component to strengthen basic health and nutrition services in the targeted areas, and (2) a family support component of activities outsourced through NGOs to help beneficiaries comply with their co-responsibilities, understand program operation, and collect their payments.

Conditions

Health	Compliance with immunization and regular health and nutrition monitoring[a]
Education	• School enrollment in primary school • School attendance rate of at least 80%[b] for children aged 5–15
Other	Families sign a contract stipulating their responsibilities
Verification of compliance–method	Health and education service personnel provide compliance information to staff of the contracted NGO, who then compile the information and pass it on to the social fund, FISDL, which implements the program.
Verification of compliance–frequency	Bimonthly
Compliance statistics	• Education: Average level of compliance from January to October 2008 was 96.18% • Health: Average level of compliance from January to October 2008 was 99.7%

Program Administration

Institutional arrangement	Technical Secretariat of the Presidency directs the Red Solidaria program. The FISDL is the implementation agency and is responsible for the coordination with the NGOs at the local level. Payments are outsourced through a commercial bank.
Program costs	Budget: $51.4 million

Sources: Program Web site: http://www.redsolidaria.gob.sv/; country context: *World Development Indicators* database 2008.

Note: FISDL = Fondo de Inversión Social para el Desarrollo Local; NGO = nongovernmental organization; PPP = purchasing power parity.

a. The health and nutrition transfer would require that households fulfill the separate co-responsibilities, specifically that (1) parents ensure that all children less than 5 years old are immunized fully under the established health protocols; and (2) children less than 5 years old, as well as pregnant mothers, participate in regular health and nutrition monitoring, again according to the established health and nutrition protocols.

b. Applies to all children in the family who are older than 5 and younger than 15, and who have not completed primary education already.

Country Context

General	
Population (total)	5.9 million (number adjusted according to the latest census [2005])
GDP per capita (PPP, 2005 $)	$5,587 (2006)
Poverty headcount ratio at $2/day	35% (2007)
Education	
Net enrollment in primary level	94% total (2006) 94.1% for girls, 93.9% for boys
Net enrollment in secondary level	54.2% total (2006) 55.5% for girls, 52.9% for boys
Health	
Prevalence of child malnutrition (stunting)	24.6% (2003)
Births attended by skilled health staff	92.4% (2003)

Guatemala

Program: Mi Familia Progresa

Year started	2008
Status	Active

Targeting

Target population	Extremely poor families with minors aged 0–15, living in the 130 most vulnerable municipalities
Targeting method	Geographic targeting and proxy means testing
Coverage	Target is about 250,000 households by end 2009
Incidence	Not available

Household Benefits

Benefit structure	• Education subsidy: in elementary school for children aged 6–15, Q 150 per month (approximately $20) regardless of the number of eligible children • Health subsidy: Q 150,000 per month (approximately $20) per family with members less than 16 years old
Payee	Mother
Payment method	Through a government-owned bank (BanRural)
Payment frequency	Bimonthly
Duration	As long as eligible
Additional benefits	Not available

Conditions

Health	Meet the growth control and regular checkups scheduled for pregnant women and children aged 0–16
Education	At least 90% school attendance
Other	None
Verification of compliance–method	Not fully implemented; program's staff at local level works with education and health institutions to verify compliance with conditions
Verification of compliance–frequency	Bimonthly
Compliance statistics	Not available

Program Administration

Institutional arrangement	Secretaria de Coordinación Ejecutiva de la Presidencia, a ministry-level secretariat
Program costs	• Budget: $200 per month (0.2% of GDP, 2007) • Administrative cost: 5.0% of program budget (1.0% is for materials related to verification of compliance), plus 3.4% in banking commissions

Source: Bank staff and *World Development Indicators* database 2008.

General	
Population (total)	13.3 million (2007)
GDP per capita (PPP, 2005 $)	$4,075
Poverty headcount ratio at $2/day	51%
Education	
Net enrollment in primary level	86.4%
Net enrollment in secondary level	37.5%
Health	
Prevalence of child malnutrition (stunting)	54.3%
Births attended by skilled health staff	41% (2002)

Honduras

Program: Programa de Asignación Familiar

Year started	1998
Status	Active

Targeting

Target population	Poor households with children aged 6–12 who have not completed grade 4 of primary school (education), and poor households with pregnant women and/or children less than 3 years old (health)
Targeting method	Geographic targeting (the poorest 1,000 communities in the poorest 17 departments) and proxy means testing (in 4 departments)
Coverage	• 240,000 households, 17 departments, 133 municipalities, 1,115 towns • 15% of population
Incidence	49.6% to poorest quintile (2004)

Household Benefits

Benefit structure	In all 17 departments, food security (nutrition) benefit is $113 per household per year In 4 departments (where IDB supports the PRAF), additional education and health benefits are • Education benefit: $60 per household • Health benefit: $40 per household • Delivery incentive: $60 per pregnant woman
Payee	Mother
Payment method	Vouchers cashed through local offices of BANHCAFE or mobile units
Payment frequency	Every 6 months (payments are made irregularly)
Duration	As long as eligible
Additional benefits	Communities where PRAF operates promote access to an integrated package of services, including nutrition (AIN-C), health care, and basic services

Conditions

Health	Compliance with required frequency of health center visits;[a] compliance enforced only in the 4 departments where PARF is supported by the IDB; in the remaining 13 departments, households are encouraged only to send children to school/take them for health visit
Education	• School enrollment • Regular school attendance of at least 85%
Other	None
Verification of compliance–method	No verification in 13 departments because of difficulty of enforcing conditions when the supply is missing. However, the program carries out promotion of co-responsibilities. The verification is enforced in 4 departments where IDB supports PRAF.
Verification of compliance–frequency	Every 6 months
Compliance statistics	Not available

Program Administration	
Institutional arrangement	PRAF is an autonomous program under the Secretaria de la Presidencia. IDB piloted a similar intervention with limited coverage (PRAF I, II, III). Each of the PRAF programs has its own independent institutional structure but efforts are in place to standardize processes and operations across PRAF.
Program costs	$20 million (2008)

Sources: Glewwe, Olinto, and de Souza 2003; Moore 2008; Morris, Flores et al. 2004; program Web site: http://www.gob.hn/portal/poder_ejecutivo/desconcentrados/praf/; country context: *World Development Indicators* database 2008.

Note: AIN-C = Atención Integral de la Niñez en la Comunidad; BANHCAFE = Banco Hondureño del Café; IDB = Inter-American Development Bank; PPP = purchasing power parity PRAF = Programa de Asignación Familiar.

a. Children aged 0–3: those less than 2 years old must have visited the health center at least once a month; those aged 2–5 must have visited the health center every three months. Main beneficiaries must have attended training courses four times per year. Mothers with children less than 2 years old must undergo AIN-C control. Pregnant mothers must have at least five prenatal checkups. Delivery at a public facility should be verified. Main beneficiary must have attended training courses at least four times per year.

Country Context

General	
Population (total)	7 million (2006)
GDP per capita (PPP, 2005 $)	$3,433 (2006)
Poverty headcount ratio at $2/day	35.7% (2003)
Education	
Net enrollment in primary level	96.4% total (2006) 97.2% for girls, 95.7% for boys
Net enrollment in secondary level	Not available
Health	
Prevalence of child malnutrition (stunting)	29.9% (2006)
Births attended by skilled health staff	66.9% (2006)

Jamaica

Program: Program of Advancement through Health and Education

Year started	2001
Status	Active

Targeting

Target population	• Children aged 0–19 (or until they graduate from secondary school) • Poor people aged 60 and older • Pregnant or lactating women up to 6 months after delivery • People with disabilities • Poor adults
Targeting method	Proxy means testing
Coverage	300,000 people or 12% of total population (September 2008); of that total, 70% are children, 11% are disabled, and 19% are elderly or are pregnant and/or lactating mothers
Incidence	59.6% to poorest quintile (2004)

Household Benefits

Benefit structure	J$650 per month per beneficiary (established limit of 20 beneficiaries in any one family).[a] Beginning December 2008, a new differentiated scheme of benefits is in place: boys receive 10% higher benefits than girls at all grades; lower-secondary students receive 50% higher than base benefit; upper-secondary students receive 75% higher than base benefit; all other categories receive the base benefit of $650.
Payee	Family representative or his/her agent
Payment method	Checks disbursed through prepaid cash cards
Payment frequency	Bimonthly
Duration	As long as eligible; recertification after 4 years
Additional benefits	• Secondary level students have free access to the government's textbook rental scheme • Free lunch in schools where there is a government-run school feeding program • Free health care for beneficiaries

Conditions

Health	• 4 health center visits per year for children aged 0–11 months (in keeping with the immunization schedule stipulated by the Ministry of Health) • 2 health center visits per year, at 6-month intervals, for children aged 12–59 months • Health center visits every 2 months for pregnant women, and at 6 weeks and 2 months postpartum for lactating women • 2 health center visits per year, at 6-month intervals, for people with disabilities, elderly people, and other adult beneficiaries
Education	Regular school attendance of at least 85% for children aged 6–19
Other	None

Verification of compliance–method	MLSS staff give schools and health providers lists of the PATH participants and forms for the providers to report school attendance/health care data for the previous 2 months. MLSS staff pick up the completed forms from the providers. Data are entered into PATH's management information system and used as the basis for compliance and payment determinations.
Verification of compliance–frequency	Every 2 months, MLSS staff provide the lists of PATH beneficiaries to service providers; 4 weeks later, they return to collect the completed forms
Compliance statistics	• 88% of girls and 84% of boys complied with education requirements • 88% of children aged 0–11 months complied with health requirements (May–June 2007)

Program Administration	
Institutional arrangement	MLSS
Program costs	• Budget: J$1.7 billion (approximately $245 million) during FY2007/08 • Administrative costs: 13% of program's overall budget

Sources: Levy and Ohls 2003; 2007; ODI 2006; Government of Jamaica 2006; program Web site: http://www.mlss.gov.jm/pub/index.php?artid=23; country context: *World Development Indicators* database 2008.

Note: MLSS = Ministry of Labour and Social Security; PPP = purchasing power parity.

a. Starting October 1, 2008, the base benefit increased to J$600 per month. Relative to the base benefit, benefits for students in lower-secondary school are increased by 50 percent (to J$990 for boys and J$900 for girls); benefits for students in upper-secondary school are increased by 75 percent (to J$1,150 for boys and J$1,050 for girls). Boys in primary grades receive J$660, and all other categories will receive J$600 per month.

Country Context

General	
Population (total)	2.7 million (2006)
GDP per capita (PPP, 2005 $)	$7,333 (2006)
Poverty headcount ratio at $2/day	14.4% (2004)

Education	
Net enrollment in primary level	90.3% total (2005) 90.4% for girls, 90.1% for boys
Net enrollment in secondary level	78.3% total (2005) 80.1% for girls, 76.5% for boys

Health	
Prevalence of child malnutrition (stunting)	4.5% (2004)
Births attended by skilled health staff	96.7% (2005)

Program: Oportunidades (formerly PROGRESA)

Year started	1997
Status	Active

Targeting

Target population	Extremely poor households
Targeting method	Geographic targeting and proxy means testing
Coverage	5 million households,[a] approximately 18% of the country's total population
Incidence	35% of poorest quintile

Household Benefits

Benefit structure	• Education: primary school—varies by grade, $12–$23 per child per month plus $23 per child per year for school materials; secondary—varies by grade and gender, $34–$43 per child per month plus $29 per child per year for school materials; middle/higher—varies by grade and gender $57–$74 per child per month plus $29 per child per year for school materials • Education: $336 in a savings account upon completion of high school (grade 12) • Health: $17 per household per month • $23 per month per adult over 69 years old who is part of a beneficiary family
Payee	Mother
Payment method	Cash at payment points and payments through beneficiary's savings account with BANSEFI
Payment frequency	Bimonthly (education benefit of $336 paid only once)
Duration	As long as eligible
Additional benefits	None

Conditions

Health	• Compliance by all household members with the required number of preventive medical checkups • Attendance of family member older than 15 years at health and nutrition lectures
Education	• School enrollment and minimum attendance rate of 80% monthly and 93% annually • Completion of middle school • Completion of grade 12 before age 22
Other	None
Verification of compliance–method	Program state coordination agency provides forms to the state education and health agencies, which pass them on to the local service providers responsible for filling in the compliance information. Forms are returned to the state coordination agency, which compiles the information and passes it on to the national coordination agency in charge of generating the list of beneficiaries and amounts to be paid each period.
Verification of compliance–frequency	Bimonthly
Compliance statistics	98% of beneficiary families receive benefits (November/December 2007)[b]

Program Administration

Institutional arrangement	Secretariat for Social Development, national and state coordination agencies of the program, and education and health service providers
Program costs	• Budget: $3,181,214,484 in 2006 (1.75% of net total expenditure; 0.4% of GDP)[c]
	• Administrative cost: 9.05% ($288,007,275)

Sources: Levy 2006; Lindert, Skoufias, and Shapiro 2006; evaluations: http://evaluacion.Oportunidades.gob.mx:8010/en/index.php; operations manual: http://www.Oportunidades.gob.mx/htmls/reglas.html; program Web site: http://www.Oportunidades.gob.mx/; country context: *World Development Indicators* database 2008.

Note: BANSEFI = Banco del Ahorro Nacional y Servicios Financieros; PPP = purchasing power parity.

a. At 92,208 localities and 2,444 municipalities (October 2007).

b. This refers to the percent of beneficiary families receiving benefits in October 2007, which reflects their compliance in July-August 2007.

c. Budget broken down by component (prorated): support to education, 47.29 percent; support to food intake, 30.02 percent; food supplement, 6.56 percent; support to the elderly, 6.29 percent; support to youngsters under Oportunidades, 0.78 percent.

Country Context

General	
Population (total)	104.2 million (2006)
GDP per capita (PPP, 2005 $)	$11,801 (2006)
Poverty headcount ratio at $2/day	11.6% (2004)
Education	
Net enrollment in primary level	97.7% total (2005) 97.3% for girls, 98.1% for boys
Net enrollment in secondary level	68.6% total (2005) 68.4% for girls, 68.8% for boys
Health	
Prevalence of child malnutrition (stunting)	15.5% (2006)
Births attended by skilled health staff	83.3% (2004)

Nicaragua

Program: Atención a Crisis

Year started	2005
Status	1-year pilot program, ended in December 2006

Targeting

Target population	Poor households residing in region affected by drought
Targeting method	Geographic targeting and proxy means testing
Coverage	3,000 households
Incidence	90% of households

Household Benefits

Benefit structure	• Food transfer: $145 per household per year • Education transfer: $90 per household per year • School "supply-side" transfer: $13 per child (1-time transfer at the beginning of the school year) • School "backpack" (supplies): $25 per child per year • Health transfer: $90 per household per year (was to be paid to health provider, but was never implemented) • $15 per household per month while participating in training courses, up to 6 months
Payee	Child's caregiver
Payment method	Cash at payment points
Payment frequency	Bimonthly
Duration	1 year
Additional benefits	• In addition to the traditional CCT component, the pilot program also included occupational training and a business grant component. These were allocated randomly across eligible households. In its final design, beneficiary households were allocated one of the following three interventions: (1) CCT component (with benefits as described above); (2) CCT plus occupational training; or (3) CCT plus a business grant. • For occupational training, additional benefits included (1) opportunity cost transfer (up to $90 per household per year), (2) course costs up to $140 per household per year • For the business grant, additional benefits included a business grant transfer of $200 per household plus technical assistance to develop a business plan

Conditions

Health	Pilot program design envisioned close coordination between the Ministry of Family and the Ministry of Health to improve the supply of health services for the beneficiaries, and to monitor health-related conditions. Despite strong and repeated efforts to reach interministry coordination and synergies, this supply-side health component was never implemented.

Education	• Enrollment in grades 1–6 for children aged 7–15
	• Regular attendance of 85%, (that is, no more than 5 absences without valid excuse every 2 months)
	• Deliver teacher transfer to teacher
Other	• For occupational training: household needed to decide on member who takes course, and payment is conditional on attendance at course
	• For the business grant: business plan approved by technical team in the Ministry of Family
Verification of compliance–method	Through forms sent to service providers (schools and health providers) and fed into the management information system
Verification of compliance–frequency	Bimonthly
Compliance statistics	• Less than 5% of beneficiaries were penalized
	• No terminations were made as a result of noncompliance

Program Administration

Institutional arrangement	• Funding and administrative oversight by the Ministry of Family.
	• A technical team at the Ministry of Family was responsible for the program design, targeting and beneficiary selection, and the program's overall implementation, monitoring, and coordinating activities (for example, with the ministries of education and health, the National Institute for Vocational Training, and each of the municipal administrations and local actors involved in different components of the program).
	• In each municipality, a local staffperson was assigned to serve as a liaison between the Ministry of Family and the beneficiary households to facilitate, coordinate, and monitor various program activities at the municipal level.
	• Private service providers were contracted to provide technical assistance for beneficiaries allocated the occupational training or the business grant.
	• In each community, beneficiaries were organized in small groups (of about 10 people), and each group elected 2 members as the group's *promotoras/es* to coordinate program-related information given to all beneficiaries, clarifying program rules and conditions, ensuring participation of all beneficiaries in program meetings and activities, and providing informal guidance and support to beneficiaries.
Program costs	• Budget: $1.8 million (0.1% of GDP)
	• Administrative cost: $0.4 million

Sources: Macours and Vakis 2008; impact evaluation Web site: www.worldbank.org/atencionacrisisevaluation; country context: *World Development Indicators* database 2008.

Note: PPP = purchasing power parity.

See page 273 for Country Context table.

Nicaragua

Program: Red de Protección Social[a]

Year started	2000
Status	Stopped

Targeting

Target population	Poor households with children aged 7–13 enrolled in primary school grades 1–4 (education); health care services are targeted to children aged 0–5
Targeting method	Geographic targeting
Coverage	20,000 households during phase 1; 16,016 additional households during phase 2
Incidence	Not available

Household Benefits

Benefit structure	• School attendance grant (*bono escolar*): C$240 ($17) per family every 2 months; school material support (*mochila escolar*): C$275 ($20) per child per year • Health and nutrition (*bono alimentario*): C$480 ($34) per family every 2 months
Payee	Child's caregiver
Payment method	Cash at payment points
Payment frequency	Bimonthly
Duration	Not available
Additional benefits	Education: supply incentive (*bono a la oferta*)—C$80 ($6) per student per year, given to teacher/school

Conditions

Health	• Bimonthly health education workshops (all households) • Attendance at prescheduled health care visits every month (aged 0–2) or bimonthly (aged 3–5), adequate weight gain and up-to-date vaccinations (aged 0–5) for all households with children aged 0–5[b]
Education	• Enrollment in grades 1–4 for children aged 7–13 • Regular attendance of 85% (that is, no more than 5 absences without valid excuse every 2 months) • Grade promotion at end of school year[c]
Other	None
Verification of compliance–method	Through forms sent to service providers (schools and health providers) and fed into the program's management information system
Verification of compliance–frequency	Not available
Compliance statistics	• Approximately 10% of beneficiaries were penalized at least once; therefore they did not receive, or received only part of, their transfer in the first 2 years of the program • Less than 1% of households terminated during the first 2 years of transfer delivery[d]

Institutional arrangement	• Funding and administrative oversight by the Emergency Social Investment Fund • Municipal planning and coordination by committees of delegates from the health and education ministries, representatives from civil society, and program personnel • At district (*comarca*) level: 12 program representatives worked with *promotoras* and local school and health care service providers • *Promotoras* were responsible for communication with beneficiary households[e]
Program costs	Budget: $3.7 million in phase I (10,000 households), (0.2% of GDP)

Sources: Maluccio and Flores 2005; country context: *World Development Indicators* database 2008.

Note: PPP = purchasing power parity.

a. Note that this table refers to the first phase of the program. During the second phase, a proxy means test was introduced and small changes to benefits were made.

b. The up-to-date vaccination condition was deemed unfair and not enforced when it was found that there was a delay in the delivery of vaccines. Also, punishment of children who did not have adequate weight gain was dropped at the end of the pilot phase because of a concern about the role of measurement error and the finding that the poorest households were more likely to be punished.

c. Because some schools practiced automatic promotion, enforcement of the grade promotion condition was deemed unfair and therefore never enforced.

d. But 5 percent voluntarily left the program, by dropping out or migrating out of the program area.

e. Their responsibilities included keeping them informed about upcoming health care appointments for their children, upcoming payments, and any failures in fulfilling the conditions. Each *promotora* had, on average, 17 beneficiaries in her charge, although that average masked substantial variation ranging from 5 to 30 beneficiaries.

Country Context

General	
Population (total)	5.5 million (2006)
GDP per capita (PPP, 2005 $)	$2,702 (2006)
Poverty headcount ratio at $2/day	79.9% (2001)
Education	
Net enrollment in primary level	89.8% total (2006) 89.9% for girls, 89.6% for boys
Net enrollment in secondary level	43.4% total (2004) 46.6% for girls, 40.2% for boys
Health	
Prevalence of child malnutrition (stunting)	25.2% (2001)
Births attended by skilled health staff	66.9% (2001)

Panama

Program: Red de Oportunidades

Year started	2006
Status	Active

Targeting

Target population	Families living under the extreme poverty line (about 16.6% of the population, 70,000 households)
Targeting method	Proxy means testing in rural nonindigenous areas, indigenous areas, and urban areas (different cut-offs)
Coverage	Nationwide
Incidence	Not available

Household Benefits

Benefit structure	$35 per month per household; the amount was increased to $50 in July 2008 as a response to food price inflation. The amount is flat per household, irrespective of the number or ages of children.[a]
Payee	Mother
Payment method	Post office in remote areas, banks in urban areas
Payment frequency	Bimonthly
Duration	5 years
Additional benefits	*Acompañamiento:* (planned) accompaniment through teams to link beneficiaries to other services, programs, and so forth

Conditions

Health	• Immunizations for children aged 0–5 • Visits to basic health services providers
Education	• Regular school attendance of children • Participation in parent-teacher conferences in school
Other	Participation in capacity-building events
Verification of compliance–method	Not available
Verification of compliance–frequency	Not available
Compliance statistics	Not available

Program Administration

Institutional arrangement	Ministry of Social Development
Program costs	• Budget: $160.1 million for transfers in 5 years • Administrative cost: 20%

Sources: Program Web site: http://www.mides.gob.pa/index.php?option=com_content&task=blogcategory&id=48&Itemid.com; country context: *World Development Indicators* database 2008.

Note: PPP = purchasing power parity.

a. Per family in indigenous areas.

General	
Population (total)	3.3 million (2006)
GDP per capita (PPP, 2005 $)	$8,969 (2006)
Poverty headcount ratio at $2/day	18% (2003)

Education	
Net enrollment in primary level	98.5% total (2006) 98.2% for girls, 98.8% for boys
Net enrollment in secondary level	64.2% total (2006) 67.5% for girls, 61.0% for boys

Health	
Prevalence of child malnutrition (stunting)	18.2% (1997)
Births attended by skilled health staff	91.3% (2004)

Paraguay

Program: Tekoporã/PROPAIS II

Year started	Tekoporã: 2005, PROPAIS II: 2006
Status	Active

Targeting

Target population	Extremely poor families with children aged 0–14 and pregnant women, rural areas only
Targeting method	Geographic targeting (Indice de Piorizacion Geografica), life quality index (Indice de Calidad de Vida) for Tekoporã and other proxy means testing for PROPAIS II
Coverage	Tekoporã: 14,000; PROPAIS II: 5,800
Incidence	Not available

Household Benefits

Benefit structure	Flat benefit (₲60,000) + variable component (₲30,000 per child up to a maximum of 4). Benefit range: ₲90,000–₲180,000 (equivalent to $18–$36)
Payee	Mother
Payment method	Mobile cashier
Payment frequency	Bimonthly
Duration	3 years
Additional benefits	Family support (counseling and advice)

Conditions

Health	Follow the vaccination calendar; child health checks, age groups 0–5 and 6–14
Education	School matriculation and attendance
Other	None
Verification of compliance–method	Compliance department at Presidential Agency for Social Assistance (Asuncion) checks the information (photocopies of certificates) handed to family guides during household visits
Verification of compliance–frequency	Bimonthly
Compliance statistics	Approximately 70% for health and education as of 2006

Program Administration

Institutional arrangement	Presidential Agency for Social Assistance
Program costs	• Budget: US$9.6 million (0.08% of GDP; 2007) • Administrative cost: approximately 10% of program budget

Sources: Bank staff; country context: *World Development Indicators* database 2008.

Country Context

General	
Population (total)	6.1 million (2006)
GDP per capita (PPP, 2005 $)	$1,967 (2006)
Poverty headcount ratio at $2/day	Not available
Education	
Net enrollment in primary level	94% total (2004) 95% for girls, 95% for boys
Net enrollment in secondary level	57% total (2004) 59% for girls, 57% for boys
Health	
Prevalence of child malnutrition (stunting)	Not available
Births attended by skilled health staff	77% (2004)

Peru

Program: Juntos

Year started	2005
Status	Active

Targeting

Target population	Poor households with children less than 14 years old
Targeting method	Geographic targeting, proxy means testing, and community validation
Coverage	453,823 (June 2008)
Incidence	Not available

Household Benefits

Benefit structure	S/.100 ($33) per month
Payee	Mother
Payment method	Through beneficiary's bank account at the Banco de la Nacion and associated debit card
Payment frequency	Monthly
Duration	4 years
Additional benefits	None

Conditions

Health	Regular health visits for pregnant women and for children less than 5 years old[a]
Education	School attendance of at least 85% for children aged 6–14 who have not completed elementary education
Other	• Participation in the Mi Nombre (My Name) program by all families with children who lack birth certificates and/or are older than 18 years and have no identification card
Verification of compliance–method	Not available
Verification of compliance–frequency	Every 3 months
Compliance statistics	• 2.7% of beneficiaries suspended for noncompliance (end-September 2007) • 96% compliance with health center visits

Program Administration

Institutional arrangement	Not available
Program costs	Budget: S/.300 million ($100 million) in 2006 (0.11% of GDP)

Sources: Jones, Vargas, and Villar 2008; program Web site: http://www.juntos.gob.pe/intro.php; country context: *World Development Indicators* database 2008.

Note: PPP = purchasing power parity.

a. For pregnant mothers: prenatal controls; postnatal controls; full inoculations schedule; vitamin A, iron, and folic acid supplements; and attendance at nutritional, reproductive health, and food cooking chats. For children up to 5 years old: full inoculations schedule, iron supplement, growth and development monitoring, and deworming.

Country Context

General	
Population (total)	27.6 million (2006)
GDP per capita (PPP, 2005 $US)	$6,872 (2006)
Poverty headcount ratio at $2/day	30.6% (2003)

Education	
Net enrollment in primary level	96.4% total (2005) 97.1% for girls, 95.7% for boys
Net enrollment in secondary level	70.2% total (2005) 69.9% for girls, 70.5% for boys

Health	
Prevalence of child malnutrition (stunting)	31.3% (2000)
Births attended by skilled health staff	86.9% (2006)

Yemen, Republic of

Program: Basic Education Development Project

Year started	2007
Status	Ongoing pilot program

Targeting

Target population	Girls in grades 4–9 in all basic schools that satisfy school selection criteria in one governorate; girls in grades 4–9 in randomly selected rural schools that satisfy selection criteria in second governorate (for impact evaluation)
Targeting method	Geographic targeting
Coverage	215 school catchment areas in one governorate and 67 areas in the second governorate
Incidence	Not available

Household Benefits

Benefit structure	• Girls in grades 4–5: $35 per year • Girls in grade 6: $35 per year, plus achievement bonus of $5 • Girls in grades 7 and 9: $40 per year • Girls in grade 8: $40 per year, plus achievement bonus of $5 conditional on performing well in an external examination
Payee	Mother or father (randomly divided between beneficiary school areas)
Payment method	Cash provided at school parent-teacher meetings; looking at mobile ATM cards option
Payment frequency	3 times per year: beginning of the school year and end of each semester
Duration	7 years maximum
Additional benefits	None

Conditions

Health	None
Education	Child attends 80% of all classes in a 2-month period
Other	Additional payment upon successful completion of a grade level; passing score on achievement test
Verification of compliance–method	Through regular attendance records collected from schools by a dedicated group of personnel hired for monitoring; also random spot-checks in place
Verification of compliance–frequency	Monthly
Compliance statistics	Not available

Program Administration

Institutional arrangement	Ministry of Education responsible for oversight under the program. Funds disbursed through the ministry with verification from the project administration unit. The various groups monitoring at various levels include the Girls Education Sector (GES), Governorate Education Office, District Education Office, postal service, project administration unit, CCT implementation team (consisting of 6 consultants who work under the GES), and CCT technical team (comprising experts from the GES and the World Bank).
Program costs	Approximately 3% of the total amount distributed

Sources: Fasih 2008; country context: *World Development Indicators* database 2008.
Note: PPP = purchasing power parity.

Country Context

General	
Population (total)	21.7 million (2006)
GDP per capita (PPP, 2005 $US)	$2,194 (2006)
Poverty headcount ratio at $2/day	45.2% (1998)

Education	
Net enrollment in primary level	75.2% total (2005) 64.9% for girls, 85.1% for boys
Net enrollment in secondary level	37.4% total (2005) 25.8% for girls, 48.5% for boys

Health	
Prevalence of child malnutrition (stunting)	Not available
Births attended by skilled health staff	26.8% (2003)

Bangladesh

Program: Female Secondary School Assistance Program[a]

Year started	1994
Status	Active (as FSSAP II)

Targeting

Target population	Unmarried girls who completed primary school and are enrolled in a recognized secondary school
Targeting method	Geographic targeting of districts (*thanas*) and gender targeting
Coverage	723,864 girls (2005)[b] or about 76% of girls in the project schools
Incidence	Not available

Household Benefits

Benefit structure	Combined stipend and tuition subsidy: Tk 906 for nongovernment schools; Tk 847 for government schools
Payee	Female student
Payment method	Direct deposit to a bank account in the girl's name
Payment frequency	Twice a year
Duration	From grade 6 to grade 10
Additional benefits	• Book allowance, paid to student • Examination fees, paid to student • Tuition subsidy paid directly to school • Additional supply-side support to school

Conditions

Health	None
Education	• Attends 75% of school days • Attains 45% of class-level test scores
Other	Remain unmarried until passing the secondary school certificate examination
Verification of compliance–method	Not available
Verification of compliance–frequency	Not available
Compliance statistics	About 4% of girls were dropped because of noncompliance with one or more of the three conditions (school attendance, passing grades, remaining unmarried) in 2005[c]

Institutional arrangement	Ministry of Education Directorate of Secondary and Higher Education
Program costs	• Budget: Tk 1.5 billion in 2004, ($40 million); more than 4 million beneficiaries annually
	• Administrative costs: approximately 18% of program cost

Sources: World Bank 2006e; Khandker, Pitt, and Fuwa 2003; program Web site: http://www.dshe.gov.bd/female_stipend.html; country context: *World Development Indicators* database 2008.

Note: FSSAP = Female Secondary School Assistance Program; PPP = purchasing power parity.

a. The Nationwide Female Stipend Program is implemented through four projects that operate in different districts and are funded by different donors. They include the FSSAP supported by the World Bank and the government, the Female Secondary Stipend Project (FSSP) supported through government funds, the Secondary Education Sector Improvement Project (SESIP) supported through the African Development Bank and government funds, and the Female Education Stipend Project (FESP) supported through the Norwegian Agency for Development Cooperation.

b. The four secondary-school girls' stipend programs (FSSAP, FSSP, SESIP, FESP) together covered 2.2 million girls in 2005, representing about 83 percent of girls in the schools covered.

c. Total number of girls dropped from the program for either noncompliance or other reasons was approximately 4.7 percent in 2005.

Country Context

General	
Population (total)	156 million (2006)
GDP per capita (PPP, 2005 $)	$1,119 (2006)
Poverty headcount ratio at $2/day	84% (2000)
Education	
Net enrollment in primary level	88.8% total (2004)
	90.5% for girls, 87.4% for boys
Net enrollment in secondary level	40.1% total (2004)
	40.2% for girls, 41.8% for boys
Health	
Prevalence of child malnutrition (stunting)	47.8% (2005)
Births attended by skilled health staff	20.1% (2006)

Bangladesh

Program: Primary Education Stipend Program[a]

Year started	2002
Status	Active

Targeting

Target population	Poor families with children of primary-school age
Targeting method	Geographic targeting combined with community assessment[b]
Coverage	More than 5.3 million beneficiaries per year
Incidence	Not available

Household Benefits

Benefit structure	Tk 100 per month (one student per family), Tk 125 per month (more than one student per family)
Payee	Beneficiary's guardian
Payment method	Direct transfer to beneficiary's bank account
Payment frequency	Quarterly
Duration	As long as eligible
Additional benefits	None

Conditions

Health	None
Education	• Attends 85% of school days • Obtains at least 40% marks in the annual examinations
Other	None
Verification of compliance–method	Not available
Verification of compliance–frequency	Not available
Compliance statistics	Not available

Program Administration

Institutional arrangement	Department of Primary Education, Ministry of Education
Program costs	• Budget: $103.63 million in FY2003/04 • Administrative costs: about 5% of program costs[c]

Sources: Tietjen 2003; World Bank 2006e; country context: *World Development Indicators* database 2008.

Note: PESP = Primary Education Stipend Program; PPP = purchasing power parity.

a. In 2002 the PESP replaced the Food for Education program, which was a food-based CCT program with objectives similar to those of the PESP.

b. The following criteria are used to identify households at the community level: (1) destitute woman-headed family (destitute means widowed, separated from husband, or divorced); (2) principal occupation of the household head is day-labor; (3) family of low-income professionals (such as those engaged in fishing, pottery, blacksmithing, weaving, and cobbling); (4) landless households or households that own 0.50 acres of land (marginal or share-cropper).

c. This does not include administrative costs of lower levels of government.

General	
Population (total)	156 million (2006)
GDP per capita (PPP, 2005 $)	$1,119 (2006)
Poverty headcount ratio at $2/day	84% (2000)
Education	
Net enrollment in primary level	88.8% total (2004) 90.5% for girls, 87.4% for boys
Net enrollment in secondary level	40.1% total (2004) 40.2% for girls, 41.8% for boys
Health	
Prevalence of child malnutrition (stunting)	47.8% (2005)
Births attended by skilled health staff	20.1% (2006)

Bangladesh

Program: Reaching Out-of-School Children

Year started	2004
Status	Ongoing

Targeting

Target population	Children who have not had an opportunity to attend primary school in remote areas and dropouts from primary school
Targeting method	Geographic targeting
Coverage	500,000 children
Incidence	Not available

Household Benefits

Benefit structure	• In 36 subdistricts: Tk 100 per month to children and approximately Tk 25,000 per year to community school • In 24 subdistricts: no stipend to children, but approximately Tk 55,000 per year to community school
Payee	Mother/guardian
Payment method	Direct transfer to beneficiary's bank account
Payment frequency	Twice a year
Duration	As long as student is in primary education (5 years)
Additional benefits	Support given to organizations (mainly NGOs) to train teachers and oversee quality of education in community schools

Conditions

Health	None
Education	75% attendance and 75% performance in examinations, as judged by school teacher
Other	None
Verification of compliance–method	Random third-party monitoring survey and project office monitoring
Verification of compliance–frequency	Third-party survey undertaken during the year covers 20% of institutions. Project office monitoring occurring on a monthly basis is also random.
Compliance statistics	Students not meeting criteria are excluded from program (about 5%)

Program Administration

Institutional arrangement	Ministry of Primary and Mass Education
Program costs	$63 million

Sources: World Bank 2004a; country context: *World Development Indicators* database 2008.
Note: NGO = nongovernmental organization; PPP = purchasing power parity.

Country Context

General	
Population (total)	156 million (2006)
GDP per capita (PPP, 2005 $)	$1,119 (2006)
Poverty headcount ratio at $2/day	84% (2000)

Education	
Net enrollment in primary level	88.8% total (2004) 90.5% for girls, 87.4% for boys
Net enrollment in secondary level	40.1% total (2004) 40.2% for girls, 41.8% for boys

Health	
Prevalence of child malnutrition (stunting)	47.8% (2005)
Births attended by skilled health staff	20.1% (2006)

India (Haryana)

Program: Apni Beti Apna Dhan (Our Daughter, Our Wealth)

Year started	1994
Status	Active

Targeting

Target population	Girls born on or after October 2, 1994, in poor households (based on official below-poverty-line estimates) and certain castes. Girls have to be first, second, or third child in the family. Families with more than 3 children are not eligible.
Targeting method	Using official poverty-line estimates
Coverage	Not available
Incidence	Not available

Household Benefits

Benefit structure	Incentive for female births plus marriage delay: within 3 months of girl's birth, Re 2,500 is invested in Indira Vikas Patras, a federal government savings bond scheme in which the invested amount doubles in 5 years. The sum is reinvested every fifth year. The girl can withdraw the maturity amount of Re 25,000 when she turns 18, provided she is unmarried.
Payee	Girl
Payment method	Savings bond
Payment frequency	Once, when girl turns 18 years of age
Duration	Girls exit the program at age 18
Additional benefits	• Mothers receive a cash amount (called postnatal assistance) of Re 500 upon daughter's birth. They receive cash at home or through local health workers or health centers. • A higher maturity amount (Re 35,000) for girls who agree to defer cashing in their securities, plus a credit subsidy for entrepreneurship loans

Conditions

Health	The program implicitly aims to reduce child mortality among girls and the abortion of female fetus
Education	Girls receive bonus for completing grade 5 and grade 8
Other	Marriage delay: girl must be unmarried at age 18
Verification of compliance–method	Beneficiaries submit application form to local early-childhood development worker (*anganwadi* worker) in rural areas, or to the health officer in urban areas. With this application form, parents must submit daughter's birth certificate.
Verification of compliance–frequency	Upon birth of girl and when the girl becomes eligible to redeem the savings certificate
Compliance statistics	Not available

Institutional arrangement	The state's Department of Women and Child Welfare manages the program. The program is implemented through the institutional apparatus of the early-childhood development program, called the Integrated Child Development Scheme.
Program costs	Not available

Sources: World Bank 2004; country context: *World Development Indicators* database 2008.
Note: PPP = purchasing power parity.

Country Context

General	
Population (total)	1.12 billion (2007)
GDP per capita (PPP, 2005 $)	2,230
Poverty headcount ratio at $2/day	Not available
Education	
Net enrollment in primary level	89% total (2005) 87% for girls, 90% for boys
Net enrollment in secondary level	Not available
Health	
Prevalence of child malnutrition (stunting)	48%
Births attended by skilled health staff	46%

Pakistan

Program: Child Support Program

Year started	2006
Status	Running on pilot basis

Targeting

Target population	Food Support Program beneficiaries with children aged 5–12
Targeting method	Proxy means testing
Coverage	13,265 being paid (March 2008)
Incidence	On launch of the program in the district

Household Benefits

Benefit structure	PRs 200 per month for family with 1 child and PRs 350 per month for family with more than 1 child
Payee	Parent/guardian
Payment method	At post offices
Payment frequency	Quarterly
Duration	Until child completes primary education
Additional benefits	Food Support Program subsidy of PRs 3,000 per year

Conditions

Health	None
Education	Admission of children, 80% attendance, and passing of final examination
Other	None
Verification of compliance–method	Compliance reports generated through the management information system.
Verification of compliance–frequency	Quarterly
Compliance statistics	Not available

Program Administration

Institutional arrangement	Program design at Pakistan Bait-ul-Maal head office, coordination at provincial office, and implementation through Pakistan Bait-ul-Maal district office, with close coordination of district education department
Program costs	• Budget: PRs 120 million per year for 5 districts • Targeting cost: PRs 7,011,000 • Enrollment cost: PRs 8,022,655 • Other administrative costs: PRs 650,000 • Total administrative costs: PRs 15,683,655

Sources: Government of Pakistan 2007; Mohammad Farooq, program official; country context: *World Development Indicators* database 2008.

Note: PPP = purchasing power parity.

Country Context

General	
Population (total)	159 million (2006)
GDP per capita (PPP, 2005 $)	$2,288 (2006)
Poverty headcount ratio at $2/day	73.6% (2002)

Education	
Net enrollment in primary level	65.6% total (2006) 57.3% for girls, 73.5% for boys
Net enrollment in secondary level	29.7% total (2006) 25.8% for girls, 33.3% for boys

Health	
Prevalence of child malnutrition (stunting)	41.5% (2001)
Births attended by skilled health staff	31% (2005)

Pakistan

Program: Participation in Education through Innovative Scheme for the Excluded Vulnerable

Year started	2003
Status	Pilot and closed
Targeting	
Target population	Children of poor and disadvantaged people
Targeting method	Geographic targeting of union councils/districts, using literacy rate; selection on the basis of poverty ranking
Coverage	8,000 students
Incidence	Not available
Household Benefits	
Benefit structure	PRs 600 quarterly for 1 child, and an additional PRs 200 quarterly if the household has 2 or more children
Payee	Student's household
Payment method	Direct transfer via postal money order
Payment frequency	Quarterly
Duration	As long as eligible
Additional benefits	None
Conditions	
Health	None
Education	• Enrollment in grades 0–5 (primary) in a government school in a target district/union council • School attendance on at least 80% of school days
Other	None
Verification of compliance–method	NGOs and education department monitor the compliance through attendance records maintained by the schools
Verification of compliance–frequency	Monthly and quarterly reports
Compliance statistics	Not available
Program Administration	
Institutional arrangement	National Education Foundation, Project Management Implementation Unit of provincial and district education departments, with district governments and local NGOs
Program costs	$706,500

Sources: Nangar Soomro, program official; country context: *World Development Indicators* database 2008.
Note: NGO = nongovernmental organization; PPP = purchasing power parity.

Country Context

General	
Population (total)	159 million (2006)
GDP per capita (PPP, 2005 $)	$2,288 (2006)
Poverty headcount ratio at $2/day	73.6% (2002)
Education	
Net enrollment in primary level	65.6% total (2006) 57.3% for girls, 73.5% for boys
Net enrollment in secondary level	29.7% total (2006) 25.8% for girls, 33.3% for boys
Health	
Prevalence of child malnutrition (stunting)	41.5% (2001)
Births attended by skilled health staff	31% (2005)

Pakistan

Program: Punjab Education Sector Reform Program/Punjab Female School Stipend Program

Year started	2004
Status	Implemented in selected districts of Punjab
Targeting	
Target population	Girls at secondary-school level
Targeting method	Geographic targeting of districts, using literacy rate
Coverage	186,503 (2003); 279,928 (2006); 455,259 (2007)
Incidence	Not available
Household Benefits	
Benefit structure	PRs 200 per student per month (about $3)
Payee	Student's household
Payment method	Direct transfer via postal money order from the education district office
Payment frequency	Quarterly
Duration	As long as eligible
Additional benefits	Provision of free textbooks to all school children in grades 1–7 across Punjab
Conditions	
Health	None
Education	• Enrollment in grades 6–8 in a government girl's school in a target district • School attendance of at least 80%
Other	None
Verification of compliance–method	Education department attendance reports and school progress reports
Verification of compliance–frequency	Quarterly
Compliance statistics	Not available
Program Administration	
Institutional arrangement	Project Management Implementation Unit of provincial and district education departments, with district governments
Program costs	• FY2005: PRs 450 million • FY2006: PRs 960 million

Sources: Chaudhury and Parajuli 2008; country context: *World Development Indicators* database 2008.
Note: PPP = purchasing power parity.

Country Context

General	
Population (total)	159 million (2006)
GDP per capita (PPP, 2005 $)	$2,288 (2006)
Poverty headcount ratio at $2/day	73.6% (2002)

Education	
Net enrollment in primary level	65.6% total (2006) 57.3% for girls, 73.5% for boys
Net enrollment in secondary level	29.7% total (2006) 25.8% for girls, 33.3% for boys

Health	
Prevalence of child malnutrition (stunting)	41.5% (2001)
Births attended by skilled health staff	31% (2005)

Review of CCT Impact Evaluations

CCTS HAVE BEEN REMARKABLE IN A VARIETY OF WAYS. ONE OF those ways is that perhaps more than any intervention in developing countries, CCTs have been evaluated credibly for their impact on a variety of outcomes—consumption, labor market participation, poverty, nutritional status, and schooling to name but a few. Indeed, it would not have been possible to write this report, at least not in its current form, without these evaluations to draw upon. This appendix discusses the strengths and weaknesses of some of the evaluations of CCTs that have been conducted. It does not, however, attempt to be an exhaustive methodological discussion of all available evaluations of CCT programs.

Impact evaluations involve credibly estimating counterfactual outcomes—the value an outcome would have taken if a given individual who benefited from a program had not received the benefit. (The same logic obviously also applies to other units, such as households, schools, or municipalities.) However, a given individual is never observed having both received and not received an intervention at the same point in time. Impact evaluation therefore can be thought of as a problem of missing data.

Drawing on the medical literature, studies of impact evaluation often refer to comparisons between a "treatment" group (those who received an intervention) and a "comparison" or "control" group (those who did not receive it). The comparison or control group is constructed in such a way as to make it an appropriate counterfactual for the treatment group. The difficulty therefore involves making those two groups comparable, except for the presence or absence of an intervention. For example, an evaluation of the impact of a CCT program on schooling would attempt to ensure that treatment and control groups are truly comparable in terms of both their "observable" characteristics (variables like parental education) and their "unobservable" characteristics (variables like the motivation or inherent ability of children). A failure to make the two groups comparable in terms of those and other characteristics could bias the results.

There are different ways of estimating counterfactual outcomes, including random assignment, "quasi-experimental" methods like instrumental variables and regression discontinuity (RDD), and nonexperimental methods like regression techniques, matching, and double (or higher-order) differencing. All of those methods have their strengths and weaknesses, and all will be more credible in some settings than in others. Indeed, one of the most important lessons from the rapidly growing literature on impact evaluation is that blindly applying a given method or technique is unlikely to be a sensible approach to the evaluation problem. Rather, what is needed is a careful and thoughtful analysis of the extent to which the assumptions made by each of those methods are likely to hold when attempting to answer a particular question with a given data set.

The evaluations of CCTs have used a variety of methods. A number of programs have been evaluated using random assignment. Randomization involves using a lottery to assign one group to treatment and another to control. If the sample is large enough, this method has the virtue of equating all characteristics, observable as well as unobservable, of the treatment and control groups. Differences in outcomes between the two groups after the intervention then can be interpreted credibly as causal estimates of program impact. Because randomization requires no further assumptions, it is often regarded as the gold standard for evaluations.

When Mexico's Oportunidades program began its operations in rural areas in the late 1990s, it randomly assigned a subsample of eligible villages to treatment and control groups. The first group of villages began receiving the program in 1998, whereas the second group was held back for approximately one year. In addition, rather than conducting an in-house evaluation, Oportunidades administrators hired the International Food Policy Research Institute and a respected consortium of international researchers to conduct the evaluation. Also, the data from the evaluation were made available to the public on the Internet so that other researchers could replicate or challenge the findings. Considering that it was difficult to predict ex ante whether the program would work,

these decisions were very brave — and influential. But the decisions have
been vindicated: the Oportunidades data have been used in dozens of
studies, and were influential in causing the spread of CCTs beyond the
countries where they first were implemented, Brazil and Mexico.

In this report, we draw heavily on the Oportunidades data, both
using existing studies and in our own calculations. Some of the more
influential papers using the Oportunidades data include Schultz
(2004), Behrman, Sengupta, and Todd (2005), and de Janvry and
Sadoulet (2006) on education outcomes; Gertler (2004), Rivera et al.
(2004), and Behrman and Hoddinott (2005) on nutrition outcomes;
and Hoddinott and Skoufias (2004) and Skoufias (2005) on consumption patterns and poverty. More recently, the random assignment
of Oportunidades has been used to estimate longer-term effects on
outcomes, including completed schooling and test scores (Behrman,
Parker, and Todd 2005), and investment and savings behavior (Gertler,
Martínez, and Rubio-Codina 2006)—and we draw heavily on those
studies as well. Finally, a handful of recent reports make use of the
randomized assignment in Oportunidades to estimate structural behavioral models (Attanasio, Meghir, and Santiago 2005; Todd and Wolpin
2006a).

Nevertheless, even the Oportunidades data have their limitations
(see, in particular, thoughtful discussions by Parker and Teruel [2005]
and Parker, Rubalcava, and Teruel [2008]). Despite the experimental
design, there appear to have been some significant differences between
individuals who received transfers and those who did not (Behrman
and Todd 1999). As a result, many studies using the Oportunidades
data have focused on differences in the growth rates of outcomes
between treated and control communities or individuals—a so-called
differences-in-differences approach—rather than on simple differences
in outcomes at follow-up. This approach is sensible and will tend to
remove the source of bias if it is time invariant and additive—probably
a reasonable assumption.

Another shortcoming of the Oportunidades data is that merging
the data across waves of the surveys, which is necessary to construct
the panels needed for a differences-in-differences approach, appears
to have been a serious problem, with large fractions that could not be
merged, especially in the evaluations that have used the data on anthro-
pometrics. This shortcoming leaves researchers analyzing the impact of
Oportunidades transfers on nutrition outcomes with the difficult choice

between two options: (1) to work with a smaller panel of households or children that could be merged effectively (the approach taken by Behrman and Hoddinott [2005]), which could result in biases associated with large and possibly nonrandom attrition out of the sample; or (2) to ignore any baseline differences between the two groups (the approach taken by Gertler [2004]), which essentially assumes that the differences between the two groups are negligible. More generally, attrition across survey rounds in Oportunidades appears to be non-negligible and correlated with the likelihood of being in the program, which also can introduce biases (see the discussion in Parker, Rubalcava, and Teruel [2008]).

Following from the Oportunidades evaluation, a number of programs in other countries launched randomized evaluations. These included evaluations of the RPS and Atención a Crisis programs in Nicaragua, PRAF in Honduras, and the BDH program in Ecuador. We use those evaluations quite extensively here, although some have limitations that we discuss below.

The evaluations of the RPS and Atención a Crisis programs in Nicaragua seem to have worked well. In both cases, the randomized design was successful—there appear to be no significant differences between treated and control households at baseline. Attrition rates in the evaluation of RPS were reasonably low (approximately 15 percent over four years) and, in the case of the evaluation of Atención a Crisis, extremely low (only 1.3 percent of households were lost between baseline and follow-up, although the period between the two surveys was short—approximately nine months). Moreover, attrition appears to be uncorrelated with treatment status, and the characteristics of attrited and other households were very similar—again, limiting the potential for important biases. Finally, there was no contamination of the control group, and take-up among eligible households was high. For all of those reasons, reports based on those evaluations—including Maluccio and Flores (2005), Maluccio (2005, 2008), and Macours, Schady, and Vakis (2008)—are likely to provide robust evidence of the impact of CCT programs in Nicaragua, at least during a pilot phase.

The randomized evaluation of PRAF in Honduras also appears to have worked reasonably well, although it faced a number of challenges. On the health side, the evaluation design originally considered four groups: (1) one group of municipalities in which households would receive the CCT, (2) another group in which there would be a supply-

side Intervention to improve health services, (3) a group of municipali
ties that would receive both interventions, and (4) a group that would
serve as a control. In practice, however, the supply-side intervention was
not implemented and so could not be evaluated (Morris, Flores et al.
2004). Moreover, because of the relatively small number of households
involved, there were some important baseline differences. For example,
at baseline, the fraction of households that had received five or more
antenatal visits was 37.9 percent in the group randomly assigned to
receive the CCT intervention only, and 48.9 percent in the control
group. That finding raises the possibility that some of the impact that
was estimated—an 18.7 percentage point impact on the probability that
a woman had received five antenatal visits—could be a result of mean
reversion, as treated households simply caught up with those in the
control group. Also, the evaluation of the effects of PRAF on education
faced a problem in that the baseline survey was collected first among
households in the treatment group (between August and October 2000)
and only then for households in the control group (between November
and December 2000). As Glewwe and Olinto (2004) discuss, that
complicates matters because November and December are important
coffee-harvesting months in Honduras and therefore baseline levels of
child labor were significantly higher in control than in treatment areas,
and school attendance levels were lower. For most outcomes, the authors
reasonably focus on single-difference estimates of program impact (differences between treatment and control groups at follow-up), rather
than differences-in-differences (differences in the growth rates between
treatment and control groups), because the latter could have been
biased by the artificially high levels of child labor at baseline among the
control group. That kind of unexpected complication underlines the
challenges of running randomized evaluations in practice, although
some of the same problems obviously can occur with nonexperimental
evaluations.

In Ecuador, there have been numerous evaluations of the BDH
program. Paxson and Schady (2008) use panel data to estimate program effects on measures of child health and cognitive development.
Households were assigned randomly to treatment and control groups,
and there were no differences in observables at baseline between the two
groups. Take-up among the treated was reasonably high (approximately
75 percent) and contamination of the control group was low (less than
4 percent). Attrition in the survey was low as well—6 percent of the

sample at baseline could not be re-interviewed at follow-up—and is uncorrelated with treatment status.

Other evaluations of the BDH pose more serious identification challenges. The data used by Edmonds and Schady (2008), Schady and Araujo (2008), and Schady and Rosero (2008) to analyze the impact of the program on school enrollment, child work, and household consumption patterns also are based on a randomized experiment. A lottery was used to assign households with school-age children to treatment and control groups, and that lottery appears to have been successful (the authors document that there are no baseline differences between the two groups in observable characteristics). However, there was a substantial contamination of the control group, 48 percent of whom received transfers. The precise reasons for the contamination are unclear. It appears that the list of households randomly excluded from the program was not passed on immediately to operational staff activating households for transfers. That situation was corrected after a few weeks but, as the authors explain, withholding transfers from households that already had begun to receive them was no longer feasible. Moreover, the contamination of the control group clearly was nonrandom: Schady and Araujo (2008) document significant differences between households that actually received transfers and those that did not (as opposed to lottery winners and lottery losers), especially with regard to education levels.

The solution adopted by Edmonds and Schady, Schady and Araujo, and Schady and Rosero is the following. They first focus on differences in outcomes between households assigned to the treatment and control groups by the lottery, rather than on differences between those who received the transfers and those who did not receive them. These so-called intent-to-treat effects abstract from the contamination of the experiment, and provide a lower-bound on the estimated impact of the BDH. The authors also present estimates in which assignment by the lottery is used as an instrument for receiving BDH transfers. That approach—using "partial randomization" as an exogenous source of variation, as proposed by Imbens and Angrist (1994)—is convincing because lottery status is clearly random, and Schady and Araujo show that there is a strong first stage. Nevertheless, it is not without costs. The estimated coefficients are local average treatment effects (LATE) that apply to "compliers"—those whose probability of receiving transfers was affected by the lottery (see Angrist, Imbens, and Rubin 1996). Those compliers cannot be identified without additional assumptions. If there is heterogeneity of treatment effects, the LATE coefficients (although unbiased for the group of compliers) may not be relevant for other households in the sample. The external validity of the results reported in these papers, as in any other instrumental-variables regression, therefore may be somewhat limited.

Another paper that uses the Ecuador data to estimate BDH program effects on school enrollment is by Oosterbeek, Ponce, and Schady (2008). The authors begin by reproducing results very similar to those in Schady and Araujo (2008). As they point out, however, the sample of households used by Schady and Araujo are all drawn from "around" the 20th percentile of the proxy means. The reason for this is that the BDH originally envisioned two tiers of transfers, corresponding to households in the first and second quintiles of the proxy means. The original evaluation design therefore was based on RDD, with two cut-offs—one at the threshold between the first and second quintiles, another at the threshold between the second and third quintiles. However, after the sample was drawn, but before any of the households started receiving transfers, President Lucio Gutiérrez announced that all households in the first and second quintiles of the proxy means would receive transfers of the same magnitude. That decision obviously invalidated the original evaluation design for households around the threshold between the first and second quintiles. As a solution to this problem, it was agreed that the sample of households around that lower threshold would be assigned randomly to treatment and control groups—regardless of whether they were "just above" or "just below" the original cut-off.

Oosterbeek, Ponce, and Schady (2008) compare BDH program effects "around" the 20th percentile of the proxy means—estimated by instrumental variables, as described above—with those "around" the 40th percentile of the proxy means. Those latter estimates use RDD. In practice, this is a case of "fuzzy" RDD—households below the cut-off established by the 40th percentile of the proxy means are much more likely to receive transfers than those above, but a small fraction of ineligibles (approximately 8 percent) nonetheless received BDH transfers. Oosterbeek, Ponce, and Schady therefore instrument receiving BDH transfers with a dummy variable that takes on the value of 1 for households below the cut-off given by the 40th percentile, after flexibly accounting for the relationship between school enrollment and the score on the proxy means test. On the basis of those estimates, they conclude that the BDH had an impact on the enrollment decisions made by "very poor" households (those around the 20th percentile of the proxy means) but no effect for "less poor" households (those around the 40th percentile). That conclusion is plausible, given that there is a good deal of evidence suggesting that CCT program effects on human capital outcomes, including school enrollment, tend to be larger among poorer households (for example, Maluccio and Flores [2005] on the RPS in Nicaragua; Filmer and Schady [2008] on the JFPR program in Cambodia). Nevertheless, the fact that the LATE estimates around the 20th and 40th percentiles of the proxy means refer to different groups of "complier" households somewhat muddies the interpretation put forward by Oosterbeek, Ponce, and Schady.

Two other evaluations of CCT programs use instrumental variables. Morris, Olinto et al. (2004) and Braido, Olinto, and Perrone (2008) evaluate the impact of the Bolsa Alimentação program in Brazil. The identification in those reports is ingenious. Both papers describe a series of administrative errors whereby some potential beneficiaries inadvertently were excluded from program benefits. Entire batches of beneficiaries were lost when files were transferred from participating municipalities to a central data-processing unit in Brasilia, and the data-processing software initially rejected applications with names having nonstandard characters, such as é, ç, or ô. Morris, Olinto et al. and Braido, Olinto, and Perrone argue that this source of variation is as good as random, and therefore is uncorrelated with potential outcomes. That argument seems convincing. But given that these are LATE, the external validity of the estimated effects is unclear.

During the Indonesian crisis of 1997–98, the government made children in poor households eligible for a "scholarship" program. Given the crisis context, it is not surprising that little attention was paid to a possible evaluation of the effect of the program. Sparrow (2007) runs ordinary least squares regressions that suggest the program increased enrollment for children aged 10–12 by about 8 percentage points. He also uses "mistargeting" resulting from outdated poverty data as an instrument for receipt of the scholarship program. On the basis of those calculations, he estimates a larger program effect on enrollment (about 10 percentage points) for children aged 10–12. However, the identifying assumption—in effect, that enrollment decisions respond to current but not lagged poverty levels—is open to question.

A reasonably large number of papers have used RDD to estimate CCT program effects. In addition to Oosterbeek, Ponce, and Schady

(2008), discussed above, these include evaluations of Chile Solidario (Galasso 2006), of the PATH program in Jamaica (Levy and Ohls 2007), of the CESSP program in Cambodia (Filmer and Schady 2009a, 2009b, 2009c), and of the Turkey Social Risk Mitigation Project (Ahmed, Adato et al. 2006; Ahmed, Gilligan et al. 2006; Ahmed et al. 2007).

Levy and Ohls (2007) report intent-to-treat estimates of the impact of PATH. Take-up was high among eligible households (those below the cut-off of the proxy means)—approximately 80 percent—and the fraction of ineligible households (those above the cut-off) was reasonably low—approximately 10 percent. The authors collected both baseline and follow-up data. They experiment with various control functions for the proxy means, and settle on a linear formulation. They also present the results from a variety of placebo experiments, all of which suggest that, controlling for a linear formulation, there are no jumps at the threshold of the proxy means at baseline in any of a large number of observables. That finding adds considerable credibility to the identification strategy. One potential source of concern is the fact that the group of households that received PATH transfers (the treatment group) appears to have applied to the program somewhat earlier than those who did not receive transfers (the comparison group). That fact raises the possibility that there was selection on some unobservable related to "eagerness" or "need." However, the solution adopted by Levy and Ohls—to control for the date of application in all of the main regressions—seems reasonable.

Ahmed, Adato et al. (2006) and Ahmed, Gilligan et al. (2006) also use RDD to estimate the impact of the CCT program in Turkey. As with other CCTs, the score on the proxy means is a significant but imperfect predictor of treatment: about 9 percent of households do not "comply" with their assignment (either eligible households that do not receive transfers, or ineligible households that do receive them). A conservative and standard approach to the problem of imperfect compliance would have been to use the initial assignment by the proxy means to calculate intent-to-treat estimates of program effects, or to calculate LATE estimates by instrumenting program participation with the eligibility rule based on the proxy means. Instead, the authors simply drop those groups of "ineligible beneficiaries" and "eligible nonbeneficiaries" from their sample, despite the fact that, as they acknowledge, "dropping those households from the sample for estimation contributes potential bias to the impact estimates" (Ahmed et al. 2007, p. 123).

Other papers have used double- or triple-differencing techniques to estimate CCT program effects. Both Filmer and Schady (2008) and Chaudhury and Parajuli (2008) estimate the effect of a CCT program for which girls, but not boys, are eligible in Cambodia and in the Punjab area of Pakistan, respectively. Filmer and Schady first compare the growth rates of girls' enrollment in districts that were eligible for the JFPR scholarship program with those that were not eligible. However, they show that preprogram growth rates in girls' enrollment were already higher in eligible districts, which suggests that the common trends assumption underlying their double-differencing estimates is unlikely to hold. They therefore use triple-differencing techniques, comparing the growth rate of girls' enrollment, relative to boys' enrollment, in JFPR-eligible and in other districts. The authors show that this growth rate is higher in JFPR-eligible districts. A similar approach (using boys as an additional control in estimation), with similar conclusions, is followed by Chaudhury and Parajuli in their analysis for the Punjab area of Pakistan.

Triple-differencing of this sort can provide credible estimates of program effects under reasonable assumptions—essentially, that in the absence of the program, the enrollment of girls, relative to that of boys, would have grown by the same amounts in treated and control districts. Showing that preexisting trends in the relative enrollment growth rate are very similar, as is done in Filmer and Schady (2008), provides reassurance on the identification strategy. In addition, both Chaudhury and Parajuli and Filmer and Schady compare the results from this triple-differencing technique with other estimates, using different data sets (for example, household data rather than administrative data), and they show that the estimated effects are very similar.

Separately estimating program effects using household and administrative data is also the basis of Khandker, Pitt, and Fuwa's (2003) analysis of the Female Stipend Program in Bangladesh. The authors show that estimates of program effects on girls' enrollment are similar using both sources of data. They also present estimates of program effects for boys, who were ineligible for the program. Using household data, they find no effect on boys' school enrollment; but using the administrative data, they estimate a worryingly large, negative effect of the program—29 percentage points, or about three times the magnitude of the positive effect on girls' enrollment. The authors point out that the administrative data cover only Female Stipend Program schools, whereas the household data cover enrollment at any school, regardless of whether it was included in the program. Khandker, Pitt, and Fuwa suggest that the difference in boys' effects in the administrative and household data is a result of the transfer of boys out of program schools.[1] Although that suggestion is plausible, the very large magnitude of the coefficient raises some concerns about the estimation strategy and results in the Bangladesh study.

Attanasio, Battistin et al. (2005), Attanasio, Gómez et al. (2005), and Attanasio et al. (2006) identify program effects on the basis of changes over time in treatment and a matched set of ineligible communities to estimate the impact of the Familias en Acción program in Colombia. The identifying assumption therefore is that outcomes would have followed the same trends in both groups of communities in the absence of the program. As with any evaluation that matches eligible and ineligible communities, there is a concern that the characteristics that define eligibility are themselves correlated with outcomes or changes in outcomes. This is untestable, but the authors provide some ancillary support for their identification strategy: They show that average per capita household labor income was higher in comparison communities than in treatment communities prior to the implementation of the Familias en Acción program, but the *trends* in income over three preprogram years are similar. Nevertheless, that evaluation faced other challenges, including the fact that participation in the Familias program made households ineligible to participate in a community-based child care program, Hogares Comunitarios.

Another complication that arose in the Familias en Acción evaluation resulted from the program already having been announced in the treatment areas at the time the baseline survey was collected. As a result, families in treatment areas may have anticipated the effect of the program by enrolling their children in school. Under those circumstances, differences-in-differences that focus on changes in enrollment $E_t - E_{t-1}$ would likely underestimate the true program effects. Foreseeing this problem, the evaluation team collected retrospective data on schooling at the time of the "baseline" survey, and constructed a "pre-baseline" measure of school enrollment, E_{t-2}. This, rather than the measure E_{t-1}, is used in the differences-in-differences estimation.

A similar estimation strategy—first differences combined with matching—is also the basis for a number of evaluations of the impact of the urban Oportunidades program in Mexico. However, the pattern of program effects estimated with those data is somewhat surprising. For example, Todd et al. (2005) estimate that the largest impacts of urban Oportunidades on school enrollment are found among children aged 6–7 years at baseline—a finding that is puzzling on a number of grounds: baseline enrollment in the urban sample for this age group is high, and decreases with child age; children in this age group would have been enrolled in grades that were ineligible for subsidies; and finally, the results for the Oportunidades sample in rural areas suggest that program effects are largest for children in age groups close to the transition from primary to secondary school, rather than for the youngest children (Schultz 2004). Although it is conceivable that the pattern of program effects in rural and urban areas of Mexico are very different, it is also possible (and perhaps more likely) that the double-differencing, matching estimation strategy introduced some hard-to-correct-for biases into the urban estimates.

Given that all communities in the original (randomized) Oportunidades rural sample started receiving payments in December 1999, more recent evaluations of the impact of Oportunidades in rural areas also have had to rely on matching to create a set of comparison communities. However, that effort has faced a number of important difficulties. One hundred fifty-two comparison communities were matched from a pool of 14,000 potential communities that had not received the program. The matching was done on the basis of the locality-level information from the 2000 Mexican census.

There are a number of reasons why this comparison group—and estimates of program effects that use it—should be treated with caution.[2] First, the comparison communities were drawn from different geographic areas than was the treatment group, and therefore they may have had other local area effects that could affect the levels or changes in the outcomes of interest. Second, although there appear to be no differences between the matched sets of treatment and comparison communities (not surprising, given that community characteristics were used to create the matches), individuals in the two sets of communities differ significantly in virtually every characteristic analyzed, and the differences often are large. For example, mean schooling levels of the household head and his spouse are approximately 2.7 in the original Oportunidades communities, but 4.5 in the matched comparison communities. Clearly, this could introduce a number of important biases. Third, to construct a "pre-intervention baseline" for the comparison communities, data were collected on households in those communities in 2003, asking them about their characteristics in 1997. It seems reasonable to assume that this would introduce a good deal of measurement error based on recall bias to those data. Indeed, some recent work on China suggests that such data collection can work quite poorly (Chen, Mu, and Ravallion 2006). Moreover, these retrospective, pre-intervention data were collected in the matched set of communities, but not in the original Oportunidades communities for which the data originally collected in 1997 were used. As a result, recall bias may affect the propensity score used for matching. Finally, migration may have introduced selection problems if the sample of people living in the comparison communities in 2003—those who were asked about their characteristics in 1997—was different from those people who actually lived there in 1997. For all of those reasons, and because of the abundance of studies on Mexico that use the original, randomized (and likely more credible) data collected in the first generation of Oportunidades evaluations, in this report we do not make extensive use of these "second-generation" data collected in recent rounds of the Oportunidades evaluations. Our choice obviously has some costs because it limits the extent to which we can discuss program impacts on outcomes that only recently have been collected in the Oportunidades surveys (for example, adult obesity, hypertension, diabetes, or child cognitive development).

Similarly, we do not make extensive use of a handful of other evaluations, including two that are available for CCT programs in Latin America. In Brazil, Cardoso and Portela Souza (2004) use data from the 2000 population census to evaluate the impact of the Bolsa Escola program. They conclude that children in households that received cash transfers were 3–4 percentage points more likely to attend school than were matched children in the control group. However, the set of covariates used to construct the propensity score is small, and it is not immediately clear why "comparable" households received transfers in some cases but not in others. Moreover, Cardoso and Portela Souza are not able to disentangle transfers made by Bolsa Escola, the CCT program, from other income transfer programs in Brazil.

An evaluation also is available for the Programa Nacional de Becas Estudiantiles in Argentina. Heinrich (2007) uses matching methods to make two sets of comparisons: first, between children who were in the Becas program and other children, and, second, between children who were in the Becas program for one year only and other children who were in the program for two years or longer. Following Behrman, Cheng, and Todd (2004), who analyze the impact of a preschool program in Bolivia, Heinrich refers to the first set of comparisons as estimates of "average" impacts of the program, and to the second set of comparisons as estimates of "marginal" effects. Heinrich argues that the marginal program effects are less likely to be biased if selection into the program is determined by student characteristics unobserved by the researcher, but the duration of program exposure is not. However, estimates of "marginal" program effects need not be free of endogeneity biases. More able students, or students who are different in hard-to-observe ways, may not only be more likely to receive Becas; they may also be likely to stay in the program for longer. Indeed, in an earlier version of the paper (Heinrich and Cabrol 2005) it appears that, after the first year, students who eventually would receive the Becas for two years had significantly lower grade repetition and significantly higher grade averages than those who would receive the program for only one year. This suggests that selection is a serious concern with this identification strategy. Also, interpretation of the estimated grade repetition effects reported by Heinrich (2007) may be problematic because there is anecdotal evidence that some teachers promoted Becas beneficiaries to ensure that they would remain eligible for the program, a point discussed by Heinrich.

In sum, there are many evaluations of CCT program effects. Broadly speaking, these evaluations can be grouped into four categories: First, there are evaluations of small-scale pilot programs, often based on random assignment. These evaluations generally have worked well, as is the case with the evaluations of the RPS and Atención a Crisis programs in Nicaragua and of the PRAF evaluation in Honduras. Random assignment appears to have equated the baseline characteristics of treatment and control groups effectively; attrition has been low. Under these circumstances, simple comparisons of means at follow-up between both groups provide credible estimates of program effects. The main limitation of these evaluations—and an important one—is the fact that the programs were small-scale pilot projects. For a variety of reasons, it is unclear how well the findings from these evaluations approximate the impacts of large, nationwide programs. Households participating in the pilot programs may be aware that they are participating in an experiment, and that may lead them to behave differently in a variety of ways—for example, they may be more likely to comply with the conditions or be receptive to the program's social marketing; staff administering these pilots may be particularly motivated to demonstrate that the pilot programs work. As a result, these small-scale pilots may not be an accurate reflection of how well a much larger program administered by average staff would work in practice. Put differently, the evaluations of the small-scale, randomized pilot programs provide very accurate estimates of the impact of those pilots, but the external validity of the findings may be somewhat open to question.

Second, there are attempts to randomize large-scale programs for a period of time —often by randomizing the timing of the expansion of a program. That was the case with the rollout of the Oportunidades program in rural areas and the expansion of the coverage of the BDH program in Ecuador. Because both programs already had been implemented on a large scale, their evaluations face fewer questions about external validity than do the evaluations of pilot programs in Nicaragua and Honduras. Nevertheless, both evaluations also faced difficulties. Pressure to enroll all eligible beneficiaries shortened the period for which the original Oportunidades control communities did not receive transfers. Moreover, the rapid expansion of the program, even before households in the original control communities started receiving transfers, meant that control communities often literally were surrounded by other communities that were already receiving them. Under such circumstances, it is likely that households in the control communities may have expected to receive Oportunidades transfers before they actually started to receive them, which complicates interpretation of the estimated program effects. In the case of the BDH evaluation, there was substantial contamination of the control group in the sample used to estimate impacts on schooling, child labor, and consumption (see Edmonds and Schady 2008; Schady and Araujo 2008; Schady and Rosero 2008), although not in the sample that was used to estimate program effects on child health and development (Paxson and Schady 2008). The general point is that maintaining random assignment in a large-scale program is extremely difficult for political reasons. In addition, the Oportunidades data have faced other problems, including what appear to be very high levels of attrition and difficulties merging data across survey rounds, particularly for the anthropometric data.

Third, a number of evaluations have used RDD, including evaluations in Cambodia, Chile, Ecuador, Jamaica, Pakistan, and Turkey. A clear advantage of RDD is that it generally does not require program administrators to alter the rules whereby potential beneficiaries are made eligible or ineligible for transfers. As a result, the pressure to incorporate households in the control group into the program tends to be less serious than with randomized experiments. Some contamination of the study design is not unusual (in a number of countries, some ineligible households received transfers and some eligible ones did not), but the solution to that problem is well known: estimating intent-to-treat effects on the basis of the initial assignment, or LATE estimates instrumenting program receipt with assignment. The main shortcoming of these RDD evaluations is that the estimated effect is "local," applying only to households around the eligibility threshold. There appears to be considerable evidence of heterogeneity of CCT treatment effects (Maluccio and Flores 2005; Filmer and Schady 2008; Paxson and Schady 2008). For this reason, it is not clear that these estimates are relevant for other households whose value of the proxy means places them well below the threshold. This heterogeneity is perhaps less of a concern for the evaluations of programs in Chile and Turkey, where the CCT attempts to reach only a very small fraction of households (around 5 percent), than for evaluations in Ecuador, where the CCT attempts to make payments to fully 40 percent of households. A second potential disadvantage of RDD is that, as the value of the threshold becomes better known, households or sympathetic local program officials may attempt to manipulate scores to place some families who would normally have been ineligible for the program "just" below the eligibility threshold. Because that kind of manipulation is likely to be selective, affecting some households more than others (possibly on the basis of unobservable household characteristics), it could introduce serious biases into estimates of program effects.[3]

Finally, a number of evaluations have used differences-in-differences, often combined with matching, to estimate program effects. In some cases, as in the evaluation of the Familias en Acción program in Colombia, matching was done before the program began. In other cases, as with the second-generation Oportunidades evaluations discussed above, matching was done after the fact on the basis of administrative and retrospective data. This second approach adds a layer of uncertainty to the matches and the estimated program effects. Many of the more convincing evaluations using differences-in-differences also present a variety of validation exercises—for example, showing that preexisting trends are not different in the two groups of households or communities, or showing that outcomes that one would not expect to have been affected by the treatment did not change differentially for the two groups. Attempts to triangulate the results with more than one source of data also can add to the credibility of the results.

CCTs truly have been unusual in how much and how seriously they have been evaluated. Few, if any, of these evaluations are without fault. However, the body of credible research on the impact of CCTs on a variety of outcomes is arguably without parallel in development. We conclude this appendix by discussing some areas that should receive high priority in impact evaluations (and research, more generally) on CCTs in the future.

First, much more needs to be known about the long-term effects of CCT programs in a variety of dimensions. Do CCTs lead to long-term reductions in poverty, as might be suggested by the results from Mexico that show households investing some of the transfer? Or does it take longer for households to respond to transfers by reducing their labor supply, in which case the short-term effects on consumption may overestimate the long-term effects? Do the children of families who received CCTs complete more schooling and eventually earn higher wages, or do the somewhat mixed and limited effects on learning and nutritional status translate into only small wage gains? Do families change their fertility and composition in the long term in response to transfers? Those are particularly difficult questions to answer because they involve revisiting households that received transfers many years earlier, and there is a great likelihood that they (or their children) have moved. Re-interview rates may be correspondingly low, and the possibility for substantial estimation biases is serious. Nevertheless, the returns to carefully constructing and studying long-term panels of this sort should be very high, and doing so is a priority for future evaluation work.

Second, although much is known about the effect of CCTs on some outcomes—such as consumption levels, school enrollment, health service utilization—much less is known about a variety of other important outcomes: Under what circumstances do CCTs affect learning outcomes, and how does that interact with the quality of the supply of schooling? Can CCTs be used to seek changes in sexual behaviors, as has been proposed in discussions about how best to limit the transmission of HIV/AIDS? In many countries, CCTs make payments through the banking system, and in some cases a fraction of payments is deposited directly into a savings account for a household. Have those payment methods resulted in positive spillover effects in households' ability to access and use financial services?

Third, more needs to be done to unpack the CCT effects on outcomes. Are the changes that are observed a result of the cash, the conditions, the social marketing that generally accompanies the program, or the fact that transfers are made to women? How much, and for what outcomes, does the magnitude of the transfer matter? Understanding the answers to these and related questions is important for the design of efficient CCT programs in the future.

Notes

Overview

1. For evidence from a variety of settings, see Thomas (1990, 1994); Lundberg, Pollak, and Wales (1997); Duflo (2003); and Ward-Batts (2008).
2. For example, see Miguel and Kremer (2004) on deworming and Gimnig et al. (2003) on insecticide-treated bednets. There is a large body of literature on externalities associated with immunization.
3. On Colombia, see Attanasio, Battistin, and Mesnard (2008); on Ecuador, see Schady and Rosero (2008); on Mexico, see Hoddinott, Skoufias, and Washburn (2000) and Angelucci and Attanasio (2008); and on Nicaragua, see Maluccio and Flores (2005) and Macours, Schady, and Vakis (2008).
4. On Brazil, see Yap, Sedlacek, and Orazem (2008); on Cambodia, see Filmer and Schady (2009c); on Ecuador, see Edmonds and Schady (2008); on Mexico, see Skoufias and Parker (2001) and Schultz (2004); and on Nicaragua, see Maluccio (2005). Exceptions are Attanasio et al. (2006), who find the Familias en Acción program has no effect on child work in Colombia (although the program does appear to have reduced the amount of time dedicated to domestic chores); and Glewwe and Olinto (2004) who find the Programa de Asignación Familiar has no effects on child work in Honduras.
5. On remittances, see Teruel and Davis (2000) and Albarran and Attanasio (2003) for Mexico, and Nielsen and Olinto (2007) for Honduras and Nicaragua. Stecklov et al. (2006) analyze fertility effects of CCT programs in Honduras, Mexico, and Nicaragua. Angelucci and de Giorgi (2008) study village-level general equilibrium effects associated with Oportunidades in Mexico. Medium-term effects of transfers are analyzed by Gertler, Martínez, and Rubio-Codina (2006) for Mexico, and by Maluccio (2008) for Nicaragua. For Mexico and Nicaragua, respectively, Skoufias (2002) and Maluccio (2005) study program effects on the extent to which recipient households can smooth income shocks.

6. The impact of CCTs on child nutritional status is analyzed by Morris, Olinto et al. (2004) for Brazil; by Attanasio, Gómez et al. (2005) for Colombia; by Paxson and Schady (2008) for Ecuador; by Gertler (2004), Rivera et al. (2004), and Behrman and Hoddinott (2005) for Mexico; and by Maluccio and Flores (2005) and Macours, Schady, and Vakis (2008) for Nicaragua.

7. CCT program effects on school attainment by adults are discussed in Behrman, Parker, and Todd (2005). The lack of impact on test scores, even among children who have received more schooling, is found by Ponce and Bedi (2008) for Ecuador; by Behrman, Sengupta, and Todd (2000) for Mexico; and most convincingly, from a methodological point of view, by Filmer and Schady (2009b) for Cambodia; and Behrman, Parker, and Todd (2005) for Mexico.

8. de Brauw and Hoddinott (2008) and Schady and Araujo (2008) exploit glitches in program implementation in Mexico and Ecuador, respectively. Filmer and Schady (2009c) analyze differences in effects across siblings for the CESSP program in Cambodia, in which transfers are conditional on the enrollment of only one sibling. Simulation methods and structural modeling also have been used to estimate the relative importance of income and price effects associated with transfers in Brazil (Bourguignon, Ferreira, and Leite 2003) and Mexico (Attanasio, Meghir, and Santiago 2005; Todd and Wolpin 2006a).

Chapter 1

1. Several programs that have most of the CCT design features transfer not cash but food stamps (the Dominican Republic's Comer es Primero program or Costa Rica's Supremos) or food (the Bangladesh Food for Education program). These programs might be expected to have effects similar to those of CCTs.

2. In Brazil, Bolsa Família is beginning to encourage more explicit links to social worker support services for families who are not complying with conditions and for especially vulnerable families. Colombia has developed the Juntos program, which provides social worker accompaniment similar to that of Chile Solidario and eventually might be linked to the CCT program. In El Salvador, the CCT program itself provides assistance to help families give birth. The government there also has designed parallel interventions in the same target municipalities to improve livelihoods for small farmers through small-scale productive projects and microcredit.

3. Most recently, CCTs have been created in New York City and Australia for use among indigenous communities. The New York City CCT built explicitly on the experience from developing countries. Staff from the office of Mayor Michael Bloomberg and a number of city agencies traveled to Mexico to learn about the program. Numerous informational meetings also were facilitated by the World Bank so that policy makers designing Opportunity NYC could learn from the experience in developing countries—an example of the North learning from the South.

Chapter 2

1. Demirgüç-Kunt and Levine (2008) have pointed out correctly that improving the functioning of financial markets in developing countries should be seen as the "first-best" response to failures that originate in those markets. The arguments to address these failures through redistribution instead should be seen as conditional on the first-best solution being too costly to implement, or be viewed as a temporary substitute.

2. The net effect of aggregate economic shocks on health and education investments varies substantially across countries, depending on the relative strength of substitution and income effects (Ferreira and Schady 2008). Severe idiosyncratic shocks often lead to investment pauses that can be costly.

3. The "true" private optimal is defined counterfactually by the absence of misguided beliefs, intrahousehold principal–agent problems, or hyperbolic discounting.

4. In an excellent survey of the theory and empirics of redistribution in kind and in cash, Currie and Gahvari (2007) note that "paternalism is intimately related to the idea of merit goods and merit wants, and may be a key reason for government intervention" (p. 6).

5. The concept of merit goods also is related closely to James Tobin's (1970) idea of *specific egalitarianism*. In the context of the United States in the late 1960s, Tobin argues that there are some instances, notably education and medical care, where "a specific egalitarian distribution today may be essential for improving the distribution of human capital and earning capacity tomorrow" (p. 277). Implicit in that claim is the notion that society would value a more egalitarian distribution of earning capacity in the future *above and beyond* the value placed by individual agents on their own (or their children's) improved capacity.

6. Das, Do, and Özler (2005) and de Janvry and Sadoulet (2006) discuss how some of those issues provide justification for CCT programs.

7. A third use of children's time—leisure—is ignored in this model. The three-way choice among education, child labor, and leisure is analyzed both theoretically and empirically by Ravallion and Wodon (2000). Those authors find that an enrollment subsidy in Bangladesh (an in-kind precursor to the CCTs) leads to increased enrollment, and that most of that increase comes from child leisure rather than from child work. The authors are careful to recognize that theirs is a very imperfect measure of child work, and that some of the time implicitly classified as leisure may be spent in homework or other cognitively important activities. The broad argument in Ferreira (2008), on which we draw here, will hold if child leisure and schooling are complements in the human capital "production function."

8. It is critical to remember that, although we do not consider other policy alternatives (such as investing in the quality of the supply of health or education services, or setting up a workfare scheme), it well may be that, in general equilibrium, those policies make more sense than either a UCT or a CCT.

9. See Piketty (1995) for the original model. Bénabou and Tirole (2006) show that stable multiple equilibria can arise in such models, with "incorrect" beliefs arising endogenously, being privately rational, and persisting.

10. There are many reasons why we should expect insufficient information in low-income settings. For example, if there is residential segregation by income, most poor households will observe very few high-education/high-income adults. Furthermore, if migration is correlated with ability so that high-ability people are more likely to migrate, and those high-education people who are left behind have low ability, the information problem may be more severe. Jensen (2006) discusses this possibility.

11. Dominitz and Manski (1996) start this line of research in the United States. They find no evidence that high school and college students underestimate the realized rates of return to schooling. In developing countries, information problems could be more severe for a variety of reasons because people have less education (and thus less ability to process information on the true returns), and less information may be available. There is also an extensive body of literature suggesting that education is particularly beneficial at times of economic disequilibria—such as times of significant technological change (see classics such as Nelson and Phelps [1966] and Foster and Rosenzweig [1996]). It is not clear that households would or could factor in these potential gains when making education decisions. Not only does education confer benefits now (the wage returns in equilibrium), but it also is likely to yield even larger benefits if things change rapidly.

12. Trang Nguyen (2007) finds that both the mean and the dispersion of perceived (by parents) and realized earnings are similar in Madagascar, a finding that suggests information is not that much of a problem. Nevertheless, an intervention in which students and their parents are informed of the mean realized returns does induce more effort (more attendance, higher test scores). Somehow, the information must (1) lead those parents who hold low-return beliefs to correct their beliefs—and therefore to exert more effort—without a countervailing effect on the effort of those who are overstating the expected returns; or (2) convey the (possibly incorrect) notion that the dispersion in returns is low—a notion that would lead risk-averse households to invest more in schooling (holding the average return constant).

13. This statement assumes that a child's education is seen only as an investment by the household. If education is at least partly seen as a consumption good (including as a source of status), there could be an income effect even under functioning credit markets.

14. As we pointed out in note 13, results change if schooling is seen, at least in part, as a consumption good. In that case, the effect of incomplete parental altruism will depend on who is seen as consuming schooling. If it is seen as the child's consumption, then the CCT will have an effect even under perfect markets. If it is seen as the consumption of the parents (for example, by affording higher status or providing child care), then the CCT is not needed.

15. An experiment whereby a specified amount is given to children rather than to adults would not solve the problem because it would be confounded

by other factors such as the likely higher discount rate of children and possibly irrational behavior among children. For example, Bettinger and Slonim (2006) find that children's choices are consistent with hyperbolic discounting: 25 percent of children in their experiment do not make rational intertemporal choices within a single two-period time frame.

16. The nonwage returns to more education are likely to be at least as large for girls as for boys—for example, in terms of health investments.

17. There is also some evidence that women and men may value boys and girls differently, with women investing more on girls than on boys (Thomas 1994; Duflo 2003). In those circumstances, conditions can act as a means to ensure "equal treatment" regardless of who receives the transfer payment.

18. The only exception to this pattern is the social assistance transfer to the elderly poor and poor disabled (known as the *Benefício de Prestação Continuada da Loas*), which is not conditioned. It should be noted, though, that the target groups (elderly, disabled) often are considered "deserving poor" because of who they are and not because of what they do.

19. See Kooreman (2000) for evidence on child benefits in the Netherlands, and see Schady and Rosero (2008) for evidence from Ecuador.

Chapter 3

1. For recent reviews of the general literature on design and implementation of social assistance programs, see, for example, Samson, van Niekerk, and MacWuene (2006); and Grosh et al. (2008).

2. To date, only Bolivia's Juancito Pinto program is targeted broadly to all first-graders in public schools.

3. Coverage is the portion of a population group (for example, decile of per capita expenditure [PCE] net of the CCT transfer) that receives the transfer. Coverage rates reflect the time at which the data were collected. Some programs have expanded rapidly since the years of the surveys used in this study. For example, Brazil's Bolsa Família program has expanded from 5.0 million households in 2004 to 11.1 million in 2006, and its coverage in figure 3.2 is therefore underestimated.

4. The CCT programs included Chile Subsidio Unitario Familiar (SUF) and Chile Solidario; Brazil's Bolsa Escola, Bolsa Alimentação, Auxílio Gás, and PETI; the Dominican Republic's Tarjeta de Asistencia Escolar (TAE); Mexico's Oportunidades; and Argentina's Jefes y Jefas.

5. Carrillo and Ponce (2008) also estimate that reducing travel time by 60 minutes to the closest town with a payment agency would increase the value of the transfer by about 4 percent—a modest amount.

6. Originally, stipends provided by the FSSAP amounted to $18–$45 per student per year, but they were reduced to $5–$16 by 2001 (World Bank 2003). Because the amount of the stipend was fixed in nominal terms, the current transfer is even lower in real terms after adjusting for inflation.

7. In Brazil, for example, costs of food and housing are nearly double in São Paulo compared with rural areas. More formally, the Laspeyres price index

based on food and housing is 1.000 for São Paulo, 0.797 for metropolitan Brazil, 0.633 for urban areas excluding metropolitan Brazil, and 0.568 in rural areas (World Bank 2007). Even in small, more geographically homogeneous Honduras, the cost of living in Tegucigalpa is 12 percent higher than in rural areas. The Laspeyres index is 1.000 nationally, 1.081 in Tegucigalpa, and 0.967 in rural areas (World Bank 2006b).

8. See chapter 4 of this report for a summary of CCT programs' impacts on fertility.

9. In Lindert, Skoufias, and Shapiro (2006), the computations are based on posttransfer welfare. In this research report, we principally present results based on welfare net of the program transfer. Thus the results for CCTs in figure 3.1 are not exactly the same as those shown in figure 11 of Lindert and her coauthors. The comparison with other programs, however, is valid.

10. For compliance, see Mutzig (2006) on Brazil, Roberts-Risden (2006) on Jamaica, and Government of El Salvador (2008) on El Salvador; for Mexico compliance information, see http://www.oportunidades.gob.mx/indicadores_gestion/main.html.

Chapter 4

1. Bolsa Alimentação is one of the pilot precursors of the larger CCT program now known as Bolsa Família. The analysis of impact in the first and second sections uses the evaluation data for Bolsa Alimentação because it included expenditure information and therefore is comparable to the other countries. In the third section, when we consider the impact of CCTs on the national level of poverty, we analyze Bolsa Família's impact on income poverty using less-robust methods.

2. These programs were chosen because (1) their evaluation studies collected consumption or income data, (2) the methods employed to measure impact are robust enough, and (3) we have access to the evaluation data and can carry out comparable analysis.

3. Two household surveys were conducted before the start of Oportunidades in Mexico. The first survey did not have a consumption module. The second one did have a consumption module, but problems in the implementation of this survey render the consumption data unusable. In 1998, a third survey with a consumption module was carried out a few months after the start of the program. The results presented in tables 4.1 and 4.2 are from that third survey and two follow-up surveys done in June and October 1999.

4. The lack of impact of Oportunidades in 1998 is not unexpected because the 1998 survey was carried out only a few months after the start of the program, and many beneficiary households had yet to receive their transfers.

5. A number of recent papers consider the impact of the Chile Solidario program on employment, consumption, and poverty. Carneiro and Galasso

(2008) use regression discontinuity techniques and report very large impacts. Their estimates suggest that Chile Solidario resulted in an increase of 11 percentage points in the probability that a head of household is employed, and a reduction in poverty of 8–11 points. However, Larrañaga, Contreras, and Ruiz Tagle (2008) use differences-in-differences techniques and find no significant impacts of the program on either employment or income. More research is needed to understand the difference between these two studies, particularly because of the innovative nature of the Chile Solidario program.

6. In the case of Brazil, we conduct this analysis for the newer Bolsa Família program. (Beginning in 2003, Bolsa Família incorporated the earlier and smaller Bolsa Alimentação program.)

7. This possibility of bias is especially the case for Brazil because there was no random assignment of program by location or individual households. Beneficiary households and poor areas were targeted purposefully. In the case of Mexico, although Oportunidades was allocated randomly at the village level, the randomization was carried out only within a set of preselected rural villages with high poverty levels. Thus, although estimates of poverty impacts within that set of preselected villages should be unbiased, that may not be true for estimations of poverty impact at the national level.

8. Encouraging effects of CCTs on national poverty are reported elsewhere. Brown and Agostini (2008) use census and survey data to estimate the extent to which Chile's success in reducing poverty results, at least in part, from a variety of cash transfer programs. The authors use the Elbers, Lanjouw, and Lanjouw (2003) methodology to combine census (a 2002 population census) and survey (the 2003 Caracterización Socioeconómica Nacional) data. On the basis of these calculations, they estimate income for every individual in the census with and without the transfers. They find that transfers significantly reduce the incidence of poverty, and that estimated headcount ratios fall by 5–68 percent, with considerable geographic variation.

9. In theory, increases in food consumption could be positive, resulting in reductions in child wasting or stunting, for example; or they could be negative, resulting in increases in obesity and adult diseases such as diabetes.

10. See Thaler (1999) for a general discussion; and see evidence in Fraker, Martini, and Ohls (1995), Kooreman (2000), Jacoby (2002), and Islam and Hoddinott (2009).

11. A similar pattern is reported by others. Averaging across the three survey rounds, Hoddinott, Skoufias, and Washburn (2000) find that the increase in monthly consumption of 151 pesos is substantially smaller than the average transfer of 197 pesos per month. Attanasio and Mesnard (2006) report that beneficiaries of Familias en Acción spend only 53,000 pesos out of an average transfer of 100,000 pesos per month.

12. Payment is made to students older than 16.

13. See also the discussion of the incentive effects of the Bolsa Alimentação program in Brazil in chapter 5.

Chapter 5

1. Also see Ravallion and Wodon (2000) for an evaluation of the Food for Education program, which antedated the FSSAP program in Bangladesh.

2. For a sample of beneficiaries around the 20th percentile of the national distribution of the proxy means, treatment by the BDH was randomized; that is the basis for the estimates by Schady and Araujo (2008). The 40th percentile of the proxy means is the cut-off point for BDH program eligibility; Oosterbeek, Ponce, and Schady (2008) use regression discontinuity techniques to estimate program impacts around that threshold, and they compare the estimated effects to those found in Schady and Araujo (2008).

3. One exception to this pattern of larger CCT program effects among poorer households is found in Bangladesh. Khandker, Pitt, and Fuwa (2003) estimate larger FSSAP effects on girls in households with larger landholdings.

4. However, the fraction of women who reported five antenatal visits was 11 percentage points lower in the treatment group at baseline, and that raises the possibility that some of the observed changes may be the product of reversion to the mean.

5. Although children who benefit from CCT programs are more likely to be enrolled in school and to attend classes more frequently than they would have otherwise, the program effects on years of schooling could be muted for a variety of reasons. First, children receiving transfers may not always be promoted to the next grade (although some programs, including Oportunidades in Mexico and the RPS in Nicaragua, place limits on the number of times a child can repeat a grade before he or she is disqualified from receiving further transfers). Second, even in the absence of grade repetition, CCTs could increase enrollment and grade attainment in the short run without affecting long-term outcomes. Consider a scenario in which school enrollment is intermittent (for example, if enrollment is determined partly by conditions in the labor market) or one in which parents have a target grade they want their children to attain (perhaps completion of primary school) and that target is not affected by the CCT program. Under such circumstances, parents who are eligible for the CCT may choose to enroll their children in school now rather than later because transfer income now is preferable to more uncertain transfer income in the future. An evaluation that focuses on the short-run impact of the CCT program then would find positive program effects on enrollment and grade completion. On the other hand, an evaluation that focuses on the "medium-run" effects might find negative program effects on enrollment (as CCT-treated children drop out of school when they have attained their target grade, whereas control group children continue to be enrolled intermittently) and muted or no program effects on grade attainment. Finally, an evaluation that focuses on long-term effects might find that there are

no differences between treated and control households in school attainment. More generally, this example points to the advantages of revisiting CCT-treated and control children when they are old enough plausibly to have completed their schooling.

6. In practice, Behrman, Parker, and Todd (2005) find much larger differences in wage income between girls who started receiving transfers in 1998 and girls who started receiving transfers in 2000 (on the order of 25 percent), and they find no effects for boys. Those estimates are noisy, however, and arguably are too large to be credible.

7. Nevertheless, even in those countries, aggregate effects on poverty in the next generation may be lower than those estimated by simple back-of-the-envelope calculations for a variety of reasons. First, a large increase in the fraction of members of an age cohort who have completed a given school cycle is likely to depress the returns to schooling. (Card and Lemieux [2001] present results for Canada, the United Kingdom, and the United States; Manacorda, Sánchez-Páramo, and Schady [2008] report on five Latin American countries.) Second, the returns to schooling for the marginal child brought into school by the CCT may be lower than those for the average child.

8. Alderman and Behrman (2006), and Galiani (2007) present calculations in a similar spirit.

9. PRAF also envisioned a program to transfer resources to health centers to improve the quality of the supply, but the transfer of resources to local health units that had been envisioned was not implemented properly (Morris, Flores et al. 2004; Hoddinott 2008).

10. It is not clear exactly how the presence of the Hogares Comunitarios child care program may have affected the estimates of Familias en Acción program effects. Hogares Comunitarios is a community-based child care program. Participating children receive a nutritional supplement, among other things. Because parents are not allowed to enroll their children in the Hogares Comunitarios program and also receive transfers made by the Familias en Acción program, participation in Hogares is lower in the municipalities where the Familias program has been implemented than in the comparison communities. That situation could introduce biases—for example, the estimates of Familias program effects in Attanasio et al. (2005) could be biased downward if Hogares Comunitarios has a positive effect on child nutritional status.

11. No baseline measures of adult health status are available, so the identification relies on comparisons between the two groups at follow-up.

12. The results for obesity and hypertension are significant at the 1 percent level, whereas those for diabetes are insignificantly different from zero, perhaps because of the relatively small number of adults who were tested for diabetes in the study.

13. A third study (Fernald, Gertler, and Neufeld 2008) assesses the impact of receiving larger Oportunidades transfers on cognitive outcomes in early childhood. The authors conclude that doubling the magnitude of the

transfer would result in substantial improvements in motor development, cognitive development, and receptive language acquisition. The paper exploits the facts that program benefits vary for girls and boys and that there is a cap on the total amount of benefits that a household can receive, regardless of the number of children it has. This feature of program design generates variations in the amount of transfers received by program-eligible households. However, it is not clear that the identification strategy is robust to the presence of economies of scale or "quantity-quality" trade-offs in child outcomes, which is a source of concern. Some specifications directly control for household size and composition. In those specifications the program impacts appear to be identified off nonlinearities in the effect of household size and composition on the amount of transfers for which a household can be eligible.

14. In Nicaragua, 82 percent of households in the sample live on less than $1 per capita per day, compared with 34 percent in the sample of households in the Ecuador evaluation

15. Lundberg, Pollak, and Wales (1997) conclude from their analysis of a British transfer program that the identity of the recipient matters—when transfers are made to women, for example, a larger fraction is spent on child clothing than when the transfers are made to men. Also see the results in Thomas (1990, 1994) and Duflo (2003).

16. For evidence on the importance of social marketing in the allocation of expenditures, see Fraker, Martini, and Ohls (1995), who show that when there are food stamp "cash-outs" (whereby food stamps are replaced with income transfers), families continue to spend a disproportionate share of their food stamp income on food in the United States; in the Netherlands, spending on children's clothing out of child benefit income is much larger than out of other sources of income (Kooreman 2000).

17. As a validation exercise to test their identification strategy, de Brauw and Hoddinott (2008) show that there are no differences in the acquisition of calories between households that did and did not receive the forms. Because both groups received the same cash transfer, and because there is no obvious reason why caloric intake should have been affected by schooling conditions attached to transfers, this exercise suggests that unobserved differences between households that did and did not receive the forms are not the main reason for the measured differences in their school enrollment behavior.

18. Specifically, local elected leaders (the heads of the *Juntas Parroquiales*) were encouraged to hold townhall-style meetings in which the BDH was presented as a compact between the state and beneficiaries: the state agreed to transfer resources to poor households, and those households in turn agreed to send their children to school; for a brief period, the BDH program aired a series of radio and television spots that explicitly linked transfers with school enrollment; some BDH administrators also appear to have stressed the enrollment requirements when they signed up households for transfers.

19. See box 6.3 for a discussion of the methods used.

Chapter 8

1. It should be noted that CCT programs can be justified also in the absence of redistributive objectives. Indeed, when private investment in human capital is socially suboptimal, monetary incentives may be needed to change behaviors—even if those incentives are not large enough to have any measurable effect on short-term poverty. Our focus, however, is on those cases in which redistribution is part of the rationale for a CCT.

2. Grant and Behrman (2008) examine a number of demographic and health surveys and find that gender differences in schooling attainment generally do not favor boys. Boys apparently fail and repeat grades a lot more often than girls do. As a result, although enrollment rates are higher for boys, attainment rates are not.

3. Miguel and Kremer (2004) find positive spillover effects of deworming both within and across neighboring schools in Kenya. They also find that simply informing parents and students of the benefits of deworming (through health education) led to no changes in behavior, and that user fees led to the collapse of the program. On that basis, and given the positive spillover effects, they argue there is a strong justification for the subsidized provision of deworming drugs. Although the free provision of drugs may be sufficient in the case of children in school, other cases may require further incentives (for example, in the form of a CCT). The presence of externalities is not a proof that a CCT is needed, but it does provide the basis to consider if one makes sense.

4. A full description would consider less than full take-up among group B households. For simplicity we do not consider it here. In essence, the extent of take-up among group B is a function of the size of the transfer.

5. It would be incorrect, however, simply to extrapolate those estimates and assume that average effects among the extremely poor would remain unchanged as a result of the retargeting, particularly because that would not be a marginal change in coverage.

6. For rural areas, Duarte Gómez et al. (2004) find that program beneficiaries have better knowledge on health practices, but the authors cannot test whether that is the result of the health education sessions. For urban areas, they are able to compare knowledge among people attending and not attending the sessions, but they must rely on propensity score matching for those comparisons. They also use qualitative methods to complement their analysis.

7. The extent to which conditions are likely to affect beneficiaries' behavior depends on a combination of implementation factors that vary from country to country. First is the frequency with which compliance with conditions is verified. Second is the speed with which information on compliance becomes available to trigger sanctions—often a function of administrative capacity. As shown in chapter 3, even in a relatively high-capacity environment like Mexico, the benefit amount paid reflects the compliance or noncompliance of the beneficiary household four months

       prior to the payment. Third, although all CCT programs specify a schedule of sanctions in the case of noncompliance with conditions, both the type of sanctions and the degree of enforcement vary quite substantially from one program to another. Moreover, as explained in chapter 3, conditions are not always viewed as "hard."

8. It could be said that, in fact, the program is operating as two separate cash transfers using the same targeting mechanism and administrative procedures. Moreover, to the extent that the conditions must be satisfied in order to receive the per-child benefit, the base benefit could be interpreted as an additional UCT.

9. *Telesecundaria* schools rely on videos shown by satellite and have fewer teachers, whereas general secondary schools have more infrastructure and more specialized instructors.

10. The cost to build a *telesecundaria* school is estimated to be 1.38 million pesos, and to build a technical secondary school 2.4 million pesos. Annual personnel and operating costs are $170,000 for *telesecundaria* and $427,000 for technical secondary schools. See Coady and Parker (2004) for a cost-effectiveness analysis of these supply-side investments.

11. See Regalía and Castro (2007) for an analysis of how the Nicaraguan Ministry of Health outsourced the delivery of health care services while it retained supervision over the providers through management agreements that were intended to align health service providers' incentives with better health care and health outcomes.

12. Most of these programs were influenced by a community nutrition model known as Atención Integral de la Niñez en la Comunidad, first established in Honduras (see Van Roekel et al. 2002; Griffiths and McGuire 2005). Typically, other primary health services have been added.

13. The earlier RPS program relied instead on nongovernmental providers.

14. Preliminary results by Leite and Olinto (2008) suggest that in Brazil, as coverage of CCT programs increased, local governments adapted the supply of education services (consolidating smaller schools, increasing the number of secondary schools and teachers, and so forth).

15. For example, Banerjee et al. (2007) argue that without changes in curriculum and pedagogy that recognize the different needs of poor/excluded children, additional educational inputs are not effective in improving learning outcomes. They evaluate two experiments that follow that approach through remedial education and find positive results on learning outcomes.

16. There are different approaches to social pensions: some countries (Bolivia, Botswana, Mauritius, Namibia, Nepal) follow universal schemes, whereby all elderly people are eligible. The cost of those programs either makes them too expensive or forces them to pay very low benefits, with correspondingly limited effects on poverty. A larger number of countries have adopted targeted schemes instead (usually through some form of proxy means test) as a way to provide meaningful support at an affordable cost. The OAP program in South Africa costs approximately 1.4 percent of GDP.

17. In principle, CCTs, like other social assistance programs, could crowd out participation in (contributive) insurance schemes. This implies there is a separate but equally important demand on coordination with social protection programs, especially with regard to the relationship between CCTs and social insurance programs (see Levy [2008] for Mexico).
18. We thank Harold Alderman for bringing this point to our attention.

Appendix B

1. Also see Filmer and Schady (2009a) for a discussion of the possible effects of selective transfers in Cambodia.
2. In particular, see the discussion in Parker, Rubalcava, and Teruel (2008).
3. One obvious check for that kind of manipulation is to test for an unusual concentration of mass in the density of the proxy means right below the eligibility cut-off—a clear indication of a problem.

References

Adato, Michelle. 2004. "CCTs, Community Participation and Empowerment." Presentation prepared for the Second International Workshop on Conditional Cash Transfers, São Paulo, Brazil, April.

Adato, Michelle, Terence Roopnaraine, Natalia Smith, Elif Altinok, Nurfer Çelebioglu, and Sema Cemal. 2007. "An Evaluation of the Conditional Cash Transfer Program in Turkey: Second Qualitative and Anthropological Study." International Food Policy Research Institute, Washington, DC.

Agüero, Jorge M., Michael R. Carter, and Ingrid Woolard. 2007. "The Impact of Unconditional Cash Transfers on Nutrition: The South African Child Support Grant." Working Paper 39, International Poverty Centre, United Nations Development Programme, New York.

Ahmed, Akhter, Michelle Adato, Ayse Kudat, Daniel Gilligan, and Refik Colasan. 2006. "Interim Impact Evaluation of the Conditional Cash Transfer Program in Turkey: A Quantitative Assessment." International Food Policy Research Institute, Washington, DC.

———. 2007. "Impact Evaluation of the Conditional Cash Transfer Program in Turkey: Final Report." International Food Policy Research Institute, Washington, DC.

Ahmed, Akhter, Daniel Gilligan, Ayse Kudat, Refik Colasan, Huseyin Tatlidil, and Bulent Ozbilgin. 2006. "Interim Impact Evaluation of the Conditional Cash Transfer Program in Turkey: A Quantitative Assessment." International Food Policy Research Institute, Washington, DC.

Ahmed, Salehuddin, and Samir R. Nath. 2003. "Public Service Delivery in Education: The BRAC Experience." Paper prepared for the Annual Bank Conference on Development Economics, sponsored by the World Bank, Bangalore, India, May 21–23.

Albarran, Pedro, and Orazio Attanasio. 2003. "Limited Commitment and Crowding Out of Private Transfers: Evidence from a Randomized Experiment." *Economic Journal* 113 (486): C77–85.

Alderman, Harold, and Jere Behrman. 2006. "Reducing the Incidence of Low Birth Weight in Low-Income Countries Has Substantial Economic Benefits." *World Bank Research Observer* 21 (1): 25–48.

Alderman Harold, and Elizabeth M. King. 1998. "Gender Differences in Parental Investment in Education." *Structural Change and Economic Dynamics* 9 (4): 453–68.

Andrews, Emily, and Dena Ringold. 1999. "Safety Nets in Transition Economies: Toward a Reform Strategy." Social Protection Discussion Paper 9914, World Bank, Washington, DC.

Angelucci, Manuela, and Orazio Attanasio. 2008. "Oportunidades: Program Effects on Consumption, Low Participation, and Methodological Issues." *Economic Development and Cultural Change.*

Angelucci, Manuela, and Giacomo de Giorgi. 2008. "Indirect Effects of an Aid Program: The Case of PROGRESA and Consumption." *American Economic Review.*

Angrist, Joshua, Guido Imbens, and Donald Rubin. 1996. "Identification of Causal Effects Using Instrumental Variables." *Journal of the American Statistical Association* 91 (434): 444–55.

Ardington, Cally, Anne Case, and Victoria Hosegood. 2008. "Labor Supply Responses to Large Social Transfers: Longitudinal Evidence from South Africa." *American Economic Journal: Applied Economics.*

Ashworth, Karl, Jay Hardman, Yvette Hartfree, Sue Maguire, Sue Middleton, Debbi Smith, Lorraine Dearden, Carl Emmerson, Christine Frayne, and Costas Meghir. 2002. "Education Maintenance Allowance: The First Two Years. A Quantitative Evaluation." Research Report RR352, Department for Education and Skills. Nottingham, UK: Queen's Printer.

Atkinson, Anthony B. 1987. "Income Maintenance and Social Insurance." In *Handbook of Public Economics,* ed. Alan J. Auerbach and Martin Feldstein, 779–908. Amsterdam, The Netherlands: Elsevier.

———. 1996. "On Targeting Social Security: Theory and Western Experience with Family Benefits." In *Public Spending and the Poor: Theory and Evidence,* ed. Dominique van de Walle and Kimberly Nead, 25–68. Baltimore, MD: Johns Hopkins University Press.

Attanasio, Orazio, Erich Battistin, Emla Fitzsimmons, Alice Mesnard, and Marcos Vera-Hernández. 2005. "How Effective Are Conditional Cash Transfers? Evidence from Colombia." Briefing note 54, Institute for Fiscal Studies, London.

Attanasio, Orazio, Erich Battistin, and Alice Mesnard. 2008. "The Structure of Consumption in Rural Colombia: Using Engel Curves to Estimate the Effect of a Welfare Program." Unpublished manuscript, Institute for Fiscal Studies, London.

Attanasio, Orazio, Emla Fitzsimmons, and Ana Gómez. 2005. "The Impact of a Conditional Education Subsidy on School Enrollment in Colombia." Unpublished manuscript, Institute for Fiscal Studies, London.

Attanasio, Orazio, Emla Fitzsimmons, Ana Gómez, David López, Costas Meghir, and Alice Mesnard. 2006. "Child Education and Work Choices in the Presence of a Conditional Cash Transfer Programme in Rural Colombia." Working Paper W06/01, Institute for Fiscal Studies, London.

Attanasio, Orazio, Luís Carlos Gómez, Patricia Heredia, and Marcos Vera-Hernández. 2005. "The Short-Term Impact of a Conditional Cash Subsidy on Child Health and Nutrition in Colombia." Report Summary: Familias 03, Institute for Fiscal Studies, London.

Attanasio, Orazio, and Katja Kaufmann. 2007. "Educational Choices, Subjective Expectations and Credit Constraints." Unpublished manuscript, University College, London.

Attanasio, Orazio, and Valérie Lechene. 2002. "Tests of Income Pooling in Household Decisions." *Review of Economic Dynamics* 5 (4): 720–48.

Attanasio, Orazio, Costas Meghir, and Ana Santiago. 2005. "Education Choices in Mexico: Using a Structural Model and a Randomized Experiment to Evaluate PROGRESA." Working Paper EWP05/01, Institute for Fiscal Studies, London.

Attanasio, Orazio, and Alice Mesnard. 2006. "The Impact of a Conditional Cash Transfer Programme on Consumption in Colombia." *Fiscal Studies* 27 (4): 421–42.

Baird, Sarah, Jed Friedman, and Norbert Schady. 2007. "Infant Mortality Over the Business Cycle in the Developing World." Policy Research Working Paper 4346, World Bank, Washington, DC.

Baland, Jean-Marie, and James A. Robinson. 2000. "Is Child Labor Inefficient?" *Journal of Political Economy* 108 (4): 663–79.

Banerjee, Abhijit V., Shawn Cole, Esther Duflo, and Leigh Linden. 2007. "Remedying Education: Evidence from Two Randomized Experiments in India." *Quarterly Journal of Economics* 122 (3): 1235–64.

Banerjee, Abhijit, Suraj Jacob, and Michael Kremer, with Jennifer Lanjouw and Peter Lanjouw. 2005. "Moving to Universal Primary Education: Costs and Tradeoffs." Unpublished manuscript, Massachusetts Institute of Technology, Cambridge, MA.

Banerjee, Abhijit V., and Andrew F. Newman. 1993. "Occupational Choice and the Process of Development." *Journal of Political Economy* 101 (2): 274–98.

Barham, Tania. 2005a. "Providing a Healthier Start to Life: The Impact of Conditional Cash Transfers on Infant Mortality." Unpublished manuscript, Department of Agriculture and Resource Economics, University of California at Berkeley, CA.

———. 2005b. "The Impact of the Mexican Conditional Cash Transfer on Immunization Rates." Unpublished manuscript, Department of Agriculture and Resource Economics, University of California at Berkeley, CA.

Barham, Tania, and John Maluccio. 2008. "The Effect of Conditional Cash Transfers on Vaccination Coverage in Nicaragua." Health and Society Working Paper HS2008-01, Institute of Behavioral Science, University of Colorado at Boulder, CO.

Barrera-Osorio, Felipe, Marianne L. Bertrand, Leigh Linden, and Francisco Perez-Calle. 2008. "Conditional Cash Transfers in Education: Design Features, Peer and Sibling Effects Evidence from a Randomized Experiment in Colombia." Policy Research Working Paper 4580, World Bank, Washington, DC.

Basu, Kaushik, and Pham Hoang Van. 1998. "The Economics of Child Labor." *American Economic Review* 88 (3): 412–27.

Behrman, Jere R., Yingmei Cheng, and Petra Todd. 2004. "Evaluating Preschool Programs When Length of Exposure to the Program Varies: A Nonparametric Approach." *Review of Economics and Statistics* 86 (1): 108–32.

Behrman, Jere R., and Anil B. Deolalikar. 1995. "Are There Differential Returns to Schooling by Gender? The Case of Indonesian Labour Markets." *Oxford Bulletin of Economics and Statistics* 57 (1): 97–117.

Behrman, Jere R., and John Hoddinott. 2000. "An Evaluation of the Impact of PROGRESA on Pre-school Child Height." Unpublished manuscript, International Food Policy Research Institute, Washington, DC.

———. 2005. "Programme Evaluation with Unobserved Heterogeneity and Selective Implementation: The Mexican PROGRESA Impact on Child Nutrition." *Oxford Bulletin of Economics and Statistics* 67 (4): 547–69.

Behrman, Jere R., Susan W. Parker, and Petra E. Todd. 2005. "Long-Term Impacts of the Oportunidades Conditional Cash Transfer Program on Rural Youth in Mexico." Discussion Paper 122, Ibero-America Institute for Economic Research, Göttingen, Germany.

Behrman, Jere R., Piyali Sengupta, and Petra Todd. 2000. "The Impact of PROGRESA on Achievement Test Scores in the First Year." Unpublished manuscript, International Food Policy Research Institute, Washington, DC.

———. 2005. "Progressing through PROGRESA: An Impact Assessment of a School Subsidy Experiment in Rural Mexico." *Economic Development and Cultural Change* 54 (1): 237–75.

Behrman, Jere R., and Petra E. Todd. 1999. "Randomness in the Experimental Samples of PROGRESA (Education, Health, and Nutrition Program)." Unpublished manuscript, International Food Policy Research Institute, Washington, DC.

Bénabou, Roland, and Jean Tirole. 2006. "Belief in a Just World and Redistributive Politics." *Quarterly Journal of Economics* 121 (2): 699–746.

Bertrand, Marianne, Sendhil Mullainathan, and Douglas Miller. 2003. "Public Policy and Extended Families: Evidence from Pensions in South Africa." *World Bank Economic Review* 17 (1): 27–50.

Besley, Timothy J. 1988. "A Simple Model for Merit Good Arguments." *Journal of Public Economics* 35: 371–83.

Bettinger, Eric, and Robert Slonim. 2006. "Using Experimental Economics to Measure the Effects of a Natural Educational Experiment on Altruism." *Journal of Public Economics* 90 (8-9): 1625–48.

Blank, Rebecca M. 2002. "Evaluating Welfare Reform in the United States." *Journal of Economic Literature* 40 (4): 1105–66.

Bloom, Dan, and Charles Michalopoulos. 2001. *How Welfare and Work Policies Affect Employment and Income: A Synthesis of Research.* New York: Manpower Demonstration Research Corporation.

Bobonis, Gustavo, and Frederico Finan. 2008. "Endogenous Social Interaction Effects in School Participation in Rural Mexico." *Review of Economics and Statistics.*

Bourguignon, François, and Francisco H. G. Ferreira. 2003. "Ex Ante Evaluation of Policy Reforms Using Behavioral Models." In *The Impact of Economic Policies on Poverty and Income Distribution: Techniques and Tools,* ed. François Bourguignon and Luis Pereira da Silva, 123–42. New York. World Bank and Oxford University Press.

Bourguignon, François, Francisco H. G. Ferreira, and Phillippe G. Leite. 2003. "Conditional Cash Transfers, Schooling, and Child Labor: Micro-Simulating Brazil's Bolsa Escola Program." *World Bank Economic Review* 17 (2): 229–54.

Bourguignon, François, Francisco Ferreira, and Michael Walton. 2007. "Equity, Efficiency and Inequality Traps: A Research Agenda." *Journal of Economic Inequality* 5: 235–56.

Braido, Luis H.B., Pedro Olinto, and Helena S. Perrone. 2008. "Gender Bias in Intrahousehold Allocation: Evidence from an Unintentional Experiment." Unpublished manuscript, World Bank, Washington, DC.

Brown, Philip H., and Claudio A. Agostini. 2008. "Cash Transfers and Poverty Reduction in Chile." Unpublished manuscript, Colby College, Waterville, ME.

Caldés, Natàlia, David Coady, and John A. Maluccio. 2006. "The Cost of Poverty Alleviation Transfer Programs: A Comparative Analysis of Three Programs in Latin America." *World Development* 34 (5): 818–37.

Camargo, José Márcio, and Francisco H. G. Ferreira. 2001. "O Benefício Social Único: Uma Proposta de Reforma da Política Social no Brasil." Discussion Paper 443, Department of Economics PUC-Rio, Rio de Janeiro, Brazil.

Cameron, Lisa A. 2002. "Did Social Safety Net Scholarships Reduce Drop-out Rates During the Indonesian Economic Crisis?" Policy Research Working Paper 2800, World Bank, Washington, DC.

Card, David. 1999. "The Causal Effect of Education on Earnings." In *Handbook of Labor Economics,* ed. Orley C. Ashenfelter and David Card, 1801–63. Amsterdam, The Netherlands: North Holland (Elsevier).

Card, David, and Thomas Lemieux. 2001. "Can Falling Supply Explain the Rising Return to College for Younger Men? A Cohort-Based Analysis." *Quarterly Journal of Economics* 116 (2): 705–46.

Cardoso, Eliana, and André Portela Souza. 2004. "The Impact of Cash Transfers on Child Labor and School Attendance in Brazil." Working paper 04-W07, Department of Economics, Vanderbilt University, Nashville, TN.

Carneiro, Pedro, and Emanuela Galasso. 2008. "Medium-Term Effects of the Program Chile Solidario: A Preliminary Assessment." Presentation prepared for the Ministry of Planning, Santiago, Chile.

Carrillo, Paul E., and Juan Ponce. 2008. "Efficient Delivery of Subsidies to the Poor: Improving the Design of a Cash Transfer Program in Ecuador." *Journal of Development Economics.*

Castañeda, Angelica. 2006. "Padrón de Beneficiarios: Entrega de Apoyos Monetarios." Presentation for the Inter-American Development Bank, Washington, DC, November 3.

Castañeda, Tarcisio, and Kathy Lindert. 2005. "Designing and Implementing Household Targeting Systems: Lessons from Latin America and the United States." Social Protection Discussion Paper 0526. World Bank, Washington, DC.

CESSP (Cambodia Education Sector Support Project) Scholarship Team, Government of Cambodia. 2005. *Targeted Assistance for Education of Poor Students and Children in Disadvantaged Areas. Operational Manual.* Phnom Penh.

Chaudhury, Nazmul, and Dilip Parajuli. 2008. "Conditional Cash Transfers and Female Schooling: The Impact of the Female School Stipend Program on Public School Enrollments in Punjab, Pakistan." *Journal of Applied Economics.*

Chen, Shaohua, Ren Mu, and Martin Ravallion. 2006. "Are There Lasting Impacts of Aid to Poor Areas? Evidence from Rural China." Policy Research Working Paper 4084, World Bank, Washington, DC.

Coady, David P., and Susan W. Parker. 2004. "Cost-Effectiveness Analysis of Demand- and Supply-Side Education Interventions: The Case of PROGRESA in Mexico." *Review of Development Economics* 8 (3): 440–51.

Cohen, Ernesto, and Rolando Franco. 2006. "Los Programas de Transferencias con Corresponsabilidad en América Latina: Similitudes y Diferencias." In *Transferencias con Corresponsabilidad: Una Mirada Latinoamericana,* ed. Ernesto Cohen and Rolando Franco, 85–136. Mexico City: SEDESOL.

Cunha, Flavio, James Heckman, L. Lochner, and Dimitriy Masterov. 2006. "Interpreting the Evidence on Life Cycle Skill Formation." In *Handbook of the Economics of Education,* ed. E. Hanushek and F. Welch. Amsterdam, The Netherlands: North Holland (Elsevier).

Currie, Janet. 2001. "Early Childhood Education Programs." *Journal of Economic Perspectives* 15 (2): 213–38.

Currie, Janet, and Firouz Gahvari. 2007. "Transfers in Cash and in Kind: Theory Meets the Data." Working Paper 13557, National Bureau of Economic Research, Cambridge, MA.

Cutler, David M., Felicia Knaul, Rafael Lonzano, Oscar Méndez, and Beatriz Zurita. 2002. "Financial Crisis, Health Outcomes and Ageing: Mexico in the 1980s and 1990s." *Journal of Public Economics* 84 (2): 279–303.

Das, Jishnu, Quy-Toan Do, and Berk Özler. 2005. "Reassessing Conditional Cash Transfer Programs." *World Bank Research Observer* 20 (1): 57–80.

Datt, Gaurav, and Martin Ravallion. 1994. "Transfer Benefits from Public Works Employment: Evidence for Rural India." *Economic Journal* 104 (427): 1346–69.

de Brauw, Alan, and John Hoddinott. 2008. "Must Conditional Cash Transfer Programs Be Conditioned to Be Effective? The Impact of Conditioning Transfers on School Enrollment in Mexico." Discussion Paper 757, International Food Policy Research Institute, Washington, DC.

de Ferranti, David M., Guillermo Perry, Francisco H. G. Ferreira, and Michael Walton. 2004. *Inequality in Latin America: Breaking With History?* Washington, DC: World Bank.

de Janvry, Alain, Frederico Finan, Elisabeth Sadoulet, Donald Nelson, Kathy Lindert, Bénédicte de la Brière, and Peter Lanjouw. 2005. "Brazil's Bolsa Escola Program: The Role of Local Governance in Decentralized

Implementation." Social Protection Discussion Paper 0542, World Bank, Washington, DC.

de Janvry, Alain, Frederico Finan, Elisabeth Sadoulet, and Renos Vakis. 2006. "Can Conditional Cash Transfer Programs Serve As Safety Nets in Keeping Children at School and from Working When Exposed to Shocks?" *Journal of Development Economics* 79 (2): 349–73.

de Janvry, Alain, and Elisabeth Sadoulet. 2005. "Conditional Cash Transfer Programs for Child Human Capital Development: Lessons Derived from Experience in Mexico and Brazil." Paper prepared for presentation at the GRADE 25th Anniversary Conference, "Investigación, Politicas y Desarrollo," Lima, Peru, November 15–17, 2005.

———. 2006. "Making Conditional Cash Transfer Programs More Efficient: Designing for Maximum Effect of the Conditionality." *World Bank Economic Review* 20 (1): 1–29.

de la Brière, Bénédicte, and Laura B. Rawlings. 2006. "Examining Conditional Cash Transfer Programs: A Role for Increased Social Inclusion?" Social Protection Discussion Paper 603, World Bank, Washington, DC.

de Mel, Suresh, David McKenzie, and Christopher Woodruff. 2008. "Returns to Capital in Microenterprises: Evidence from a Field Experiment." *Quarterly Journal of Economics* 123 (4): 1329–72.

de Walque, Damien. 2007. "How Does the Impact of an HIV/AIDS Information Campaign Vary with Educational Attainment? Evidence from Rural Uganda." *Journal of Development Economics* 84 (2): 686–714.

Demirgüç-Kunt, Asli, and Ross Levine. 2008. "Finance and Economic Opportunity." In *Proceedings of the World Bank Annual Conference on Development Economics on Private Sector Development,* ed. François Bourguignon and Boris Pleskovic. Washington, DC: World Bank.

Dominitz, Jeff, and Charles F. Manski. 1996. "Eliciting Student Expectations of the Returns to Schooling." *Journal of Human Resources* 31 (1): 1–26.

Doss, Cheryl. 2006. "The Effects of Intrahousehold Property Ownership on Expenditure Patterns in Ghana." *Journal of African Economics* 15 (1): 149–80.

Drèze, Jean. 2004 "Employment As a Social Responsibility," *The Hindu,* November 22. http://www.hindu.com/2004/11/22/stories/2004112205071000.htm.

Drèze, Jean, and Amartya Sen. 1991. *Hunger and Public Action.* New York: Oxford University Press.

Duarte Gómez, María Beatriz, Sonia Morales Miranda, Alvaro Javier Idrovo Velandia, Sandra Catalina Ochoa Marín, Siemon Bult van der Wal, Marta Caballero García, and Mauricio Hernández Ávila. 2004. "Impact of *Oportunidades* on Knowledge and Practices of Beneficiary Mothers and Young Scholarship Recipients: An Evaluation of the Educational Health Sessions." In *External Evaluation of the Impact of the Human Development Program Oportunidades 2004,* ed. Bernardo Hernández Prado and Mauricio Hernández Ávila. Cuernavaca, Morales, Mexico: National Institute of Public Health.

Duflo, Esther. 2003. "Grandmothers and Granddaughters: Old-Age Pensions and Intrahousehold Allocation in South Africa." *World Bank Economic Review* 17 (1): 1–25.

Duflo, Esther, Pascaline Dupas, and Michael Kremer. 2008. "Peer Effects and the Impact of Tracking: Evidence from a Randomized Evaluation in Kenya." Unpublished manuscript, Abdul Latif Jameel Poverty Action Lab, Cambridge, MA.

Dugger, Celia W. 2004. "To Help Poor Be Pupils, Not Wage Earners, Brazil Pays Parents." *The New York Times.* http://query.nytimes.com/gst/full-page.html?res=9D02E7DA1731F930A35752C0A9629C8B63&sec=health [accessed April 16, 2008].

Dupas, Pascaline. 2007. "Relative Risks and the Market for Sex: Teenagers, Sugar Daddies and HIV in Kenya?" Unpublished manuscript, Dartmouth College, Hanover, NH.

Edmonds, Eric V., and Norbert Schady. 2008. "Poverty Alleviation and Child Labor." Policy Research Working Paper 4702, World Bank, Washington, DC.

Elbers, Chris, Jean O. Lanjouw, and Peter Lanjouw. 2003. "Micro-Level Estimation of Poverty and Inequality." *Econometrica* 71 (1): 355–64.

Fasih, Tazeen. 2008. "Concept Note: Impact Evaluation of a Conditional Cash Transfer Scheme in Yemen." Unpublished manuscript, World Bank, Washington, DC.

Fehr, Ernst, and Simon Gächter. 2000. "Cooperation and Punishment in Public Goods Experiments." *American Economic Review* 90 (4): 980–94.

Fehr, Ernst, and Klaus M. Schmidt. 1999. "A Theory of Fairness, Competition, and Cooperation." *Quarterly Journal of Economics* 114 (3): 817–68.

Fernald, Lia, Paul Gertler, and Lynette Neufeld. 2008. "Role of Cash in Conditional Cash Transfer Programmes for Child Health, Growth, and Development: An Analysis of Mexico's Oportunidades." *The Lancet* 371: 828–37.

Fernald, Lia C., Paul J. Gertler, and G. Olaiz. 2005. "Impacto de Mediano Plazo del Programa Oportunidades sobre la Obesidad y las Enfermedades Crónicas en Áreas Rurales." In *Evaluación Externa de Impacto del Programa Oportunidades 2004: Alimentación,* ed. Bernardo Hernández Prado and Mauricio Hernández Ávila, 247–330. Cuernavaca, Morales, México: National Institute of Public Health.

Ferreira, Francisco H. G. 2008. "The Economic Rationale for Conditional Cash Transfers." Unpublished manuscript, World Bank, Washington, DC.

Ferreira, Francisco H. G., and Norbert Schady. 2008. "Aggregate Economic Shocks, Child Schooling and Child Health." *World Bank Research Observer.*

Fields, Gary, Robert Duval, Samuel Freije, and M. L. Sánchez Puerta. 2007. "Intragenerational Income Mobility in Latin America." *Economía* 7 (2): 101–54.

Filmer, Deon, and Norbert Schady. 2006. "Getting Girls into School: Evidence from a Scholarship Program in Cambodia." Policy Research Working Paper 3910, World Bank, Washington, DC.

———. 2008. "Getting Girls into School: Evidence from a Scholarship Program in Cambodia." *Economic Development and Cultural Change* 56: 581–617.

———. 2009a. "Are There Diminishing Returns to Transfer Size in Conditional Cash Transfers?" Unpublished manuscript, World Bank, Washington, DC.

———. 2009b. "In School But Not Learning: The Impact of a Scholarship Program on School Enrollment and Achievement." Unpublished manuscript, World Bank, Washington, DC.

———. 2009c. "Who Benefits? Scholarships, School Enrollment and Work of Recipients and Their Siblings." Unpublished manuscript, World Bank, Washington, DC.

Fiszbein, Ariel. 2005. *Citizens, Politicians and Providers: The Latin American Experience with Service Delivery Reform.* Washington, DC: World Bank.

Foster, Andrew D., and Mark R. Rosenzweig. 1995. "Learning by Doing and Learning from Others: Human Capital and Technical Change in Agriculture." *Journal of Political Economy* 103 (6): 1176–209.

———. 1996. "Technical Change and Human-Capital Returns and Investments: Evidence from the Green Revolution." *American Economic Review* 86 (4): 931–53.

Fraker, Thomas M., Alberto P. Martini, and James C. Ohls. 1995. "The Effect of Food Stamp Cashout on Food Expenditures: An Assessment of the Findings from Four Demonstrations." *Journal of Human Resources* 30 (4): 633–49.

Freeland, Nicholas. 2007. "Superfluous, Pernicious, Atrocious and Abominable? The Case Against Conditional Cash Transfers." *IDS Bulletin* 38 (3): 75–78.

Galasso, Emanuela. 2006. "With Their Effort and One Opportunity: Alleviating Extreme Poverty in Chile." Unpublished manuscript, World Bank, Washington, DC.

Galiani, Sebastián. 2007. "Reducing Poverty in Latin America and the Caribbean." Report prepared for the Copenhagen Consensus Center and the Inter-American Development Bank. Washington University, St. Louis, MO.

Galor, Oded, and Joseph Zeira. 1993. "Income Distribution and Macroeconomics." *Review of Economic Studies* 60 (1): 35–52.

Gelbach, Jonah B., and Lant Pritchett. 2002. "Is More for the Poor Less for the Poor? The Politics of Means-Tested Targeting." *B. E. Journal of Economic Analysis & Policy* 2 (1): article 6.

Gertler, Paul. 2000. "Final Report: The Impact of PROGESA on Health." International Food Policy Research Institute, Washington, DC.

———. 2004. "Do Conditional Cash Transfers Improve Child Health? Evidence from PROGRESA's Control Randomized Experiment." *American Economic Review* 94 (2): 336–41.

Gertler, Paul, Sebastián Martínez, and Marta Rubio-Codina. 2006. "Investing Cash Transfers to Raise Long-Term Living Standards." Policy Research Working Paper 3994, World Bank, Washington, DC.

Gimnig, John E., Margarette S. Kolczak, Allen W. Hightower, John M. Vulule, Erik Schoute, Luna Kamau, Penelope A. Phillips-Howard, Feiko O. Ter Kuile, Bernard L. Nahlen, and William A. Hawley. 2003. "Effect of Permethrin-Treated Bed Nets on the Spatial Distribution of Malaria Vectors in Western Kenya." *American Journal of Tropical Medicine and Hygiene* 68 (4 suppl): 115–20.

Glewwe, Paul, Michael Kremer, and Sylvie Moulin. 2008. "Many Children Left Behind? Textbooks and Test Scores in Kenya." *American Economic Journal: Applied Economics.*

Glewwe, Paul, and Pedro Olinto. 2004. "Evaluating the Impact of Conditional Cash Transfers on Schooling: An Experimental Analysis of Honduras." Unpublished manuscript, University of Minnesota, Minneapolis.

Glewwe, Paul, Pedro Olinto, and Priscila Z. de Souza. 2003. "Evaluating the Impact of Conditional Cash Transfers on Schooling in Honduras: An Experimental Approach." Unpublished manuscript, University of Minnesota, Minneapolis.

Goldin, Claudia. 1999. "Egalitarianism and the Returns to Education During the Great Transformation of American Education." *Journal of Political Economy* 107 (6): 65–94.

Goldstein, Markus, and Christopher Udry. 1999. "Agricultural Innovation and Resource Management in Ghana." Unpublished manuscript, Yale University, New Haven, CT.

Gómez-Hermosillo, Rogelio. 2006. "Oportunidades: Achievements and Future Challenges." Presentation prepared for the Inter-American Development Bank, Washington, DC, November 3.

González-Pier, Eduardo, Cristina Gutiérrez-Delgado, Gretchen Stevens, Mariana Barraza-Lloréns, Raúl Porras-Condey, Natalie Caravalho, Kristen Loncich, Rodrigo H. Dias, Sandeep Kulkarni, Anna Casey, Yuki Murakami, Majid Ezzati, and Joshua A. Salomon. 2006. "Priority Setting for Health Interventions in Mexico's System of Social Protection in Health." *The Lancet* 368 (9547): 1608–18.

Government of Brazil, Ministry of Health. 2004. "Avaliação do Programa Bolsa Alimentação, Primeira Fase e Segunda Fase. (Evaluation of the Bolsa Alimentação Program, First and Second Phases)." Brasilia.

Government of El Salvador. 2008. "Informes Red Solidaria." Unpublished manuscript, San Salvador.

Government of Indonesia. 2007a. *Pedoman Umum Keluarga Harapan-PKH 2007 (General Manual of the PKH Program 2007).* Jakarta.

———. 2007b. *Petunjuk Teknis Kelembagaan Program Keluarga Harapan-PKH Daerah (Technical Instruction PKH Manual for Local Institution).* Jakarta.

———. 2007c. *Petunjuk Teknis Program Keluarga Harapan-PKH bagi Pemberi Palayanan Kesehatan (Technical Instruction PKH Manual for Health Services Providers).* Jakarta.

———. 2007d. *Petunjuk Teknis Program Keluarga Harapan-PKH bagi Pemberi Palayanan Pendidikan (Technical Instruction PKH Manual for Education Services Providers).* Jakarta.

Government of Jamaica. 2006. "Ministry of Labour and Social Security Programme of Advancement through Health and Education (PATH) Operational Audits, Compliance Report #7 and #8." Unpublished manuscript, Kingston.

Government of Kenya, Office of the Vice President and Ministry of Home Affairs. 2006a. *Cash Transfer Programme for Orphans and Vulnerable Children (CT-OVC) Operational Manual, Version 1.0.* Nairobi.

———. 2006b. "Program Design, Cash Transfer Pilot Project." Version April 18. Nairobi.

———. 2007. *Cash Transfer Programme for Orphans and Vulnerable Children (CT-OVC) Operational Manual, Version 2.0.* Nairobi.

Government of Pakistan, Ministry of Social Welfare and Special Education. 2007. *Child Support Programme Operational Manual, Version 1.0.* Islamabad, Pakistan: Bait-Ul-Mal.

Grant, Monica J., and Jere H. Behrman. 2008. *Gender Gaps in Educational Attainment in Less Developed Countries.* Unpublished manuscript, University of Pennsylvania, Philadelphia.

Grantham-McGregor, Sally, Y. Cheung, S. Cueto, P. Glewwe, L. Richter, and B. Sharp. 2007. "Developmental Potential in the First 5 Years for Children in Developing Countries." *The Lancet* 369 (9555): 60–70.

Griffiths, Marcia, and Judith S. McGuire. 2005. "A New Dimension for Health Reform: The Integrated Community Child Health Program in Honduras." In *Health System Innovations in Central America: Lessons and Impact of New Approaches,* ed. Gerard M. La Forgia, 173–96. Washington, DC: World Bank.

Grogger, Jeffrey. 2003. "The Effects of Time Limits, the EITC, and Other Policy Changes on Welfare Use, Work, and Income among Female-Headed Families." *Review of Economics and Statistics* 85 (2): 394–408.

Grosh, Margaret E., Carlo del Ninno, Emil Tesliuc, and Azedine Oueghi, with Annamaria Milazzo and Christine Weigand. 2008. *For Protection and Promotion: The Design and Implementation of Effective Safety Nets.* Washington, DC: World Bank.

Gutiérrez, Juan Pablo, Paul Gertler, Mauricio Hernández Ávila, and Stefano Bertozzi. 2005. "Impacto de Oportunidades en los Comportamientos de Riesgo de los Adolescentes y en sus Consecuencias Inmediatas: Resultados del Corto Plazo en Zonas Urbanas y de Mediano Plazo en Zonas Rurales." In *Evaluación Externa de Impacto del Programa Oportunidades 2004: Alimentación,* ed. Bernardo Hernández Prado and Mauricio Hernández Ávila. Cuernavaca, Morales, Mexico: National Institute of Public Health.

Hamoudi, Amar, and Duncan Thomas. 2005. "Pension Income and the Well-Being of Children and Grandchildren: New Evidence from South Africa." On-Line Working Paper 043-05, California Center for Population Research, University of California, Los Angeles, CA.

Heckman, James J. 2006a. "Investing in Disadvantaged Young Children Is an Economically Efficient Policy." Presentation prepared for the Forum on Building the Economic Case for Investments in Preschool, Committee for

Economic Development, Pew Charitable Trusts/PNC Financial Services Group, New York City, January 10.

———. 2006b. "Skill Formation and the Economics of Investing in Disadvantaged Children." *Science* 312 (5782): 1900–02.

———. 2008. "Schools, Skills, and Synapses." *Economic Inquiry* 46 (3): 289–324.

Heckman, James J., and Pedro Carneiro. 2003. "Human Capital Policy." Working Paper W9495, National Bureau of Economic Research, Cambridge, MA.

Heckman, James J., and Dimitriy V. Masterov. 2007. "The Productivity Argument for Investing in Young Children." Working Paper 13016, National Bureau of Economic Research, Cambridge, MA.

Heinrich, Carolyn J. 2007. "Demand and Supply-Side Determinants of Conditional Cash Transfer Program Effectiveness." *World Development* 35 (1): 121–43.

Heinrich, Carolyn J., and Marcelo Cabrol. 2005. "Programa Nacional de *Becas Estudiantiles* Impact Evaluation Findings." Working Paper WP-06, Inter-American Development Bank, Washington, DC.

Hernández, Bernardo, Dolores Ramírez, Hortensia Moreno, and Nan Laird. 2005. "Evaluación del Impacto de *Oportunidades* en la Mortalidad Materna e Infantil." In *External Evaluation of the Impact of the Human Development Program Oportunidades 2004,* ed. Bernardo Hernández Prado and Mauricio Hernández Ávila, 73–95. Cuernavaca, Morales, Mexico: National Institute of Public Health.

Hernández, Gonzalo. 2006. "The Construction of an Integrated Monitoring and Evaluation System for Social Programs: A Public Policy Challenge with Technical Elements." Presentation prepared for the National Council for Evaluation of Social Development Policy, Mexico City.

Hernanz, Virginia, Franck Malherbet, and Michele Pellizzari. 2004. "Take-Up of Welfare Benefits in OECD Countries: A Review of the Evidence." Social, Employment and Migration Working Paper 17, OECD Directorate for Employment, Labour and Social Affairs, Paris.

Hirschman, Albert O. 1958. *The Strategy of Economic Development.* New Haven, CT: Yale University Press.

———. 1990. "The Case Against 'One Thing at a Time.'" *World Development* 18 (8): 1119–22.

Hoddinott, John. 2008. "Nutrition and Conditional Cash Transfer (CCT) Programs." Unpublished manuscript, International Food Policy Research Institute, Washington, DC.

Hoddinott, John, and Lawrence Haddad. 1995. "Does Female Income Share Influence Household Expenditures? Evidence from Côte d'Ivoire." *Oxford Bulletin of Economics and Statistics* 57 (1): 77–96.

Hoddinott, John, and Emmanuel Skoufias. 2004. "The Impact of PROGRESA on Food Consumption." *Economic Development and Cultural Change* 53 (1): 37–61.

Hoddinott, John, Emmanuel Skoufias, and Ryan Washburn. 2000. "The Impact of PROGRESA on Consumption: A Final Report." International Food Policy Research Institute, Washington, DC.

Hoffman, Elizabeth, Kevin McCabe, Keith Schachat, and Vernon Smith.1994. "Preferences, Property Rights and Anonymity in Bargaining Games." *Games and Economic Behavior* 7 (3): 346–80.

Hossain, Naomi. 2004. "Access to Education for the Poor and Girls: Education Achievements in Bangladesh." Scaling Up Poverty Reduction: A Global Learning Process and Conference, sponsored by the World Bank, Shanghai, May 25–27.

IFPRI (International Food Policy Research Institute). 2000. *Evaluation of PROGRESA*. Washington, DC.

———. 2003. *Sexto Informe. Proyecto PRAF/BID Fase II: Impacto Intermedio*. Washington, DC.

Imbens, Guido, and Joshua Angrist. 1994. "Identification and Estimation of Local Average Treatment Effects." *Econometrica* 62 (2): 467–75.

Institute for Fiscal Studies, Econometría, and Sistemas Especializados de Información. 2006. "Evaluación del Impacto del Programa Familias en Acción–Subsidios Condicionados de la Red de Apoyo Social." National Planning Department, Bogotá, Colombia.

Islam, Mahnaz, and John Hoddinott. 2009. "Evidence of Intra-Household Flypaper Effects from a Nutrition Intervention in Rural Guatemala." *Economic Development and Cultural Change* 57 (2): 215–38.

Jacoby, Hanan G. 2002. "Is There an Intrahousehold 'Flypaper Effect'? Evidence from a School Feeding Programme." *Economic Journal* 112 (476): 196–221.

Jalan, Jyotsna, and Martin Ravallion. 2003a. "Does Piped Water Reduce Diarrhea for Children in Rural India?" *Journal of Econometrics* 112 (1): 153–73.

———. 2003b. "Estimating the Benefit Incidence of an Antipoverty Program by Propensity-Score Matching." *Journal of Business & Economic Statistics* 21 (1): 19–31.

Jensen, Robert. 2000. "Agricultural Volatility and Investments in Children." *American Economic Review* 90 (2): 399–404.

———. 2006. "Do the Perceived Returns to Education Affect Schooling Decisions? Evidence from a Randomized Experiment." Unpublished manuscript, Harvard University, Cambridge, MA.

Jones, Nicola, Rosana Vargas, and Eliana Villar. 2008. "Conditional Cash Transfers in Peru: Tackling the Multi-Dimensionality of Poverty and Vulnerability." http://www.unicef.org/policyanalysis/files/Conditional_Cash_Transfers_In_Peru_-_Tackling_The_Multi-Dimensionality_Of_Poverty_And_Vulnerability.pdf [accessed November 2008].

Khandker, Shahid R., Mark M. Pitt, and Nubuhiko Fuwa. 2003. "Subsidy to Promote Girls' Secondary Education: The Female Stipend Program in Bangladesh." Unpublished manuscript, World Bank, Washington, DC.

Knudsen, Eric I., James J. Heckman, Judy L. Cameron, and Jack. P. Shonkoff. 2006. "Economic, Neurobiological, and Behavioral Perspectives on Building America's Future Workforce." *Proceedings of the National Academy of Sciences* 103 (27): 10155–62.

Kooreman, Peter. 2000. "The Labeling Effect of a Child Benefit System." *American Economic Review* 90 (3): 571–83.

Krueger, Alan B., and Bruce D. Meyer. 2002. "Labor Supply Effects of Social Insurance." In *Handbook of Public Economics,* ed. Alan J. Auerbach and Martin Feldstein, 2327–92. Amsterdam, The Netherlands: Elsevier.

Kudat, Ayse. 2006. "Evaluating the Conditional Cash Transfer Program in Turkey: A Qualitative Assessment." Unpublished manuscript, International Food Policy Research Institute, Washington, DC.

Lafaurie, Maria Teresa, and Claudia A. Velasquez Leiva. 2004. "Transferring Cash Benefits through the Banking Sector in Colombia." Social Protection Discussion Paper 0409, World Bank, Washington, DC.

Larrañaga, Osvaldo, Dante Contreras, and Jaime Ruiz Tagle. 2008. "Evaluación del Sistema Chile Solidario." Unpublished manuscript, Economics Department, Universidad de Chile, Santiago, Chile.

Leite, Phillippe, and Pedro Olinto. 2008. "Investigating the Relationship between CCTs and Supply of Education." Unpublished manuscript, World Bank, Washington, DC.

Levy, Dan, and James Ohls. 2003. "Evaluation of Jamaica's PATH Program: Methodology Report." Mathematica Policy Research, Washington, DC.

———. 2007. "Evaluation of Jamaica's PATH Program: Final Report." Mathematica Policy Research, Washington, DC.

Levy, Santiago. 2006. *Progress Against Poverty: Sustaining Mexico's PROGRESA-Oportunidades Program.* Washington, DC: Brookings Institution Press.

———. 2008. *Good Intentions, Bad Outcomes: Social Policy, Informality and Economic Growth in Mexico.* Washington, DC: Brookings Institution Press.

Levy, Santiago, and Evelyne Rodríguez. 2004. "Economic Crisis, Political Transition and Poverty Policy Reform: Mexico's PROGRESA/Oportunidades Program." Unpublished manuscript, Inter-American Development Bank, Washington, DC.

Lindert, Kathy, Anja Linder, Jason Hobbs, and Bénédicte de la Brière. 2007. "The Nuts and Bolts of Brazil's Bolsa Família Program: Implementing Conditional Cash Transfers in a Decentralized Context." Social Protection Discussion Paper 0709, World Bank, Washington, DC.

Lindert, Kathy, Emmanuel Skoufias, and Joseph Shapiro. 2006. *Redistributing Income to the Poor and the Rich: Public Transfers in Latin America and the Caribbean.* Washington, DC: World Bank.

Lindert, Kathy, and Vanina Vincensini. 2008. "Bolsa Família nas Manchetes." Presentation at the World Bank, Washington, DC, July 1.

Loury, Glenn C. 1981. "Intergenerational Transfers and the Distribution of Earnings." *Econometrica* 49 (4): 843–67.

Lundberg, Shelly J., Robert A. Pollak, and Terence J. Wales. 1997. "Do Husbands and Wives Pool Their Resources? Evidence from the United Kingdom Child Benefit." *Journal of Human Resources* 32 (3): 463–80.

Mackay, Keith Robin. 2007. *How to Build M&E Systems to Support Better Government.* Washington, DC: World Bank.

Macours, Karen, Norbert Schady, and Renos Vakis. 2008. "Cash Transfers, Behavioral Changes, and the Cognitive Development of Young Children:

Evidence from a Randomized Experiment." Policy Research Working Paper 4,59, World Bank, Washington, DC.

Macours, Karen, and Renos Vakis. 2008. "Changing Households' Investments and Aspirations Through Social Interactions: Evidence from a Randomized Transfer Program in a Low-Income Country." Unpublished manuscript, Johns Hopkins University, Baltimore, MD, and World Bank, Washington, DC.

Maluccio, John A. 2005. "Coping with the 'Coffee Crisis' in Central America: The Role of the Nicaraguan *Red de Protección Social*." Discussion Paper 188, Food Consumption and Nutrition Division, International Food Policy Research Institute, Washington, DC.

———. 2008. "The Impact of Conditional Cash Transfers in Nicaragua on Consumption, Productive Investments, and Labor Allocation." *Journal of Development Studies*.

Maluccio, John A., and Rafael Flores. 2005. "Impact Evaluation of a Conditional Cash Transfer Program: The Nicaraguan *Red de Protección Social*." Research Report 141, International Food Policy Research Institute, Washington, DC.

Maluccio, John A., Alexis Murphy, and Ferdinando Regalía. 2006. "Does Supply Matter? Initial Supply Conditions and the Effectiveness of Conditional Cash Transfers for Grade Progression in Nicaragua." Unpublished manuscript, Inter-American Development Bank, Washington, DC.

Manacorda, Marco, Carolina Sánchez-Páramo, and Norbert Schady. 2008. "Changes in the Returns to Education in Latin America: The Role of Demand and Supply of Skills." *Industrial and Labor Relations Review*.

Martorell, Reynaldo. 1995. "Results and Implications of the INCAP Follow-up Study." *Journal of Nutrition* 125 (4 suppl): 1127S–38S.

McKenzie, David J. 2003. "How Do Households Cope with Aggregate Shocks? Evidence from the Mexican Peso Crisis." *World Development* 31 (7): 1179–99.

Miguel, Edward, and Michael Kremer. 2004. "Worms: Identifying Impacts on Education and Health in the Presence of Treatment Externalities." *Econometrica* 72 (1): 159–217.

Moffitt, Robert A. 2002. "Welfare Programs and Labor Supply." In *Handbook of Public Economics,* ed. Alan J. Auerbach and Martin Feldstein, 2393–430. Amsterdam, The Netherlands: Elsevier.

———. 2007. "Welfare Reform: The US Experience." Report prepared for the From Welfare to Work Conference, sponsored by the Economic Council of Sweden, Stockholm, May 7.

Mont, Daniel. 2006. "Disability in Conditional Cash Transfer Programs: Drawing on Experience in LAC." Report prepared for the Third International Conference on Conditional Cash Transfers, Istanbul, Turkey, June 26–30.

Moore, Charity. 2008. "Assessing Honduras' CCT Programme PRAF, Programa de Asignación Familiar: Expected and Unexpected Realities." Country Study 15, International Poverty Center, Brasilia, Brazil.

Moretti, Enrico. 2004a. "Estimating the Social Return to Higher Education: Evidence from Longitudinal and Repeated Cross-Sectional Data." *Journal of Econometrics* 121 (1-2): 175–212.

————. 2004b. "Workers' Education, Spillovers, and Productivity: Evidence from Plant-Level Production Functions." *American Economic Review* 94 (3): 656–90.

Morris, Pamela A., Aletha Huston, Greg Duncan, Danielle Crosby, and Johannes Bos. 2001. *How Welfare and Work Policies Affect Children: A Synthesis of Research.* New York: Manpower Demonstration Research Corporation.

Morris, Saul, Rafael Flores, Pedro Olinto, and Juan Manuel Medina. 2004. "Monetary Incentives in Primary Health Care and Effects on Use and Coverage of Preventive Health Care Interventions in Rural Honduras: Cluster Randomised Trial." *The Lancet* 364 (9450): 2030–37.

Morris, Saul, Pedro Olinto, Rafael Flores, Eduardo A.F. Nilson, and Ana C. Figueiró. 2004. "Conditional Cash Transfers Are Associated with a Small Reduction in the Weight Gain of Preschool Children in Northeast Brazil." *Journal of Nutrition* 134: 2336–41.

Murgai, Rinku, and Martin Ravallion. 2005. "Is a Guaranteed Living Wage a Good Anti-poverty Policy?" Policy Research Working Paper 3640, World Bank, Washington, DC.

Musgrave, Richard Abel. 1959. *The Theory of Public Finance: A Study in Public Economy.* New York: McGraw-Hill.

Mutzig, Jean-Marc. 2006. "The Bolsa Família Grants Program." Report prepared for the Third International Conference on Conditional Cash Transfers, Istanbul, Turkey, June 26–30.

Nath, Samir R., Kathy Sylva, and Janice Grimes. 1999. "Raising Basic Education Levels in Rural Bangladesh: The Impact of a Non-formal Education Programme." *International Review of Education* 45 (1): 5–26.

Nelson, Richard R., and Edmund S. Phelps. 1966. "Investment in Humans, Technological Diffusion, and Economic Growth." *American Economic Review* 56 (1/2): 69–75.

Neufeld, Lynette M. 2006. "Nutrition in the Oportunidades Conditional Cash Transfer Program: Strengths and Challenges." Report prepared for the Third International Conference on Conditional Cash Transfers, Istanbul, Turkey, June 26–30.

Neufeld, Lynette M., Daniela Sotres-Álvarez, Paul Gertler, Lizbeth Tonlentino Mayo, Jorge Jiménez Ruiz, Lia Fernald, Salvador Villalpando, Teresa Shamah, and Juan Rivera Dommarco. 2005. "Impacto de Oportunidades en el Crecimiento y Estado Nutricional de Niños en Zonas Rurales." In *Evaluación Externa de Impacto del Programa Oportunidades 2004: Alimentación,* ed. Bernardo Hernández Prado and Mauricio Hernández Ávila. Cuernavaca, Morales, México: Instituto Nacional de Salud Pública.

Nguyen, Trang. 2007. "Information, Role Models and Perceived Returns to Education: Experimental Evidence from Madagascar." Unpublished job market paper, Massachusetts Institute of Technology, Cambridge, MA.

Niaz Asadullah, Mohammad, and Nazmul Chaudhury. 2007. "Do Religious Schools Respond to Financial Incentives? Islamic High Schools, Public Subsidies, and Female Schooling in Bangladesh." Unpublished manuscript, World Bank, Washington, DC.

Nichols, Albert L., and Richard J. Zeckhauser. 1982. "Targeting Transfers through Restrictions on Recipients." *American Economic Review* 72 (2): 372–77.

Nielsen, Mette E., and Pedro Olinto. 2007. "Do Conditional Cash Transfers Crowd Out Private Transfers? Evidence from Randomized Trials in Honduras and Nicaragua." Unpublished manuscript, Princeton University, Princeton, NJ.

ODI (Overseas Development Institute). 2006. "Jamaica: The Programme for Advancement through Health and Education (PATH)." Policy Brief 4, Inter-Regional Inequality Facility, London.

O'Donoghue, Ted, and Matthew Rabin. 1999. "Doing It Now or Later." *American Economic Review* 89 (1): 103–24.

Oosterbeek, Hessel, Juan Ponce, and Norbert Schady. 2008. "The Impact of Unconditional Cash Transfers on School Enrollment: Evidence from Ecuador." Policy Research Working Paper 4645, World Bank, Washington, DC.

Paes de Barros, Ricardo, Miguel Nathan Foguel, and Gabriel Ulyssea. 2006. "Desigualdade de Renda no Brasil: Uma Análise da Queda Recente." Instituto de Pesquisa Econômica Aplicada, Brasilia, Brazil.

Parker, Susan W., Luis Rubalcava, and Graciela Teruel. 2008. "Evaluating Conditional Schooling and Health Programs." In *Handbook of Development Economics,* ed. T. Schultz and John Strauss, 3963–4065. Amsterdam, The Netherlands: New Holland-Elsevier.

Parker, Susan W., and Emmanuel Skoufias. 2000. "The Impact of PROGRESA on Work, Leisure, and Allocation." Unpublished manuscript, International Food Policy Research Institute, Washington, DC.

Parker, Susan W., and Graciela Teruel. 2005. "Randomization and Social Program Evaluation: The Case of Progresa." *Annals of the American Academy of Political and Social Science* 599: 199–219.

Paxson, Christina, and Norbert Schady. 2005. "Child Health and Economic Crisis in Peru." *World Bank Economic Review* 19 (2): 203–23.

———. 2007. "Cognitive Development among Young Children in Ecuador: The Roles of Wealth, Health, and Parenting." *Journal of Human Resources* 42 (1): 49–84.

———. 2008. "Does Money Matter? The Effects of Cash Transfers on Child Health and Development in Rural Ecuador." Unpublished manuscript, World Bank, Washington, DC.

Pearson, R., and C. Alviar. 2006. "The Evolution of the Government of Kenya Cash Transfer Programme for Vulnerable Children between 2002 to 2006 and Prospects for Nationwide Scale-Up." UNICEF Kenya Country Office, Nairobi.

Petry, Nancy M. 2000. "A Comprehensive Guide to the Application of Contingency Management Procedures in Clinical Settings." *Drug and Alcohol Dependence* 58 (1-2): 9–25.

———. 2002. "Contingency Management in Addiction Treatment." *Psychiatric Times* 19 (2).

Petry, Nancy M., and Michael J. Bohn. 2003. "Fishbowls and Candy Bars: Using Low-Cost Incentives to Increase Treatment Retention." *Science & Practice Perspectives* 2 (1): 55–61.

345

Piketty, Thomas. 1995. "Social Mobility and Redistributive Politics." *Quarterly Journal of Economics* 110 (3): 551–84.

Pitt, Mark M., and Shahid R. Khandker. 1998. "The Impact of Group-Based Credit Programs on Poor Households in Bangladesh: Does the Gender of Participants Matter?" *Journal of Political Economy* 106 (5): 958–96.

Ponce, Juan, and Arjun S. Bedi. 2008. "The Impact of a Cash Transfer Program on Cognitive Achievement: The Bono de Desarrollo Humano of Ecuador." Discussion Paper 3658, Institute for the Study of Labor, Bonn, Germany.

Pritchett, Lant, Sudarno Sumarto, and Asep Suryahadia. 2003. "Targeted Programs in an Economic Crisis: Empirical Findings from Indonesia's Experience." Working Paper 030, Bureau for Research and Economic Analysis of Development, Cambridge, MA.

Quisumbing, Agnes, and John A. Maluccio. 2000. "Intra-household Allocation and Gender Relations: New Empirical Evidence from Four Developing Countries." Discussion Paper 84, Food Consumption and Nutrition Division, International Food Policy Research Institute, Washington, DC.

Rangel, Marcos A. 2006. "Alimony Rights and Intrahousehold Allocation of Resources: Evidence from Brazil." *Economic Journal* 116 (513): 627–58.

Ravallion, Martin. 1999. "Appraising Workfare." *World Bank Research Observer* 14 (1): 31–48.

———. 2008. "How Relevant Is Targeting to the Success of an Antipoverty Program?" *World Bank Research Observer.*

———. 2009. "Bailing Out the World's Poorest." Unpublished manuscript, World Bank, Washington, DC.

Ravallion, Martin, and Gaurav Datt. 1995. "Is Targeting through a Work Requirement Efficient?" In *Public Spending and the Poor: Theory and Evidence,* ed. Dominique van de Walle and Kimberly Nead. Baltimore, MD: Johns Hopkins University Press.

Ravallion, Martin, Gaurav Datt, and Shubham Chaudhuri. 1993. "Does Maharashtra's Employment Guarantee Scheme Guarantee Employment? Effects of the 1988 Wage Increase." *Economic Development and Cultural Change* 41 (2): 251–75.

Ravallion, Martin, and Quentin Wodon. 2000. "Does Child Labour Displace Schooling? Evidence on Behavioural Responses to an Enrollment Subsidy." *Economic Journal* 110 (462): C158–75.

Regalía, Ferdinando, and Leslie Castro. 2007. "Performance-Based Incentives for Health: Demand- and Supply-Side Incentives in the Nicaraguan Red de Protección Social." Working Paper 119, Center for Global Development, Washington, DC.

Regalía, Ferdinando, and Marcos Robles. 2005. "Social Assistance, Poverty and Equity in the Dominican Republic." Report RE2-05-007, Inter-American Development Bank, Washington, DC.

Reimers, Fernando, Carlo Da Silva, and Ernesto Trevino. 2006. "Where Is the Education in the Conditional Cash Transfers in Education?" Working Paper 4, UNESCO Institute for Statistics, Montreal, Canada.

Rivera, Juan A., Daniela Sotres-Álvarez, Jean-Pierre Habicht, Teresa Shamah, and Salvador Villalpando. 2004. "Impact of the Mexican Program for Education, Health, and Nutrition (PROGRESA) on Rates of Growth and Anemia in Infants and Young Children: A Randomized Effectiveness Study." *Journal of the American Medical Association* 291 (21): 2563–70.

Roberts-Risden, Collette. 2006. "Monitoring Performance: Jamaican Programme of Advancement through Health and Education." Report prepared for the Third International Conference on Conditional Cash Transfers, Istanbul, Turkey, June 26–30.

Rodríguez, Evelyne. 2003. "Some Notes on Changing Social Policy: Mexico's Experience." Presentation at the World Bank Safety Net Primer Launch, Washington, DC, December 1.

Roemer, John E. 1998. *Equality of Opportunity.* Cambridge, MA: Harvard University Press.

Royal Government of Cambodia. 2005. *CESSP Scholarship Team: Operational Manual.* Phnom Penh.

Rubalcava, Luis, Graciela Teruel, and Duncan Thomas. 2004. "Spending, Saving and Public Transfers Paid to Women." On-Line Working Paper 024-04, California Center for Population Research, University of California, Los Angeles, CA.

Rubio, Gloria M. 2007. "Construyendo un Sistema de Evaluación y Monitoreo Basado en Resultados de los Programas Sociales." Presentation, Subsecretaría de Prospectiva, Planeación y Evaluación, Dirección General de Evaluación y Monitoreo de los Programas Sociales, SEDESOL, Mexico City.

Samson, Michael, Ingrid van Niekerk, and Kenneth MacWuene. 2006. *Designing and Implementing Social Transfer Programmes.* Cape Town, South Africa: Economic Policy Research Institute.

Schady, Norbert. 2004. "Do Macroeconomic Crises Always Slow Human Capital Accumulation?" *World Bank Economic Review* 18 (2): 131–54.

———. 2006. "Early Childhood Development in Latin America and the Caribbean." *Economía* 6 (2): 185–225.

Schady, Norbert, and María Caridad Araujo. 2008. "Cash Transfers, Conditions, and School Enrollment in Ecuador." *Economía* 8 (2): 43–70.

Schady, Norbert, and José Rosero. 2007. "Are Cash Transfers Made to Women Spent Like Other Sources of Income?" Policy Research Working Paper 4282, World Bank, Washington, DC.

———. 2008. "Are Cash Transfers Made to Women Spent Like Other Sources of Income?" *Economics Letters* 101 (3): 246–48.

Schultz, T. Paul. 2004. "School Subsidies for the Poor: Evaluating the Mexican PROGRESA Poverty Program." *Journal of Development Economics* 74 (1): 199–250.

Schweinhart, Lawrence J. 2004. *The High/Scope Perry Preschool Study Through Age 40: Summary, Conclusions, and Frequently Asked Questions.* Ypsilanti, MI: High/Scope Educational Research Foundation.

Scott, John. 2002. "Public Spending and Inequality of Opportunities in Mexico, 1970–2000." Working Paper 235, Division de Economía, Centro de Investigación y Docencia Económicas, Mexico, DF.

347

Sen, Amartya K. 1985. *Commodities and Capabilities.* Amsterdam, The Netherlands: North Holland (Elsevier).

———. 1999. *Development As Freedom.* Oxford, UK: Oxford University Press.

Shrimpton, Roger, Cesar G. Victora, Mercedes de Onis, Rosângela Costa Lima, Monka Blössner, and Graeme Clugston. 2001. "Worldwide Timing of Growth Faltering: Implications for Nutritional Interventions." *Pediatrics* 107 (5): 75–81.

Skoufias, Emmanuel. 2002. "Rural Poverty Alleviation and Household Consumption Smoothing: Evidence from PROGRESA in Mexico." Unpublished manuscript, International Food Policy Research Institute, Washington, DC.

———. 2005. "PROGRESA and Its Impacts on the Welfare of Rural Households in Mexico." Research Report 139, International Food Policy Research Institute, Washington, DC.

Skoufias, Emmanuel, and Vincenzo di Maro. 2006. "Conditional Cash Transfers, Work Incentives, and Poverty." Policy Research Working Paper 3973, World Bank, Washington, DC.

Skoufias, Emmanuel, and Susan W. Parker. 2001. "Conditional Cash Transfers and Their Impact on Child Work and Schooling: Evidence from the PROGRESA Program in Mexico." *Economía* 2 (1): 45–96.

Sparrow, Robert. 2007. "Protecting Education for the Poor in Times of Crisis: An Evaluation of a Scholarship Programme in Indonesia." *Oxford Bulletin of Economics and Statistics* 69 (1): 99–122.

Stecklov, Guy, Paul Winters, Jessica Todd, and Ferdinando Regalía. 2006. "Demographic Externalities from Poverty Programs in Developing Countries: Experimental Evidence from Latin America." Working Paper 2006-1, Department of Economics, American University, Washington, DC.

Subbarao, Kalanidhi, Carol Graham, Kene Ezemenari, Jeanine Braithwaite, Aniruddha Bonnerjee, Soniya Carvalho, and Alan Thompson. 1997. *Safety Net Programs and Poverty Reduction: Lessons from Cross-Country Experience.* Washington, DC: World Bank.

Teruel, Graciela, and Benjamin Davis. 2000. *Final Report: An Evaluation of the Impact of PROGRESA Cash Payments on Private Inter-Household Transfers.* Washington, DC: International Food Policy Research Institute.

Tesliuc, Emil, David Coady, Margaret Grosh, and Lucian Pop. 2006. "Program Implementation Matters for Targeting Performance: Evidence and Lessons from Eastern and Central Europe." Unpublished manuscript, World Bank, Washington, DC.

Thaler, Richard H. 1999. "Mental Accounting Matters." *Journal of Behavioral Decision Making* 12: 183–206.

Thomas, Duncan. 1990. "Intra-Household Resource Allocation: An Inferential Approach." *Journal of Human Resources* 25 (4): 635–64.

———. 1994. "Like Father, Like Son; Like Mother, Like Daughter: Parental Resources and Child Height." *Journal of Human Resources* 29 (4): 950–88.

Thomas, Duncan, and John Strauss. 1997. "Health and Wages: Evidence on Men and Women in Urban Brazil." *Journal of Econometrics* 77 (1): 159–85.

Thomas, Duncan, Kathleen Beegle, Elizabeth Frankenberg, Bondan Sikoki, John Strauss, and Graciela Teruel. 2004. "Education in a Crisis." *Journal of Development Economics* 74 (1): 53–85.

Tietjen, Karen. 2003. "The Bangladesh Primary Education Stipend Project: A Descriptive Analysis." World Bank, Washington, DC.

Tobin, James. 1970. "On Limiting the Domain of Inequality." *Journal of Law & Economics* 13 (2): 263–77.

Todd, Petra E., Jorge Gallardo-García, Jere R. Behrman, and Susan W. Parker. 2005. "Impacto de Oportunidades Sobre la Educación de Niños y Jóvenes en Áreas Urbanas Después de un Año de Participación en el Programa." In *Evaluación Externa de Impacto del Programa Oportunidades 2004: Educación,* ed. Bernardo Hernández Prado and Mauricio Hernández Ávila. Cuernavaca, Morales, México: Instituto Nacional de Salud Pública.

Todd, Petra E., and Kenneth I. Wolpin. 2006a. "Assessing the Impact of a School Subsidy Program in Mexico: Using a Social Experiment to Validate a Dynamic Behavioral Model of Child Schooling and Fertility." *American Economic Review* 96 (5): 1384–417.

———. 2006b. "Ex Ante Evaluation of Social Programs." Working Paper 06-022, Penn Institute for Economic Research, Department of Economics, University of Pennsylvania, Philadelphia.

Van Roekel, Karen, Beth Plowman, Marcia Griffiths, Victoria de Alvarado, Jorge Matute, and Miguel Calderón. 2002. "BASICS II: Midterm Evaluation of the AIN Program in Honduras, 2002." Basic Support for Institutionalizing Child Survival Project, United States Agency for International Development, Arlington, VA.

Varangis, Panos, Paul Siegel, Daniele Giovannucci, and Bryan Lewin. 2003. "Dealing with the Coffee Crisis in Central America: Impacts and Strategies." Policy Research Working Paper 2993, World Bank, Washington, DC.

Vermeersch, Christel, and Michael Kremer. 2004. "School Meals, Educational Achievement, and School Competition: Evidence from a Randomized Evaluation." Policy Research Working Paper 3523, World Bank, Washington, DC.

Walker, Susan P., Theodore D. Wachs, Julie Meeks Gardner, Betsy Lozoff, Gail A. Wasserman, Ernesto Pollitt, and Julie A. Carter. 2007. "Child Development: Risk Factors for Adverse Outcomes in Developing Countries." *The Lancet* 369 (9556): 145–57.

Ward-Batts, Jennifer. 2008. "Out of the Wallet and into the Purse: Using Micro Data to Test Income Pooling." *Journal of Human Resources* 43 (2): 325–51.

World Bank. 2001a. "Brazil: An Assessment of the Bolsa Escola Programs." Report 20208-BR, Washington, DC.

———. 2001b. "Brazil: Eradicating Child Labor in Brazil." Report 21858-BR, Washington, DC.

———. 2003. *World Development Report 2004: Making Services Work for Poor People.* Washington, DC.

———. 2004a. "Bangladesh: Reaching Out-of-School Children Project." Project Appraisal Document 29019, Washington, DC.

———. 2004b. "Education Sector Adjustment Credit for the Government of Punjab Province." Washington, DC.

———. 2005. *World Development Report 2006: Equity and Development.* Washington, DC.

———. 2006a. "Dominican Republic Poverty Assessment: Achieving More Pro-Poor Growth." Report 32422-DO, Washington, DC.

———. 2006b. "First Phase of the Bono de Desarrollo Humano Reform Project." Washington, DC.

———. 2006c. "Making the New Indonesia Work for the Poor." Report 37349-ID, Washington, DC.

———. 2006d. "Panama Poverty Assessment: Toward Effective Poverty Reduction." Unpublished manuscript, Washington, DC.

———. 2006e. "Social Safety Nets in Bangladesh: An Assessment." Bangladesh Development Series Paper 9, Dakar, Bangladesh.

———. 2007. "Proposed Third Education Sector Development Support Credit." Washington, DC.

———. 2008a. "Bulgaria: Social Inclusion Project." Project Appraisal Document, Report 38604-BG, Washington, DC.

———. 2008b. "¿Cuál es el camino a seguir para fomentar políticas públicas más amplias y sostenibles?" Proceedings of the Workshop of the CCT Community of Practitioners, Cuernavaca, Mexico, January 15–18.

———. 2008c. "Guidance for Responses from the Human Development Sectors to Rising Food Prices." Human Development Network, Washington, DC.

Yap, Yoon-Tien, Guilherme Sedlacek, and Peter Orazem. 2008. "Limiting Child Labor through Behavior-Based Income Transfers: An Experimental Evaluation of the PETI Program in Rural Brazil." In *Child Labor and Education in Latin America: An Economic Perspective,* ed. Peter Orazem, Guilherme Sedlacek, and Zafiris Tzannatos. Palgrave.

Index